FRATERNAL CAPITAL

FRATERNAL CAPITAL

Peasant-Workers, Self-Made Men, and Globalization in Provincial India

SHARAD CHARI

Stanford University Press
Stanford, California 2004

Stanford University Press
Stanford, California

Printed in the United States of America on acid-free,
archival-quality paper

Library of Congress Cataloging-in-Publication Data

Chari, Sharad.
Peasant-workers, self-made men, and globalization in provincial India /
Sharad Chari.
    p. cm.
Includes bibliographical references and index.
ISBN 0-8047-4873-X (cloth : alk. paper)
1. Working class—Social conditions—India—Tiruppur. 2. Working
class—Economic conditions—India—Tiruppur.
3. Industrialization—Social aspects—India—Tiruppur. 4. Rural
development—India—Tiruppur. 5. Tiruppur (India) —Economic
conditions. I. Title.
HD8689.T52C43 2004
306.3'6'095482—dc22
                                        2004002486

Original Printing 2004

Last figure below indicates year of this printing:
    13 12 11 10 09 08 07 06 05 04

Typeset by Guru Typograph Technology, in Adobe Garamond

for
Ma and Pa

Contents

Tables

Maps and Figures

Illustrations

(All photos by the author)

Note on Transliteration*

1. I distinguish long vowels from short vowels with an accent over the appropriate roman letter.

   a (as in 'about')   á (as in 'art')
   i (as in 'ink')   í (as in 'eel')
   u (as in 'put')   ú (as in 'pool')
   e (as in 'end')   é (as in 'ale')
   o (as in 'box')   ó (as in 'bowl')

2. I distinguish long or stressed consonants from short or unstressed consonants by doubling the appropriate roman letter.

3. I distinguish retroflexes from dentals by underlining the particular letter, either t, n, l, or r. Also, since retroflex r and l are often interchangeable, I opt for l as it is more common in practice. Hence, I write *Tamil* or *ulaippu*.

4. The sounds s and ch are represented by c.

5. I sometimes distinguish voiced sounds—b, d, j, g—from the corresponding sounds of p, t, cc, or k/ h, although the Tamil letters are the same and the rules for voice sounds are based on placement. The voiced sounds b, d, j, g follow nasals; and p, t and t are voiced between vowels; k is pronounced h or g.

---

* I have drawn from E. Valentine Daniel's (1984) method of transliteration.

Preface

A Tale of Banians, "Toil," and Miracles

Banian (n, pronounced baníyan): Indian word for sleeveless undershirt, also a generic term for knitted cloth and for garments made from knitted cloth (like T-shirts, underwear, sweatshirts, fleece, etc.)

Looking up from underneath the knitting machine, Nalasamy said once more, "Owner isn't here. Come back later." He was a jovial enough sort, wearing a white *vécti* hitched and tied around the waist, under an old, sweat-encrusted banian. Jovial, but stern. He shouted to another worker to get the machine started again: precious time was being lost. "Come back again," he reiterated, meaning come back if you have to, but leave now.

The next day I bicycled back through side alleys to get to the clearing around a banyan tree under which four old men sat still while the town engulfed their village world. With the midday *namáz* filling the air, I found my way around a little *Puḻiár* temple back to Texaco Knitting Company, resolved to meet its owner. The survey had forced me to find precise companies, with precise owners: both daunting tasks. I nodded, right palm chest-ward, to the smart young man and woman in the office. I had interviewed her already, Leelavathi. At first exchanging embarrassed glances with Kannan, the office clerk, she spoke of her move from Madurai with her husband, a "cutting master," and of their careers in Tiruppur. When I asked if the owner was there, they said no, but this time they added, "probably not." I imagined I had their confidence. I sat for a little while in the office, until Kannan abruptly glanced at the door and shot back at me, "What will he know anyway? He only has a second grade education!" I was taken aback by this sudden and complicated admission, unsure of how to respond. Instead, I asked if I could go back inside to see what work was being done.

This time I walked directly to the powertable section, where two tables were in operation. Each had seven or eight stitching machines on it, worked by rows of young men and women stitching sleeves onto unfinished chests of knitted shirts. I had met Palanisamy at the South Indian Hosiery Manufacturers' Association, where he had come to pay his company dues. He smiled as I approached the table. A young girl handed him cut pieces of knitted cloth in quick succession as he stitched. She giggled and handed him piece after piece, watching the strange intruder with his tape recorder and quizzical look from the corner of her eye. "Back again, California? Tell me, you have this kind of work in California?" he shouted rhetorically over the whirring of stitching machines. The lady on the opposite side smiled to herself as she continued to stitch shirt after shirt. Another little boy put ironed shirts in a box with a tag in German and a picture of two very blond children wearing brightly colored knitted garments. As he chatted, Palanisamy called Nalasamy his *annan*, elder brother.

Responding to a sudden racket outside, Palanisamy shook his head. "Those union men again." I went to the window and looked down at a group of men I recognized from the Congress of International Trade Unions (CITU), affiliated with the Communist Party of India—Marxist (CPM). The CITU men were chanting slogans in favour of travel allowances for workers, while one among them planted a small red flag in front of the company. The group quickly dispersed when a snazzy foreign car pulled up in front of the building. A man in a bright green safari suit with large, trapezoidal sunglasses bounded out and headed straight for the front door. Was this the owner, at last?

I went back to the accountant's office to find a dapper but perturbed man of about thirty. Just as I was about to extend my hand to introduce myself, Nalasamy of the knitting section came hastily out, calling out, "Welcome, welcome son-in-law. Tell me!" Nalasamy, whom I'd taken on so many occasions to be a senior worker, was addressing this sharp young man as his son-in-law?! The younger man sputtered on about problems with his loans, late orders to France and Italy, an impending trip to New York for which his visa wasn't ready. On and on he went, as Nalasamy took him into the owner's office in the corner, a room with characteristic tinted windows. An airconditioner was turned on and all further conversation grew muffled. A sign above the door read: "OM *Lápam:*" OM, the cosmic utterance; and Profit.

As I realized the central role of men like Nalasamy in the industrial boom in Tiruppur, I also gained more confidence in the reasons that brought me to study the cultural politics of work. Owners of working-class origins like this man appreciated that I was less interested in their mastery of formal languages of business administration than in their memories and experiences of work. Moreover, as I collected the life histories of men like Nalasamy, I found their personal accounts of class mobility invariably hinged on their *u̠laippu* or toil. In taking these renderings of self and circumstance seriously and critically, I ask in this book how these men have turned toil into capital, to profit from a culturally and historically specific labor theory of value. Indeed, many of these owners, while of modest origins, are far from being independent owner-operators isolated from broader processes of capital accumulation and globalization. *Fraternal Capital* asks how such owners of capital, from modest agrarian and proletarian origins, continue to work in networks of small firms, producing for global markets. Rather than explaining capital accumulation as a consequence of global and national shifts, I explore the local labors that animate the lives of Tiruppur's self-made men, allowing them to take advantage of broader opportunities which make Tiruppur a centerpiece of globalization in provincial India.

The chapters that follow explore how these Gounder men of modest origins came to the industry as peasant-workers from Tiruppur's rural hinterland and gradually made it their own through toil. Along the way they outcompeted their ex-bosses, beat the communist unions that had won them some measure of job security, and forged a gendered hegemony through a fraternity of decentralized capital. Life histories of men like Nalasamy provide windows into Gounder self-presentations of class mobility and transition from country to city. I show how Tiruppur's fraternal capitalism renovates meanings and practices from a regional agrarian and colonial past in order to selectively remake class, gender and the geography of work in today's knitwear firms. In Tiruppur's subsequent shift to global production, I ask how fraternal Gounder capital reworks broader gender discourses of the feminization of labor, linking sexed bodies to processes of differentiation in new ways. In brief, this agrarian history of the industrial present asks how peasant-workers have remade place, gender and class while creating global production in provincial India.

Acknowledgments

Early in my research I had the disarming experience of *being thanked* by an old man I was interviewing. This grandfather, having narrated the story of his life in a village on the outskirts of Tiruppur, broke into tears and thanked me, his fellow Tamilian, for coming all the way from America to bear witness to his difficult life. What surprised me—an ethnographer-in-training—was that the old man had not in fact provided any precise details of his difficulties but had assumed that I knew how to interpret his pain. This act of opening a shared space of solidarity gave me a sense of purpose that I have tried to maintain. My first debt of gratitude is to that grandfather, who will never read these words, but who infused my wide-eyed claims to speak truth with a practical call to listen.

When rewriting version after version of this book I have felt deeply fortunate for all the stories that animate my thoughts on development in Tiruppur. My thanks go to a host of people there, and its environs, who gave generously of their time, whether in garment companies, villages, offices, homes, streets, tea stalls or rustic bars. I cannot name the hundreds of people I had conversations with, but I can say that my education was made complete only by the practical knowledge I was taught through fieldwork.

Several people made living in Tiruppur more rewarding. Dr Visvasam's family graciously provided a home for me while in mourning. Mrs Padmini Visvasam was instrumental in introducing me to several people after inducing me, on my very first day in Tiruppur, to speak to a large crowd of owners at a "Felicitation to Mohan P. Kandasamy Gounder," the head of the South Indian Hosiery Manufacturers' Association. Had I not been confused for the son of a State Bank of India official from the 1970s who then moved to the USA, Sri Kandasamy may not have stood up and extended "all support to *tambi*," a public gesture which eased my entry into a world of knitwear owners who would otherwise have been difficult to crack. I am grateful to the Visvasam family, and to their domestic servants, who helped make my first year productive and comfortable.

I am also thankful to Sri Krishnamurthy "Kittu" Iyer for opening his home–factory for me to stay during my second trip. I was afforded an entirely unusual and wonderful sense of Tiruppur by living in a century-old wooden house with beams and pillars, and a strange assortment of objects—including a bat living in a decaying deer-head mounted in the beautiful attic room where I wrote—all presided over by a wonderful and eccentric bachelor. I realized later how much I learnt about the older style of industry by living in this factory–home, watching heirarchical power relations linking Kittu Iyer to his foremen and to a series of Dickensian boy "helpers." I felt a sense of camaraderie among these men as Iyer's music sessions, accompanied by an electronic harmonium, slipped effortlessly from Bing Crosby to Bollywood and classic MGR Tamil tunes via Morocco, or . . . China! The young men who lived in the factory–home and who ate, worked and slept around Kittu Iyer in the great central room were a joy to hang out with. Three guys called Venkatesh and the indomitable Sasikumar provided many hours of entertainment, with furtive trips to eat fried fish while the Brahmin owner's head was turned. A visit to Sasi's village was a treat, as he showed me all the places and ways in which he plays on the one day of the week that he can return from being an industrial worker to being a kid.

Several people offered their friendship in Tiruppur: I am particularly thankful to Bala, Mohan, Jhansi, Sriram, Venkatesh, "Disco" Ravi, Karuppusamy, Dastan Bannatic Kings and the City Leaves guys. Mohan, Bala and Sriram valiantly joined the local gym with me, only to filter in sporadically to spirit me off to The Topp, Tiruppur's open-air bar, for American chopsuey and whisky. Mohan and Jhansi's families were also very warm to me. Siva deserves my special thanks for being a trusty assistant during my survey phase, ferrying me to companies I couldn't as easily find either on my own or on my bicycle. "MTech" Fantom Nataraj gave me very useful advice as an organic intellectual of Tiruppur's left. Similarly, G. Karthikeyan gave me time, insight, and good cheer every time I spoke to him. I am also grateful to Sujana Krishnamoorthy, activist and scholar from New Delhi, with whom I could access a group of younger women workers. Finally, Hari Santharam and his father, R. Santharam, provided hospitality and insight into the Coimbatore industrial elite's relations with Tiruppur.

I am also grateful to the officials and staff of the South Indian Hosiery Manufacturers' Union, the Tiruppur Exporters Association, and to the Congress of Indian Trade Unions (CITU), the labor union of the Communist Party of India—Marxist. The South India Hosiery Manufacturers' Association (SIHMA) staff wrote me a letter of introduction that did wonders to expedite my survey research, and they let me use their files and spend time with their old bulletins lying at the bindery. Likewise, CITU provided me their files on strikes, and let me use a room for a week with a kind old lady periodically bringing me tea. I would also like to thank the Factories Inspectorate in Tiruppur and the District Industries Center, Coimbatore, for letting me use their material. A special word of thanks must go to the Tamilnad State Archives in Chennai, where I was rewarded with many articles for which I had not even requested.

Also in Chennai, I am grateful to the Madras Institute of Development Studies (MIDS) for providing me affiliation during my research. Padmini Swaminathan, J. Jeyaranjan, S. Janakrajan and M.S.S. Pandian were always available for stimulating intellectual engagement. I am particularly thankful for the encouragement, support and incisive comments provided periodically by Padmini Swaminathan, whose work on industry, gender and poverty I find inspirational. I am grateful to Jeyaranjan for arranging a presentation through the Institute for Development Alternatives in conjunction with Katha South Publishers. Also in Chennai, Sarah Hodges, Steve Hughes, Yigal and Galila Bronner, little Amosi and Maheshwari provided the best respite from the field and the perfect place to work out my ideas after I emerged. Sarah and Yigal were my partners in crime years ago in Madurai, when we learnt Tamil from Dr Bharathy; it was indeed a gift to spend time with them again, "in the family way." Thanks also to the Chennai and New Delhi staff of the United States Educational Foundation in India for help in the course of my research. For a home away from home in India, I thank my aunt and uncle, Mr and Mrs M.S. Sundarajan. I remain fortunate for the memory of my grandmother, Jayalakshmi Jagannathan, a compassionate supporter who did not live to see this work completed.

For research support I would like to thank the Social Science Research Council's International Pre-Dissertation Fellowship Program (IPFP), to the US Department of Education's Fulbright-Hayes Doctoral Dissertation Award, and the University of California at Berkeley for Foreign Language and Area Studies Fellowships, a Simpson Memorial Fellowship and a Chancellor's Dissertation Writing Fellowship.

My intellectual and personal debts at Berkeley are manifold. This book is *dakṣina* for my teachers. Had Michael Watts not seen promise in me as an undergraduate student of physics who had wandered into his class to make sense of the 1991 Gulf War, I would not have been able to return to be his student. Gillian Hart has been no less a guiding force in the development of this project since its inception, and her creativity and commitment have inspired my shift to research in South Africa. Michael Burawoy has been an inspiration as a passionately engaged teacher and ethnographer of the labor process, and his lessons are central to this book. I cannot repay the debts their guidance and wisdom have afforded, but I can register gratitude for their efforts to enable the scholarship of others.

Friends and colleagues at U.C. Berkeley and the vibrant Bay Area also provided a range of insight, argument, solidarity and care. Of several people, I would like to acknowledge Aditya Advani, Jaishri Abichandani, Ayaz Ahmad, Chitra Aiyar, Swati Argade, Pranab Bardhan, Subham Basu, Matthew Berson, Rakesh Bhandari, Aaron Bobrow-Strain, William Boyd, Preeti Chopra, Lawrence Cohen, Marsha Colby, Ben Crow, Kavita Datla, Navroz Dubash, Jehanbux Edulbehram, Donnett Flash, Suzanne Freidberg, Vinay Gidwani, Will Glover, Julie Guthman, Kausalya Hart, Patrick Heller, Eugene Irschick, Priya Jagannathan, Michael Johns, James McCarthy, Melanie and David McDermott-Hughes, Donald Moore, Rinku Murgai, Tad Mutersbaugh, Tahir Naqvi, Urvashi Narain, Elizabeth Oglesby, Anand

Pandian, Robert Pollock, Allan Pred, Manohar Raju, Tara Raman, Haripriya Rangan, Raka Ray, Amy Ross, Ananya Roy, Sandip Roy, Simona Sawhney, Annalee Saxenian, Gautam Sethi, Mona Shah, Padmini Srikantiah, Janet Sturgeon, Michael Tarr, Steve Thorne, Richard Walker, Wendy Wolford and Dave Wilson. "The Alcatraz 5.5," comprising David, James, Janet, Melanie and Jesse "the Bear," provided the right mix of critique and comfort to keep me writing.

The University of Michigan, Ann Arbor, has provided a strong web of intellectual and personal support. My thanks go to the Michigan Society of Fellows and the anthropology and history departments for keeping my mind open while finishing this book. I am grateful for opportunities to present sections of this research to lively audiences through the Anthropology and History Reading Group, the Center for South Asian Studies, Sonya Rose's seminar on gender and history, and the Michigan Society of Fellows. I was provided constant intellectual stimulation through the Center for the Study of Social Transformation (CSST), Lee Schlessinger's *Kitabmandal,* and numerous formal and informal reading groups. Of this vibrant community, I would like to acknowledge support, stimulation and friendship from Jane Burbank, Frank Cody, David Cohen, Fred Cooper, Fernando Coronil, Naisargi Dave, Grace Davie, Geoff Eley, Eric Firstenberg, Dario Gaggio, Chandan Gowda, Thomas Guglielmo, Maya Jasanoff, Andreas Kalyvas, Stuart Kirsch, Val Kivelson, Lisa Klopfer, Nita Kumar, Jayati Lal, Ching Kwan Lee, Rama Mantana, Laurie Marx, Christie Merrill, Gina Morantz-Sanchez, David Pedersen, Kathy Pence, Steven Pierce, Monica Prasad, Helmut Puff, Mary Rader, Bhavani Raman, Sumathi Ramaswamy, Sonya Rose, Lee Schlessinger, Jordan Shapiro, Julie Skurski, Genese Sodikoff, Scott Spector, Jeremy Straughn, Ann Stoler, Rachel Sturman, Sam Temple, Tom Trautman, Katherine Verdery, Marina Welker and Jim White.

Two sets of incredible students in graduate seminars at Michigan, one co-taught with Fernando Coronil, provided challenging readings of my manuscript to help me finish. Thanks go to Carlton Basmajian, Sayan Bhattacharya, Frank Cody, Leland Davis, Matt Dore-Weeks, Alissa Kendall, Bree Kessler, Daniel Latea, Ed Murphy, Eric Phillipson, Bhavani Raman, Rhea Rehman, Karen Smid, Genese Sodikoff, and

Caleb Zigas. Though I decided against Leland's "Horatio Alger Gounder" and Caleb's "Capitalism's (dirty) Underwear" as titles for this book, Caleb's literal representation adorns my mantelpiece. Fernando came through with the title, and with the challenge of writing about capitalism without fetishizing its fetishisms.

Several scholars who I respect tremendously provided considered comments on drafts or on papers linked to this project. Besides those already mentioned, I am thankful for encouragement at various stages from Vinay Gidwani, Barbara Harriss-White, John Harriss, Karin Kapadia, Janaki Nair, and Mellissa Wright. Barbara and Karin have been very generous in engaging my work in theirs. For thoughtful and challenging readings of the whole manuscript, I am very grateful to Keith Breckenridge, Laura Brown, Catherine Burns, Dipesh Chakrabarty, Sandra Comstock, Stuart Corbridge, Ramachandra Guha, Anand Pandian, Chandan Reddy, K. Sivaramakrishnan, and two anonymous reviewers for Stanford University Press.

I am grateful to my editors, Pat Katayama and Mariana Raykov, as well as Kate Wahl and Carmen Borbon-Wu, at Stanford University Press, and Rukun Advani at Permanent Black, for taking on this project. A global product, this book relies on the work of many across New Delhi and California, to whom I remain grateful. A special thanks to Sujata Keshavan and Ray + Keshavan for the jacket.

I have finished this book while learning of new places and politics, in Durban, South Africa. I am grateful to the School of Development Studies, University of KwaZulu Natal, for allowing me to present this work to a lively South African audience. I will not list a host of new friends in South Africa, but would like to express thanks for care and support from Ismail Jazbhay, Monique Marks, Vishnu Padayachee, Michelle Simon, and Caroline Skinner.

Not least, I rely on my family, for constancy. I am grateful for Arvind and Jeannie, especially for giving us Nikhil and Maya. This book is for the joys I receive from my parents: to Pa, Srinivas Chari, for his ceaseless imagination of alternative worlds, and to Ma, Prema Chari, for her resolute engagement with this imperfect one. Ma has engaged my thoughts with critical interest for as long as I can remember. Pa has shared his dreams long before returning to graduate school, to valiantly resist the discipline of teachers and term papers. Their strange and wonderful combination guides me through each possible new day.

In the charge of an old farmer in Coimbatore District, to bear witness to the unspoken sufferings of many who will never read this text, lies a utopian spark I share. If globalization is to mean anything for the mass of the world's peoples, many stories of exploitation will have to be told, translated, and accounted for.

FRATERNAL CAPITAL

CHAPTER 1

A Worker Path to Capital?

I. First Impressions

T he whole town was a decentralized factory, or so it seemed on my first stroll around Tiruppur, on the main railway line across South India from Madras, through Coimbatore and on to Kerala. Map 1 locates Tiruppur in western Tamil Nadu state as one of several specialist towns, each specializing in particular commodities. During the months for which Tiruppur became my home I found the railway line an important spatial marker. I either scurried under it through a tiny causeway covered with dye-stained sludge, or I darted over it in a bumping row of pedestrians and cyclists. I begin with a walk through Tiruppur's lived geographies, pointing along the way to the key questions I ask. A detour through conventional scholarship on industry in Tiruppur and on industrial clusters in the Third World more generally takes the reader to the broader theoretical issues at stake in my research. I then state my central question in terms of a cultural political economy that speaks to the lived experience of Nalasamy, as suggested in the Preface. The test of my choice of theory will be in its ability to translate diversely situated stories without losing sight either of the analytical power of critical social science or the singularity of life in Tiruppur.

II. Factory Town: A Walk through Tiruppur and Its Industry

In Tiruppur, knitwear is king. The five main roads leading into the town from the countryside proclaim: "Welcome to Knit City!" and "Welcome to Banian Capital!" As one enters the town, bus or train,

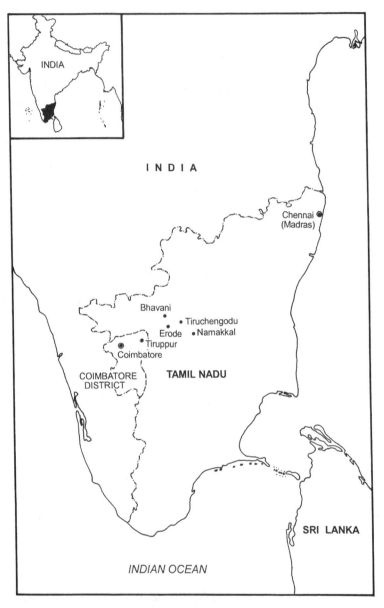

Map 1: Specialist Towns of Western Tamil Nadu, India

large posters of bras and underwear accost the eye. Bus-stops bustle with commuters each morning and evening, making journeys on private and public busses from surrounding villages. Flower-sellers intercept young working women in the mornings, before they join streams of lunch-toting workers into the maze of neighborhoods and colonies. In the export season, cardboard signs hang on posts, trees and walls announcing "Packing women needed" or "Ironing man needed," a company name scrawled on one corner. Everyone who can, finds work through these cardboard signs, the hallmark of calls to informal work for today's flexible proletariat.

Tiruppur lies between eight radial roads from the countryside, intersecting across the railway tracks on the new and rather remarkable bridge that makes any self-respecting Tirupurian, and the occasional temporary resident, proud. The area between these main roads can be confusing to an outsider. Note the number of streets halting into nothingness on Map 2 that the mapmakers have left almost every neighborhood between these spines unmapped.

Tiruppur's main road is named for its hero, Kumaran. To many South Indians, Tiruppur is "Tiruppur Kumaran." Born within a prosperous Chettiar merchant family, Kumaran was Tiruppur's contribution to the nationalist Congress movement. Martyred as yet another regional cog in the imagined geography of anti-colonial nationalism, Kumaran now stands in bas-relief on an unremarkable concrete pillar in a small park by the railway station. Further south, on the banks of the dye-stained trickle that is the Noyil river, stands the ex-chief minister M.G. Ramachandran (MGR), whose celluloid charisma tapped the rural poor and made him a leader of the Dravidian Movement, one of South India's most important modern social reform movements. With bright red lips, yellow *vécti*, trademark cap and sunglasses, MGR basks on the shores of the Noyil river to announce the arrival of the Tamil people on the global economic stage, with putrid waters and the outlines of smokestacks an ironic background. The main memorial in Tiruppur, however, is at the heart of the traffic, where Kumaran Road enters the bustling city center and old bus stand. At the center of the commotion, in front of his old seat of power, the Tiruppur municipality, rises the dazzling silver-painted statue of *Tiruppur Tantai*, Father

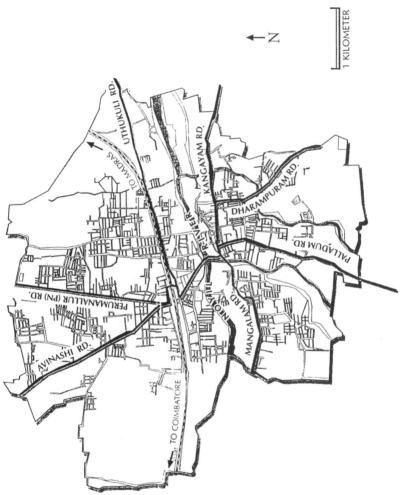

Map 2: Tiruppur: Coimbatore District, Tamil Nadu State

of Tiruppur, K.N. Palanisamy Gounder (KNP). An aristocrat, KNP served multiple terms as chairman of the Tiruppur municipality, and is venerated as the man who brought water to this parched town from the foot of the Nilgiri mountains, under the First Municipal Scheme. In Tiruppur, all other statues pale in significance.

Behind KNP lies the bustle of the central market and old bus station, the heart of an older Tiruppur. To one side is the old Muslim neighborhood along Demand Street, identified by some as the original village. On the other side, near the bus station, lie numerous little streets named for famous Chettiar and Mudaliar merchants. As in most Indian towns, trades cluster along streets, with numerous open shops selling wholesale grain at one end, woven fabric at another. The main temple of Tiruppur also lies near the crowded center. Eswaran Koil, temple of the god Siva, is simultaneously dedicated to its erstwhile patron Eswaramurthy Gounder, another aristocrat and relative of the silvered KNP. This man, with the name "statue of Eswaran," now stands in stone facing his namesake god, his ownership caught in a messy legal battle between his kin and the state trustees of this nationalized temple. Farther east, his grandson roosts in an opulent bungalow opposite his three-star hotel, Velan Hotel Greenfields, which offers generic Western comforts to cater to the tastes of foreign buyers. Velan has become an icon of foreign presence as it commands the country to the south-east with the psychological weight of a plantation mansion or manor house. Much of the area near Kangayam Road was owned by the family of Eswaramurthy Gounder and has been converted into posh new residential space in which each home tries to out-Westernize the next.

The older affluent residential areas lie closer to the center and to its west. Sherief Colony was a tract once owned by the father-in-law of Hitech Kandasamy, leader of the South India Hosiery Manufacturers' Association (SIHMA)—the domestic knitwear owners' association. His house, like many of the older houses in this area, is a complex of large, flat bungalows with prominent front verandahs from which he continues to hold court. Guests approach and shed footwear at the steps to the verandah, then sit on rows of cane chairs of different types to await an audience. After following suit, when I made it into the main house for lunch served by his daughters, I knew indeed that I was home free. When it came time for me to conduct surveys, a signature from Mohan Kandasamy on a Tamil letter written by his staff at the very same verandah was enough to open innumerable doors of owners.

Returning to the main spine as its name changes slowly from Kamaraj to Palladam Road as it heads south, one encounters the marketplaces for which Tiruppur was once known. Behind a string of small cotton commission agents lies the compound of the Tiruppur Cotton Market, once one of the most important cotton markets in India and which, in local lore, used to set the price of cotton in Bombay. Beside it is the more recently established Agricultural Regulated Market, fought for and built by a section of the farmers' movement emanating from the south of Tiruppur. Further south still is the old Tiruppur *cantai*, periodic market, once the site of an annual cattle fair. Mixed with these older sites of commerce are the few remaining knitwear factories from the 1950s. Khader Knitting Company, Spider Knitting Company and Mohan Knitting Company, built a decade later, are all large bungalows in spacious compounds. I lived for six months in a company of the same era, Design Knitting Company, near the railway tracks and on the edge of the *agraháram* or Brahmin section. The two century-old buildings that comprise home and company are modeled on well-to-do homes, with a series of multi-functional rooms leading into a central hall where general work and life activities are carried on.

My first home in Tiruppur was in the west, in Petha Chetty Puram (P.C. Puram), named for one of the early Chettiar founding entrepreneurs of hosiery in these parts. I found no resident, over the ten months I lived there, who knew anything about Petha Chetty. Adjoining P.C. Puram is a small colony of Dalits known by the disparaging term Sakkilian or Chakklian, or by their affirmative self-identification, Madari. These Madari continue in large part in their ancestral leather crafts, but what is striking is that they live as if in their own private village, complete with its own canals and administrative body.

Further along, en route to the railway station, is a sudden maze of streets populated mainly by Muslims and North Indians, in a mixture of homes and shops selling knitwear-seconds pieces. Khadarpet, as this area is called after the old Muslim patriarch and company owner

S.A. Khadar, is a thriving conduit for the unregulated and largely un-taxed market in a range of knitwear products that are variously called export seconds or export surplus. Whatever the quality norms might be—and my sense is that they fluctuate with the fortunes of the in-dustry as a whole and provide a vent for any possible glut in export production—this market is the one place in Tiruppur in which knit-wear meets the bazaar economy. Each week goods proceed from the shops of Khadarpet to the much larger Erode *cantai*, the periodic market in Erode city which has, at least through the twentieth century, specialized in all manner of regional textile goods. Mosques broadcast prayers periodically, and in the evenings I sometimes followed the lights of Khadarpet's "hotels" for tantalizing mutton biryani.

The new bridge eases some of the congestion for trucks and buses, while other means of conveyance dodge trains at level crossings, or squeeze through a few tiny tunnels under the tracks. Beyond the bridge, north Tiruppur opens out like a pair of scissors through two main roads, Avinashi Road and Perumanallur (or P.N.) Road. These roads have the strongest reach into a commuting countryside, from which rural workers ply to and fro each day. These are also the streets where the two communist labor unions stand, corresponding to the Communist Part of India (CPI) and the Communist Party of India—Marxist (CPM). The large and freshly painted union buildings rival their counterparts in the four Indian metros, announcing that this is indeed a workers' town. Directions here, as in many localities in Tiruppur, are most often given in relation to the most popular of mod-ern temples, cinema theaters. The theaters on Avinashi and P.N. Road are perennially packed with young men without work, loathe to return home until nightfall. The final milestone on the north-east, along Avi-nashi Road, is Asher Textiles Mill, one of the few functional monuments in Tiruppur to the beginnings of modern industry in South India.

Certain streets between the railway tracks and the river betray an earlier era of industry and trade. Art deco buildings peek over bill-boards onto crowded roads adjoining the ramparts of spinning mills and Dickensian cotton gins, now industrial ruins. A turn-off to the west from Kumaran Road on the banks of the river can lead the unwary through a maze of factory walls, the occasional break in the parapet offering a glimpse of the courtyard of a cotton gin, relatively unchanged for fifty years. On these antiquated machines equally antiquated-looking women sort cotton, picking out the larger seeds before the *kapas* are thrown into the hungry gin. These *parutti offices*—or cotton offices, as gins are known locally—along with the cotton market and the railroad, were the nexus of the cotton trade that brought Tiruppur into this century of development, tying its fortunes to the booming spinning mills of Coimbatore city as well as a vibrant cotton-growing hinterland. The largest *offices* were those set up by British mills, and these compounds are still known by their old names: Binny Office is now a shopping complex; Harvey Office is an industrial estate on the north, just below the bridge; and Kearny Office is the name of a neighborhood. The spinning mill gates are important artifacts of a strong, masculinist, communist labor union past which is revived on many occasions. The Asher Mills gate and the Dhanalakshmi Mills gate are important places where older workers and union men have associated, and labor unions continue to make public statements and begin processions from the mill gates.

Where in this urban landscape are the knitwear factories? Everywhere. I realized this on my first night's sleep in Tiruppur, as I heard the constant hum of knitting machines even in my residential neighborhood. I began my enquiries first, of course, in the official industrial parks, the state-subsidized SIDCO estates at the base of the bridge and another outside town in the countryside to the west. Yet these estates could not contain the mushrooming of this industry since the 1980s. Every neighborhood includes its own companies, some just tiny enough to fit a table, a motor and a couple of machines, others scarcely big enough for one worker on a collar loom, yet others in sprawling mansions. Even working-class localities contain tiny units stuck somewhere between the alleys, some with no name but just an icon to ward off the evil eye. Most companies have no names, but many have multiple addresses for a variety of purposes. In one instance, while exasperated searching for a particular company, I stood at the place I thought it should be and asked a worker on his break where the company was. "I have worked here for years. There is only one company in this building, the one I work in. Your address is wrong or your company just does not exist," he said resolutely. As it turned out, the door on his right led to a basement beneath his company in which my prospective interview lay buried.

Walking by the factories of Tiruppur's official industrial parks and the factories of its old posh residential areas, the factories of its village suburbs and the factories of its slums, I began to see that the whole town is a decentralized factory. This fact was only heightened as I watched in amazement at how flows of materials—thread, knitted cloth, dyes or printed shirts—are carted in all manner of conveyances between far-flung workplaces. Men balance precarious piles of T-shirts on mopeds. Bullock carts carry rolls of yarn or knitted cloth while a Mercedes or BMW behind honks mercilessly. At times the flow of traffic is so chaotic one wonders how the industry meets any success at all.

Quite the contrary: the signs of success are everywhere. Of all the buildings in view, it is the opulent facades of the newly rich that catch the eye: the haphazard gaudiness of Greco-Tamil mansions with tinted windows and polished granite exteriors. Whether they are houses or knitwear companies, these monstrosities are more striking for sharing space with myriad makeshift workshops. This is most striking in the north-east, in the neighborhoods of Lakshminagar, Bridgeway Colony and Kongu Nagar, areas at the core of stories of class mobility like Nalasamy's. Here, grotesque architectural hybrids spring up like weeds. It is even more surprising to wander into various pockets of town to find these buildings alongside the occasional stubborn agricultural field or century-old open well. To the north, I often chanced upon images of rural life, of elements of a village surrounded but not entirely engulfed by the expanding town: a cluster of huts, a small field for fodder crops, a banyan tree under which old men meet. This rurality was always within sight of a palatial company or of a four-star hotel catering to foreign buyers.

Farther to the north the rural landscape becomes parched, with little agriculture in the first twenty kilometers on either side of Avinashi Road and P.N. Road save the occasional patch of fodder crop. At one point to the north, along a tributary of the Noyil river, a cluster of smokestacks is the telltale sign of bleaching and dyeing units. Another cluster of bleaching and dyeing firms lies upstream from the city in the western view behind the statue of MGR, along Mangalam Road, and indeed there are more along the course of the river downstream. Bleaching firms provide the most physically degrading work, and a glance into the compounds reveals scantily clad men, predominantly Dalits, standing inside tanks of bleach water beating the cloth against the sides of these tanks under the hot midday sun. What is striking is how little these men look as they have left the world of agricultural labor. These workers are most unlike others from the countryside who dress as far removed from the trappings of village custom as possible. Men discard *véctis* for baggy pants, fancy tailored polyester shirts and filmstar hairstyles. Women wear blouses with "puff" shoulders and do themselves up with beauty products and *fancy itengal,* or fashion accesories. A boy I knew who went home to his village about 50 kms to the west of Tiruppur wore his best outfits for his Sunday visits when he went dressed to impress with special clothes, a baseball cap and "scent" or cologne. Knitwear firms in the north thin out into parched countryside, while in the south and south-east, what is striking is that there is some farming as close as 5 kms away. Most of the farms grow fodder crops or coconut trees, and indeed there is even some irrigation water to be had as one reaches Palladam. Villages along the railway line running east and west show signs of diversification into various rural industries, as in rice trading and milling in the village of Vanjipalayam to the east. The countryside is replete with local pockets of collective diversification with peculiar stories of their own. Each dawn, for instance, lines of bullock carts come into Tiruppur from a village hamlet of Naickers in the west, which now controls much of the inter-firm bullock cart transportation of goods. On the other hand there are Dalit hamlets quite close to town which seem untouched by change. A young Dalit man told me quite incidentally that his childhood was spent as a bonded laborer to a Gounder farmer to pay off his parents' debts before work in Tiruppur was ever an option.

Most rural workers in town are never far from the artifacts of village life. The footloose global entrepreneur with a flashy marbled house— part Parthenon, part Swiss chalet—has still to get his car through a bumpy unpaved road, avoiding oncoming bullock carts. The jagged

1. Lunch-toting workers, smartly dressed for industrial work,
heading into North Tiruppur in the
early morning, 1997.

2. Haphazard cardboard signs outside the walls of a large company
announce "Singer Tailor Needed" and "Iron Master Needed,"
displaying the political marginality of
flexible labor, 1997.

3. The impressive office of the Congress of Indian Trade Unions, CITU, 1996.

4. Small unmarked company in Khadarpet, with only an icon to ward off the evil eye, and a cardboard sign to attract footloose labor, 1996.

5. Company with no name, only political graffiti, and a cardboard sign advertising temporary work, 1997.

6. Bleaching and dyeing firms along the polluted Noyil River, 1996.

7. Construction of gaudy façades proceeds all over formerly working-class North Tiruppur, 1997.

8. A photocopy shop displays new services for the
internet age, 1997.

9. Bullock carts ply between firms, piled high with yarn and knitted cloth, 1996.

10. Bleaching workers inside vats of chemical-saturated water and under the fierce sun, which drying cloth is shielded from, 1997.

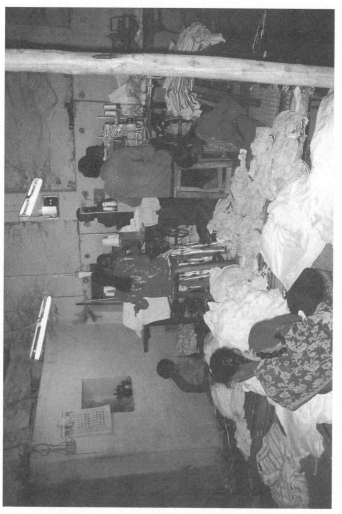

11. A small unit comprising primarily a stitching section, in which the owner is entirely immersed in work alongside his workers, 1997.

12. A small finishing firm that announces its capacities: "drimmar, scalaping, picoting, and zigzag," 1997.

13. A young girl folding banians, 1996.

historical layers of this built environment are testimony to dramatic accumulation with minimal public regulation, culminating in an export boom between the mid 1980s and early 1990s. While the mid 1990s, since 1993 to be precise, were difficult for the industry for various reasons, the same 1990s saw the adoption of technology to meet the requirements of high- and mid-market fashion buyers from Europe and North America, and Tiruppur made a decisive shift from basic T-shirts that are sourced cheaper from China, Bangladesh or Pakistan, to mid-market fashion knit garments for diversified Northern markets.

III. Explaining the Boom in the 1990s:
The Problematic

There are many indicators of the boom in Tiruppur knitwear since the late 1980s. Figure 1 shows that nominal export earnings shot up from $25 million in 1986 to $636 million in 1997; Figure 2 shows that the number of garments exported increased more than ninefold over the same period. The types of garments also changed as Tiruppur shifted to exporting diversified, multi-product fashion garments. As an example of the type of garment exported, I saw a brand name shirt that I had seen in production in Tiruppur, at a department store in California retailing for $65 in 1997.

I present these indicators as do spokespeople for the knitwear industry in Tiruppur, while noting that statistics are most important for their rhetorical power. This data is not adjusted for inflation or for changes in the exchange rate, so that it stands to exaggerate the boom, to some extent. Other official data helps broaden the vantage on industrial structure. Table 1, in Appendix 2, indicates the spatial and sectoral concentration of Small Scale Industries (SSIs) engaged in "hosiery and garments" in Tiruppur Block of Coimbatore District. Table 2, Appendix 2, also draws on SSI data to show the concentration of garment firms within the knitwear cluster. Data on all registered factories, whether or not they are SSIs, recorded in Table 3, Appendix 2, shows that "hosiery and garments" accounts for half the working factories and about a third of employment in Tiruppur. A comparison with data from 1986 in Table 4, Appendix 2, indicates a dramatic

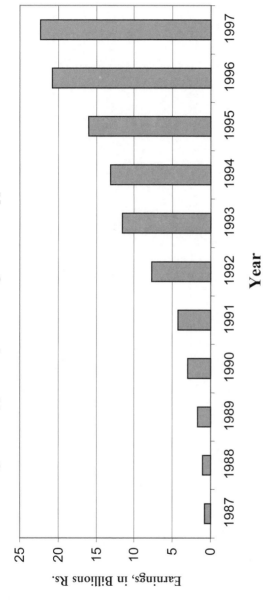

Figure 1: Apparel Export Earnings from Tiruppur, 1987–97

Source: Apparel Export Promotion Council, 1997.

Note: Rupees in the AEPC figures are in nominal prices and are used as such by the Tiruppur Exporters Association to represent dramatic growth.

Figure 2: Quantity of Apparel Export from Tiruppur

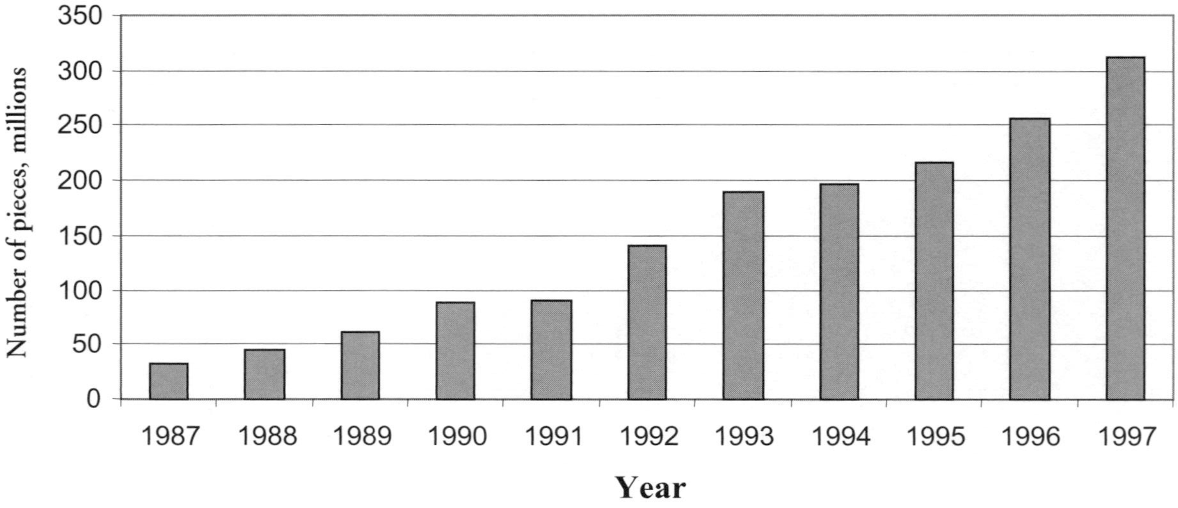

Source: Apparel Export Promotion Council, 1997.

increase in employment in the decentralized powerloom sector and a more modest but substantial increase in knitwear, but I argue that this is primarily an indicator of evasion of factory legislation. Factories Inspectorate data disaggregated by size in employment terms in Table 5, Appendix 2, reveals the predominance of units with 10–20 workers and particularly with 20–50 workers. Note below that the lion's share of 82 percent of firms in Hosiery and Garments fall in the range of 10–50 workers.

How has growth in Tiruppur been related to this decentralized industrial form and to extremes of wealth and insecurity visible in people's fortunes? Research on Tiruppur has been a study in contrasts. Scholars of the early 1980s either portray Tiruppur as mired in a despotic informal sector or on an upward spiral of capital accumulation without centralisation. While Krishnaswami's research attends to the detail of the labor process, Cawthorne uses the metaphor of "amoebic capitalism" to describe expanding firms breaking off into smaller units of production that give the appearance of small-scale industry while also opening up opportunities for upward mobility. Cawthorne subsequently reframes her results as demonstating a "low road" to industrial flexibility. I return to explore these formulations in their broader intellectual contexts in the following section.[1]

A comparison of Table 5 with Cawthorne's data from 1986, in Table 6, does suggest an elaboration of industrial decentralization.

Table 6: Decadal Change in Distribution of Factories by Employment, Tiruppur Division, 1996

Factory Size	No. Firms, 1986	No. Firms, 1996	Decadal Change
<10 workers	0	130	–
10—19	0	310	–
29—49	151	497	229%
50—99	89	37	–58%
100—499	12	7	–42%
500—999	20	0	–100%
>1000 workers	0	0	0

Source: "Statement III,"1996, at the Office of the Deputy Inspector of Factories, Tiruppur.

The entire spectrum has shifted upwards to smaller units than reported ten years earlier, particularly so in the "20–49" workers range, against a dramatic decline in the "> 500" workers range. This evidence suggests a deepening of industrial decentralization in the decade since the mid 1980s.

By the early 1990s some firms were also crossing the hurdles of product diversification and technological change. Padmini Swaminathan and J. Jeyaranjan asked how local entrepreneurs have "leapfrogged" into multi-product fashion garment exports, enhancing technologies in key sections of the labor process while maintaining a smallholder form.[2] The inevitable question posed was whether Tiruppur represents a sort of "industrial district" in the manner of some of the towns in the Third Italy, a point I return to in the next section. While small-firm networks and active owners' associations have been important in both cases, the Italian towns continue to have strong local unions and municipal regulation, which is where superficial similarities fail. The deeper question in this line of reasoning is whether Tiruppur's capitalists have forged new forms of cooperation to forge a local culture of innovation.[3]

As I found out more about Tiruppur and its industry, I approached a set of peculiarities that I found more centrally to do with its production politics. First, a dogged communist union presence means that both Communist Parties of India, CPM and CPI, have union buildings large enough to rival those in Chennai or Delhi. However, there is a wide gap between remarkable collective bargaining mechanisms set up and revised every three years by unions' and employers' associations, and their dismal level of enforcement. In practice, wage rates vary from firm to neighboring firm. Why does such a strong symbolic veneer of class compromise persist?

Second, there is something peculiar about what people in Tiruppur sometimes call its "work culture": it seems to outsiders as unprofessional, it takes a lot of personal grease to get orders through subcontracting chains, and at the end of the day local bosses of the Gounder caste say they respect bosses just like themselves. Outsiders, including the textile corporate giants of India, have had a difficult if not impossible time attempting to harness this work culture. Some North Indian merchant families have made it in Tiruppur, but only by giving up direct control of production and surviving as traders. Why do outsiders have a hard time breaking into the heart of production in this peculiar "work culture"?

Third, the majority of owners are Gounder men, from modest caste and class origins, coming from villages within 50 kms of Tiruppur. After several months of interviews I found people would stop in their narratives predictably to say, "there is only one reason for Tiruppur's growth: toil." Not capital, not cheap labor, not credit or yarn, but the toil of self-made men. During the last year in which sales taxes were collected from domestic firms, sales tax information reveals that most firms concentrate in the old working-class neighborhoods of north Tiruppur, as indicated in Map 3. Former working-class neighborhoods like Bridgeway Colony are now packed with knitwear factories. As I hedged around these stories of class mobility and conducted a survey to find their statistical significance, I found there was no way out of the fact that most owners in Tiruppur, especially the most successful ones, are of working-class origin. Tiruppur is a town of rags-to-riches stories. My research asks how peasant workers have become owners and transformed the knitwear industry into a powerhouse of small-firm networks.

I approached this problematic through the work histories and practices of the class fraction of owners who now have the knitwear industry in their grip: Gounders of worker-peasant origins. Once these owners had consolidated their hold on the industry, they were able to outcompete the old guard of industrialists of mercantile origins, the landlord elite as well as big industrial capital that has tried to make inroads into Tiruppur. Key to the ways in which these Gounder men remade relations of place, class and gender were their ways of refashioning the space of industry into networks of firms. In order to understand why and how work has taken this "smallholder" form, I turn to processes through which peasant-workers have become fraternal capitalists, using agrarian history to remake the industrial present. The following section asks how industrial subcontracting in Tiruppur speaks to a series of wider questions concerning Indian development and the globalization of capital in provincial India.

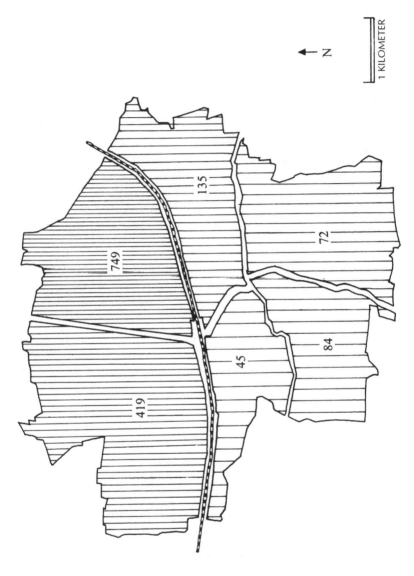

Map 3: Tiruppur: Density of Firms by Area

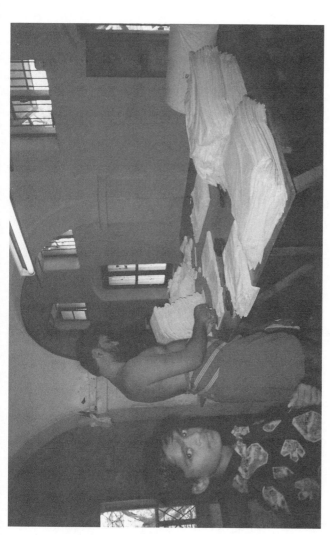

14. Gendered Articulations 1: The old order of "masculine" labor for domestic markets. An established worker with his young apprentice in an older domestic firm with an all-male workforce, making masculine garments the worker himself might buy and wear, 1997. This image presents gender in older firms in contrast with what is on offer in Photograph 18.

IV. Explaining the Globalization of Capital in Provincial India

"The need of a constantly expanding market for its products chases the bourgeoisie over the whole surface of the globe. It must nestle everywhere, settle everywhere, establish connections everywhere." Marx and Engels, *The Communist Manifesto*

While globalization has become a keyword only since the late twentieth century, nineteenth-century radicals like Marx and Engels were centrally concerned with the combined predatory and emancipatory possibilities unleashed by the globalization of capital. The internationalism of Marx's *Capital* lies in the way it relates the specific conditions of transition to capitalism in Britain not just to the bloody, and multiple, origins of capitalism, but also to capital's immanent globalizing imperative.[4] What is more, the penultimate chapter of *Capital* on "so-called primitive accumulation" also details a specific geographical imagination of the English elite displaced through colonial rule. In this imagined geography, an ideal rendition of English capitalism, capital and labor *require* forced dispossession, and metropolitan capital constituted in a landscape of full proletarianization is the driver of global change.[5] David Harvey uses these insights to effect in arguing against the spatial myopia of organized capital and labor alike in using mobility to *resolve* the contradictions of capitalist accumulation, as any such spatial fix remains a mirage, for contradictions ramify in new spatial configurations. Hence, as the globalization of capital has deepened inequalities between differentiated regions and populations, radical writers in the late twentieth century began speaking of the globalization of the Third World, the deepening of internal peripheries through sweatshops and prisons within advanced capitalism, and of the casualization of low-wage work everywhere. Some kind of internationalism remains necessary to account for the mixed predatory and emancipatory possibilities brought on by the globalization of capital. The question that remains is—what kind of internationalism?

Economic geography tends to replicate the Eurocentrism endemic in metropolitan Marxism, even when it invokes universalist conceptions of primitive accumulation to temper the progressivism of globalization. A dramatic challenge to this Eurocentrism has emerged from transitions to capitalism in East Asia. In Taiwan, South Korea, Japan, and post-Maoist China, capitalist development has not been premised on widespread dispossession. Instead, these Asian trajectories of capitalism without full proletarianization suggest a range of processes of partial dispossession and ongoing state power entailed in articulating production and reproduction, states and households, agriculture and industry.[6] What is clear in explaining these Asian trajectories is the importance of intersecting politics of inter-imperial rivalries, nation states, and a range of social institutions between states and households. This book asks how Tiruppur's Gounder peasant-workers have forged a less dramatic local capitalism without widespread dispossession, at least in its constitution, and without active state intervention.

In using the term globalization I refer to the globalization of capital as a spatial process that revives rather than buries the politics of development. How do space and power provide an alternative to an undifferentiated globalism? First, attention to social space implies, as is commonplace in social histories, that geographies are imposed, used, remade, imagined, moved, fought for and lost.[7] The chapters to follow document the dialectics of place and space, of fixity and motion, and of the unstable spatial hegemonies that make Tiruppur's global connections work. Second, the continuing importance of development politics strikes against the grain of post-leftist and neoliberal skepticism about development and planning in an era of globalization.[8] Against this skepticism, subaltern groups in the postcolony persist in making claims under the sign of development precisely because these claims cannot be subsumed into a legible logic of capital, especially where capital is not hegemonic through bourgeois-democratic politics. In the postcolony *par excellence*, the anarchic movements of uneven capitalist development continue to make space for contestations over what development ought to mean. The post-left critique of development suffers also from an essentialized, monolithic rendering of the Enlightenment and its legacies, which has come to be questioned by revisionist historians.[9] Focus on contestation over Enlightenment legacies makes it difficult to dismiss development as totalizing domination rather than as an aspect of the contested lived experience of modernity. Equally, subaltern critiques of Enlightenment legacies make it all the more important to decenter metropolitan accounts of capitalism rather than to presume European ideal types as guides to global processes.[10]

In framing a decentered account of Tiruppur's capitalism, I rely on three elements of radical thought, as emerging from the Enlightenment, Southern nationalism and postcolonial or subaltern critique.[11] Rather than seeing these as historical stages, requiring a defense of one or the other, I pose the elements as relational and configured differently across geographic contexts. Hence, Latin American postcolonial studies has emerged in relation to dependency theory to critique unequal global trade as well as Occidentalist accounts of modernity.[12] On the other hand, South Asian subaltern studies has emerged against left-nationalist historiography, as well as against the inability of progressive analytics like development economics, to grasp the conditions of power and knowledge that maintain subaltern domination.[13] I analyze Tiruppur through a specific mix of these three forms of knowledge: metropolitan radicalism, understandings of Indian development and Gounder self-presentations. The metropolitan disciplinary tradition I find most useful in understanding developments in Tiruppur is agrarian studies. In the rest of this section, I sketch out the insights from agrarian studies that I have found useful to understand Indian development theory and practice in an industrial town in a time of neoliberal ascendancy.

What is Indian neoliberalism? Industry and trade deregulation in the 1980s had deepened into a broader platform of economic liberalization by the 1990s that was supported in practice by all political parties.[14] The rhetoric of liberalization had by the 1990s taken over a large share of public discourse, so much so that the Indian popular press portrayed small towns like Tiruppur as natural successes without government support, in contrast to government-sponsored Export Processing Zones of the 1970s.[15] Key elisions in this market-centrism were the roles of small-scale industries policy and the work of regional elites and local political authorities in promoting decentralized growth.[16] In parallel, development theory and practice in India, as elsewhere, came under assault from both neoliberal critics of dirigisme, or state intervention in the economy, as well as by post-leftist critiques of governmental domination of society. Stuart Corbridge and John Harriss argue persuasively that what is striking about India in the 1990s is the lack of clear convergence between the two elite revolts of economic liberalization and ascendant Hindu nationalism, or Hindutva, in a reactionary Hindu capitalism. Countercurrents of public action from politicized plebeian castes and other marginalized populations across India's uneven geographies have made such a convergence tenuous, though the 2002 anti-Muslim pogrom in the state of Gujarat is cause for alarm on this count.[17] Certainly, both liberalization and Hindutva mark the exhaustion of Nehruvian secular, national development, a vision once supported by Cold War geopolitics and global circuits of development ideology.[18] Both are elite revolts in the wake of uneven processes of capitalist development and plebeian politicization through piecemeal postcolonial state action.

To briefly trace the background to these processes: the coalition of dominant classes represented by the postcolonial Indian state have had to address several legacies of colonialism, including the partition of the subcontinent, the linguistic demarcation of subnational states, the politicization of caste, and deepening constraints on structural transformation of the economy.[19] The elite-dominated nationalist movement chose to avoid radical social change in the face of a differentiated agrarian scene, seeking rather to entrench rural power-brokers and endemic rural poverty, to contain inequality through bureaucratic means. In the absence of both land reform and bourgeois revolution, Nehruvian planning relied on what Antonio Gramsci called a passive revolution. In other words, in the absence of Jacobin popular-nationalist consciousness, the elite coalition had to enlist the support of subaltern classes in fits and starts. This provisional, incomplete, shifting hegemony had to make space for intermediaries to seek consent for state projects, but passive revolution also provided fertile ground for plebeian counter-hegemonic movements.[20] The power of Congress Party nationalism was in this sense always tenuously linked to the persisting localization of power relations, documented by several decades of research on agrarian India. Local power and the political incapacity to finance public sector investment through direct taxes—both in

complex ways the consequence of the Indian state's inability to transform agrarian production relations—effectively prevented the emergence of a developmental state akin to the East Asian "Tigers." Passive
revolution also allowed mechanisms of political mobilization to be
ruralized, captured by plebeian constituencies for alternative ends.
Nehru's optimistic nationalism and state-making has been undone by
the ruralization of the state and the dissolution of Congress Party hegemony, and the consequence is today's landscape of plebeian politicization and elite counter-revolt.[21]

These shifts in Indian development speak to the importance of
rooting claims of globalization and social change in provincial, rural,
and small-town India, where most Indians live, work, and die. This provincial India is a space of informal economy and informal state, of incomplete regulation and of multiple forms of social control of activity
between proletarianization and self-employment. Barbara Harriss-
White has painstakingly demonstrated that the uneven implementation of economic liberalization in provincial India stands not to
replace state regulation by "good government" through market forces
but rather to create new opportunities for rent-seeking and corruption. Non-state modes of power continue to confound neoliberal
"good government" because of actually existing social and spatial
structures of accumulation, mediated by caste and gender. This book
is a historical ethnography of one such socio-spatial configuration as
it actually works in provincial India.[22]

In this wider context, Tiruppur's entry into academic debates in the
1980s and 1990s has been as an instance of flexible specialization in
India. These debates draw from the experience of the "Third Italy,"
North-East and Central Italy, from which theorists suggested flexible
specialization as an alternative form of capitalist industrialization that
could elide economies of scale and corporate dominance. Industrial
districts and inter-firm networks were seen through this frame as
balancing workers' rights with efficiency enhancement and innovation.[23] At the center of the industrial district literature was an emphasis
on small producers in a sort of yeoman's capitalism. Consequently, a
range of studies of industrial clusters in Third World contexts began
to see flexible specialization and post-Fordism as the new Holy Grail

to replace the older goals of import substitution and self-reliance under state-centered development planning.[24] These debates have brought space and geography back into the analysis of work and industry, particularly in asking whether and how specialized spatial agglomerations mitigate capitalism's contradictions. Industrial district scholars were most interested in the ways in which collective capital benefits through the division of labor, through collective efficiency, a concept that reworks older concerns in industrial studies drawing from Alfred Marshall's classic work on British textile and metalworking clusters. The new industrial studies extend Marshall's interest in the non-pecuniary gains of spatial agglomeration, particularly through new kinds of capitalist collective action or "joint action" to enhance regional innovation.[25]

Certain scholars in the 1990s saw flexible specialization as a model for Third World countries after the decline of import substitution industrialization, and hence for economic liberalization in India.[26] The primary concern in studies of Indian industrial clusters was to ask whether inter-firm relations of competition could complement cooperation, whether in Agra's footwear, Ludhiana's light engineering, or Pakistani Punjab's surgical instruments clusters. This body of research is primarily interested in forms of "horizontal" inter-firm relations that combine competition and cooperation, as in "capacity contracting" or the sharing of production orders, pooled marketing strategies or collective lobbying of the state.[27]

Cultural and communicative aspects of inter-firm relations enter this perspective through the notions of a "local social milieu," "work ethos," or "non-confrontational spirit." The social milieu, for instance, is a site of learning through which technology and innovation are endogenized in the cluster. Like scholars rethinking Weber on Asian business, these researchers wrestle with explaining why South Asian clusters are dominated by particular castes or communities, such as Patels in Surat's diamond polishing cluster, Sikh Ramgarhias in Ludhiana, Ansari Muslim *biradaris* or fraternities in textiles, and Lohar ironsmith *biradaris* in metalworking clusters in Pakistani Punjab. Where industrial cluster scholars fall short is in explaining how social milieux differentially shape economic action, to reinforce

the power of certain social identities and the stability of specific practices. An underlying assumption is that power, meaning and practice
are a kind of baggage that fixed identities carry around with them, so
identities can only really have a positive or negative effect *vis-à-vis* the
possibility of collaboration.[28]

Meenu Tewari's research on Ludhiana, Punjab, addresses some of
these concerns through social history. The key to Ludhiana's industrial growth was agrarian colonial policy in the form of the Punjab
Land Alienation Bill of 1900, which sought to preserve "traditional"
farming communities, thereby defining a range of non-farm communities excluded from agrarian accumulation. One such community,
Ramgarhia artisans, shifted as a whole from the countryside to investment and skill-development in Ludhiana's industry. When state defense contracts fueled demand for knitwear and large firms started
subcontracting to smaller units on credit, another regional community stepped in. Credit for small firms came in large part from *arha-
tiyas*, grain brokers and regional financiers who straddled rural and
urban spheres, mediating agrarian surpluses and industrial investment,
allowing a slow process of transfer of resources before Punjab's Green
Revolution. Subsequently, the state government in the 1960s used
bureaucratic innovations to work around the "red tape" of import
substitution industrialization, to fuel industrial accumulation in
Ludhiana. This analysis is rare in looking at the historical dynamics of
rural–urban classes, their roles in the intersectoral transfers of resources,
and the ways in which regional institutions used the dirigiste state.[29]

As mentioned in the last section, my analysis of Tiruppur responds
to Cawthorne's research in the 1980s by situating knitwear work in
processes and practices of agrarian and regional change. Before I turn
to the ways in which I conceive of these broader processes, I want to
note that Cawthorne writes as if the histories and self-presentations of
Tiruppur's inhabitants are exogenous to political economy. In the face
of qualitative evidence of workers becoming, or interested in becoming, owners, this researcher is resolutely skeptical: "What, *cannot* be
assumed, contrary to popular Tiruppur ideology, is that workers who
do begin [as small owners] will become particularly 'successful' . . . Just
as the picture of a small-scale industry is assiduously promoted by
interested institutional parties and by the owners of firms (and is, in

some very important respects a distorted view) so are the prospects for the 'entrepreneurially-minded worker' overstated."[30] Certainly, local ideology cannot be taken at face value in light of considerable economic differentiation between firms and classes. However, in not analyzing local interpretations of political economy, the label "distortion" misses the links between ways of signifying self and conventional interaction.[31] An ethnographic and historical critique of subaltern self-presentation is essential if one is to grasp how specific work histories and agrarian or regional legacies are deployed by participants in knitwear work today, let alone how these articulate wider shifts in the political economy of India in the late twentieth century.

As I have hinted, I explain these regional processes and broader shifts through the tradition of agrarian studies, a longstanding counter-tradition to the Eurocentrism of metropolitan Marxism. The classical "agrarian question" of nineteenth-century German and Russian political economy decenters Marxism by looking at capitalism from the fields rather than the factory gates. In asking how capitalism transforms agriculture differently, the agrarians conceptualize "difference" through the persistence of peasant households and their constitutive non-capitalist dynamics, as well as through the natural dynamics of agriculture and the worked environment.[32] Fundamental to classical agrarian theorists is some sense of "natural economy," with singular characteristics, that is somehow altered in the modern world; and the question is what these shifts mean for peasant livelihoods. While this problematic could not see subaltern rationalities in non-Occidentalist terms, the peasant has always been a reminder of singularities and of the unevenness of capitalist development. This point has consistently differentiated agrarian studies from metropolitan Marxism, and it provides a tradition of radical thought derived from the Enlightenment that can be used to decenter conventional accounts of capitalism.

Terry Byres has engaged in an important comparative account of agrarian transitions, distinguishing the English tripartite division of landlord, tenant farmer, and waged laborer; the Prussian dual economy of semi-proletarian labor and neo-feudal capitalist landlord reliant on state largesse; petty commodity production in the US North; an impoverished French small peasantry beholden to the monarchy; and state-led East Asian transitions based on land reform and high rates of extraction from the peasantry through the intersectoral terms of trade.[33] In India, the colonial attempt to create improving landlords through the Permanent Settlement of Bengal met with little or no success, resulting in practice in the consolidation of a parasitic class of absentee landlords and the stagnation of agriculture.[34] Agrarian capitalism in India has taken root in areas of the north-west and south that were *ryotwari* areas, where the colonial state granted long-term leases to smallholders, and where the postcolonial Indian state has supported the interests of rich peasants, or "kulaks," against parasitic landlords. What is striking in contrast to this general rendition of Indian agrarian transition, is that agrarian transition in Tiruppur's hinterland has been effected not by a "kulak" class but by the poorer end of a differentiating peasantry. A deeper problem in this orthodox approach is the reduction of social power relations to the agency of the state or a carrier class, a position questioned by revisionist scholarship which sees agrarian transitions through complex negotiations across institutions and social domains.[35]

Three key debates in Indian agrarian studies are central to understanding Tiruppur's development in broader terms. The corresponding features to the agrarian question in India concern the localization and fragmentation of work; regional divergence and processes of agro-industrial linkage; and new forms of agrarian mobilization linked to the rising power of rural capitalists in prosperous regions.[36] These three themes concerning agrarian India converge in the dynamics of development in Tiruppur.

First, as I have argued, local power relations have been central to the workings of modern India, as both colonial and postcolonial regimes have had to realize in practice. Indian agrarian studies has a tradition of research on local arrangements of land, labor, and credit, since the pioneering work of Krishna Bharadwaj. One general observation of this literature is the overwhelming evidence that forms of attachment such as tied-labor arrangements or interlinked transactions in land, labor, credit, and other services need not be obstacles to the development of capitalism, but might be instruments of class struggle and accumulation.[37] Scholars of gender and caste relations in agrarian India arrive at a similar point on the modernity of "traditional" institutions and conventions, but with a stress on the politics and negotiation implied by specific uses. Another strand, since T.S. Epstein's classic village ethnography, indicates that technological and economic development might strengthen Dalit and women's subjection, while regional diversification and pluriactivity might weaken them. Subsequent work takes this argument further to show how gender politics operates at wider spatial scales to mediate the reproduction of a differentiated system of accumulation and impoverishment. These studies take gender out of the household and family to see gender ideology as constitutive of labor market segmentation and of social inequality more generally.[38] These ethnographically informed studies of local power relations in agrarian India provide an analytic for understanding articulations of work regimes with broader social processes. In this task, this work shares space with historical, ethnographic scholarship on labor regimes and the modern career of caste in Tamil Nadu and India more generally.[39]

Second, questions concerning sectoral and social biases in Indian development have centered on the politics of intersectoral resource transfers, and its relation to rising prosperity in the west and south, and also to the charge that Indian development suffers from an "urban bias." The problematic of intersectoral resource transfers emerged from the Soviet Industrialization Debates in the early USSR, in which the question of whether an agrarian surplus was necessary to fuel rapid industrialization had intense political consequences. Ensuing debates show that competing interpretations of resource transfers rest crucially on how sectors are defined and on how class relations are elided in the definition of sectors.[40] Similar debates, with similarly disastrous political implications, were played out in postcolonial contexts such as India. In a useful recapitulation of India in this comparative frame, Massoud Karshenas shows, first, that the Indian state maintained a high agricultural price policy and steep terms-of-trade in favor of agriculture since the mid 1960s; second, that farm households were net borrowers from the 1950s; and, third, that the state has been politically unable to skim off farm incomes, leading to a positive inflow of resources *into* agriculture until 1970. This counters Michael Lipton's urban bias argument, in which the state drained the countryside through the manipulation of relative prices; this argument neglects the

ways in which rural elites maintain power in alliance with urban elites
and state agents. In light of the brutal repression of urban worker militancy leading to the Emergency of 1977, the urban bias thesis ignores
the state's inability to use taxes or the terms-of-trade to secure cheap
food in order to keep industrial wages low. Subsequent research showed how struggles between fractions of rural and urban capital differentiate by region and crop, so that those dominated by politically
active large farmers tended to receive the benefits of farm pricing
policy. Relations between classes and the state have been profoundly
geographical. To counter this geography of rural inequality, John
Mellor argued that growth in foodgrains can forge demand and consumption linkages to ensure cheap food, and growth with relative equity. This policy outcome is, however, premised on a developmental
state committed to an alliance of the rural and urban poor, rather than
to a farm lobby mobilized to maintain price supports and input subsidies across India's divided geography.[41]

Subsequent research on rural diversification in a more ethnographic vein, by Rutten in rural–urban Kheda District, Gujarat, demonstrates the cultural and economic activities that link large farmers and
small-scale industrialists into a class of rural capitalists. These Patidar
capitalists use kin and caste ties in mobilizing managerial and financial resources across rural and urban industry. Upadhya's research on
Kamma Naidu farmers diversifying into the urban sphere in coastal
Andhra Pradesh is important for similar reasons, and these cases are in
line with Byres's presumption that the "carrier class" of successful local
agrarian transitions is rich peasants/capitalist farmers. Culture functions
in these accounts as superstructural reinforcement for entrepreneurial
class solidarity. Tiruppur's Gounders, in my analysis, disrupt this picture in multiple ways. First, entrepreneurs must be understood in
relation to other classes. Second, the cultural politics of classes have to
be seen relationally in explaining the simultaneity of class mobility and
differentiation. Third, culture–economy dialectics must show how
cultural "lifestyles" make a difference to economic action. Particularly
useful in this respect is Jan Breman's work on the "footloose proletariat"
stretched across agrarian and migrant labor in rural and urban South
Gujarat. *Mukadars* or labor recruiters must prove to employers that

they can get migrant workers to work through a mix of verbal abuse and persuasion, and, in order to secure migrants, *mukadams* renovate relations of indenture and control that mirror an older agrarian system of Hali unfree labor. Intersecting class, caste and gender loyalties prevent the emergence of fully mobile permanent migrants, reinforcing labor contractors' tendency to locate in labor-sourcing regions; people explain this geographical sourcing of labor by essentializing skills as caste-specific. In the absence of unionization and as a response to extremely arduous work regimes, the footloose proletariat chooses "fugitive behavior" as its only recourse in gaining time for recuperation. This ethnography of movement shows how subordinate groups without much in the way of material resources carry traces of agrarian social relations into non-farm and urban work environs. I elaborate on this ethnographic approach to intersectoral linkages, by attending to the ways in which peasant-worker migrants to Tiruppur rework relations of space and place while remaking themselves through specific uses of their agrarian past.[42]

The third debate concerns the politics of the agrarian question, and in particular the rise of "New Farmers" Movements premised on fighting "urban bias." The debate surrounding these movements arises from the fact that rather than the "Green Revolution turning red," as many left scholars of the 1970s expected,[43] certain Green Revolution regions saw the emergence of New Farmers' Movements centered on input and output prices.[44] These farmers' movements tied the agrarian sector more closely to the populist state's politics of prices and subsidies. Consequently, agrarian capitalism transformed the geography of Indian development, "ruralizing" party politics while fostering state populism directed at rescuing rural "Bharat." The ruralization of politics and the related explosion in state subsidies only deepened the fiscal crisis of the state and fueled, in complex ways, challenges to Indian federalism. These forces have come together in two major elite revolts in contemporary India: first, the ascent of the Hindu fundamentalist Bharatiya Janata Party (BJP) as a response to the reservation of government jobs for underprivileged "Backward Classes" under the Mandal Commission; second, the rise of an ideology of a "new middle class" in the wake of rural and provincial accumulation, and the attack on *dirigiste* development through economic liberalization. What is important to note is that economic liberalization has hardly touched the agrarian sector, because of the continuing power of rural and provincial elites. Instead, the populism of agrarian subsidies extended its contradictions into the reform process.[45]

Incomplete neoliberal reforms have tended, moreover, to perpetuate primitive accumulation in the informal economy governed by an informal state rife with decentralized violence and corruption. Barbara Harriss-White has shown how liberalization has deepened state failure in social development while legitimating more virulent, often violent, forms of class domination at local levels. This insight shifts focus from "kulaks" as a carrier class of agrarian transitions to uneven processes of accumulation in provincial India. This book uses an ethnographic method to understand how accumulation in provincial India works through local articulations of caste, class, and gender.

As a final note to this tracing of theory relevant to Tiruppur, the state of Kerala demonstrates how counter-hegemonic forces have linked local struggles with political decentralization to challenge the unholy alliance of informal economy and informal state, while reconfiguring the nature and function of the state profoundly. Kerala's development with relative equity has been enabled through the articulation of difference by Gramscian organic intellectuals within the regional Communist Part of India who infiltrated a range of social movements to link mass literacy, public health, women's capabilities, agitations against caste inequality, and the unionization of informal sector workers. These movements brought not only the first popularly elected communist government in the world, but also a set of grassroots institutions that have maintained counter-hegemonic public action for working-class Keralites even when the communist party has not been in power in the state. Kerala's developmental trajectory, based on the extension of social support enforced by popular public action, provides an implicit normative contrast for this account of agrarian transition in Tiruppur.[46]

I have sought in this section to situate Tiruppur in a broader set of debates on development and agrarian change in provincial India. In the tradition of agrarian studies I find useful intellectual tools for radical analysis of local power relations and the persistence of singular "unfreedoms" within capitalist geographies. This makes little sense in the abstract, without ethnography that critically engages subaltern self-presentation. I turn in the following section from theory to my research practice.

V. Method: Significance and Causality, Social Locations and Solidarities

I realized while conducting research that I was just as surely being located by people I interacted with. A stranger on the bus asked me how my research was going, and on more than one occasion other researchers in Tiruppur were referred by locals to talk to the strange *Americakarrar* who bicycled around town with a tape recorder. I turn to my research experience to relate how I wrestled with questions of significance and causality, objectivity and reflexivity, while finding myself located socially through a series of compromises and solidarities. All the while, I sought to collect evidence for a cultural political economy of development, combining ethnographic, survey and archival methods.

I conducted research over 1996–8 in two research trips. During the first trip of ten months in India, I was in residence in Tiruppur for nine months between November 1996 and August 1997, primarily collecting life histories. After a short trip back to the US and to the archives in London, I returned for a second trip of six months to India. This time I spent four months in Tiruppur, between October 1997 and March 1998, primarily conducting surveys. I kept a diary of ethnographic reflections through my stay in Tiruppur.

I began with open-ended interviews in the form of life histories to gain access to a wide array of events that respondents saw as significant in linking their lives to local development. I also tried to speak to a range of people of all walks of life and from various locations in the city and surrounding countryside. By the end of my first trip I completed 201 life histories, almost all in Tamil, and recorded on tape, so that I could revisit narratives. I sought to link details of events and practices with interpretations and narrative strategies emerging from particular social locations. In collecting these narratives, I sought a set of intersecting, relational accounts that I could link to the social processes that were of interest to me: histories and practices of work. In creating an oral archive of situated knowledges, I tried to be conscious of the ways in which my interpretive apparatus mediated the social relations in which I sought to situate my interlocutors.[47]

During the first research trip, I also conducted research at the Tamil Nadu Archives, Chennai; the Madras Institute of Development Studies Library, Chennai; the District Collectorate Library, Coimbatore; the District Industries Centre, Coimbatore; the Factories Inspectorate, Tiruppur; Apparel Export Promotion Council, Tiruppur; SIHMA, Tiruppur; and at CITU, the union of the Communist Party of India—Marxist, Tiruppur. I also spent a short two weeks in August 1997 conducting library research at the India Office Records, London.

Returning to California, I used the life histories of knitwear company owners to think through different sorts of "routes of entry and accumulation," or ways in which owners' histories could be linked to their identities and work practices. These stylized "routes," constructed after close examination of life histories collected, provided the questions for a survey instrument, designed to assess the validity of what appeared to be widespread class mobility.

My second research trip was concentrated on administering the survey to randomly selected 15 percent of members of the two main owners' associations, SIHMA, and the Tiruppur Exporters Association (TEA). Finding 218 specific firms selected from association lists by a random number generator proved to be a very difficult task, but I completed both surveys with a 95 percent success rate. I administered all the surveys myself, almost always in Tamil, and on many occasions the survey would spill out into a broader discussion around particular themes of interest. I tried to frame questions following local talk. For instance, in asking "*Nínga vélai paḷakkitingḷa?*" ("Did you get accustomed to the work?"), I wanted to ask today's owners if they had been workers, but I use a local euphemism that emphasizes skill-acquisition rather than wage labor. This is one way in which I sought to use local knowledge from my first research phase in constructing an ethnographically precise survey.

Implicit in my fieldwork is an argument about mixed research methods. I constructed my study to see the agrarian origins of industry in Tiruppur as a particular case that reconstructs the theory of agrarian transition. Indeed, the anomaly of peasant-workers being at the center of this local transition to global production provided an opportunity to reconsider the paths and means through which capitalism develops.[48] However, I foreground the acts of translation that allow a mapping of singular cultural historic evidence onto a particular case study of general processes. My commitment to the notion of a case study is circumscribed by the importance of the work of translating conversations that enable social scientific knowledge about actual social processes.

Life histories and ethnography allow me to make claims about causal mechanisms as well as about how these mechanisms are interpreted. Surveys allow me to make statistic claims about the incidence of particular causal mechanisms. Moreover, in laying out a diversity of trajectories of capital within the knitwear industry, I use internal comparisons to also speak comparatively within the case study. The scale of most of my research has been local, primarily because the questions I ask took me increasingly close to micro-level meanings and practices. While the processes that work through this locality are much wider in scale and scope, I focus on how they work through the lives of people seeking to inhabit a particular capitalist modernity.

This has meant that I was drawn to a multiplicity of habitations in Tiruppur, some of which I was much more welcome in than others. As a "Tambram" or Tamil Brahmin by birth, I was lucky to be conducting research in a region that is not numerically or socially dominated by Brahmins. As far as I can gauge from my friendships in Tiruppur, I could be taken seriously for affirming a dislike of anything to do with casteism or Brahminism, even as these forms of social domination have undoubtedly shaped my character in a variety of unintended ways. I certainly did not partake of the most obvious markers of Brahminism, like wearing a "crossbelt" or sacred thread, and speaking in a Sanskritized Tamil. This was vindicated by the uneasy reactions of several in my own extended family for my choice of speaking Tamil without displaying Brahmin affiliation.

When it came to gender, however, I found I could make common cause with some men who shared progressive views regarding women's rights. In practice, most of my friends were young men, and though I had friends across class I only saw a group of working-class friends during short interludes between work and exhaustion at a particular tea stall. Although I had a few friends with somewhat progressive views on gender and sexuality, most men I spent time with held such different views and engaged in such different practices that I decided not to be argumentative or moralistic on this count, but to be circumspect. While women would speak to me alone for a while, unmarried or recently married women would often become embarrassed after an initial period. Older women, women at workplaces or in groups, and women I knew through my daily activities were exceptions, as I perhaps did not pose a threat. I could only spend substantial time with young working-class women and girls when, for a short period, I accompanied Ms Sujana Krishnamoorthy, an academic and activist from New Delhi, on her interviews in Tiruppur's working-class neighborhoods.

Beyond the ways in which I sought to place myself ideologically, in terms of caste, class and gender, the details of my housing and movement around town profoundly shaped the types of compromises and solidarities I made. During my first research trip, I resided with the family of a wealthy doctor in an affluent residential neighborhood, with comforts that made my initial stage of research much easier. Moreover, because Dr Visvasam was very well known, with the reputation of a doctor from a bygone era who would make frequent house calls, I received the advantages of familiarity with a wide swathe of local society. I also met some key owners and public figures through Mrs Visvasam's introductions after the doctor's premature death. Moreover, when I was desperate to arrange an interview and had to play all my cards, I would introduce myself as from America, California University, and from the home of Visvasam Doctor, before mumbling my name. This connection to a deceased local professional afforded autonomy from inter-owner competition and local politics, and the respect it offered, thankfully, never backfired.

I began moving around town by foot, then switched to a bicycle through which I accomplished most of my research, save occasional excursions into the countryside. Bicycling gave me the opportunity to stop where I chose, and, as I discovered from ways in which certain locals later described my activities, it conveyed a sense of *my toil*! I know that on one occasion an owner of working-class origins was impressed that I was ready to bike across town to meet his ex-worker who now runs his own factory; he got on the phone and arranged the meeting for me immediately.

During my second research trip I resided in an old factory–home owned by a quirky bachelor of the Iyer Brahmin caste. There were two 100-year-old buildings adjacent to each other housing Kittu Iyer's home and factory. Though I had a room upstairs in the home, it was too dusty to use for anything except the occasional private writing time. I ate, slept, performed ablutions, and wrote my notes along with the group of boys whose daily lives surrounded Kittu Iyer in his large multipurpose central room. My living experience could not have been more different from the first research trip, as I no longer had a place to use a laptop nor the leisure to rest and work as I pleased. I was, however, afforded insights into a dying form of patriarchal management and work practice found in few of the remaining older banian companies oriented to the domestic market, relying entirely on male labor and particular kinds of homosocial relations surrounding work. This factory/home was my window into a form of capital that has been displaced by Gounders of worker origins.

Deprived of an easy place to retreat from research, I was forced into the rhythms of company owners as I relentlessly pursued their schedules, from 9 a.m. to 2 p.m., then 4 p.m. to 8 or 9 p.m., after which I would go to a local gym and then, occasionally, to a local bar to write up notes. There was nothing like uncomfortable lodgings with extremely congenial hosts to keep me working to finish a tedious survey.

My social class position as an Indian from the US also afforded me the opportunity to meet foreign buyers and members of the Coimbatore elite. Moreover, as I had built a rapport with several of the leading figures in Tiruppur's industry early on, much of it through sheer persistence, I began to greet them in each other's company at various events in town. As leading men of the Gounder community from both the owner and labor union sides were like kin in these events, I could present myself as a somewhat objective figure even if the labor union leaders tended to know that my sympathies lay on the side of workers.

My research is most thin on Dalits and women partly because they have been excluded from the processes I sought to explain, but partly for my own embodied limitations as an elite male. While I did have some very engaging discussions in Dalit neighborhoods, I sometimes did not. On one occasion, in a far-flung Dalit village, I drew a throng of unhappy faces, one among whom said, after a long silence, "Tell him we are the Paraiyar, we are the Chakkiliar, we are the Harijan!" The implication in this statement of disgust was that I only wanted to be told things that were said pejoratively about them. My most informative interviews in Dalit neighborhoods were with young people who found work outside, and with it, perhaps, a sense that they could find a shared arena of conversation with me. Apart from the most abject subalterns, many poor people who traverse Tiruppur and its surrounding villages were open to translating their particular stories in broader terms, opening a space both for understanding and for solidarity.

While I had a good rapport with male workers, there was one incident that gave me considerable pause. A worker had promised that I could see the diary he had kept over many years as an alternative to narrating his life history, and I thought this a gold mine. In my excitement I let someone at the labor union know that I anticipated accessing this man's diary. After this the man changed his mind entirely and became much more resistant to sharing his story. Although a costly lesson, this event taught me that my equation of the worker's views with his union was naïve and uncognizant of the complex relations of power between union organizers, rank-and-file workers, and researchers. I have sought to retain a sense that the biographies I have collected do not "speak for themselves" as they are situated in experiences saturated with multiple power relations, involving a range of other narratives, not least my own. Finally, this has only confirmed my sense that Marxist ethnography need not be narrowly "laborist" but can retain a sense of objectivity as long as it also takes stock of the multiple fetishisms that mediate the possibility of speaking truth to power. In the following section, I briefly summarize my argument.

VI. Plan of This Work: An Agrarian History
of the Industrial Present

This book is written in the form of a spiral. I begin with the industrial present, then turn to agrarian history to make sense of memories of toil in reshaping industrial work practices today. I do not want to prove that the past has marched inevitably to *this* present, but that today's industrial practice has been forged through a selective reworking of meanings and practices from partial locations, with divergent visions of the future. The present with which I conclude is brittle, fraught with the contradictions of its construction, and from which alternative futures might be forged.

To put flesh on all this abstraction, I briefly rehearse the arguments in the chapters to follow. Part I begins with the industrial present. Chapter 2 responds to ways of seeing Tiruppur as an industrial district with potentials actualized in the Third Italy. Through the notion of social labor, I show how the accumulation of capital through small-firm networks is related to new forms of labor market insecurity, so that Tiruppur combines technological change with intensified insecurity of employment. Chapter 3 turns within the division of labor to find multiple accumulation strategies taken by fractions of capital of different social origins. Through an internal comparison of "routes of entry and accumulation," I find one fraction of capital advantaged in its power over production. Part I concludes by asking why and how Gounders of working-class origin wield power over the knitwear cluster like no other fraction of capital.

Part II turns to the agrarian past and its use in remaking urban industry. Chapter 4 turns to the colonial and agrarian history of Coimbatore District to explore how agrarian production politics, regional geographical processes, and colonial representations of Gounders as an entrepreneurial caste came together as social and cultural preconditions for Tiruppur's rapid transformation as the fastest growing town in Tamil Nadu in the first half of the twentieth century. In particular, this chapter explores how a flexible production politics forged in the smallholder agriculture of the 1930s combined with strong links between country and city in a process of geographical specialization that produced a series of specialist towns, including Tiruppur. These two agrarian legacies—flexibility based on a particular production politics, on the one hand, and geographical specialization based on intersectoral linkage and rural diversification on the other hand—came together in Tiruppur, and Gounder peasants remained key actors in a processes of rural diversification, trade and industrialization.

Chapter 5 begins by setting the stage for the character of industry and unionism in Tiruppur between the 1920s and 1950s, when Gounder peasant-workers came to town as industrial workers. While the older elite organized work through a mercantilist vision in which labor was embodied in things, this would be in sharp contrast to the Gounder owners who saw their labor as toil. I then turn to the question "can the subaltern accumulate capital?" which I address by tracing a series of moments through which certain Gounder men could use to turn their toil into capital by renovating elements of their agrarian past. I show that toil was indeed the advantage that Gounders still say it was, but the more important question is what this cultural construction indexes and how it is used in practice to remake class and place in gendered terms.

Chapter 6 picks up on this theme in the era of exports, as an unintended consequence of the agrarian transition through Gounder toil was the making of a Gounder fraternity controlling dispersed capital and of a feminized, insecure workforce. In this last respect, feminization has meant not only the entry of women workers and deepened gender divisions of labor but also the articulation of sexed bodies to differentiation in new ways. The consequence has been a diversification of work contracts, types of security, exposures to violence, and forms of sexualization in a widening gap between institutionalized rights and workplace realities. Simultaneously, a class of exporters has risen to dominate the entire production cluster through new forms of cosmopolitan Gounder masculinity and institutionalized class power *vis-à-vis* the state.

Chapter 7 sews up the seams and concludes with broader reflections on agrarian questions and gendered accumulation in the globalization of provincial India.

PART I

Social Labor and the Industrial Present

CHAPTER 2

Social Labor, or
How a Town Works, 1996–1998

I. Introduction: A Capitalist Order
of Things

Garment work in Tiruppur appears first as a world of people and things: subjects and objects, owners of factories, workers, raw materials, and goods that travel through the system as if of their own accord. Foreign buyers encounter only final products, fashion garments, while labeling a diversity of producers with the generic term "suppliers." From the buyer's perspective, suppliers must agree to the lowest price for particular products delivered at the right time. Beneath the membrane that keeps foreign buyers from the turmoil of production lies a messy ensemble of labors that come together in making the whole town work for the global economy. This chapter explores the social character of this variety of labors, as they constitute a working town. In detailing social labor, I show how capital, labor, uncertainty and seasonality, credit, and regulatory institutions are mobilized in production. I show how at the center of this baroque organization of work is a section of the labor process that has most to tell about Tiruppur and its self-made men: the stitching section. I concur that industrial cluster studies use the notion of "collective efficiency" to good effect in understanding capitalist action in organizing social labor.[1] This chapter demonstrates how, through the work of social labor, value that is a product of cooperation and coordination of diverse labors is offered to capital as a gift.[2]

After describing the categories through which people in Tiruppur experience the order of things, Section II turns to the organization of work through networked worksites. In Section III, I think more deeply about the concept of social labor in relation to power and contracting in Tiruppur. Section IV asks how global demand constructs the types of uncertainty and seasonality producers of export knitwear must contend with in organizing work. Section V uses the countervailing circuit of money capital to discuss the crucial role of short-term credit or "working capital" in decentralized production. Section VI turns to regulatory institutions, which guide inter-capitalist competition in the interests of accumulation and control. Finally, Section VII returns to exploitation at the heart of the organization of social labor, to considerations of labor and labor-time in spatially and temporally fragmented work. Through this journey, I show how Tiruppur draws a motley crew of workers, owner-operators and dependent contractors into a web of class subjection.

Who are the various agents in Tiruppur's order of things? Tiruppur's residents distinguish two types of owners by their products: banians, underwear for the home market; or fashion garments for export. People in Tiruppur also distinguish owners by their ways of organizing work. Manufacturers, engaged in *taiyárippu*, might own plant and machinery while being minimally involved in the labor process, either by sourcing out more than they produce in-shop, by leasing, or contracting out their machines. Some business families and larger textile concerns operate in Tiruppur purely as traders, but the convention is to include them among manufacturers as long as they purchase the main raw material, yarn. Buyers of yarn who are sellers of knitwear are manufacturers by local convention. Below them a layer of local producers makes garments on jobwork subcontract. The crucial distinction among domestic owners is in producing for the market rather than for another firm, which one owner disdainfully called *kottatimai*, indenture or bonded labor. Among exporters, similarly, some actually make garments and others are traders. Most people in Tiruppur distinguish direct exporters from merchant exporters in much the same way that domestic manufacturers are distinguished from jobworkers. Direct exporters contract with foreign buyers or buying houses while merchant exporters produce export garments on subcontract for final exporters. Merchant exporters never enter the process of contract negotiation with foreign buyers and rarely even see the export contract. I follow local convention in distinguishing firm owners by whom they supply products to.[3]

Members of the owners' associations are domestic manufacturers, direct exporters or merchant exporters, but none of these designations imply whether they own production units, let alone organize production themselves. What owners own are companies, and a mass of job-workers supplies these companies with goods and services at various stages of production. The sheer range of types of activities that might comprise a knitwear company or group of companies, and the myriad ways in which neat firm boundaries are violated, motivates my use of "unit" to speak of actual workplaces. The unit may be a part of a larger company or set of companies that comprises something like a capitalist firm.

Older firms combine secretarial-managerial functions in the *kanak-kupiḻḻai*, or accountant, who is second to the boss, while large export houses employ an army of managers, secretaries and roving quality controllers to oversee dispersed worksites. Production managers and contractors are also best seen as part of this upper tier of the workforce as they share the prized possession of a regular, year-round income. Below them lie industrial workers with varying degrees of freedom and insecurity, and with varying degrees of socially recognized skill. The *kanakkupiḻḻai* has an awkward role to play in small firms, in which he may in fact be as beholden to the boss as any other worker, but his literacy and distance from manual labor set him off from industrial labor. In many small units where the boss has himself risen from the ranks of industrial labor and is often less educated than today's workers, the boss manages work (*vēlai*) while the accountant manages "business."

Figure 3 diagrams the interrelations between units engaged in production in Tiruppur. The nerve center of interfirm relations is the knitwear company that purchases yarn and sells knitwear garments. The knitwear company is the hub of contractual relations with external buyers and local subcontractors. Since all or part of the production of garments from knitted cloth can be contracted or leased out, either internally or through external units, the knitwear company might just be a shell which puts out everything; this is why Figure 3 represents it as a hollowed box. All elements of the labor process can be separately located and owned, which is why this diagram presumes separable units contracting with a hollow knitwear company that is merely a trader. This is the basic order of things in Tiruppur knitwear.

Most companies only assemble garments, farming out fabrication, processing and accessorizing on jobwork. Jobwork is the most common contractual relation between units of production that are formally independent. Jobworkers identify themselves with their stage in Figure 3, by whether they own knitwear production units, small stitching sections, or various sections in processing, accessorizing, packaging or fabrication. These units may be independent in terms of direct control of production, though they may be dependent on buyer firms through credit. Jobwork relations range from spot-market relationships to durable ties between units of a larger group of firms with common partners. Many small units in garment stitching say they are not in *taiyárippu* or manufacture because they only work for *coolie*, a wage. These petty commodity producers struggle to reproduce their production unit rather than to accumulate capital. The institution of jobwork breeds a mass of such petty units to take on a variety of functions on contract from the central company. There is significant differentiation between small jobwork units producing local goods for the Erode *cantai*, or periodic market, on *coolie* just enough to pay the owner-operator a wage, and larger units producing export garments for export firms engaged in capacity subcontracting; that is, for exporters who take on orders far above their own capacity and put out most of the production on jobwork.

Jobwork differs from inter-unit relations known as "contract," which refer specifically to sections of production owned by the company where the control of the labor process is left in the hands of an individual contractor.[4] Often the company owner describes these arrangements as, "I own the machines but I don't own the work." The *taiyal nilayam* or stitching section is usually "given on contract" in the charge of a Power Table Contractor. In fact, contract is almost always a term referring to stitching sections, whether formally within or outside the company. Sometimes companies refer to all piecerated

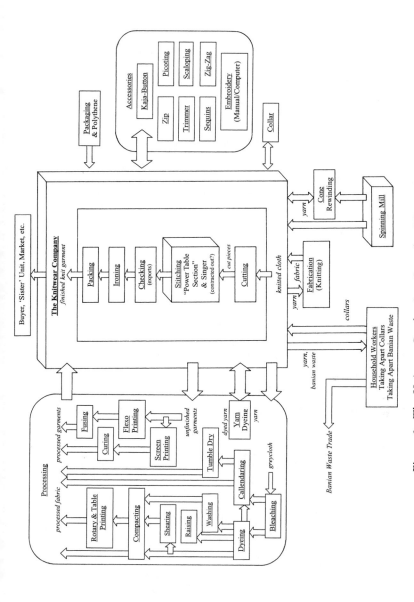

Figure 3: The Knitwear Production Complex, Tiruppur, c. 1998.

workers as contract workers, but these individual labor contracts based on piece-rates are different from group- and task-based contractual arrangements; and, as will become clear in chapters to come, the latter are a much more recent labor arrangement. Contracting in this specific sense of decentralizing not ownership but production control has proliferated since the mid 1980s through internal and external task-based contracts using company machines and raw materials, with contractors mediating the irregular supply of laborpower.

This is not to say that companies don't also consolidate operations to achieve economies of scale, but, as Section IV shows, they do so through different ways of handling the contradiction between standardized products and dedicated production, and between predictability and uncertainty. North Indian owners, particularly those who have entered since the export boom of the 1980s on a merchant putting-out model, have in many instances integrated their processing, fabrication and accessorizing operations *without* investing in knitwear manufacturing companies. However, small manufacturing firms with one power table and a combination of hired and "known" labor constitute the quintessential petty producer in Tiruppur.[5] These are jobwork firms working for *coolie*.

A layer of traders deals in commodities ranging from crucial raw materials such as yarn, chemical dyes, and water for processing to the illicit trade in rejected or surplus export fabric and garments, and to the trade in "banian waste."[6] Yarn traders are some of the older business families of the region, who have served as intermediaries for spinning mills' relations with in-weavers and knitters for at least fifty years. Chapter 1 described the streets in the old city center named for prominent Chettiar and Mudaliar traders, many of whom made their fortunes in the yarn trade. The trade in water is a recent phenomenon that has emerged in relation to Tiruppur's boom, and much of it is for the captive use of large dyeing and processing operations. A mass of small, unregulated traders deal in export surplus cloth and garments, as well as in lower quality products for the Erode *cantai*, the regional periodic market specialized in the textile products of western Tamil Nadu. These traders concentrate in the Khadarpet area near the railway station, where North Indian traders typically come to buy batches in spot

15. Gendered Articulations 2: A contractor of an old domestic firm
with the Factory Acts, in Tamil and English, at the entrance, 1997.
This image links the "masculine" domestic workplace of Photograph 14
to the public labor unionism of an all-male workforce.

market transactions. The Erode *cantai* provides an outlet for goods produced and marketed in firms that are for the most part outside state regulation, in relation to sales tax.

Providers of various services, concerning export and domestic marketing, management, computers, transport, finance, communications, and even astrology and numerology, form the next component of this production system. The mushrooming of export buying offices and trading houses shows how Tiruppur's globalization makes room for a range of intermediary trade and quality-related services. A sign of the global times hangs outside a local xerox store in the process of diversifying into internet services: "Sail Your Company Profile on the Internet: Get Solid Buyers!" Many of these subsidiary activities are truly tiny. A friend who provided customized business software to exporters from an old PC in a small rented office was loath to call himself an owner given his shiftless, insecure operations. Another roving consultant specialized in *Vactu*, the Vedic science of architecture, with which he advised industrialists on how rearranging their walls could improve business. From computer services to warding off the evil eye, there are all sorts of business opportunities around the magic of money, particularly where most firms do not accumulate capital.

Tiruppur provides opportunities for the tiniest of units engaged in garment accessories, often in the most temporary of shacks. To call some of these owners would be to deny their own self-representations, and indeed many petty owners say they only work for *coolie*, or task-based wages. When jobwork is called *coolie*, it blurs distinctions between owner and worker, just as sharecropping blurs tenancy and labor contracts in agriculture. I turn next to relations of work through the blizzard of small firms that comprise Tiruppur's capitalism.

II. Working through Networked Worksites

Cotton thread arrives in Tiruppur a stranger, leaving as a surfer T-shirt for French teenagers, and though it will never speak a word it has learnt the entire geography of the town. The components of the T-shirt must traverse several workplaces and types of labors before the latter leaves the industrial cluster as a knitted garment. With Figure 3 as a guide,

I sketch the labor process as things move through the division of labor on the way to making garments, all the while highlighting the centrality of the stitching section.

The main raw material, cotton, is processed in a *parutti office*, or ginning mill, before being sent to spinning mills to be converted into yarn or woven cloth. Spinning mills, as opposed to composite mills that also weave cloth, send yarn either to handloom or powerloom workshops to make woven cloth, or to the knitwear sector. Yarn comes to Tiruppur from mills which are far-flung from town, from the nearby mill center of Coimbatore City to the southern districts of Tamil Nadu state. Hosiery yarn is brought to Tiruppur either through yarn merchants or, increasingly in the past decade, through direct sales by mills to manufacturers. Tiruppur's small-firm owners consistently contrast themselves to Coimbatore's Mill owners, who are perceived as lordly industrial capitalists. Indeed, a few large owners integrated backward into spinning in the 1990s without much success.[7] As spinning is a distinct sector in terms of investment and work, peripheral to the knitwear production complex, I do not include it in this analysis.

Yarn is bought by the central knitwear company in Figure 3, the command control in coordinating work contracts across multiple worksites simultaneously and in parallel. First, yarn may be sent for processing, to be dyed to precise specifications. Yarn dyeing is the least technically developed section in Tiruppur, and it is not unusual for yarn to be sent as far as Ludhiana in Punjab to take advantage of the latest yarn-dyeing technology. Yarn is then sent to a "cone rewinding" unit to be wound into cones to fit onto circular knitting machines. Cone rewinding requires little investment and is often a makeshift shack with a woman watching a series of machines. Cones of yarn are dispatched to a fabrication unit for conversion into knitted cloth. Fabrication is either part of a composite factory or is an externally contracted unit. These workspaces have anywhere from one to a dozen circular knitting machines making cloth in the form of a tube.

In fabrication, a crucial characteristic of knitwear takes shape. Unlike weaving, which is the manufacture of cloth in two dimensions, warp and weft, knitting is done in one dimension: one strand of yarn is looped back into itself. This gives knitted cloth its unique quality of one-dimensional elasticity for form-fitting apparel. Most fabrication units use antiquated Indian machines, mainly from Ludhiana, unchanged since the 1960s. Imported machines from Japan, Germany or the USA fill entire rooms like majestic spiders churning out complex Jacquard textures and color combinations that local machines cannot match. Imported machines are so expensive that the amortization of fixed capital forces owners to keep the machines running as much as possible. There has been an expansion in imports of fabrication machines since the liberalized import policies of the early 1990s. On the estimate of Cobalt Devaraj, a fabrication owner, 50 percent of knitting machines by the mid 1990s were imports. By 1997, it had become common to buy a Rs 20 lakh machine, once unimaginable in Tiruppur, and it was possible to buy the latest machines.[8]

Fabrication workers tend to be middle-aged or older men, responsible for running up to four machines, night and day. The main tasks are to fit machines to the specific requirements of the order and to minimize damage in the process. Most machines stop automatically if a thread is broken, when the machinist must quickly re-spool the thread for fabrication to resume. Fabrication workers gain the skills that machine "tenders" typically have in industries that are not fully automated, where there is a premium on learning ways of tinkering and adjusting machines to deliver different sorts of qualities.[9] The premium placed on this knack lends to fabrication a reputation as one of the most skilled occupational categories, kept completely out of reach for women. Female exclusion is often defended as a consequence of year-round night shifts, but it is more likely the consequence of an older sector of all-male, semi-permanent workers retaining their relative privileges as long as possible. Skill is crucial to the language of gendered labor market exclusion.[10]

The movement of yarn and knitted cloth between knitwear companies and fabrication units is most often carried out by independent owners or hired operators of bullock carts, who are entirely male. On occasion, bullock cart drivers are dedicated, or linked in dependence, to specific companies, but they are never employees with regular wages. These men engage in transporting goods between units in a spot market for particular transport tasks. Several bullock cart drivers are

Naickers by caste, from a particular village east of Tiruppur. Their "central office," as one driver called it, is the bullock cart stand near Miller bus-stop, the most important intersection in northern Tiruppur. Despite this organization, bullock cart driving is an easily transferred skill from rural life, and this remains a buyer's market even in the busy export season. On one occasion, a bullock cart driver was telling me precisely how much he could expect for a load only to be interrupted by a curt young man from an export company who went on to strike a deal for a delivery on much lower terms. The driver was entirely at a loss.

The knitting of collars is carried out on flat, manual looms in the most makeshift of locations. The home-factory in which I lived for six months had two collar looms in the backyard, stuck between the kitchen and bathing area. Two men swung these looms deftly back and forth all day to knit rolls of collars. Some large units invest in automated collar machines, but, despite their much lower productivity, antiquated manual collar looms persist in the nooks and crannies of this working town. Gopikrishnan's collar unit is a shed with rows of manual looms worked by migrant labor.[11] Venkatesh was a collar worker at the factory-home I lived in, until he was dismissed for insubordination: he asked why work was given to him so erratically. Collar workers are among the most insecure sections of the working class in Tiruppur.

Collar work moves from the insecure to the invisible, to the section in which rolls of collars are separated. Early each morning, collar rolls are taken out from knitwear companies and dispersed by scooter to working-class households contracted through word-of-mouth. Women and girls separate collars during their "leisure" at "home," where they are not recognized as workers, let alone with skills and rights. The pile is left in one corner and tended to between household chores, waged work, and rest. Many workers consider this a subsidiary activity, an addition to the family wage. Some, particularly women with infants, prefer to work at home as long as possible and rely on this activity as primary income. Women and girls in working-class families also engage in taking apart "banian waste" from all leftover pieces of knitted cloth that can no longer be used for low quality or seconds production.

Discarded pieces of cloth are taken to households for manual separation by needle, to un-knit cloth into springy, tangled banian waste
with good resale value as sponge material for mechanic shops and
garages. Banian waste is then taken to the market by traders, while both
cloth and collars return to the main company.

No sooner does fabric return to the company than it is sent out
again for processing. "Greycloth," unprocessed fabric, must be bleached
and steam calendared to make Tiruppur's white banians. Calendaring
or machine ironing turns rolled fabric into a folded stack, ready to be
cut. For more complicated knitted products, particularly for export,
greycloth goes through bleaching, dyeing and finally "compacting," in
which shrinkage is controlled and roll sizes adjusted to precise needs.
Between dyeing and compacting, fabric may be machine washed, tumble dried, and, for velour, raised and sheared. In addition, fabric may
also go through rotary or table printing.[12] Processing admits a range in
levels of technology and forms of labor use. Several new techniques
and technologies in sections like compacting, raising, shearing and
rotary printing are responses to the export boom.

In contrast, bleaching is almost always carried out through an antiquated open-tank system, in which workers stand inside vats of chemical-saturated water, beating fabric against the sides of the vat. On
going to the bleaching *tóttams* or garden farms along the tributaries of
the Noyil river outside town along Kangeyam Road and Perumanallur
Road, I was immediately struck by how archaic the labor process remains. Bleaching is a reminder of how uneven the possibility of capital
accumulation is across the division of labor.[13] Rows of open sheds
shelter drying fabric, and beyond these sheds, under the open sun, are
vats within which bleaching workers labor. Drying fabric is permitted
shade from the sweltering sun that the bleaching worker is not. Bleaching is the most immediately physically degrading work I saw in Tiruppur. I surmised through their manner of dress, and their subservience
to the Gounder boss, that bleaching workers are likely to be from the
lowest regional Dalit caste, Madaris.

Many bleaching units have diversified into dyeing with the expansion of exports. Dyeing work is not degrading in the way that bleaching is, even if the techniques are also antiquated. Workers must add

dyes and chemicals in precise quantities and at precise times to winches which turn rolls of fabric round in vats of dye, and running time must be uniform for there to be minimal variation across the entire batch. The backwardness of technology in this particular sector has proven to be one of the major failings of the industry. There are, however, some large dyeing units that use new "soft flow" dyeing technology requiring major capital investments, and some of these large units are dedicated, linked in dependent relations, to particular exporters who are often partners in ownership. Other processing sections detailed in Figure 3 are most often independent units that have invested in one or two particular machines. In these, male machinists are not unlike the machine tenders in fabrication, who tinker and adapt machines to particular needs, as well as unskilled helpers and lesser attendants to do a variety of supportive tasks. At the end of their combined effort, processed fabric is sent back to the knitwear company, or, on its behalf, to a jobwork manufacturing unit.

The processed fabric is then cut into appropriate shapes in preparation for stitching. Cutting is almost completely manual, by scissors. "Cutting masters," as these workers are known, sometimes use a handheld lathe to cut out the armpits on the body of a T-shirt, but it is extremely rare for cutting to be fully mechanized; one estimate was 10 percent. Of the hundreds of units I visited during 1996–8, I never saw one. With the sheer variation in shapes and patterns, and the importance of minimizing waste, cutting masters are most often men working on piece-rates or under direct supervision. On one occasion, I found an owner of a knitwear company denying having any stitching labor at all, while behind him was a shopfloor full of contract workers. In this instance, the owner said that only his cutting masters were his *sonda-al*, or "own" labor, meaning that he owned their labor power directly, in contrast to contract labor. The cutting master piles bundles of cut pieces ready for the stitching section, where the garment comes into its own.

The power table or stitching section is the central process in Tiruppur knitwear, not least because it is here that pieces of cloth become a recognizable garment. The power table consists of six to eight stitching machines mounted on a table, all powered by a motorized shaft running under its length. A typical six-seat power table consists of the assortment of stitching machines necessary to stitch a knitted garment: two flatlock machines, two overlocks, one rib-cut and perhaps one button-sewing machine. Flatlock and overlock stitching machines are not single-needle stitching machines such as those used to make woven garments. These multiple-needle machines provide a stronger, more complex bond between knitted cut pieces which are elastic in one dimension and which can unravel easily. Knitted cloth's elasticity introduces a high degree of risk into stitching work, which continues to provide a rationale for capital to outsource the stitching of cut pieces to quasi-independent producers who rely on manual labor. Hence, stitching is manually performed even in the otherwise fully mechanized center of global knitwear production, the town Modena in Italy. This lack of mechanization at the core of global knitwear demonstrates how contracting provides a substitute for technical modernization.

In Tiruppur's form of contracting, the stitching section affords manual labor a central role while allowing this section a degree of apparent autonomy. Workers at the power table are typically young men and women who began their careers as child helpers, handing cut-pieces or receiving garments from stitchers, turning garments inside out and performing various odd tasks. Stitchers deftly assemble cut pieces until the section has completed the task of making the batch of garments at hand. Most power-table sections work on a task basis and the contractor or section leader is paid for the batch, to cover workers' wages and his own share. The relative autonomy of the power table, and its centrality in the labor process, play a key role, as I argue in the course of this book, in the construction of Tiruppur's self-made men. This first glimpse of the stitching section contains the gist of the argument I make through this book on the historical and ongoing links between fraternity and capital in Tiruppur's knitwear industry.

Once the garments are made, they are passed to "Singer tailors" who often work alongside the power-table section. Singer tailors use single-needle stitching machines, typically classic Singer-brand manually operated machines, sometimes power-driven single-needle machines. Their main job is to stitch garment labels on. Power machines are used for more complicated operations—using woven pieces for lapels or

16. Gendered Articulations 3: The abject woman worker submits to the light of global capital? This kind of image, constantly on offer in Tiruppur, is a gendered presentation of class that must be seen against many others, such as Photographs 14–20.

17. Gendered Articulations 4: This image of a boisterous flower-seller
may be seen not just as an empowered micro-entrepreneur, but as a
participant in a sex/gender order at work which requires or allows women
workers to buy beauty products for work. Photographs 16 and 17 have
to be seen against the grain so as not fetishize domination/resistance.

18. Gendered Articulations 5: The new order of "feminized" labor
for foreign markets. These young women stitching gigantic T-shirts
with Italian slogans for foreign tastes portray a very different
gendered articulation of work and consumption than that
in Photograph 14.

19. Gendered Articulations 6: Men on bikes, May Day 1997. Smart young male rank and file activists display a masculinist labor activism on their motorbikes.

20. Gendered Articulations 7: Working women take the streets. Despite low rates of formal membership in the labor unions, women fill the streets for the May Day parade, 1997.

collars, for instance. Singer tailors are typically piece-rated workers and there are still some roving Singer tailors who cart around their own machines on wheels, looking for contract work. Once all stitching is done, the garment is ready to return to the central company.

Back in the company, garments are inspected before the final stages. In export units, garments go to "checking" sections, where rows of women carefully check for stains, dangling strings and other quality mistakes. Certain errors such as stains are corrected immediately, while defective garments are set aside for repair or for the seconds' market. Either before or after checking, garments may be sent for further processing, typically to screen printing or the more capital intensive "flexo printing," a system through which images are heat-transferred in the manner of an iron-on. Both forms of printing then go through a stage of treatment to preserve the print quality, called curing or fusing, respectively. Women workers check garments after each stage of processing. The garment returns to the main unit only to leave for various other accessories, such as "*kaja*-button": tiny units specializing in making *kajas*, or buttonholes, with Singer machines, along with hand-stitched buttons. Embroidery units use either manual machines, employing rows of male tailors under common supervision, or, more rarely, computer-embroidery machines that trace out encoded patterns. Other accessory tasks include "zip," "sequins" and several specialized forms of stitching particularly for garment edges, including "trimmer," "scaloping," "zig-zag," and "picoting." The last four are operations that provide special effects for lingerie and babies' clothing. "Picoting" is a new operation in Tiruppur, named after the Picoeta embroidery machine. Tiny units often offer several of these accessory services. Once these are complete, the garment returns to the main unit to be checked, ironed and packed.

Ironing is usually done manually, by male workers, with electric irons. Ironing is entirely adult work, unlike stitching, checking and packing sections, where child laborers are everywhere. Child helpers often work between stages of the labor process, preparing batches for the next stage or for the final stage of packing. After ironing, the garment is packed. Here, the final consumption tag and price tag is attached in the case of export garments. Young workers sling on

German or French tags they will never read, with prices they could never afford. After the package is made, the garment is boxed or crated and ready to be shipped. I leave the T-shirt as it leaves Tiruppur, to return to the concept of social labor and what it can do for an understanding of contracting across this fragmented labor process.

III. Contracting as Power over Social Labor

"[L]abor is always social, for it is always mobilized and deployed by an organized social plurality . . . Labor thus presupposes intentionality, and therefore information and meaning . . . Social labor with both hand and head is deployed to cope with nature; the deployment of social labor, in turn, reproduces both the material and ideational ties of human sociality." Eric Wolf[14]

In reworking Marx's notion of the relations of production, Eric Wolf links the material and cultural as forms of "deployment of social labor by organized human pluralities," a phrase worth unpacking with caution. Focus on social labor shifts from production to a broader set of activities through which value is accrued and redistributed. Deployment shifts view to the ways in which groups, classes, states, and institutions strategize and compete across the multiple domains that constitute the social.[15] What I find compelling for the purposes of understanding Tiruppur is a reading of Wolf specific to capitalism, that "*once it became possible to talk about labor in general,* it also became possible to visualize how human beings forming organized pluralities assign labor to the technical processes of work and apportion the products of social labor among themselves" (my emphasis).[16] That is, once a multiplicity of concrete labors can be equated through abstract labor circulating through the division of labor in the money form of capital, the organized plurality thereby constituted can be interrogated for its specific ways of deploying social labor. In the last decade of his work, Wolf returned to think more deeply about power over the deployment of social labor, pressed by Foucault's notion of governmentality as structuring the conditions of possibility of action. If the notion of structural power could reveal anything about political economies it would have to contend with the centrality of power over social labor.[17]

Attention to social labor forces one to see capitalist collective action as related to local hegemony over work. Capital accumulation requires the exercise of class power in a politics of production, the praxis through which capital both secures and obscures value.[18] Power over social labor spans both the detail division of labor and relations across networks of firms. Capital cannot mechanistically resolve the multiple contradictions of capitalism for long-term place-based accumulation. Instead, short-term rapaciousness and the rents derived thereof drive an anarchic process of accumulation.

Observing the industrial revolution in Britain, Marx considered "accumulation" essential to capitalist development in two senses: as the accumulation of capital and of a reserve army of labor.[19] My analysis uses these twin processes of the accumulation of capital and surplus labor to understand how Tiruppur combines elements of informal sector and industrial district. As the reserve army of labor returns home or hangs around movie theaters without a job for the day, the politics of social labor are all to do with why and how flexible workers wait for the next insecure job. Indeed, labor market insecurity has only deepened alongside uneven technical change and dramatic growth. Under these conditions, I return to the prosaic and prescient question Michael Burawoy asks of the detail division of labor: "why do workers work?"[20] This question calls for ethnography to understand how and why workers participate in the production of relative surplus value, in exploitation based on raising productivity rather than only on sweating labor. Industrial clusters like Tiruppur rely on a powerful source of relative surplus value through organizational innovation.[21] However, as the tour through the labor process in the last section details, the organization of work allows technical change to recombine with forms of absolute surplus value, or sweating. How, in this case, is value secured and obscured? How does one explain workers' volitional and involuntary consent, indeed complicity, in their own exploitation?[22]

To return to Eric Wolf, I ask how participants in Tiruppur's industry assign labors to the division of labor as a plurality, and how they distribute the gains of their collective work. The fetishism of complex and connected labors as an "industrial cluster" takes a multitude of imaginative labors that emerge in various ways through the ethnography in this book. Tiruppur exporters, for instance, like to project a fetish-ism of integrated manufacture despite the appearance of a decentralized, fragmented production form, with uneven technologies and work arrangements. They claim integration to say that all this mania is in fact under their thumb:

> Even though there are not many integrated manufacturing facilities in Tiruppur, there has been a vertical integration of production facilities of exporters. This is the latest trend in Tiruppur and hence we find exporters having effective control of all production activities even though they are located in various places. (Ganeshan, *TEA Bulletin*, May 1997, p. 2)

This prominent exporter is arguing to foreign buyers that effective control rather than spatial contiguity can ensure meeting requirements of time and quality. This is not to say that dispersed firms do not integrate, but that they do so in flexible ways, to maintain control of contracting networks. Owners use jobwork and contract relations to combine capacity subcontracting and labor market flexibility to respond to uncertainty, to minimize investment in fixed capital, and, most importantly, to control social labor.

As a caveat, it is important to note that technological advancement has been coterminous with the shift to exports. New machines were brought in first to stitching after 1980, to fabrication from around 1992 and in printing from 1994. Dyeing houses with the latest technology are few and far between, but they emerged by the late 1990s. Technological change has been primarily in fabrication and processing. Stitching machines have been replaced slowly, and cutting has not been mechanized to any significant extent. This landscape of uneven technical change is as much cause as consequence of owners' strategies through dispersed production as of a landscape of uneven labor control.

From her research in Tiruppur around 1984, Pamela Cawthorne argues that firms that combined manufacturing and fabrication were the preserve of "large capitalists."[23] In 1997–8, I found no correlation between firm size and knitting machines owned among owners in the exporter and domestic owners' associations.[24] I return to disaggregated survey information in Chapter 3, but it suffices to say that economies of scale do not hold in any simple sense, as firms that do more business do not necessarily own more machines. On integrating operations, Cawthorne argues for a process of firm "expansion without vertical integration."[25] I find it heuristically useful to separate vertical integration (sequential links across sectors, principally spinning, knitwear and marketing), from horizontal integration (parallel or sequential links within the knitwear sector, including manufacture, knitting, processing and accessorizing). As Chapter 3 details, neither form of integration correlates with business volume.[26] Hence, there is evidence to ask what forces counter economies of scale. Since there is no *negative* correlation either, however, there is no reason to presume, as Cawthorne does through cross-sectional data, that there is an underlying systemic process at work which she calls "amoebic capitalism," in which firm growth and expansion *causes* disintegration.[27]

What is clear is that contracting reduces entry costs for all firms, large and small, while providing a means for evading the labor problems of larger factory establishments.[28] The more fundamental question is how contracting in Tiruppur allows a mode of deployment of social labor that deepens cooperation, the elementary form of relative surplus value. This requires venturing into the ways in which contracting affords firms flexibility with respect to production time. On the one hand, this flexibility allows the flexible exploitation of the working class; on the other hand, this flexibility is necessitated by the seasonality of global garment sourcing. The next section turns to the imperatives of global demand as it structures perceptions and practices of uncertainty and value in the rough and tumble of work in Tiruppur.

IV. Uncertainty, Seasonality, and Global Demand

The producer of garments, like any producer, has to supply a *useful* commodity. This begs the question of how usefulness, or use-value, must be construed by producers, including workers who will never consume the products of their labor. As representations of demand, use-values must be produced alongside material production in order for the commodity to live out its cycle from production to consumption. Since usefulness is a social product of ever-shifting and uneven geographies of marketing and consumption, its determination by agents at various locations in the life of a commodity is always partial and uncertain. Yet, one might identify characteristic ways in which producers organize work to make useful commodities in relation to market and commodity character. Producers act under conditions of material and semiotic uncertainty that are constitutive of the production of particular commodities for particular types of markets.[29] I want to stress that the meanings employed in designing fashion garments are structurally removed from the labor process in Tiruppur by a separation of conception and execution across global garment commodity chains. Hence, work in this export site, and indeed in most peripheral export production sites, draws on meanings of commodities that are entirely removed from local knowledge, and that appear to be characteristics of things.[30] If the commodity character of knitwear is seen to provide specific advantages to knitwear capitalists in very different contexts, it is also important to ask how this character becomes part of the ideology of peripheralization that marks working bodies who will not consume the export products they make. This section ventures into the specific ways in which Tiruppur's organization of global production relies on fetishizing the use-value of export garments.

To begin with, it is important to note that demand for Tiruppur knitwear is extremely diversified. Domestic owners sell to market agents, traders or directly to retailers, or to illicit spot markets in town or at the Erode *cantai*, which requires the lowest quality goods. Exports are bound primarily for the US and EC, often through intermediary locations if the export quotas for the final destination have not been secured. Shanmugam, a Tiruppur exporter, once asked me point blank what I thought the main problem for a knitwear owner is, and while I fumbled for answers he shot back, "China." Tiruppur exporters are acutely aware of the shifting reaches of global garment sourcing networks in the last years of the Multi Fiber Agreement, and Shanmugam saw China, and secondarily Bangladesh and Pakistan, as a threat because they can deliver cheaper garments after the end of quota restrictions on global garment production. Producers like Shanmugam have therefore had to stay ahead of the ball by moving up-market into the volatile world of fashion garments. Fashion garments bound primarily for European and North American markets are the highest-value commodities from Tiruppur, and their use-values set what are perceived as the "external" conditions of profitability in Tiruppur today. Spoken of in terms of "adherence to quality standards," the effects of fashion garment demand in Europe and North America are mediated by several layers of producers and subcontractors, as detailed in Section II.

The global market in fashion garments is understood in Tiruppur in terms of national tastes and changing seasons. However, knowledge of consumption and the means of creating new tastes are closely guarded elements of the advertising and design phases of production concentrated in Europe and North America. The structure of the global garment trade also differs broadly between the more dense North American sourcing networks, which admit large numbers of intermediaries for gigantic retail and wholesale chains, and thinner European sourcing networks. Many European buyers who come to Tiruppur own or work for their own brands, while most American buyers are buyer–supplier intermediaries or traders. To the extent possible, all foreign buyers secure knitwear orders only when they know they can sell them on the other end. This, they argue, is necessary because of the physical characteristics of knitwear. This emphasis on physicality is then deployed in the organization of social labor, so it is worth dwelling on more carefully.

Knitwear differs from woven garments, as I have mentioned, by its form-fitting elasticity, made by turning one dimension of thread into two dimensions of cloth. In contrast, weaving is a process of intertwining two dimensions of warp and weft thread, so that woven garments are not meant to stretch. This characteristic elasticity means that knitwear is made in small quantities and multiple varieties, with narrow ranges of sizes, shapes and forms. Unlike woven garments made in large, standardized lots, unsold knits cannot be dumped as easily on the market, and buyers are well aware of this risk. Global knitwear fashion markets tend to be more volatile than woven apparel markets, with more risk transferred down commodity chains to producers. This transfer of risk to peripheral production sites is made to appear natural rather than an effect of postcolonial geopolitics through appeal to the physical character of knitwear.

Fashion garment sourcing takes a particular form that can be explained to a certain extent by the nature of risk and uncertainty that are involved in producing standardized, dedicated products.[31] Dedicated production refers to relations between specific firms for specific goods, as opposed to mass production of standardized goods for the best buyer. Even the simplest types of fashion knitwear are sourced through dedicated production runs along specific requirements put forth by the buyer to a specific supplier. Both foreign buyer and local supplier share a common, standardized language through which the garment's characteristics are specified. This specification does not use a unique aesthetic vocabulary as it does in crafts sourcing, where artisanal knowledge and ethnic difference are exploited to signify uniqueness rather than standardization. Neither do these standardized commodities face uncertainty as predictable risk, a consequence of codified norms concerning quality and technology, and routinized adjustment to price signals.[32] Dedicated production of standardized commodities works to the advantage of buyers by preventing the formation of loyalty or obligation with sellers, and by stoking competition between sellers in price and speed. Dedicated sellers therefore operate as if in a spot market where they confront a kind of "true uncertainty" that appears entirely out of their control.[33] Sellers cannot respond to market fluctuations by consolidating routinized and relatively invariant instances from a known range of options to arrive at probabilistic assessments of risk and corresponding response. Dedicated sourcing confers a degree of uniqueness to each transaction that makes quantification and probabilistic resolution of risk extremely difficult, if not impossible, in practical terms. Where true uncertainty is concerned with standardized and not specialized products, as in fashion knitwear, the burden of uncertainty is passed almost entirely to the producer. Knitwear producers in Tiruppur, therefore, face an export market that is uncertain in terms of both price and quality, and they are subject to fierce competition both between firms and across production sites. Local exporters are painfully aware of the latter when they bemoan cheaper labor in other Asian garment sourcing sites as a key reason for their shift to higher quality fashion garments.

The "external" competitive pressures faced by exporters have also fueled rampant undercutting of prices to the extent that buyers have been able to ask for higher levels of quality at lower prices. The rationale suppliers use in explaining undercutting one another is the hope of hooking an order with a foreign buyer in the hope of building sustained ties. Invariably this hope turns to folly and leads many firms into deeper indebtedness in a downward spiral of unprofitability. However, new entrants quickly realize that Tiruppur does not attach stigma to loss, but instead provides institutional support for closing "sick" units and starting new ones with separate lines of credit. Hence, loss among new entrants is often an early stage in learning how to think of knitwear production in terms of the dedicated production of standardized products rather than of specialized products.

Firms that have been engaged in exports for at least a few years have adapted routines for managing uncertainty through a combination of product diversification, subcontracting and labor market flexibility. Contracting can either be in the form of capacity subcontracts or jobwork contracts that increase product diversification. Therefore, while standardized products compel firms to pursue scale economies, these forms of internal and labor market flexibility act as a counter to the tendency towards overproduction. Buyers rely on a system of suppliers and subcontractors engaged according to conventions of quick response and adjustment down the subcontract chain, as a way of dealing with constantly changing prices and quantities. Storper and Salais call these relations "network markets" in which buyer–supplier relations are bound through "non-market mechanisms, ties that bind the participants . . . more durably than pure spot market relations."[34] What I try to address ethnographically in this book are the relations of power that allow the dispersal of risk through these ties that bind.

Within the knitwear cluster, buyer–supplier relations are in large part characterized by network market relations. A significant share of owners, 42 percent of domestic owners and 18 percent of exporters, engage in dedicated production. What is key is that these dedicated buyer–supplier relations are seen as local strategies forged in relation to true uncertainty. Global knitwear production fosters this type of uncertainty that cannot be mitigated through quantitative means alone, but through qualitative, organizational means. Hence, the manipulation of social labor becomes central to capitalist strategy in accumulating capital and dispersing risks to an increasingly insecure workforce.

Another major structural constraint on global production in Tiruppur has to do with time and the profound seasonality of knitwear production, following the seasons of Northern fashion markets. Agents of global garment sourcing usually explain this seasonality in terms of style change on retail shelves. Knitwear is worn, due to its elastic and absorptive properties, mainly in warm weather. Hence, T-shirts have been essential summer attire in the North, and summer has been the most important knitwear season for the cotton knitwear market. However, since the 1980s, knitted garments have become popular year-round and the world over, and the diversity of fabrics and styles has increased tremendously. Given these changes in taste, why has production retained its seasonality? The American Apparel Manufacturers Association provides a clue as to why foreign buyers favor seasonality, particularly in European apparel sourcing from Asia in the mid 1990s: "With more apparel contracting capacity available to European sourcers in one form or another, both retailers and manufacturers are now more interested in wider choices of low cost textiles and the ability to delay sourcing commitments to the last minute in order to respond flexibly to consumer demand. This has made India's textile strengths, closer proximity and historic orientation even more appealing to European sourcers than the Far East."[35]

Seasonality persists despite changing Northern, and global, consumption because garment sourcing networks use competition over market share to exert pressure on producers through extremely short periods of involvement. Exporters in Tiruppur always complain of the strict schedules required by buyers, and they often agree to these requirements despite the implausibility of completing production within the allotted time. Often goods are shipped by air rather than by ship because of delays. Most importantly, strict schedules and probable delays increase buyers' control over price, ex-post and through fines and debits ex-ante. The temporal dimension of production in Tiruppur is therefore highly seasonal, and exporters are at pains to divest some of the pressure to their subcontractors and workers. This seasonality is primarily an expression of the class power of North American and European garment sourcing capital. However, Tiruppur owners participate in naturalizing this class power in order to share in its effects and to pass the burden onto the flexible proletariat. Indeed, workers who couldn't find work during the export season would often tell me "season *pattalai*" or "the season wasn't enough," in the terms used to discuss the failure of the monsoon. Similarly, differentiated wage payments are routinely explained in terms of "changing fashions" rather than in terms of class politics.

Hence, owners use jobwork and contract relations to combine capacity subcontracting and labor market flexibility in response to the uncertainties and seasonality of global production in Tiruppur. These modes of deployment of social labor foster both the accumulation of capital and surplus labor, as the two intertwine and support each other in a dispersed, dynamic and insecure organization of work. Before turning to the ways in which labor experiences this flexible production complex, the following sections turn to the countervailing circuit of money and credit, and the regulation of capital and the industrial cluster.

V. Money, Credit, and Working Capital

I have considered the flows of material objects between units in the social division of labor by focusing on commodities and their transformation by various forms of work. The circulation of commodities is mirrored in reverse in the circulation of money, the measure of value in all commodities. As a lubricant of exchange, money allows the separation of buying and selling, and credit allows for the purchase of means of production and labor power necessary for the production of new value to proceed. Credit is key in organizing dispersed production in Tiruppur, where contracting feeds the disjuncture between the ownership of means of production and the control of labor processes. While credit, like money, presents itself as neutral in the sphere of circulation, its centrality to production foregrounds its social power. Moreover, precisely because the social power of money can be disengaged from production relations and because productive capitalists take on different embodiments as moneylender and producer, credit highlights functionally separate fractions of capital, both of which can claim property rights to the social product. In this section, I begin by exploring the different sources of credit that producers in Tiruppur rely on, to begin to understand the tangled class relations between owners of capital and users of capital, or commodity producers.[36]

In 1998, 80–82 percent of owners utilized formal bank credit, and these percentages shot up for owners from Tiruppur in contrast to North Indian business families.[37] As I detail in Chapter 3, the latter often bring in capital through intra-familial/firm networks, with relations to banks or moneylending in Calcutta or Bombay.[38] Formal bank credit is the main source of credit for Tiruppur knitwear.

This bank credit is primarily of two forms. First are term loans for plant and machinery. More important, however, are short-term loans for working capital through "bill discounting" in domestic production and "packing credit" in exports. These arrangements between banks of Tiruppur suppliers and far-flung buyers advance working capital so that production can proceed well before foreign buyers pay for orders. Once shipments clear on the other end, bills are settled across banks involved. The volume of bank credit in the form of working capital loans is now gigantic and involves agreements with banks around the world. Working capital loans first require credit to be needs-assessed based on performance, turnover and assets; then a loan is extended for a period of 30 to 90 days. The bills drawn against buyers' orders are kept with the bank as promissory notes agreed to by buyer and seller, and the document is used to loan money for the working-capital needs of the contract. This is called bill discounting in domestic production. For exports, the foreign buyer provides a similar promissory note known as a letter of credit against which producers borrow working capital. By allowing production of garments to proceed far before final payments are made, short-term credit is essential to this dispersed industrial form.

Firms from various sections in subcontracting networks do not have equal access to these forms of credit. One limiting factor is that access to institutional credit requires some form of collateral security.[39] Furthermore, one modest domestic producer said he could never access institutional loans because he did not have the kinds of connections and reputation that others had. Another important point about credit in production is that one cannot assume that credit is passed on down the subcontract chain by firms with strong capacities to draw on institutional credit. In actual fact, many knitwear companies, particularly the powerful domestic and export groups, receive goods and services from fabrication, processing, and jobwork manufacture units without any outlay of money capital in the organization of production. Some large companies advance just enough capital to pay the weekly wages of supplier firms, and it is in this sense that jobwork units often say they work for *coolie*. Several merchant exporters report being compelled to take orders from exporters who never settle accounts fully but always maintain just enough of a balance so that the merchant exporters remain in a sense debt-bonded to them. While these forms of indebtedness provide credit to exporters, this begs the question of where jobworkers seek money capital required to secure the means of production.

A large and diverse market in private and informal credit exists to make the whole production complex function. Non-bank sources of credit in Tiruppur include private finance companies, rotating credit unions called chit funds, moneylenders, and forms of mutual assistance between friends, family or kin. Finance companies generally charge high rates of interest. Many large landholding families and traditional business families have established finance companies. Chit funds operate like credit unions, where depositors are allowed periodically to bid for much larger amounts than they invest, at low rates of interest but with the assurance of monthly repayments. Many small producers begin and persist through chit funds. Moneylenders are more likely to charge higher rates of interest than banks. The moneylending interest rate peaks on Saturday afternoons after banks close and when weekly wages must be settled. Desperate jobworkers must often agree to usurious interest rates for very-short-term private loans to tide them over until Monday morning.

Consequently, small owners have also developed forms of mutual aid to circulate capital around their concerns. One Saturday evening I met a young owner called Eswaran paying back Rs 1000 borrowed from his friend and fellow small company owner, Mohan; Eswaran had intercepted Mohan after his morning trip to the bank and "rotated" the money by the evening in time for Mohan to pay his workers.[40]

Finally, locals often have recourse to kin and familial networks to secure capital.

Traders who supply the main raw material, yarn, have extended another form of credit since the early period of this industry. Yarn credit, or yarn on credit, was as important as bill discounting for the expansion of production for the domestic banian market. With the growth of direct sales of yarn from spinning mills, yarn credit has declined. Finally, while some families are involved in both knitwear production and the yarn trade, they have not become leading players through the kind of mercantile putting-out system that prevails in the regional powerloom sector. Most knitwear companies, particularly those producing for export, procure their own yarn so as to control quality to some extent. The irony is that many knitwear companies then supply yarn to their jobworkers in the form of yarn credit. Credit in this sort of case becomes a means for concealing unequal power relations in the contract between buyer and supplier. In many instances, dependence and indenture are wrapped in the rhetoric of preferential access to yarn.

The social power of money in the credit system in Tiruppur is concentrated in the hands of large producers who receive credit from institutional sources and provide yarn "gratis" to numerous suppliers, paying them off for production only when they have to. Smaller, informal credit moneys circulate to keep suppliers afloat. At the apex of lending, the banks that provide crucial short-term credit stay away from the realm of production. In effect, this provides free rein to large knitwear companies. A local who left work in knitwear spoke to me of a drying up of credit in the recent years of instability: banks and even chit funds don't lend that easily any more. On the other hand, in his view today's "owners want to do business without investment": they take yarn loans for a month, fabrication loans for 1–2 months, dyeing loans for two months and in the end one kilo fabric ends up costing Rs 60–70 in credit whereas it used to cost Rs 40.[41] As the credit supply has tightened, it would seem that larger, more powerful firms with access to credit would have the upper hand.

One such large firm called Sargam, however, closed up and the owner, Agarwal claimed that insufficient credit led to his demise. When I interviewed Sargam Agarwal in 1997, before this event, I was so struck that a North Indian could convey his story so eloquently in Tamil that by the end I was convinced of his deep roots and commitments in Tiruppur. Later in the year, he left his company with a small briefcase, announcing to his staff that he was bound for a pilgrimage to the important temple of Tirupati. He has never returned to date. Instead, in a letter to the State Bank of India explaining his reasons for absconding and leaving banks, suppliers and his workers in the lurch, he blames the inadequate supply of credit for his actions.[42] This case only highlights how little discipline can be imposed on large concerns, and the result of this and several other defaults in the rocky period of the mid 1990s has been a tightening of credit money by local banks. Money as means of exchange hits dead against money as the measure of value when production systems fail to deliver: garments lie unsold and workers remain unpaid.

Where the ownership of means of production and the organization of production are not isomorphic but are severed as in Tiruppur, credit is an important mechanism to enable both the appearance of neutrality and the persistence of complex dependent relations. At any moment, if the production system fails for a variety of reasons, the capitalist can cry out that the fault lies in the system of credit itself, as did Sargam Agarwal. For a while, Agarwal's default created a climate of suspicion against his caste-fellows from Rajasthan, who own firms in Tiruppur. In this extreme case, local regulatory institutions were at a loss in providing redress. Opportunism such as Agarwal's is only one form of social problem that the cluster as a whole must resolve through institutional means in regulating social labor. In the following section, I turn to the cluster-level associations that exist to mitigate such problems as well as to facilitate the development of the cluster as a whole.

VI. Regulation, Capital, and Collective Efficiency

The mills may wonder why knitwear exporters are very touchy about yarn prices. The reason is simple. While mills can pass on any increase in cost of production to buyers we cannot pass on any increase to our foreign buyers as we are bound by contracts and commitments. Export is a national effort . . . On difficult situations every section of the industry should sacrifice something. It is not our intention to deny anybody of their right to earn profits; but consumers, especially consumers catering to export markets need to be careful.[43]

The leader of TEA, Sakthivel, appeals here to a blend of "consumer" rights and nationalism ironically in defense of export production and commitments to foreign buyers. The guilty party, charged with undue profiteering, is in this case the spinning Mill owner. What is interesting is that exports are the symbol of national pride, a far cry from the days of import substitution. Moreover, capitalists are portrayed as consumers, and the question of "passing on prices" is seen solely in terms of effects on buyers' prices rather than in terms of squeezing subcontractors and workers. "Contracts and commitments" are seen in relations linking exporters to the globalization of India, not to unequal relations of social labor. This vision brings together some of the key contradictions within owner associations in Tiruppur. In what follows, I lay out the functions of these associations while critiquing what the industrial districts literature calls joint action and collective efficiency. As mentioned in Chapter 1, collective efficiency refers to collective gains from the clustering of interlinked specializations, and related non-pecuniary gains are sources of innovation. Joint action refers to collective capital taking on planning functions in turning competition into a virtuous spiral of innovation. This section is concerned with the extent to which owners' associations, in consort with labor unions and local government, engage in joint action to enhance collective efficiency.[44]

To return to the TEA leader, Sakthivel calls attention to the central function of owners' associations in Tiruppur, to lobby the state in the economic interests of knitwear exporters. Yarn is the main raw material cost for knitwear companies, and the price of yarn links directly to state regulation of quantities of yarn and raw cotton exported. TEA began as a small group of exporters who could not tolerate extended labor strikes in the heavy-handed manner of the older, primarily domestic SIHMA. From providing a voice for upstart exporters in collective bargaining with labor unions, TEA has grown as an exporters' lobby to state and national governments. TEA's incursions into the organization of production have also been minimal but not insignificant. First, TEA gained an industrial estate for export-oriented units, located outside town in Mudalipalayam, from the state government of Tamil Nadu. The estate has had a slow rate of success because of its distance from town and the lack of services, but has managed to provide space for subsidiary units with easy access to rural labor. Second, TEA built an industrial estate in Kanjikode, Kerala, near Pallakad across the state border from Coimbatore, with joint support from the Kerala state government capital for advanced processing technology. Attempts were made to exclude organized labor from the estate. The processing facility is entirely captive for Tiruppur exporters and was in operation for a few years, but was shut down in 1998 due to labor union disputes and it is unclear what its future will be.

Third, TEA is involved in a massive overhaul of the organization of production in Tiruppur through a public–private hybrid development scheme to the tune of $160 million. The board of the New Tiruppur Area Development Corporation (NTADC), a public limited corporation formed in 1995, includes representatives of the Government of India, the Tamil Nadu state government, and the Infrastructure Loans and Financial Services (IL&FS), a quasi-governmental body with representation from the World Bank. NTADC was created to undertake a massive overhaul of the rural–urban production system, including a new commercial water scheme (which would sell water to industrial, rural and municipal consumers), a sewage and effluent treatment plan (since the Tiruppur Dyers Association has been in the courts fighting against the Tamil Nadu state pollution board), and a model township and industrial estate on the main highway from Madras to Coimbatore. The entire scheme costs Rs 570 crore, $160 million in 1997 prices, and the capital is to be raised by loans (69 percent, primarily from the World Bank and US capital markets with USAID standing guarantor), equity shares (14 percent) and the resale of rural land (18 percent.) In 1998, negotiations over how NTADC was to be financed were fraught with politics. If indeed this contention can be bought out, which in all probability it will if it has not been already, NTADC will mark a consolidation of the class power of the major exporters in TEA and of the cluster-level conditions for their longer-term accumulation strategies. On June 20, 2002, the foundation stone was laid by the Tamil Nadu chief minister, Jayalalitha, for "the first public–private partnership project to access commercial funds for the water sector in India."[45]

Furthermore, TEA has been involved in the lead along with a set of local employer associations in developing an arbitration council to take care of various sorts of disputes in inter-firm and buyer–supplier relations. However, TEA has not made any incursions of consequence in the arena of collective negotiations with buyers for export contracts, or in collective marketing of products. Neither has TEA worked as a marketing association because there are strong individual interests within it that are unwilling to give up their personal gain for collective efficiency.

SIHMA is located in the SIDCO Industrial Estate near the railway station, in an old building with a somewhat dilapidated exterior, but with a historic presence. SIHMA has expanded from representing domestic producers—about 95 percent of whom are members—to merchant exporters.[46] SIHMA has also broadened its reach over the latter by lobbying for the end of excise taxes, and its efforts paid off in a stay on the collection of taxes followed by an end to excise taxes for all domestic and merchant knitwear production. Merchant export items, because they are manufactured for a final exporter, are subject to domestic taxes, but these had not been collected until 1996.[47] SIHMA's raison d'être has been in obtaining pecuniary concessions for its members, whether through lobbying the state for cheaper yarn and an end to excise duties or through ongoing negotiations with labor unions.

The Tiruppur Export Knitwear Manufacturers Association (TEKMA) is ostensibly the association of merchant exporters, whom it represents in collective bargaining and in the new arbitration council that oversees disputes between firms. TEKMA is much weaker than SIHMA in Tiruppur; it has an entirely forgettable office and a relatively weak presence in the public sphere. TEKMA's leader, moreover, treats the association more like his political party.

TEA, as I have mentioned, is the most powerful owners' association in Tiruppur. About 70–80 percent of direct exporters are members of TEA.[48] Housed in a snazzy new building in an older working-class neighborhood that is now a cluster of the largest export houses, in Kongu Nagar, TEA is headed by Mr Sakthivel. In a recent function to "felicitate" him, Sakthivel sat on the stage with a row of Gounder leaders in industry and politics, all in traditionally sober starched white shirts and *veshtis*, while he wore a shocking-pink silk shirt, tinted glasses and gold jewelry. TEA promotes itself as the new export community. As Sakthivel snapped at me once when I attempted to talk to him about caste, "Tiruppur exporters are a cosmopolitan people," and this was precisely what he sought to enact in pink silk. TEA is global Tiruppur, and is not meant to represent decidedly local or regional concerns of caste or party politics.

While many of the functions provided by TEA were prefigured and developed by SIHMA, particularly in representing the interests of the industry to government, TEA has also been responsible for bringing the quasi-government Apparel Export Promotion Council (AEPC) to Tiruppur. AEPC is an agency registered under the Companies Act and sponsored by the Government of India, Ministry of Textiles, with the express purpose of facilitating garment exports and disbursing quotas under various categories of entitlement for exports to countries under the Multi-Fiber Agreement. Sakthivel has been an executive committee member of AEPC since 1984, and he accepts full credit for bringing an AEPC office to Tiruppur to address the needs of knitwear exporters within the cluster. Sakthivel also takes credit for starting a technical training center on the same premises in conjunction with a large Coimbatore-based quasi-governmental agency called South India Textile Research Association (SITRA). AEPC came to Tiruppur with strong ties to TEA, and the AEPC director in Tiruppur enjoys close relations with TEA leaders with obvious effects, until the passing of the quota system. One consequence of these relations is a steady use of state funds for trade fairs, promotional events, delegations and so on. The India Knit Fair, sponsored by AEPC and TEA, has become a bi-annual event in its own building in the outskirts of Tiruppur, and this trade fair allows local exporters to showcase their products to foreign buyers and buying agents. A walk through the Knit Fair is amazing, as booth after booth of goods display fashions entirely removed from the world of labor. When I went to the fair in 1997, Sakthivel walked through like a movie star, sporting sunglasses indoors and trailed by bright lights and video cameras.

TEA has, along with AEPC, been able to engage in some provision of real or non-pecuniary services such as technical, marketing and business support. These real services are certainly not spread evenly across the cluster. Moreover, the AEPC-SITRA training center is not the hub of technical training it purports to be, and most technology and technical consulting comes to firms through market relations.[49]

Another type of joint action in Tiruppur has to do with regularizing business relationships and settling contractual disputes between firms. TEA began to engage in inter-firm arbitration in 1992, but the independent Arbitration Council of Tiruppur, registered under the Tamil Nadu Societies Act, was begun in 1996. The council can only make recommendations, as it has no enforcement powers, but is presented as an alternative to long and cumbersome formal litigation. TEA claims to have begun the council, but this is neither accepted by other members nor is it written in the council documentation. The council portrays itself as equally represented by all major owner associations: SIHMA, TEA, TEKMA, the Banian Cloth Manufacturers Association (BCMA, the association for fabrication owners), Tiruppur Screen Printing Owners Association (TSPOA), Tiruppur Dyers Association (TDA) and Tiruppur Hosiery Yarn Manufacturers Association (THYMA).[50] The Arbitration Council deals with disputes between foreign buyers and direct exporters, direct exporters and merchant exporters, yarn merchants and exporters, dyers and exporters, cloth fabricators and exporters, and between owners and staff; the last because staff are not represented by labor unions. The main problem is that most agreements exporters make are non-binding, particularly as many firms export without letters of credit. The Arbitration Council allows agents involved in multiple transactions to continue to do business in Tiruppur without constraining their choices through unresolved disputes and without long and messy court litigation.[51] The council tries to capitalize on time, emphasizing its commitment to fast-track resolution without any appeals. It must be said that the council had considered 325 cases by March 1998, and of 70 disputes between exporters and foreign buyers it had met 5 successes, from the perspective of TEA exporters.[52]

On the internationally sensitive issue of child labor, TEA has taken the lead in projecting Tiruppur exporters as progressive, caring and willing to change. Sakthivel says that TEA has been advising its members for the past two or three years not to hire child labor, but it is the jobworkers down the chain who continue to hire child labor. He reiterated that they want to stop child labor, but "we want to do it voluntarily." When I arrived in Tiruppur, TEA held a grand function called "Chilabolition 1996," with members of a major European buyer, C&A, involved alongside all the major leaders of employer associations and labor unions, with representatives from government and political parties present. "Chilabolition" displayed a rhetorical rejection and collective accommodation to child labor, and should be seen as one act in the theater of class struggle and compromise in Tiruppur.[53]

One of the things that TEA has been particularly proud of is the arrival of a local branch of the National Institute of Fashion Technology (NIFT), called NIFT–TEA Knitwear Fashion Institute. This fashion design institute provides skills on modern techniques for meeting buyers' standards and for preparing samples through computerized color shade matching, color recipe formulation, batch correction, and so on. It remains to be seen whether this will bring fashion design to Tiruppur or whether it will only help Tiruppur firms conform to fashion standards set elsewhere. The former would threaten the structural conditions of export knitwear that I have argued allow owners to pass down the risks of global production to peripheral firms and their flexible proletariat. Needless to say, global garment sourcers have little incentive to allow their crucial advantage to slip, so that it remains unlikely that Tiruppur will be at the cutting edge of R&D until owners begin to brand fashion garments for the domestic market.[54]

As I have mentioned, TEA has had mixed success in joint action for expanding the industrial cluster on its periphery and through an industrial estate in Kerala. The crowning glory of joint action in Tiruppur might well be the NTADC, which, as Sakthivel reminds me, is "the first fully privatized water supply in Asia; the government is on the board but it is fully privatized." For now the scheme is fraught with politics, and time will tell whether the big TEA exporters, whose interests it serves best, will be able to ride roughshod over the rest.

Finally, I turn briefly to the leader of TEA, Sakthivel, who sees himself as TEA personified. Indeed, most owners associations in Tiruppur are led by prominent men who treat their appointments as ways of amassing supporters. However, Sakthivel has remained remarkably aloof from party politics and portrays his interests as the interests of exporters alone. In a letter to the Bombay-based Federation of Hosiery Manufacturers' Association of India (FOHMA), Sakthivel requests for representation in AEPC, which has representatives according to different regions in India, for a "knitwear region" comprising six members, with "a minimum value of export of knitwear as qualification." Six big exporters would represent this knitwear region at this apex body for apparel exports. What I want to highlight is the *spatial* imaginary in Sakthivel's representation of the regional class power of Tiruppur exporters. Rather than representing a regionally dominant fraction of capital, Sakthivel claims to speak for a sectorally demarcated space, which entirely erases the messy world of class struggle and domination entailed in maintaining regional class power.

Clearly, owners' associations, and particularly TEA, have played a major role in joint action to keep the district competitive. Tiruppur's structurally subordinate location in global garment production constrains TEA from taking on the more important joint action of collective negotiations with buyers for production contracts, marketing of locally developed export brands, collective technology importing, or collective innovation and design development. In these matters, competition between exporters has not been overruled by cooperation. The major test of TEA's leadership in joint action may well be its ability to manage a privatized water and waste system through NTADC.

To the extent that it has been forged in Tiruppur, collective efficiency remains an uncertain goal that is secondary to the accumulation strategies of capitalists and their tenuous attempts at maintaining hegemony over spatially and temporally fragmented work. The expansion of exports seems to have fueled competition, and owners' associations can do little to dampen competition through inter-firm cooperation. The secretary of TEA said to me in exasperation that there are simply too many firms to truly coordinate production here.[55] Instead, competition fuels cost-cutting and heightened exploitation of workers and dependent owners. As Sakthivel put it: "People here start by seeing the neighbor start working. The owner comes first and leaves last. Work, work, work: that is the culture of Tiruppur."[56] How are meanings and practices of work stabilized in this frenetic atmosphere in which people work, work, work? What happens beyond the reach of the most powerful local institution, TEA, which in its own analysis can only get so far in achieving collective efficiency? How do production and intensified exploitation hang together in a period of dramatic growth? These are questions that require considering the deployment of social labor from the experience of workers.

VII. Giving Labor Its Due

"Employers are terrible. It's a dog's life. There is no permanent work here," says "Iron" Lokanathan, an ironing worker and active unionist, while relating his incessant work on two hours of sleep a day during the three months of "season."[57] During the height of the export season, from October to February, haphazardly strung cardboard signs crop up around town announcing short-term work. When these signs of labor market insecurity are taken down in Tiruppur's lean months, those who can return to their rural origins and those who can't take out consumption loans from moneylenders who descend into working-class neighborhoods. A group of migrant women workers spoke to me candidly on the roof of their company at lunchtime about how work is "dull" for about six months, and virtually absent for another one or two months. In the latter periods, they are forced to take out loans from moneylenders at monthly interest rates of as high as 40 percent until work picks up again.[58] In this section I move closer into how labor time is organized and remunerated across a spatially and temporally fragmented division of labor.

Most workers I interviewed spoke of the pressure of seasons across firm sizes, despite the claims made by some owners of large firms about stable, year-round production. This is not to say that there aren't differences between firms in their ability to transfer the effects of seasonality to subcontractors and workers. I begin by looking at how labor time is organized across sectors and firm sizes across Tiruppur's industrial structure. Much of this data distinguishes knitting, or the fabrication of knitted cloth, from knit apparel, or knitted garment manufacture. Factories Inspectorate data in Table 7 shows that the average number of working days per year is significantly lower for knitting ("knitted cotton textiles") and knitwear ("Total textile products with apparel") workers than for workers in food products, light industry, the cotton textiles sector—comprising ginning, weaving, spinning and composite mills—or in the average for private sector industry.

Table 8 disaggregates numbers of factories and employees under different ranges of working days per year. Knitting and knitwear stand out in concentrating numbers of working factories in the range of 180–239 days per year, and numbers of working employees in the range of 120–179 days per year. Across the row for knitwear, it seems that some firms work all year, many continue to work for only about half the year, and as many work all year as for less than two months. Most workers are employed for less than half the year, demonstrating that knitwear work is profoundly seasonal.

Table 7: Average Working Days Per Year

Industry	Average Days/ Year
Food Products Manufacture	235
Cotton Ginning	233
Powerloom weaving	225
Cotton spinning mills	305
Cotton composite mills	339
Total cotton textiles manufacture	350
Knitted cotton textiles	103
Total textile products with apparel	112
Total Private Sector	247
Light industrial machinery	293

Source: "Statement II," 1996, the Office of the Deputy Inspector of Factories, Tiruppur.

Table 8: Number of Firms and Workers, by Working Days Per Year

Industry	Number of firms (and workers) across ranges of days/year					
	<60 days	60–119	120–79	180–239	240–99	>299 days
Food Products	3	11	33	13	15	36
	(308)	(123)	(778)	(255)	(457)	(2189)
Total Cotton	4	46	120	63	96	246
Textiles	(30)	(859)	(4438)	(1282)	(3005)	(21331)
Knits, Apparel	99	191	156	257	182	96
	(319)	(4657)	(6437)	(6295)	(3423)	(3261)
Total Private	109	255	321	360	336	537
Sector	(867)	(5982)	(11821)	(8177)	(10252)	(36939)

Source: "Statement IV—Distribution of Working Factories According to No. of Days, 1996," Office of the Deputy Inspector of Factories, Tiruppur.

Further indication that the weight of seasonality is borne by the working class comes from a quick perusal of wages in the Factory Inspectorate data. Gross wages, including allowances and supplements, reveal that knitwear and knitting workers receive handsome daily wages of Rs 68.55/day for knitting and Rs 69.35/day for knitwear. These are considerably higher than that of cotton textile Mill workers, at Rs 60.35/day let alone that of food products workers, at Rs 33.73/day. This contrast becomes starker in comparing gross annual wages: with workers in knitting and knitwear averaging Rs 7,525 in contrast to cotton textiles at Rs 21,146 and food processing at Rs 7,920. Factories Inspectorate data provides one indicator that knitwear uses low-wage labor relative to comparable local jobs, though average statistics do not reveal whether or not this workforce may be segmented into permanent and temporary workers with different wage bills.[59]

A different window into wage rates comes from the union of the Communist Party of India-Marxist, the Congress for Indian Trade Unions (CITU). These are the wage rates for 1998 as agreed to by unions and employer associations through the tri-annual General

Agreements between owners' associations and labor unions which set basic wage rates and increments over three years. The figures are for eight-hour shifts, though most workers work 1.5 shifts. As I have suggested, there is no concept of overtime as an increment to the normal wage. Indeed, each time I asked about overtime, I was told, "Yes, workers can work overtime, for 1.5 shifts." Overtime means workers have the right to work all hours with no supplementary wage because their insecurity pushes them to be beholden to the boss. Table 9 presents basic rates as well as rates with "Dearness Allowance" or DA, an inflation-indexed bonus or "living wage" supplement won by unions in 1984 for all workers, including piece-rated workers, a feat I return to in Chapter 5.

Many workers in Tiruppur are misled to think the figures on the CITU flysheet are a minimum and maximum. Nevertheless, the wide dissemination of wage information has proven to be an ingenious union tactic under conditions of high labor mobility, low union membership and near-absent government intervention in ensuring employer compliance with labor law. My conversations with workers over 1996–9 indicate that they were almost always paid between the basic wage rates and the wages with DA as publicized widely by the flysheet.

Table 9: General Agreement Shift Wage Rates, 1998

Tasks	Union Basic Rates	With DA˙ & Raise
Cutting, Stitching, Ironing		
Fabrication Machinist (Export)	57.03	83.66
Checking	32.58	57.98
Label	29.34	54.58
Kaimadi (Folding Helper)	28.52	53.72
Damage	22.81	47.73
Adikkuthal (Arranging Helper)	16.29	40.88
Fabrication Machinist (Domestic)	53.14	79.57

Source: "Cambala Uyarvù Vibaram" (News of Wage Increase), CITU Flysheet, 1998.

Notes: Shifts are eight hours; raises are annual; DA or "Dearness Allowance" is an inflation-indexed supplement; 1998 prices.

A group interview with workers also confirmed that average wage rates for different sorts of work varied within this band.[60]

Migrant workers often told me that Tiruppur's wages are high compared to other rural and town industries.[61] Disco Ravi, a cutting master and friend, confirmed that wage rates were generally higher here than in nearby Coimbatore city, but so were expenses. The working couple mentioned in the Preface, a cutting master and typist, told me they need a minimum of Rs 1500 per month to make ends meet.[62] Migrant workers often live in surrounding villages such as Pandiyanagar because rents in Tiruppur are too high.[63] On one occasion I met a North Indian non-Dalit worker family living in the Dalit section of a nearby village, and if this family had casteist concerns it would be safe to surmise that necessity pushed them to think first of affordable housing. A group of migrant women workers said they could get by with about Rs 1000 per month, not including the fact that the home villages of these migrants also shouldered some of their reproductive costs in child-rearing, as many left smaller children behind.[64] Expenses could be considerably higher for workers who could not return to their villages or draw on support services from home. One such worker from Tiruppur, Ravi, outlined his household budget "for a good month," when he makes Rs 2500 and does not have to rely on loans.[65] These migrant and resident workers are lucky if they can rely on credit and subsidies from home to support their insecure livelihoods as industrial workers.

The most important aspects of labor relations in Tiruppur knitwear prove to be beyond the scope of statistical and survey research because of the sheer diversity of labor arrangements. I therefore turn to comparative observations with Cawthorne's research to suggest how labor relations changed between the mid 1980s and the late 1990s. My research corroborates Cawthorne's findings that wages continue to be well above minimum daily wages. My first major disagreement is that I draw different conclusions as to what this means for securing a "family wage" in a context rife with gender bias, whether in wages or in contributions to the household. Despite seeing major gender differences in wage rates, Cawthorne argues that since the whole family can get opportunities to work in knitwear, and because wages are "simply handed over to their mothers," it follows that "where the whole family is working, the actual family wage . . . compares with the salaries [of] middle class professionals."[66] There is too much presumed here in the relative security of different types of work as well as of women as natural conduits for a family wage. My interviews with working-class families spoke instead of sharp gender differences in job security as well as in contributions to family accounts, calling such a rosy view of the family wage into question. I return to this point in Chapter 6.

The second distinction my research draws from Cawthorne's findings has to do with what she calls the "classic sweating" of labor. During the export season, workers work 1.5 shifts for six days a week with no overtime supplements to the wage, save "tea money" of a few rupees. When export schedules come due, the working day can be lengthened to as much as twenty hours. Most workers are piece-rated and without much access to Employees' State Insurance (ESI) or Provident Fund (PF), the institutionalized gains of unionism.[67] Cawthorne argues that absolute surplus value, or value extracted by increasing the working day rather than by enhancing productivity, rules the town.[68] The notion of absolute surplus value draws focus within particular enterprises and to particular ways in which workers are worked harder, while capital in Tiruppur benefits from the insecurity of workers across the division of labor. Absolute surplus value and cheap labor are inadequate concepts for describing Tiruppur in the 1990s, when pervasive labor market insecurity allows a political dominance of capital over organized labor. This dominance means that capital can combine sweatshop labor processes with organizational innovation and uneven technical change. Tiruppur's advantage does not lie simply in labor's price or effort, but in capital's control of the deployment of social labor in coordinating dispersed worksites. Foreign buyers know this all too well. The American Apparel Manufacturers' Association warns against the "cheap labor" argument in explaining to global buyers the important shifts in apparel sourcing between 1986 and 1997: "Labor Cost. Once the predominant factor in sourcing decisions, labor cost has lost some of its weight. When buying a complete package, as is common in Asia, labor is combined with material and other component costs, giving the sourcer little control over (or knowledge of) any of them . . . When weighing this factor, include the costs of benefits and local work rules, as well as the stability of the labor force."[69] The implication is that places like Tiruppur don't just offer cheap labor, they offer the benefits of a complete package of social relations, of which low wages and insecure workers' rights are ingredients. More important are "local work rules," forms of knowledge and control through which work across dispersed worksites is integrated; in other words, social labor.

Typically, the contribution of social labor is represented in the narrow rhetoric of skill formation. Workers acquire and diversify their skills through on-the-job training and mobility between firms. However, most jobs have been routinized and, as in fabrication and stitching, have been slow and uneven in relation to technical change. Consequently, unions have treated job classifications as fixed categories, contributing to the notion that skill inheres in jobs rather than in workers' actions. One result of this notion of the given-ness of job classifications is that union-mediated conflict over promotions, upgrading of standards, and transfer of personnel have been extremely rare.[70] Job duties and payments vary by skill, age, and gender, each form of distinction seemingly supporting the given-ness of job types. In this context of rigid jobs, possibilities of multi-skilling and class mobility are surprising. Cawthorne found her own notions of "classic sweating" challenged by what she took to be workers' aspirations: "I encountered, to my own consternation, a considerable contrast between the way in which workers . . . perceive their situation [as] one of opportunity and the way in which the same situation might be 'objectively' perceived . . . [T]he argument I have made . . . about 'poor' overall conditions in the industry is not necessarily one which most of the workers in it would have endorsed."[71]

I was similarly confronted with workers' aspirations of class mobility against the odds, but not because they didn't also have powerful and poignant critiques of their poverty and insecurity. These aspirations matter politically and ideologically rather than simply as truth claims.[72]

My friend Disco Ravi, a cutting master, persisted in the hope of starting a unit some day, despite being under no illusions as to the difficulties that workers face. The circulation of successful rags-to-riches
stories, which I explain in the course of this book, allows even workers
who suffer the indignities of seasonal work to envision the faint possibility of class mobility. This is not to say they don't also mock the idea,
or realize—as I came to—how deeply exclusionary such opportunities
are. After returning from a break to the US, a group of working-class
men I met occasionally at a local café, including Ravi, joked to me
sarcastically, "At least you could have brought back some [export]
orders for us. Then we'd all be Big Owners . . ." At which point they
would all, on cue, twist their large and imaginary moustaches like the
classic Big Owner might! One of these men, a Dalit Christian with the
improbable name Dastan Bannatic Kings, did in fact start a processing
unit in partnership with other workers the following year. The ambi-
guities in workers' aspirations are linked to the experience of work in
Tiruppur. My worker friends at the tea stall were commenting on this
tension in their sarcasm, on the one hand realizing a basis for Tiruppur's rags-to-riches stories while on the other hand replying, "It's not
quite me." My friends knew that the ideology of self-made men operates selectively, relying crucially on their misrecognition as workers
who can certainly not all make the class leap. I return to these dynamics
of interpellation and misrecognition in Chapter 5.[73]

In contrast to Cawthorne's pessimism, Swaminathan and Jeyaranjan,
researching in the early 1990s, stress the variety of trajectories workers
take through firms in the process of multi-skilling. They explain on-
the-job learning as linked to extensive horizontal mobility across
Tiruppur's firm-networks, in marked contrast to the heirarchical
formal sector with its rigid Taylorist organizational structure and
comparative lack of mobility. Some workers do in fact acquire a knowledge of the entire production process through their mobile careers,
giving them the skills to start small jobwork units of their own. Key to
this mobility is the acquisition of informal procedures and conventions
rather than formal degrees. In this context, the imposition of formal
sector norms that link pay scales to formal degrees and qualifications

could be particularly disastrous for workers.[74] This is an important caution, one that requires further explanation of the conventions that enable multiskilling through mobility.

Questions of on-the-job skill formation, in contrast to school-based or formal technical education, crystallize in the problem of child labor. While numbers are very difficult to ascertain with certainty, the most reliable information on child labor is that of SAVE, an NGO in Tiruppur focused and organized around the problem of child labor. SAVE reported 25,000 child laborers in 3000 units, or an average of 8.3 per unit in 1997.[75] Labor unions do not treat child labor as a priority issue, and seem to concur with owners' association representations of this as a social ill. Moreover, because the acquisition of skills by child workers is gendered from an early age, young boys can aspire to skill acquisition and future job security while young girls, for the most part, cannot.[76]

Gender and family mediate a variety of aspects of work, particularly the forms of underpaid family labor accessed through households, as described in Section II. S. Bhuvana, a woman in her late forties, works in companies and does various forms of work at home along with her daughter, who works outside in a knitwear retail showroom. They get "collar separation" work for Rs 0.08/collar, "half finishing" for Rs 2/dozen pieces, and "banian waste" work for Rs 8/kg. Bhuvana's landlady, in the next small cluster of rooms facing their common courtyard, does cone-rewinding, having invested in a small machine that rewinds yarn for powerlooms; some households do similar work, as in rewinding yarn into cones for knitting machines. Bhuvana wanted to save Rs 1 lakh for a button machine, so as to earn Rs 0.18 per button.[77] Another lady in a village on the outskirts of the town engaged in collar-separation spoke of stable and uniformly low piece rates, at Rs 0.8 per collar. When I asked how much they do, the daughter continued pulling apart collars on their rural porch and responded with some puzzlement, "As many as we can!"[78]

There are other forms of petty enterprise in which workers or members of working-class families participate. For instance, male workers sometimes collect collars to put out to households for collar separation, performing the same function that Bhuvana does. Companies prefer to have their own trusted employees, typically men, in these intermediary positions. One man called Mohammad Rafi was a Singer tailor who also bought seconds pieces from his company to sell in a shop in Khadarpet, the export surplus and seconds sales market in Tiruppur. He said he would get a Rs 5 margin on each piece he sold.[79] Other workers buy and sell banian waste on the side. While these activities can be risky, they also provide opportunities for poaching, and are therefore not always encouraged. A stitching worker also involved in the seconds trade would, for instance, have an incentive to make more mistakes. These types of workers must be careful in marketing seconds pieces and waste material, as they can be held responsible for making mistakes for personal gain.[80]

Turning back to factory work, I found it difficult to make strict correlations between firm size and conditions of work. I found large units, usually arrayed in complexes, more airy and methodically organized, while small units were stuck into the most unlikely places with equally haphazard interiors. This, however, says precious little of how rigorous work might be or how much autonomy it might grant workers. My friend Karuppusamy would wander in and out of the tiny unit he worked in, located in the working-class neighborhood in which he also lived. Between jobs for his sister's provision shack (*malligaikkatai*) on the main road, he would come back to the unit to iron banians or press stacks of shirts in the hydraulic press. Karuppusamy's job description was broad, and he also enjoyed closeness with the two young working-class brothers who owned the unit. Workers often said that while they began their careers at large companies, they preferred to settle into smaller and more secure workplaces that tended also to be better paying and less taxing.

What was certainly not clear was that large firms paid all workers better-than-average wages. For instance, one prominent large company which I call Ginwin has several units over a large *tóttam* or farm outside town along Palladam Road.[81] Cutting masters and ironing workers are all male and paid very well at Ginwin. Checking workers, all women, and overlock stitchers, sometimes women, are paid very low wages that dip below the union basic rates. Women engaged in single-needle power stitching are paid considerably less than men.

Gender divisions are therefore one way by which some workers in large units are paid more than the average wage at the cost of other workers, who might even be paid less than the union minimum wage.

Gender discrimination permeates social labor but is never seen as such because it works through localized labor arrangements facilitated through contracting. From a conversation with two workers who co-manage an internal contract group from cutting to packing, I found that in fact contracting might be a way to pay women and men different wages even for the same job. Management and union leaders would never admit to this in Tiruppur. Furthermore, a comparison of wages reported by the contractors and the group of workers mentioned earlier suggests that workers in contract groups might be paid slightly less. In this case, a small margin goes directly to the contractors, who make around Rs 500–600 per week. Wages paid by contractors "include bonus and DA," they assured me, despite the fact that the "bonus" in particular is supposed to be independent of wages and annual raises, and is given for the Deepavali holiday in October. However, it is significant that these contractors pay between the union-negotiated basic and full wages, so that contracting has not allowed wage payments to sink below the union basic rates. This may be because contractors don't make much more than other workers; one told me he makes Rs 2500 a month, which is what any skilled worker working 1.5 shifts/day in the season can make. Pressure by organized labor has certainly not been overcome by contracting.

A fascinating point made by these internal contractors was that they pay most workers, with the exception of ironing and packing, by time rather than by the piece. Stitching, checking and labeling or Singer tailoring jobs, usually paid in piece wages, are here arranged on time wages. The contractor claims to include all the rights earned by organized labor into this time wage. Most importantly, workers have no reason to intensify work at the expense of quality. Instead, time wages allow workers in internal contract groups to integrate more smoothly into the collective endeavor of batch production.[82]

Indeed, it is an understanding of these collective endeavors in the logic of batch production that the American Apparel Manufacturers' Association alludes to in cautioning foreign buyers against thinking narrowly about cheap labor. An understanding of social labor is, however, crucially incomplete without a sense of the subjective or ideological aspects of work. Owners and managers often told me that there is something peculiar about workers here: they will work like no other workers, they can work night and day, they are particularly "hard workers," and so on. Some would contrast them explicitly to Keralite labor who are seen conversely as bold, oppositional, and unwilling to work. My argument, as it unfolds, is that these fragments of consciousness are a part of ways in which value is secured and obscured in a particular production politics in which contracting and exclusionary class mobility are intertwined.

How do owners of working-class origins think of workers who respond to the cardboard signs outside lavish polished granite exteriors today? One owner of working-class origins told me his workforce was "mainly permanent" in the sense that they keep coming back to check if there's work. He says 20 percent of his 90 workers "freelance," but it's no loss to him because all the work is piece-rated.[83] Many owners use the term "freelancing" disparagingly, as if to suggest that workers choose their mobility over loyalty to bosses. There might be a grain of truth in that mobility between jobs allows some workers to place themselves in ways that can allow them to become multi-skilled and socially connected, allowing them to move up the ranks to contractor or dependent jobworker. For the mass of workers, however, "freelancing" appears not as choice but as necessity.

VIII. Conclusion: The Politics of Social Labor

This chapter has traveled through Tiruppur's baroque industrial cluster to explain how the movements of things, people, labors, credit, uncertainties and seasonalities, and forms of regulation together shape the mode of deployment of social labor. While social labor provides a window into the uneven accumulation of capital, Marx saw accumulation proceed in two dimensions: as the accumulation of capital and of the reserve army of labor. Organizational and technical change in the knitwear industry can be consistent with a mass of flexible workers. The accumulation of capital through small firm networks mirrors the accumulation of surplus labor: of workers scouring the streets in the export season for cardboard signs. The point of seeing accumulation in both senses is to recognize how they *combine*, as they do in Tiruppur. Rather than the antipodes of the informal sector *vs* the industrial district, or of high and low roads to industrial flexibility, Marx's analytical tools allow one to ask how the social relations of production create the conditions for accumulation. In other words, the mode of deployment of social labor becomes a means for securing relative surplus value as well as for dominating a differentiated and insecure workforce. The following chapter dissects the division of labor into multiple accumulation strategies, to ask how knitwear owners' social and historical identities make a difference to their industrial practice.

CHAPTER 3

Accumulation Strategies and Gounder Dominance, 1996–1998

I. Introduction: Divisions Over the Division of Labor

Rather than a seamless whole, the division of labor in Tiruppur knitwear is a place of multiple strategies of work organization and accumulation. This chapter asks how owners' accumulation strategies derive from divergent backgrounds, social affiliations, and trajectories of work and ownership. Through an engagement with multiplicity, I begin to explain the most successful accumulation strategy, pursued by Gounders of working-class origins. This internal comparison then allows me to pose the central question of this book: why and how have certain Gounders of working-class origins come to control knitwear work as they do today? As the dominant accumulation strategy must then be explained through processes that are not common to the rest, I turn in Part II to the regional and agrarian histories and legacies through which Gounder dominance over Tiruppur knitwear was made.

In my first cut at survey analysis, I used an inductive approach to deconstruct the division of labor into more-or-less-discrete accumulation strategies.[1] Here, I present the results of that exercise using the heuristic of "routes of entry and accumulation" in order to differentiate owners' backgrounds, work histories, transitions to small business, and consequent industrial practice. Section II describes the five possible trajectories, or accumulation strategies, this heuristic provides. I begin with the results of survey analysis in determining three main strategies: hierarchical producer subcontracting engaged by Gounders of working-class origins, commercial subcontracting by North Indian elites, and a form of proprietorship undertaken by South Indian elite families. I then detail the ways in which the Gounder ex-Worker strategy sets the rules of industry for the cluster as a whole. Finally, I demonstrate two spin-offs from this dominant strategy, corresponding to well-off Gounders and non-Gounder South Indian ex-Workers. Section III turns to elite failures and accumulation strategies that ended in loss or stagnation. These counterexamples of elite attempts at transition to knitwear from agrarian, mercantile, South Indian and North Indian business family origins clarify the peculiarity of the dominant route taken by Gounders of working-class origins.

In interrogating accumulation strategies, I argue that while owners are engaged in production they simultaneously attempt to regulate social labor across workplaces to make a cheap garment of the right quality, at the right time. This view questions Marx's understanding of power over capitalist work, in which despotism in the labor process has as its foil anarchy in the market.[2] Michael Burawoy has questioned the despotism of capital in the labor process by asking how workers consent to work under conditions of improving productivity.[3] While Burawoy's notion of the politics of production breaks from the teleology and functionalism of an orthodox Marxist model of power on the shopfloor, it does so to the neglect of social labor.[4] David Harvey's response is to concede that class struggle in the labor process pressures capital to enter a terrain of compromise, to dampen competition and help stabilize the anarchic process of constant technological change. Like scholars of industrial clusters and firm networks, Harvey recognizes social labor, but without the attention to praxis central to Burawoy's shopfloor ethnographies.[5] What I mean by the politics of social labor is this realm of industrial praxis, which I approach here through survey results. In the following section I ask how fractions of capital of different social origins seek to deploy and control social labor.

II. Multiple Trajectories and "Gounder Domination"

I approach conventions of work in Tiruppur through surveys conducted over 1996–8 over 15 percent random samples of owners in SIHMA and TEA. In exploring how different sorts of owners organize production and control work differently, I began by sorting owners into five "routes of entry and affiliation," which link owners' backgrounds and social affiliations with their production strategies.[6] These routes are distinguished by two parameters: owner's caste/ religious/ regional affiliation[7] and whether the owner was once a worker in Tiruppur knitwear. The five non-overlapping routes to ownership constituted through this heuristic are:

(1) *Gounder ex-Worker*: Gounder ex-Worker owners,
(2) *Gounder*: Gounder non-ex-Workers,
(3) *Other ex-Worker*: non-Gounder ex-Workers (South Indian),
(4) *Southern*: non-Gounder non-ex-Workers (South Indian), and
(5) *Northern*: North Indians, mainly Marwaris, non ex-Workers.

The motivation for these routes came from a year's ethnographic and life history research, so qualitative methods were key in constructing the questionnaire. Figure 4 represents percentages of each route in the domestic association, SIHMA, and the exporters association, TEA, to show that *Gounder ex-Workers* numerically dominate both associations. Moreover, the union of Gounder and ex-Worker affiliations (*Gounder ex-Workers, Gounders and Other ex-Workers* taken together) constitutes the lion's share in SIHMA and TEA. Furthermore, a large share of *Gounders* and *Other ex-Workers* owe their entry into the industry to *Gounder ex-Workers*, through ties of family, work or partnership. Hence, the causal significance of the *Gounder ex-Worker* route is underestimated by the restricted way in which I relate caste affiliation to work history here. My argument is that even this restricted definition of routes reveals the importance of the *Gounder ex-Worker* route of entry and affiliation. A comprehensive understanding of the causal significance of this route must await the historical and ethnographic analysis in the chapters to follow.

Figure 4: Composition of Employers' Associations by Routes

Decomposition of SIHMA Owners

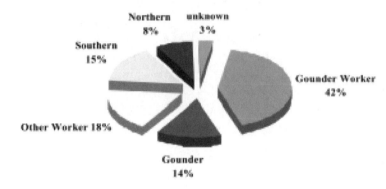

Decomposition of TEA Owners

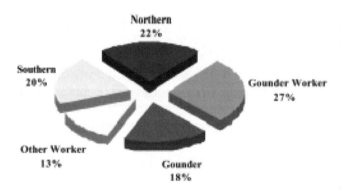

Accumulation Strategies and the Dominant Route

Using this heuristic of five routes, the evidence bears out three distinct accumulation strategies: *Gounder ex-Worker, Southern* and *Northern*. The less clearly distinct *Gounder* and *Other ex-Worker* routes inter-twine with the dominant *Gounder ex-Worker* route, from which these owners are often kin or ex-worker spin-offs. I begin by summarizing the characteristics that can be induced of each accumulation strategy, then work through some of the key evidence that supports these conclusions.

The strongest route in Tiruppur is that of *Gounder ex-Workers* who engage in a strategy of hierarchical producer subcontracting that links labor-intensive production in garment stitching with control across contract units. These owners have the highest productivity to fixed capital ratios and their units are the most labor intensive. Domestic owners in this route tend to be differentiated, the majority reliant on control at the point of production as their primary advantage. On the other hand, some domestic owners and the majority of exporters forge control over social labor either through subsidiary "sister concerns," or through external or internal contract units. Among exporters, these owners are most likely to engage in internal and external contracting. Domestic owners are likely to contract internally, but not externally, the latter reflecting their differentiation. *Gounder ex-Workers'* entry into the ranks of ownership was primarily through stitching sections, where there is a premium on participant control of production. Hence, these owners spent several initial years as owners working alongside their labor. What is more, *Gounder ex-Workers* began in partnerships through strong infusions of capital from their ex-bosses and kin, and the majority of domestic owners continue to be in dedicated inter-firm relations. Dedication, or dependent production, is much less prevalent among exporters, implying class consolidation at the apex. These are the firms to which others dedicate themselves.

The next strongest route is that of *Northerns* who engage in commercial subcontracting that builds on their mercantile and business strengths as arms of larger pan-Indian business houses. Business volumes reported by these owners reflect these larger family operations. Domestic owners are the least labor intensive of all. *Northerns* tend to emerge through apprenticeships in family business networks from which they receive large infusions of capital to become proprietors. Pan-Indian business networks also become a means for quick downstream diversification into domestic marketing. Moreover, because this strategy shies away from risky investment in garment manufacture, domestic owners tend to invest horizontally in processing. Horizontal integration is one strategy for lowering uncertainties in production without investing in sections where risk is determined by direct control of labor. *Northerns* do not engage in much dedicated domestic production, unlike the dominant route. Exports are another story. Mercantile putting-out, an older form of engagement by Marwaris in Calcutta and other parts of North India, has renewed its presence in Tiruppur's export production through access to export houses and marketing networks. However, this trajectory must conform to the production norms set by the dominant route of *Gounder ex-Workers*.

The third important route is that of *Southerns* who engage in an older model of proprietorship that has since also attempted to adapt to the new rules of the game instituted by the dominant route. Hence, for instance, many *Southerns* in the domestic market began as composite units that combined fabrication and manufacture. These domestic units did not start sister concerns in the manner of *Gounder ex-Workers*, and certainly not when Gounders were doing so in large numbers since the 1970s. *Southerns* have begun starting sister concerns only in the area of exports. Exporters tend not to be labor-intensive, nor do they tend towards dedication, reflecting an older type of disengagement between the business of the owner and work of labor. Put simply, these owners do not spend all hours alongside their workers on the factory floor. Moreover, these owners also view dedicated production in derogatory terms as akin to working for someone else. *Southerns*, particularly in domestic production, retain enough of the conservatism of an older model to constitute a distinct, if dying, route.

Turning to the two less distinct routes, *Other ex-Workers* have taken a route that has its own peculiarities, despite its relative insignificance in comparison with the three main fractions of capital. This route was initiated with much more initial capital than the *Gounder ex-Worker* route, implying that the dominant route relied on not just capital but also specific types of social relations. Unlike *Gounder ex-Workers*, these owners sought support from ex-bosses in jobwork and contacts rather than in capital and machines. However, it is not clear that *Other ex-Workers* organize industry through a different strategy, as in many respects the strategy is much like that of *Gounder ex-Workers*; one exception is that *Other ex-Workers* are more likely to have sister concerns "in name." This may be because non-Gounders lack the kin or caste relations Gounders can use in controlling production networks. This may also be a reason why *Other ex-Workers* also rarely engage in dedicated merchant export.

Finally, *Gounders* share many characteristics with *Gounder ex-Workers*; indeed several *Gounders* are partners of *Gounder ex-Workers* in the domestic market, or their sons or sons-in-law in exports. Curiously, however, the main feature that distinguishes this route from the dominant route is that *Gounders* do not tend to start sister concerns, perhaps because they have consolidated themselves as lead firms contracting out to units owned entirely by others. I use this information to interrogate the *Gounder ex-Worker* route by asking whether the immediate class origins of Gounders may have something to do with their propensity to start multiple units. On the other hand, domestic *Gounders* tend also to be dedicated, in significant part as spin-offs from the dominant route.

In the rest of this section, I detail some of the evidence for these routes and their divergent modes of deployment of social labor, and for the dominance of *Gounder ex-Workers.* I work through the survey evidence along three themes: ownership and control of means of production, control of labor and contracting, and control of production networks and class mobility.

Ownership and Control of Means of Production

In exploring how owners approach machines and work in Tiruppur, I had quickly to make sense of why many owners say: "I own the machines, but not the work." In exploring this disjuncture between ownership of means of production and control of the labor process, I asked how firms and means of production are owned privately, how firms integrate operations, and how ownership is shared in production networks.[8]

As I suggested in the previous chapter, ownership of stitching machines correlates weakly with business volume for domestic owners, but big exporters tend to own more stitching machines.[9] Vertical and horizontal integration also correlates weakly for both domestic and export owners.[10] The evidence is more interesting when it's taken apart through the heuristic of "routes of entry and affiliation."

Table 10 shows that domestic *Gounder ex-Workers* tend to own more fabrication machines than others, while non-Gounders own significant numbers of stitching machines. Using the ratio of average annual turnover to machine capital as an approximation of productivity to fixed capital, what is striking is that domestic *Gounder ex-Workers* have the highest ratios, followed by *Gounders*. Among exporters, *Northerns* have an extremely high turnover to machine capital ratio, an abberation that reflects that they are part of much larger mercantile concerns that put-out to jobworkers in Tiruppur. This is a first indication that *Gounder ex-Workers* achieve a higher ratio of productivity to fixed capital investment than all other entrepreneurs.

The following three charts of frequencies of ownership of machine capital and annual turnover or business volume show considerable differentiation among domestic owners.[11] Figure 5 plots numbers of firms across ranges of machines owned in each association. The spectrum of domestic owners shows strong evidence of differentiation between a substantial 33 percent of owners with less than 10 machines,

Table 10: Machines and Productivity–Capital Ratios

Routes	Fabrication Machines	Stitching Machines	Productivity/ Capital
Domestic (SIHMA)			
Gounder ex-worker	8	17	17.8
Gounder	3	20	15.0
Other ex-worker	2	18	9.8
Southern	4	15	9.5
Northern	5	43	5.6
Export (TEA)			
Gounder ex-worker	7	70	10.4
Gounder	9	67	4.2
Other ex-worker	2	49	4.3
Southern	3	87	3.4
Northern	0	23	59.1

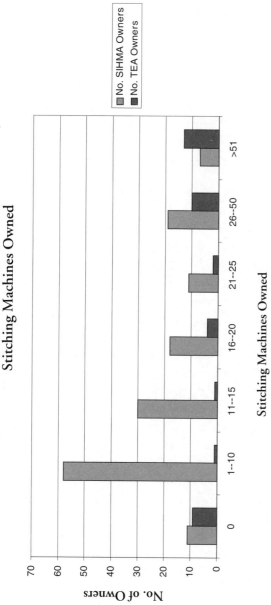

Figure 5: Distribution of SIHMA and TEA Owners by Stitching Machines Owned

in all probability a power table with 8 machines. On the other end, 10 percent own 26–50 machines and 4 percent own more than 50. There is no such evidence of differentiation among exporters, on the other hand, where economies of scale prevail. As Gounder and ex-worker affiliations dominate within both peaks of the domestic owners' spectrum, I suggest that these affiliations are better equipped to take on the risks endemic to stitching.

The machine capital spectrum in Figure 6 looks similar. A high peak early in the domestic spectrum indicates differentiation in the ownership of machines, with 34 percent of domestic owners owning machines in the frequency range of Rs 0.1 to 0.5 million while 6 percent own machines in the largest three frequency ranges, over Rs 5 million. On the other hand, the exporter spectrum does not indicate such differentiation, as most firms concentrate in the middle range of Rs 1–5 million, with a second peak at Rs 10–50 million, where several firms have integrated horizontally into processing facilities.[12]

Figure 7 turns to data on average annual turnover, or business volume. The domestic spectrum shows 66 percent of owners reporting business volumes of Rs 1–50 million, a concentration in the middle, which indicates the persistence of small firms. Indeed, domestic firms are much less differentiated in terms of business volume than machine capital. The exporter spectrum, on the other hand, concentrates 72 percent of its members in the ranges from Rs 10–500 million. I conclude from this evidence that the export association represents a more concentrated form of class power than the domestic association.[13]

A key problem in discussing firms in Tiruppur has to do with meanings of ownership where forms of shared ownership abound. Only 25 percent of domestic owners and 20 percent of exporters began as proprietors, while most started in partnerships of three, on average. In their accumulation strategies, many owners began subsidiary units called sister concerns, which are either allied proprietorships, partnerships or parts of groups with overlapping ownership and conventions for sharing production contracts. Table 11 returns to the five routes to ask how owners integrate and start sister concerns. Among domestic owners, all but the Gounder routes are more likely to start phantom

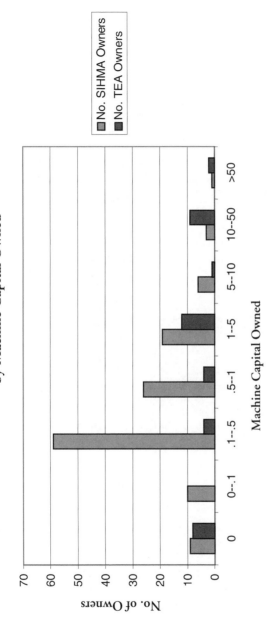

Figure 6: Distribution of SIHMA and TEA Owners by Machine Capital Owned

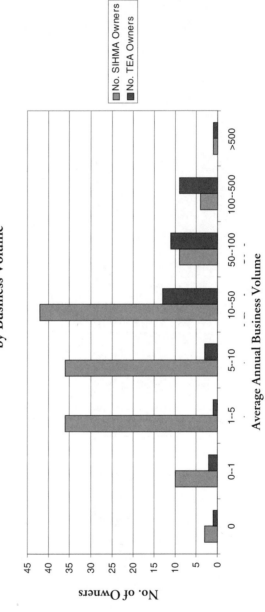

Figure 7: Distribution of SIHMA and TEA Owners by Business Volume

Table 11: Sister Concerns

Routes	Sister Concerns	Phantom Sister Concerns	Real Sister Concerns
Domestic (SIHMA)			
Gounder ex-Worker	60%	53%	28%
Gounder	48%	63%	18%
Other ex-Worker	58%	93%	4%
Southern	56%	90%	6%
Northern	92%	91%	8%
Export (TEA)			
Gounder ex-Worker	92%	57%	40%
Gounder	88%	83%	15%
Other ex-Worker	60%	67%	20%
Southern	75%	25%	56%
Northern	50%	80%	10%

sister concerns that exist only on the books, while *Gounder ex-Workers* are most inclined to start real sister concerns with investment in plant and machinery. Of exporters, *Southerns* and *Gounder ex-Workers* are most likely to start real sister concerns, while *Northerns* tend to start phantom sister concerns. The latter is not surprising, as *Northerns* do not have access to the same kinds of networks as South Indians. Many *Southerns* are in fact older proprietorships which only emulated later entrants, predominantly Gounders, in starting sister concerns once exports became dominant, and often the export units were begun for their sons or sons-in-law.

The routes diverge more strongly by ways in which owners pursue integration.[14] Table 12 shows that forward integration is the domain of business communities like *Southerns* and particularly *Northerns*. The latter enter with strong distribution and sourcing networks from North India, particularly in the domestic trade, and are therefore primed to integrate forward into marketing. Backward integration into spinning has only been pursued to a significant extent by both *Gounder ex-Workers* and *Gounders* in exports. As I mentioned in Chapter 2, this has been a limited and recent attempt to resolve some of the problems of the 1990s. Despite state subsidies for mini-mills in

Table 12: Forms of Integration

Routes	Backward Integration (Spinning)	Forward Integration (Marketing)	Horizontal Integration (Processing)
Domestic (SIHMA)			
Gounder ex-Worker	2%	0%	26%
Gounder	0%	0%	25%
Other ex-Worker	4%	4%	21%
Southern	5%	10%	14%
Northern	0%	38%	50%
Export (TEA)			
Gounder ex-Worker	18%	0%	91%
Gounder	13%	0%	63%
Other ex-Worker	0%	0%	43%
Southern	0%	13%	50%
Northern	0%	20%	10%

state-designated backward areas, however, integration into spinning has not been a profitable path in a region with long-established spinning mill concerns.

Horizontal integration into processing is pursued most strongly by *Northerns* among domestic owners and by *Gounder ex-Workers* among exporters. Bleaching, the main processing activity for domestic production, is almost entirely in the hands of Gounders who have shifted from farming to bleaching. Low entry costs allowed Gounders from adjacent villages to convert their farms into bleaching firms as long as water was within reach. This largely obviated the need for domestic producers to integrate horizontally into bleaching. *Northerns*, with access to capital from family businesses elsewhere, who also tend to shy away from investing in the riskier sections of production—such as garment stitching and manufacture—have invested in modernized processing plants to stabilize their production systems. The majority of new sorts of processing activities, however, are primarily for the export sector, where *Gounder ex-Workers* in exports lead in horizontal integration. *Northerns* in exports steer clear of horizontal integration, which fits with their strategy of sourcing in Tiruppur.[15]

Given the gendered language of sister concerns, I met only one woman running one. Only after she was widowed did this Gounder step into the company premises, to prevent her brothers-in-law and brothers from usurping her deceased husband's firms entirely. Property is bound in gender and caste relations, as will become clearer further in this book. The crucial question of property relations I pursue in this section concerns why economies of scale are not the order of the day. The existence of state incentives to small-scale industry, with ineffectual enforcement mechanisms, can be resolved through the proliferation of phantom units rather than through the decentralization of plant and machinery. Without the information to do the quick math of doubling inputs and outputs, I cannot ascertain whether economies of scale prevail for the five routes. In the absence of strong forces that propel owners to integrate, there is considerable room for owners to decide on viable strategies of decentralization by considering sister concerns in terms of the not-always-commensurable lenses of property and production.

On the one hand, viewing sister concerns in terms of property points to high transactions costs in the market for firms or machines. In other words, because it is difficult to buy or sell firms at the precise time when one needs to, it becomes easier to disintegrate investment across firms or to own less and contract out. When property was an expressed reason for starting sister concerns, it was most often Gounders who claimed to be constructing an inheritance or dowry, or as fixed capital for "raising" kin or caste fellows to become bosses, phenomena I return to in Chapter 5. A sizeable share of owners explain sister concerns as property division or ways of making inheritance.[16] Among affiliations, the expressed rationale of Gounders is most strongly concerned with property, while Chettiars and North Indians, particularly Marwaris, is least so.[17]

On the other hand, viewing sister concerns in terms of production points to ongoing attempts to resolve supervision problems in an industry in which manual labor and "labor problems" remain central.[18] Indeed, a sizeable share of owners explain starting sister concerns in terms of "labor problems"—whether understood as numbers of workers, strikes, labor market segmentation, or labor supervision.[19] The problem of sister concerns provides a bridge between dispersed ownership and the politics of production. Even big exporters would admit to me that among their major headaches are labor problems in various guises. I therefore turn next to different ways in which Tiruppur owners address problems of labor control at the heart of knitwear, in garment stitching.

Control of Labor and Contracting

Using the ratio of numbers of workers[20] to machine capital as an index of labor intensity, companies with larger volumes of business are less labor intensive.[21] Again, internal differences show up through the five routes. Table 13 shows that labor intensity is much higher for *Gounder ex-Workers* than others, and by orders of magnitude in contrast to domestic *Northerns*. Even among exporters, ex-workers—*Gounder ex-Workers* and *Other ex-Workers*—stand out as combining half as much machine capital with labor than other owners. In other words, Gounders in domestic production and ex-workers in export production tend to engage in more labor-intensive or sweated production.

Yet, the route most associated with sweating is also, as Table 14 indicates, most significant in its use of the owner's own labor and

Table 13: Average Labor and Labor Intensity

Routes	Average Number of Workers	Labor Intensity (Worker/R.)
Domestic (SIHMA)		
Gounder ex-worker	77	76.3
Gounder	66	52.6
Other ex-worker	75	32.7
Southern	45	40.0
Northern	143	5.3
Export (TEA)		
Gounder ex-worker	212	20.4
Gounder	177	9.7
Other ex-worker	186	24.3
Southern	217	10.5
Northern	23	9.2

family labor: 74 percent of *Gounder ex-Workers* in domestic production, and 70 percent in exports, worked in their own firms for an average of 7.8 and 4.9 years respectively. A fifth of *Southern* domestic owners also worked in their own companies for a significantly longer average of 14 years. While *Gounder ex-workers* in both associations have been the main users of family labor, percentages of family labor reported are on the low side in general. This anticipates an argument I will make in Part II of this book, that gender and kinship, which are assumed to have their locus in the family, are writ large across social labor. *Gounder ex-Workers* worked in their own firms while creating markedly more labor-intensive work regimes.

An important elision in this data on labor intensity centers on whether contract labor is counted as "own" labor. Most employers were at pains to say that contract labor in their companies was not their own, but was secured independently by the contractor. On one occasion I sat with an owner on the shopfloor, in full view of about twenty workers, while he repeated several times without batting an eyelid that he employed no labor whatsoever. How, then, do direct and indirect employers engage in Tiruppur's brand of relational contracting?

In approaching labor arrangements across production units, I follow local convention in distinguishing between contracting within and across companies. External contracting refers to formally separate knitwear manufacturing or stitching sister concerns owned by the parent company but run by a contractor. These are the arrangements for which owners say, "I own the machines, but not the work." External contracting units make garments, so, whatever else they might include, they always include stitching sections.[22] Internal contracting usually means contracting out the stitching section to a contractor within the company who manages all labor related to the power table. Internal contracting is often used as a strategy to separate stitching workers from cutting and packing workers who report directly to the boss.

Big exporters have a strong tendency to contract internally while domestic firms with larger business volumes do not engage as much in internal contracting.[23] Exporters show slight differences, in that Gounders tend slightly more toward internal contracting, while North Indian

Table 14: Self and Family Work

Route	Self Work	. . . years of	Family Labor
Domestic (SIHMA)			
Gounder ex-worker	74%	7.8	39%
Gounder	35%	6.2	19%
Other ex-worker	39%	7.6	23%
Southern	20%	14.0	8%
Northern	0%	0.0	0%
Export (TEA)			
Gounder ex-worker	70%	4.9	20%
Gounder	0%	0.0	0%
Other ex-worker	0%	0.0	0%
Southern	0%	0.0	0%
Northern	0%	0.0	0%

Marwaris tend not to. Among domestic owners, however, Chettiars and Marwaris show weak tendencies to contract internally. Gounders in domestic production do not tend to vary much, as many are small owners supervising workers directly.[24] The disaggregated data indicates that internal contracting is a widespread phenomenon, which around 50–75 percent of all owners engage in, and there are no clear statistical differences. Among exporters, *Gounder ex-Workers* are the only ones engaging in external contracting, while many of their counterparts among domestic owners are too small to contract externally.[25]

A key reason for contracting expressed by owners is to minimize the power of labor. Contracting allows owners to hire and fire labor at will, and it allows differentiated terms of payment. Export owners claim to pay wages by the fashion, even when tasks remain relatively unchanged. Maximum Natarajan, the son of a prominent *Gounder ex-Worker*, whose elder brother squandered most of his father's fortune, said: "Previously we were employing our own employees." He has switched to internal contractors in the factory, and "now salaries, bonus and so on are the contractor's headache."[26] Power seems to be wielded, as Marx would have it, through contractor control in the detailed division of labor and the whip of the market in the social division of labor.

However, contracting has not been a foolproof strategy for labor control. Yellowbee Velusamy, a *Gounder ex-Worker,* said that he has switched back from contracting to "own labor" because "contracting will eat up management . . . The turmoil is louder in contract units."[27] One of Maximum Natarajan's contractors is a young man called Mani, who I found engrossed in preparing an elaborate table of wage rates for his contract work group. The advantage that Mani and his partner have is not in their wages of Rs 500–600 per week, not much higher than those of other workers, but the fact of regular wages. The extent to which Mani can fiddle with his table and pay workers differently depends not only on the whip of the market, but also on ongoing negotiations within his contract group. A push too hard could take Mani right back to being another insecure worker.[28]

From the perspective of labor, contracting should be the death knell of hard-won union rights. However, this does not seem to be the case. In my observations, workers on contract were still paid somewhere between the basic rates and the wages-with-benefits as per the General Agreements. When workers have a problem that cannot be settled with the contractor, or when the contractor absconds without paying wages, workers continue to go directly or through their union to the boss. Hence, labor problems continue to plague owners, and I interpret *Gounder ex-Worker* propensity to sweat labor and to contract stitching as indications of their better propensity to handle ongoing labor problems.

If there were only a binary choice between despotism in the workplace and anarchy in the market, there would be no way to understand why *Gounder ex-Workers* invest in the riskiest aspects of work. Nor would there be reason for *Northerns* who prefer to put-out all manufacturing on jobwork to rue their inability to control labor. The fact remains that even in contracting, the owner remains the owner, despite his protests to only owning machines, not the work. The contractor is only a shade above the workers he controls and far from the social world of owners. Owners must retain strong control over contractors in order to get work done without "being eaten" by them. Control over contracts amounts to control of "network market" relations across social labor.

Control of Production Networks and
Class Mobility

Contracting redistributes machines to allow some workers, particularly in garment stitching and manufacture, to make a class leap into the ranks of small ownership. Owners pursuing an accumulation strategy of hierarchical producer subcontracting must always confront the possibility of unruly networks that spin off into independent units. Owners must contend with the countervailing dynamics of fostering start-ups as dedicated production units, while retaining a tight hold on who can become a boss and how. This section works through the ways in which routes diverge in the control of production networks, as they embody the twin pressures of class mobility and dedicated production.

Table 15 on initial firm location shows where in the social division of labor owners began their first firms. Note that there is considerable double counting between the first two columns, as is clear in the case of exporter *Other Workers.* The table points clearly to the centrality of stitching/ garment manufacture as the main entry point for new owners in Tiruppur knitwear. Among domestic owners, *Gounder ex-Workers, Gounders,* and *Other ex-Workers* were the main users of this

Table 15: Initial Firm Location in the Social Division
of Labor

Route	Fabrication/ "Composite"	Stitching Manufacture	Cutting	Trade	Other
Domestic (SIHMA)					
Gounder ex-Worker	3%	91%	4%	0%	3%
Gounder	17%	83%	0%	0%	0%
Other ex-Worker	3%	81%	10%	3%	0%
Southern	28%	64%	20%	0%	0%
Northern	0%	50%	17%	50%	0%
Export (TEA)					
Gounder ex-Worker	0%	75%	17%	0%	8%
Gounder	25%	75%	13%	13%	0%
Other ex-Worker	20%	100%	0%	0%	0%
Southern	13%	88%	0%	13%	0%
Northern	10%	60%	10%	40%	0%

entry strategy. Among exporters, all *Other ex-Workers* entered through stitching or manufacture, followed by *Southerns* and the two Gounder routes. In both domestics and exports, *Gounder ex-Workers* almost never entered through fabrication, or through composite units combining manufacturing and fabrication.[29] The large percentage of *Southerns* in fabrication reflects early entrants who began composite units before the tendency to disintegrate production began to accelerate. What is important to emphasize is that both worker routes across associations entered mainly through stitching or manufacture, while some *Gounder ex-Worker* exporters entered through cutting sections. It is surprising at first that cutting sections, which require very little labor and almost no fixed capital—save a table and pair of scissors—have *not* been the favored route of ex-workers. This anticipates an important point, that cutting does not provide a location for *Gounder ex-Workers'* advantage in participant-supervision, while power-table stitching does; hence, cutting has not emerged as the primary location of entry. In contrast, *Northerns* tended in large measure to enter the division of labor via trade, that is, through mercantile putting-out.

Turning to how these first firms were started, routes diverge in forms of support and supporters, which I detail in Chari (2000).[30] To summarize the key findings on this count, domestic and export *Northerns* express strong support in capital, and in jobwork for domestic production, confirming that these firms must be seen as subsidiaries of larger North Indian family businesses. However, *Gounder ex-Workers* stand out among exporters and domestic producers for receiving the strongest support in machines, along with support in the other forms investigated. Both ex-worker routes, among exporters and domestics, received strong support through initial jobwork, and both acknowledge their ex-boss as their key supporter. *Other ex-Worker* exporters, it must be noted, made it not with the support of capital or machines, but primarily through jobwork and business contacts. Gounders have also been the strongest beneficiaries of recommendations for bank loans, as well as of "other recommendations" to access raw materials, particularly yarn on credit. Both ex-worker routes admit to support from relatives (especially *Gounder ex-Workers*) and ex-employers (particularly *Other ex-Workers*) and these advantages were substantial both in directly material terms, as capital and machinery, and in social relations to secure and maintain material advantage: through recommendations for loans and yarn credit, business contacts, and regular relations of jobwork. However, neither ex-worker route claimed high percentages of supporters of any particular type, with the exception of *Other ex-Workers* in exports who acknowledged their business relations as their only supporters.

Tables 16a and 16b take a closer look at initial conditions and sources of initial capital. Both domestic and export *Gounder ex-Workers* had the highest percentage of family members in knitwear when they started firms. However, in both cases, *Gounder ex-Workers* came in with substantially less initial capital than others, except domestic *Southerns*. In capital brought into the initial firm, the two ex-worker roads diverge strongly, particularly among exporters. *Other ex-Workers* relied strongly on family sources and prior earnings, while *Gounder ex-Workers* also had substantial recourse to capital from agriculture— though this is often double-counted with family. Land sale was an occasional source of initial capital, but dowries were in all probability more important than informants admit.[31] Non-Gounders were often stronger in accessing bank credit for fixed capital investments, as opposed to working capital, and this was often in the form of term-loans given on government schemes to backward and scheduled castes.

The evidence thus far indicates that mobility has been primarily through ownership in stitching and manufacturing sections, and mainly through partnerships. Of owners who began as workers, many admit to a variety of forms of support, and *Gounder ex-Workers* stand out in both material forms of support, in capital and machines, and non-material support through relationships crucial for sustained business. The latter include jobwork relations and recommendations for bank loans, particularly for working capital necessary for business through networks. Both ex-worker routes relied strongly on family and prior earnings to bring their initial capital into being. However, *Gounder ex-Workers* stand out for how *little* capital they brought into firms. Note, for instance, that the average *Gounder ex-Worker* exporter began with Rs 50,000 which, over the 1980s and 1990s, was in the order of a few thousand US dollars, while *Other ex-Worker* exporters

Table 16: Initial Conditions and Sources of Initial Capital

a. Initial Conditions

Route	Family in this Industry	Initial Capital (1000 Rs)	Proprietor	Average No. of Partners	Own Capital
Domestic (SIHMA)					
Gounder ex-Worker	73%	159	21%	3	81
Gounder	61%	578	13%	3	94
Other ex-Worker	28%	236	24%	3	107
Southern	57%	159	42%	3.2	131
Northern	36%	1251	73%	2.3	822
Export (TEA)					
Gounder ex-Worker	91%	103	9%	3.3	47
Gounder	75%	501	38%	4	258
Other ex-Worker	40%	2080	20%	3.25	1366
Southern	38%	411	14%	3	369
Northern	50%	1571	33%	3	344

b. Sources of Initial Capital

Route	Source: Family	Agri	Prior Earning	Chit Fund	Bank	Dowry	Land Sale	Other
Domestic (SIHMA)								
Gounder ex-Worker	49%	17%	49%	16%	7%	22%	6%	0%
Gounder	35%	45%	50%	0%	20%	10%	0%	0%
Other ex-Worker	47%	7%	47%	13%	10%	10%	3%	3%
Southern	77%	0%	36%	0%	9%	14%	0%	0%
Northern	18%	0%	55%	0%	18%	0%	0%	9%
Export (TEA)								
Gounder ex-Worker	55%	18%	36%	9%	0%	0%	9%	0%
Gounder	13%	25%	75%	13%	13%	0%	13%	0%
Other ex-Worker	80%	0%	40%	0%	20%	0%	0%	0%
Southern	88%	0%	50%	0%	25%	0%	0%	0%
Northern	67%	0%	33%	0%	0%	0%	0%	0%

began with capital in the order of hundreds of thousands of US dollars. So the successful stories of mobility are not entirely driven by the amount of initial capital, nor were these routes through the least capital-intensive section of production, cutting. Among non-material forms of support, jobworking was particularly important for *Gounder ex-Workers.*

Another important form of support was the pooling of skills and assets as groups of workers started small firms. Collection and analysis of the survey data here is premised on individuals, which makes partnerships and their dynamics difficult to discern or reconstruct. I return to this challenge in Chapter 5, but what can be supported thus far is that the primary route in the making of owners, *Gounder ex-Worker*, was crucially enabled by the mobilization of social relations that fostered entry into the place in the social division of labor fraught with labor problems: garment stitching.

There are two more sorts of inter-firm relations I turn to in the rest of this section: partnerships and firms bound by production contracts. Two types of partnerships spoken of in Tiruppur are "sleeping partners" and "working partners." Sleeping partners invest in initial fixed capital and perhaps in expansion into new plant and machinery, but they do not involve themselves in the day-to-day operations of the firm. Working partners mirror arrangements, observed in western Tamil Nadu called *kactakkoottu*, literally "effort-share," in which one partner provides capital while the working partner or *kactakkoottáli* provides skilled labor in exchange for a profit-share of 10 to 25 percent.[32] The term *kactakkoottáli* is rarely used because of its pejorative connotations, but similar relationships have enabled several instances of class mobility.[33] In this context, it is important that ex-worker routes in both associations invested slightly *more* of their own capital than the average partner, and *Other ex-Worker* exporters invested more than double the average partner. Hence, non-Gounders in these types of arrangements were not necessarily *kactakkoottáli.* Conversely, domestic *Gounders* invested half the average partner's share. This anomaly might be explained through the fact that initial capital is far less important for decentralized production than access to working capital. In this respect, Gounders were poised to use their agricultural land as collateral security for accessing institutional credit, as I will demonstrate in Chapter 5.

Turning to production contracts between firms, Table 17 details evidence of dedicated production for another firm through jobwork

Table 17: Extent of Dedication

Route	Dedication
Domestic (SIHMA)	
Gounder ex-Worker	48.6%
Gounder	52.2%
Other ex-Worker	32.3%
Southern	36.0%
Northern	16.7%
Export (TEA)	
Gounder ex-Worker	8.3%
Gounder	25.0%
Other ex-Worker	16.7%
Southern	12.5%
Northern	30.0%

or merchant export relations. Half of *Gounder ex-Worker* and *Gounder* domestic firms produce dedicated goods. This is a significantly larger share of dedication than that of other sorts of routes among domestic owners. Among exporters, however, *Gounder ex-Worker* owners are remarkably low in terms of dedication through merchant export relations, described in Chapter 2. On the other hand, a significant share of *Northerns* and *Gounders* engage in dedicated exports often alongside direct exports.[34]

There is no way to collect reliable information concerning firms dedicated to those surveyed because the numbers keep changing, relationships are tenuous and many owners simply do not know how many suppliers they have. Dedication in Tiruppur is rarely a tight form of dependence that the contract-giver cannot be released from.[35] Several jobworkers are tied to lead firms by partial or "rolling" payments, through which large exporters not only refuse to pay their suppliers in full, but only pay enough for jobworkers to pay their workers each Saturday. Jobworkers, in turn, are beholden to exporters and they receive payments in exchange for new orders, in a system they call working for *coolie*. In effect, the relationship between firms resembles external contracting, but without investment in plant and machinery. Dedicated relations are highly variegated and left to localized forms of negotiation, the implications of which are refracted into relations with different types of workers within dedicated units.[36]

The main weapon that dedicated firms can wield in negotiations is their threat of exit. Local producers have recourse to non-local export houses in Bombay or Delhi, and this is an important check against unfair business practices within Tiruppur. Several interviews suggested that local exporters are more unscrupulous in providing rolling payments rather than payments-in-full, and they get away with it because they feel they are beyond reproach because of their social standing. I asked the unofficial don of the Tiruppur underworld, the traditional *úr* Gounder, or town leader, who now takes part in various forms of arbitration in industrial disputes, about differences between locals and outsiders in this regard. His colleagues, or henchmen, rose to their feet nervous at my question, as he let out an unfriendly laugh and said that it's easy enough to intimidate a local. In other words, since there are no clear norms on dedicated inter-firm relations, enforcement problems lurk behind every contract and local owners can resort to brute force when inter-firm contracts break down altogether. There are no advantages to particular affiliations in this ability to break inter-firm contracts by force.

I have gone through this exercise of identifying multiple routes of capital for two key reasons. First, a diversity of accumulation strategies requires a specific historical explanation of the ways in which the dominant fraction of capital has forged its advantage. Second, the dominant strategy of mobility and accumulation is crucially linked to the spatial dynamics of contracting, and in particular to the centrality of labor control in stitching sections. Hence, a historical explanation of the *Gounder ex-Worker* route must also be an account of the changing spatial organization of work in Tiruppur. Before turning to a different type of explanation, it remains for me to turn outside my survey to routes of entry and accumulation that simply did not work.

III. Elite Failures and Routes Not Taken

A smart man came in to the office of a Gounder owner of modest origins. The stranger introduced himself as a manager from one of the largest industrial houses from North India, and his purpose was to arrange to source garments from Tiruppur. The enraged Gounder owner just shouted, "Get out!" and pointed to the door. What had happened? Why was the owner enraged when the manager had only been professional? This owner explained to me that the stranger was a mere white-collar manager who could not give him enough respect as a boss.[37] This failed manager of a major business house is one type of elite failure in taking hold of Tiruppur's opportunities. This section lays out the range of such failures and routes not taken.

I found three types of elite failures in the margins of my survey reports and through conversations with many who have watched their neighbors and ex-workers become rich beyond their dreams. The first failed route to accumulation is of the rural aristocracy, sometimes called *Kániyálar* Gounders, who were large landholders with wide political and economic power. The second failed route is of the old guard business elite of *Southern* owners whose strategies were routed by wider transformations in industrial structure. I have mentioned that few *Southerns* have adapted to new rules of the game, while several did not. The third type of failed route is that of outsiders who have attempted to outsource from Tiruppur without working with the dominant accumulation strategy, unlike *Northerns*, particularly Marwaris who have made their mark in Tiruppur. These counterfactuals do not just reveal sources of failure; they also highlight the exceptional character of the dominant route.

The first route not taken is of the aristocratic *Kániyálar* Gounders, large landholders who would never touch the plough and who are now left in the lurch in their rural palaces. There were two major attempts by the older generation of these agrarian lords to enter the domestic knitwear industry with the large amounts of capital, semi-bonded labor and political influence they had ready at hand. Both ventures failed. In fact their sons tried and failed in the era of exports. Victory Knitting was started by "Kittu" Gounder, who now sits in his abandoned cotton gin on prime real estate near the river. Victory was begun in 1958 with a then-astronomical initial investment of Rs 600,000 and about thirty stitching machines. This was a large unit, and it ran for 10 years before grinding to a halt at a dead loss. Kittu Gounder said: "One has to live there, in the knitting factory. You have to *be* there.

We are a *type* of family. We cannot go and *sit* personally. Our relatives are also equally important men. They cannot go and *sit* either." His son Ramesh is a savvy young man who started a large unit called Kalinga Fabrics in the early 1990s with a Rs 2 million investment, twenty local knitting machines and thirty stitching machines. The unit was at a loss because processing remained uncontrollable, and Ramesh confessed that "in this trade the boss is the manager and he has to be on the shopfloor eighteen hours a day."[38]

Another major joint venture of these aristocratic Gounders in-volved relatives of a prominent ex-minister who referred to himself in an interview to me as "the Pope of the Gounders." K.M. Gounder's Vinayaka knitting begun in 1955 with eleven fabrication and eight stitching machines, and forty-five workers. The company ran with managers until it stagnated in the mid 1960s. His son Rajan attempted to revive the unit in the mid 1970s with an injection of Rs 700,000 and attempted merchant production for the export market. Rajan lost and left knitwear decisively in the late 1980s because he said he was alone. Sitting near his posh hotel on an edge of his ancestral holdings on the outskirts of town, he stressed that for export "one needs 2–3 partners or family involvement: one person in the company 24 hours, one per-son on finance and banking, and a third on buyers and marketing." His main problem was in management: "There's lots of loss and theft. The cutting master may not be cutting enough, or sometimes they don't cut around holes, or piece-rate workers want speed and numbers and they need to be supervised." By the late 1990s, 70 percent to 80 percent of new entrants, in Rajan's view, resolved this dilemma by teaming up with a "working partner who works 24 hours, invests no capital and gets a salary plus a profit share." Until the late 1980s, however, aristo-crats like him were entirely removed from appreciating the work of the average "toiling" Gounder.[39]

Similarly, the *úr* or "town" *Gounder*, the traditional leader of the Gounders in town, who is something of a *mafioso*, met a similar fate. These aristocratic Gounders would simply admit to me that staying late at work, really mingling with their workers and supervising mun-dane activities was beneath their dignity, and none of their relatives would do these jobs either because they were also of the same status.

Nor could they stomach the idea of dedicated production, that is, production for an established domestic or export firm; they felt this was too much like working for someone else. The agrarian elite failed because they just couldn't shake off their aristocratic relationship to work.[40]

The second failed route is that of the old guard of industrialists, of traditional "business communities," who have been slow or in many cases unable to adapt to the supervision requirements of the new, decentralizing production form. I lived for four months in a kind of Dickensian factory-home owned by an Iyer Brahmin owner of this type. There were two hundred year-old buildings next to each other, with great halls and wooden pillars. The company was in one, with the Factory Acts posted in English and Tamil at the entrance, and only male labor inside—both features one would not see in export companies today. The owner sat at the center of the second building, like a god in the middle of a series of concentric rooms. Work was in one place, "business" in the other. The company has remained stagnant for a good twenty years. In fact he'd say to me, "this is Delight Knitting Limited: business is very limited." He never ventured next door to the shopfloor, and was disdainful of those of his ex-workers who have gone on to become exporters wealthy beyond his dreams. He'd say "they are only workers" with a sort of sneer, as he sat and watched train after train go by the main line of South India. Work in this older factory has continued to be organized through a pyramid of patriarchal relations down from the manager to skilled male workers and young boy apprentices.[41]

Another old guard owner, a Muslim in Khadarpet, had a similarly stagnant business because he said he did not have the kinds of relatives and kinship networks that Gounders could muster to multiply their sister concerns.[42] Industrial decentralization increased the importance of direct control, and Gounders were simply best at it.

The third route that has failed is of large industrial houses that have tried to make inroads into Tiruppur. I went to nearby Coimbatore city to find out why one of the great Naidu industrial families of South India had failed in its venture in Tiruppur knitwear.[43] Sathyaraj, a scion of the Coimbatore textile mill elite, set up a knitting fabrication and manufacturing concern in the mid 1980s, when the government was encouraging exports. For several years the concern broke even, but then it lost everything with one big failed export order to the United States in 1991. One set of reasons for this loss has to do with unfair, indeed illegal, business practices on the part of the buyer. The other major problem was mismanagement. Production control was deputed to a manager who gave out subcontracts to family members but could not deliver the goods for an order that was far beyond their combined capacities. Sathyaraj faults himself: "Unless you are involved, it is too risky to do business in Tiruppur." He explained to me that because product specifications vary so much in knitwear, as opposed to his familiar world of spinning and weaving, one has to rely a lot more on subcontractors who have more "opportunities to cheat." Sathyaraj was also frustrated by the way in which dyeing units in Tiruppur take on multiple orders and then execute them in a seemingly random order. When I pressed him on how locals do it, he exclaimed, "Gounders are able to manage their own brother-in-laws [*sic*], brothers and so on . . . in Tiruppur the whole family might be involved in the business. Here [in Coimbatore] it is not like that." In the end, this industrial tycoon from only 50 kms away found Tiruppur's work culture alien and unmanageable because of what he called "family supervision" over production networks. Seven years after closing shop, he is still trying to get payments from ex-suppliers in Tiruppur through legal means, as he won't take recourse in the local techniques of *goondaism*, or gangsterism, or the threat of violence wielded by local "collection agencies." He said with a sigh, "Tiruppur people know how to get things done. We [Coimbatore Naidus] are soft, not violent people."[44]

The secretary of TEA, Subramaniam, a thoughtful man who worked for several years for the Mill owners' association in Coimbatore, reiterated similar views based on his comparative experience.

> Knitwear export is a highly personalized business. North Indians like Fulchand or Arora who do business here, they are *here*. The owner must be at the spot. This is not mass production. In big factories you can have absentee management and control. Professional management has not succeeded here. It is because Tiruppur is full of small people who have become big, and they cannot get over the habit of direct control. They

won't talk to subordinates, only equals. The boss will only talk to another boss. Big firms like Tata face barriers despite their advanced systems because their overheads are higher. The inherent advantages here are of a mobile workforce and highly segmentalized industry.[45]

Subramaniam pins the advantages of direct control in Tiruppur's social division of labor as a consequence of, not despite, the informalized and fractured organization of work. Moreover, he attributes the importance of direct control by the boss to his typically humble origins. Another owner, Kamaraj, told me from his experience in Tiruppur that "even today exporters go around to suppliers and say "*enna máppilai*," meaning 'what's going on, brother-in-law,' and sweet talk the boss . . . but the big industrial houses send their man to look after different segments of production and he will only talk to the corresponding management." In Kamaraj's view, "our fathers were on the production floor . . . *that* was *ulaippu* [toil] . . . not this sweet talking, this is P.R."[46] A Tiruppur industrialist makes a similar point in historical terms:

> Hosiery needs personal involvement, otherwise there are a number of chances to take money out. In the low stages of development, local production was low profits and one had to watch workers. The first workers who became owners couldn't go into banking or government lobbying because of their low educational levels, but they knew how to work. Now exporters have higher profits and owners have a lot more duties. Now there aren't responsible financial practices or prompt delivery. Still, personal involvement is necessary because all the power is concentrated in the owner. If you give chances, your subordinates will go out and start their own companies, and they are treated as traitors.[47]

Srinivasan distrusts the decentralization of production for the increased opportunities it provides for poaching, and he sees "personal involvement" as key to rectifying this problem. He also suggests that Gounders from working-class origins concentrated on control over the detail division of labor. In time, their sphere of control has extended over a broader set of activities involved in making garments, necessitating control across social labor. What is clear through these views on Tiruppur is that there is something particular about the activities of *Gounder ex-Workers* in Tiruppur having to do with their presence and active involvement in the organization of production.

IV. Conclusion: Gounder Power over Production

This chapter has used survey information, complemented by ethnography, to discern evidence of multiple accumulation strategies, of which Gounders of working class origins stand out as the strongest. In opening up the division of labor as a site of competing accumulation *strategies*, I began by presuming a diversity of fractions of capital that wield power over production differently. Through the heuristic of routes of entry and affiliation, and an inductive method based on hypotheses drawn from extensive ethnographic research, I found three strong routes of capital accumulation in Tiruppur knitwear. Gounders of working-class origins are the dominant route of these fractions of capital, and their accumulation strategies work closest to the social and spatial dynamics of hierarchical producer subcontracting.

How was the *Gounder ex-Worker* advantage constituted and how did certain Gounders use it in transforming industrial work? While my analysis of routes in this chapter has kept identities fixed, I have yet to ask how forms of affiliation and industrial practice have been forged in tandem. Part II of this book turns to the agrarian histories of toil through which *Gounder ex-Workers* refashioned industrial practice. I ask how Gounder dominance over social labor today is formed from a specific agrarian transition and from singular understandings and memories of labor control in stitching sections at the heart of the knitwear industry.

PART II

The Agrarian Past in an Unstable Present

CHAPTER 4

Agrarian and Colonial Questions in Coimbatore's Capitalism, 1890–1970

I. Introduction: Agrarian and Colonial Traces

Our literature frequently contains too stereotyped an understanding of the theoretical proposition that capitalism requires the free, landless worker . . . [C]apitalism penetrates into agriculture particularly slowly and in extremely varied forms. The allotment-holding rural worker . . . assumes different forms in different countries: the English cottager is not the same as the small-holding peasant of France or the Rhine provinces, and the latter again is not the same as the Knecht in Prussia. *Each of these bears traces of a specific agrarian system, of a specific history of agrarian relations.*—V.I. Lenin.[1]

Coimbatore District is one of the few regions in the Indian subcontinent where a vibrant agrarian capitalism has laid the foundations for dispersed industrialization under the auspices of a diversifying peasantry. Part II of this book explores these processes of agrarian transition, or ways in which agriculture has contributed to non-agricultural development. Intertwined with an explanation of historical process, I explicate how agrarian transition is represented in colonial and postcolonial historiography, as well as in the popular consciousness of certain of Tiruppur's residents. What is crucial about the agrarian transition in the environs of Tiruppur is that it was led not by the richer end of a diversifying peasantry, but by worker-peasants. This chapter explores the origins and character of this regional capitalism that took hold in colonial and agrarian Coimbatore in the early twentieth century. I show how the making of this colonial capitalism parallels the construction of its hero, the yeoman Gounder entrepreneur, an ideological form that has become a popular prejudice.[2] The following chapter is a closer analysis of the life histories and self-presentations of Gounder worker-peasants, who have come to see themselves as the architects of agrarian transition and industrial decentralization in Tiruppur. To revisit Lenin in our time, the central question of Part II of this book is: how do Gounder peasant-workers renovate traces of a singular agrarian past as their toil, to forge their industrial advantage in the present?

There are three main arguments I make in the course of this chapter, having to do with the way in which agrarian and colonial politics have shaped conditions for the emergence of Tiruppur's vibrant industry. First, I argue in Section II that the period from about 1890 to the Great Depression both fundamentally changed the geography of South India and also concentrated expertise in bringing a particular kind of modernization theory into historical consciousness. Tamil Nadu began to be seen and written about as the periphery of a global economy, and Coimbatore's Gounders began to be seen as progressive peasants, agents of the right future. I then show in Section III that this notion of a progressive Gounder has a social historic basis in the fields of rural Coimbatore in the early twentieth century. By the 1930s Gounder smallholders had forged particular ways of working and controlling work in Gounder *tóttams* or garden farms in the early commercialization of Kongunad agriculture.[3] This production politics could be recalled and renovated for new ends in Tiruppur's future. In Section IV, I argue that these processes were part of a regional spatial dynamics of agricultural specialization and agro-industrial linkage which produced a series of specialist towns centered on specific commodities and regional monopolies. I detail the character of industrialization in Coimbatore's textile mills as well as in the fastest growing specialist town, Tiruppur. Finally, I show how industry and labor unionism in Tiruppur fashioned a plebeian public culture valorizing fairness in the sphere of exchange. The subsequent chapter shows how knitwear took root in this context, and how Gounder peasant-workers moving into this milieu drew on agrarian work politics to fundamentally question the centrality of exchange through a specific labor theory of value.

I begin my argument with transformations in rural Coimbatore, and in historiography, in the decades leading up to the Great Depression.

II. Colonial Knowledge and
Social Change, 1890—the Great Depression

If the Coimbatore ryot is compared with the peasant proprietors of Europe, he undoubtedly suffers by the comparison. In mere agriculture he is behind them, not so much in empirical knowledge as in energy of practice . . . [T]he minute and patient industry with which the French ryots [*sic*] cultivate [the land], the assiduity with which they spend every possible moment on it, the economy with which they utilize every foot of it, and the thrift—amounting almost to miserliness—with which they deny themselves in food and pleasure in order to devote more capital to it, find little parallel amongst the Coimbatore ryots, and a striking feature of the Coimbatore rural economy is the want of energy and thrift in dealing with space and time . . . What then can be expected for the Coimbatore peasant proprietor not many years emancipated from the rigours of tyranny, from barbarous invasions, and from a tyrannous fiscal system . . . F. A. Nicholson[4]

In writing the most important ethnographic source on *fin-de-siècle* Coimbatore, both for history and colonial rule, Frederick Nicholson is profoundly ambivalent about Coimbatore's ryots, as singularly lacking in industriousness while also investing in wells and helping other laborers access land to become owner-cultivators in their own right. Nicholson's ambivalence reflects his close observation of transformations in rural Coimbatore from the late nineteenth century onward. By the 1930s and 1940s these Gounder peasant-proprietors will have been known as a caste whose virtues lay precisely in their thrift and industry. Nicholson's normative position, that Gounders might rather emulate French "ryots'" rational use of space and time, seems to have been borne out in practice. The presumption in this colonial order of things is that Pax Britannica has allowed both Tamil and French to occupy the same spectrum of possibility, even if racial difference defers actual parity. I argue that for certain well-positioned subaltern classes, this normative gesture also suggests a new possibility, of a progressive *caste* whose conduct supports the currents of colonial capitalism.

I want to make two general points in this section. First, by the late nineteenth century several pre-colonial geographies in the Madras Presidency had become parts of a colonial periphery while retaining distinct regional trajectories. By the Depression, these peripheries could then be seen by historians and political economists as reeling from the shared effects of a global economy. Globalization had arrived in South India as tragedy. Second, in the process of making this differentiated colonial periphery, ethnographic experts brought modernization theory into historical consciousness. While colonial experts marked Indians as different, increasingly through the ideology of caste, this historiography also marked in normative gestures how Indians should rather be. In this framework, Gounder peasants in the frontier country of Coimbatore were primed to be a progressive caste precisely as Madras was becoming part of a global economy.

Precolonial South India was a landscape of decentralized polities with overlapping spheres of authority. The region of Kongunad, today's Coimbatore and Salem Districts, has been written of as a frontier country colonized around the ninth and tenth centuries by the dominant peasant supra-castes of South India and Ceylon, Vellalas. These Vellalas joined with locals in Kongunad to form a community called Kongu Vellalas or Gounders. Using anthropological evidence from the present, Chris Baker argues that Gounders created a hybrid caste structure linking Brahmanical customs and pretensions with patri-lineage relations and supra-lineage political chiefs called *pattagars* or *palayagars*, Anglicized as *poligars*, such as the *Poligar* of Utukuli south of Tiruppur.[5]

Coimbatore was "settled," that is mechanisms of revenue assessment put in place, by the East India Company in 1799 after the second defeat of Tipu Sultan of Mysore. While the Raj may have first had ambitious plans for ruling this frontier region, it settled on a minimal style of governance. At first the British attempted variants of the Permanent Settlement of Bengal, which sought to convert local agrarian revenue farmers and potentates into a kind of English gentry.[6] Yet, after much experimentation with revenue systems, victory in South India went to the advocates of the *ryotwari* system, which called for

direct settlement between peasant and state, and direct revenue collection from the cultivator.[7] However, the *ryotwari* settlement did not
create a class of capitalist *ryots* or smallholders, as some proponents
imagined it would, primarily because of the ambiguity of land deeds,
which only intensified with their transfer through inheritance and
debt. Well into the 1930s, it seems that the colonial state did not even
know *who* the ryot was, so that implementation was inevitably left to
local communities. Hence, in the outbreak of court cases over small-
holdings in the early twentieth century, which prompted a frustrated
colonial state to think Tamilians to be "litigious by nature," it is more
likely that Tamilians were using the state to endorse locally negotiated
claims.[8]

The agrarian economy expanded unsteadily, undercut by price
slumps and periodic famine in the late nineteenth century. The building of the railroads of South India by 1880, and the expansion of
commerce, brought people to scattered *kottai pettai* or "fort-market"
settlements in which warrior-merchant castes who had migrated south
in the medieval era were key commercial intermediaries.[9] Telugu-
speaking Naidus and Kannada-speaking Devanga Chettiars found
fortune in the *cantais* or periodic markets of the dry plains and Kongunad. By the late nineteenth century, Kongunad had diverged from
the plains in that its rural economy was not based only on cattle-ranch-
ing but also on well-based agriculture. Investment in wells had increased the value of land and farm families maintained a closeness to
their fields, particularly in peak agricultural seasons, resembling patterns of habitation in paddy-growing river valleys.[10] What was distinct-
ive in Kongunad's regional economy was the opportunity it provided
both to "left" and "right" castes, vertical caste groupings corresponding to mercantile-artisan and agrarian social economies.[11]

As the nineteenth century drew to a close, Madras proved laggardly
in fulfilling the functions of a colonial periphery.[12] With the growth
in steamship trade after the opening of the Suez Canal, Madras began exporting hides, skins and oilseeds, increasingly to continental
Europe, as well as short-staple cotton to Japan. In effect, stunted
colonial trade relations facilitated diversification in external trade. As

European plantation capital moved into South East Asia, Madras began exporting labor.[13] Even as Madras was being tied into much larger flows of capital and resources, it was only in the dramatic price fluctuations of the early twentieth century that it began to be seen as exposed to a global economy.

The Great Depression reflected crises in industrial capitalist nations as well as in the global trade of primary products. The bullish global markets in primary products since the 1860s came to an abrupt halt in the late 1920s, forcing Madras from its peripheral role as an exporter of cash crops and importer of wage goods to turn inwards. Export agriculture in Madras had also been crucially reliant on an elaborate system of credit provision orchestrated by export houses, the government, and the bazaar money market. When demand for primary products fell in the mid 1920s, so did prices, and with the colonial state's deflationary responses, foreign export houses swiftly withdrew credit. The repatriation of American dollars led to a global contraction in foreign lending, and the colonial Government of India intensified remittances of sterling to London. In 1931, the Government of India devalued the rupee against sterling, now off the gold standard, allowing the colonial state to solve its balance of trade problems while intensifying deteriorating terms of trade against India. Consequently, massive exports of gold broke apart the bazaar money market and the capital necessary for rural commerce. The terms of trade moved considerably against rural Madras, and the focus of the South Indian economy turned sharply from the country to the city.

While the Depression and World War provided effective protection for many poor nations, the low level of development of the home market and of capital goods did not make for robust conditions for import substitution industrialization. Therefore the kinds of industries that took root in the towns of Madras in this period were labor intensive, like the manufacture of foods, apparel and tobacco. Knitwear in Tiruppur emerged precisely under these conditions and retained this limited technical character for the next several decades because of the inadequate development of the home market and of capital goods. What is key is that this labor-intensive industrialization grew out of the shocks of the Depression, accentuated by the colonial state's lack of interest in technological transformation in agriculture and industry. Increasingly, industrial workers came from the ranks of peasants pauperized by the turning tide against agriculture.[14]

The imposition of cash-based land revenues simultaneously forced a process of agrarian commercialization across Madras during the late nineteenth century. The plains produced cotton and groundnut for the western trade, the valleys produced rice for the eastern trade and for urban populations, and Kongunad produced cotton, sugar and foodgrains for regional towns. Despite the anti-developmental colonial state, commerce opened opportunities for an innovative farming system forged in rural Kongunad.

The modern career of caste in Coimbatore saw important shifts in the early twentieth century. Consider that the ethnographic appendices of the 1901 *Census of India* make no mention of the "progressive" character of Kongu Vellalas in their elaborate delineations of castes by cranial forms and "orbito-nasal" indices.[15] The colonial ethnography of experts like Frederick Nicholson began to make an ideology of an entrepreneurial peasant caste possible by shifting the grounds of caste to peasant practice. In the wake of new opportunities for development in rural Kongunad, certain ryots could then seem to become more like their French counterparts. The construction of colonial knowledge took place across fields, factories and colonial archives, providing opportunities for a variety of agents. In the construction of colonial hegemony, I argue that the colonial state and its successor have been relatively weak in shaping rural Coimbatore, leaving considerable room for non-state forms of power and knowledge to thrive well into the era of postcolonial neoliberalism.[16] In the following section, I turn to the farming system forged by Gounders as they came to be seen as progressive agents of an agrarian capitalism in a rural periphery now part of a global economy.

III. Agrarian Work Politics on Gounder Farms, 1880–1955

Until the late nineteenth century, agrarian Coimbatore grew food crops destined for local markets, with the largest percentage of farmland under dry grains and pulses of all districts in Madras Presidency.[17] By the mid-twentieth century, rural Coimbatore would become a bastion of commercial agriculture in the south. This section looks at how a new politics of production in Gounder farms of this period created the ground for the industrious Gounder. I explore how this farming system took shape, and how it inculcated work practices that could be retrospectively recalled as the grounds for "Gounder toil," principally in the participant supervision of a gender- and caste-differentiated workforce. I conclude with shifts in this farming system through processes of differentiation and mobility.

Kongunad is marked by sparse rainfall and soil conditions that differentiate this region from the dry plains to the east and north-east. The heavy black soils of central Kongunad tended to waterlog when wet and tessellate when dry, requiring more labor than the minimal style of labor use in the plains. In other parts of Kongunad, lighter red soils required much more irrigation, but on the whole Kongunad's soil series were too absorbent and temperatures too high for tank-based irrigation systems. Under these conditions, agriculture was based on wells cut through the hard gneissic rock to the deep water table below. Well irrigation required masonry and draught power, but well-irrigated *tóttams* or "gardens" could recover these investments through year-round farming.[18] A form of intensive smallholder farming took root in Kongunad even as new black soil was being brought under the plough up through the 1920s. By 1930, about a third of the agrarian population was engaged in cultivation, roughly half as agricultural laborers and 40 percent as cultivating owners.[19]

The commercialization of land was well under way by the early twentieth century. The persistence of a land frontier prompted observations that laborers could access land and become cultivators. Struggles over land were key in records of criminality, and the deepening of the land market by the 1930s parallels Kongunad's rise to notoriety for its crime rate.[20] By the 1940s, there were more land sales and the price of land was higher in Kongunad than in other parts of Madras Presidency, including the rich paddy-growing banks of the Cauvery River. A 1946 tenancy survey shows the highest rental values of well-irrigated land in Coimbatore. Money and land markets were tightly connected, as defaults on loans were often the impetus to land transfers, so much so that a Coimbatore banker claimed that entire village lands changed hands every forty to fifty years. Along with active land markets, Coimbatore saw the early development of tenancy markets with varying degrees of lessor involvement in the rented farm. As a measure of their commitment to the market, farmers would often exchange plots of land to consolidate their holdings around the most rational use of water.[21]

Gounder farming changed qualitatively with the arrival of the American strain of long-staple Cambodia cotton, introduced in Madras in the early twentieth century. Cambodia cotton grew well in red soils under irrigation, and found domestic demand in the mills of Coimbatore and Bombay. As early as 1909, a key institution for crop research and development, the Agricultural University, moved to Coimbatore and became a center for research on varieties of cotton. Areas of Coimbatore subsequently went through a dramatic shift from coarse cereals to Cambodia cotton, and this shift in cropping patterns was most pronounced in Palladam Taluk, the sub-district where Tiruppur lies. While Gounder *tóttams* also grew tobacco and groundnut with success, irrigated Cambodia led the expansion of cash cropping in the 1920s. Between the 1920s and the 1950s, Coimbatore increased production of cotton *vis-à-vis* all cash crops, more so than any other district in Madras Presidency. Kongunad farmers also intensified farming rather than expanding incomes by cutting costs and wages. However, more important changes were at work within the labor process in Gounder *tóttams*.[22]

What was key about Gounder *tóttams* in this period is that they are represented as highly flexible in relation to changing agricultural markets. In part, this flexibility had to do with secure and perennial access to groundwater. During the two decades between 1909 and 1929, farmers in Tiruppur and nearby Dharapuram Taluks led the district in using state loans for sinking new wells, and in Avinashi and Tiruppur Taluks for repairing existing wells. Indeed, the government Department of Industries claimed to have played a key role in boring existing wells, particularly in the late 1920s.[23] Another aspect of the flexibility of Gounder farms had to do with their ability to spread risks borne of market and nature by simultaneously growing a variety of crops, shifting emphasis as needed. As the price of cattle increased costs of ploughing as well as of the draught-powered *kavalai* system of irrigation, farmers either shifted to hiring in professional ploughing teams or to commanding more fodder crops either by growing them or by leasing land for straw.

Flexibility in Gounder farming is also explained as a product of labor arrangements forged in this period of agricultural intensification. In other parts of Tamil Nadu, elites tried to revive or invent forms of forced labor or debt bondage in the wake of caste tensions in the first decade of the twentieth century. In contrast, Gounder farmers in Kongunad are framed as having moved toward "a more commercially rational use of labour" which afforded landless laborers better wages and higher status than elsewhere in Tamil Nadu.[24] Landless labor in Kongunad took the form of attached "permanent farm servants" who were often indebted to landholders, but were unlike the *pannaiyáls* of the river valleys who were in varying forms of servitude. Permanent laborers in Kongunad were not held at a ritual and economic distance from landowners, as in the Brahmin-dominated valleys. Rather, as Chris Baker's now canonical history puts it, they were "more like an extension of *family labour*." Permanent workers were often housed and fed with the cultivator's family, and they received both kind and cash payments. In the early twentieth century and through the Depression, Kongunad laborers were often better paid than casual laborers in other regions of Madras, and migrants drew in from other parts of the south through the 1930s and 1940s. By the 1950s, Baker's history has it that "Kongunad had a large, reasonably well-paid and apparently reasonably well-satisfied labor force." This rendition of agrarian relations has become staple in all writing on rural South India, while its foundations were laid in the writings of Frederick Nicholson.[25]

I turn next to two village studies from the 1930s that provide the ethnographic basis for many of Baker's claims, particularly on "familial labor relations" in Gounder farms, in order to understand the contours of production politics in Kongunad in the 1930s. I first revisit the evidence behind "familial" labor relations to ask who worked Gounder farms and how, drawing on village studies of Perumanallur and Madathupalayam, in the vicinity of Tiruppur.[26] These studies provide valuable insights on the labor process, land and tenancy, the spatial separation of work and home, gender relations, local markets and indebtedness. I then turn to the ways in which Gounder farm families were pulled into processes of differentiation and indebtedness that broke from the notion of peasant entrepreneurialism.

What these village studies show most strikingly are multiple ways in which labor was secured on Gounder farms. Perumanallur Village relied on three kinds of agricultural laborers: (i) permanent laborers "attached to the farm who are mainly Goundars," paid in coarse cereals "according to age and efficiency;" (ii) "*Madharis* or *Chakkiliars* [Dalits, henceforth Madaris] stitching *mhote* buckets [leather irrigation bags], sandals and helping in agricultural operations . . . advanced Rs 10 free of interest on arrival to be returned on departure," and also paid in kind both monthly and as a share of coarse cereal harvest; and finally (iii) casual laborers, "the majority being women engaged when necessary for hoeing, weeding, harvesting of paddy/*ragi*, picking *kapas* and paid in kind . . . for crops *and in cash* 2½ annas for picking cotton *kapas*" (for which men were paid 4 annas). Labor relations were strongly differentiated by caste and gender. Gounder men and their families were "permanent laborers" with annual contracts who could join or quit each year in the month of *tai*, at the spring festival of *Pongal*. Gounder male wages in kind were linked to their productivity and hence provided economic incentives as caste-fellows who could not have been easily made to work harder through force or intimidation. Madaris, on the other hand, were retained through loans that they would have been hard pressed to repay since they were paid for work in kind. Moreover, Madaris had to buy dead cattle to make leather irrigation buckets and sandals, to which they had exclusive production rights. Finally, women were engaged in casualized waged work within agriculture very early in the development of regional labor markets and at lower wages. Gounder farmers relied on caste- and gender-differentiated labor relations with varying rights and obligations attached.[27]

Madari families in Madathupalayam were attached to landed Gounder households through gender-specific arrangements: men worked year-round in cultivation, principally in distributing water and taking care of irrigation technology, while women "occasionally render help in odd works."[28] Gunnel Cederlöf's revisionist scholarship on Madaris of this region shows that they were *mamools*, permanent servants engaged by custom in specific jobs, but with extra-contractual obligations. Only for what was considered the ritually polluting work of mending or stitching leather buckets—tasks central to traditional *kavalai* irrigation technology that these farms depended on—were Madaris "paid extra."[29] As Gounders were reliant on Madari work in this sense, they spoke of this dependence through an ideology of *urimai* or rights. While Madari *urimai* was primarily about exclusive entitlement to handling hides, this *urimai* was also manifest in particular roles in Gounder religious ceremonies as well as non-work-related duties as messengers in Gounder family affairs. Through a dense web of practice, *urimai* reinforced Gounder-Madari dependence at least until the coming of electric pumpsets.[30] While Tiruppur Taluk was second to Coimbatore Taluk in the number of oil and steam engines used for lifting water across the district, the number of engines was only thirteen in 1932, only among "influential ryots."[31] Only with the expansion of rural electrification did electric pumps really transform rural social relations in the 1940s, by which time Coimbatore District had more than any other district in the Presidency, at 1763 pumpsets in 1944.[32] In effect, the formal subsumption of Madari family labor through ritual and economic relations was central to agricultural expansion without significant mechanization in the 1930s.[33]

Cederlöf's scholarship and Baker's sources decisively critique a utopian rendition of familial labor relations on the Gounder farm, which seems to correspond to the situation of Gounder men in annual work contracts, not the bulk of Madari *pannaiyáls* tied through debt and custom. As Sir George Paddison, veteran of the Indian Civil Service and erstwhile Collector of Madura, reported in 1926:

> The most fortunate type of farm servant is the one whose caste position approximates that of his master and who "lives in." Such a man is often treated as one of the family and shares their fortunes in good and bad times. On the other hand, a large number, especially of the lower castes, are frequently very badly off. They are given an advance on some special occasion such as a wedding and nominally the loan is to be repaid in

service. If the workman is invaluable the master takes care that this loan shall not be worked off and this man is attached compulsorily to the master for life, and sometimes also his sons inherit the debt after his father's death. [34]

Official sources registered only men as "permanent servants," while wives and children who were also beholden to work for the landholder were recorded as "casual labor." Families of tied *pannaiyáḷs* provided a captive sphere of casual labor for Gounder farmers. These familial workers neither had the security of contractual relations nor customary rights. Between "customary" and "free" labor, in effect, women and children formed a gendered reserve army of labor. Gounder farmers managed these differentiated labor relations while working alongside their workers. This was a production politics that used caste and gender difference as well as participant supervision to subordinate working-class families to the farmer who tilled with them. These practices of work and labor control, I argue, provided fertile ground for an exclusionary notion of "Gounder toil" to recall. Other aspects of the regio-nal farming system would also leave a trace in the organization of work in Tiruppur.[35]

Tenancy relations in Gounder farming prefigured the practice of "working partners" that would reappear in Tiruppur. A significant number of tenant farmers worked alongside landowning farmers in Perumanallur village. Tenancy contracts were typically for six acres of well-irrigated land and twelve acres of dryland, sufficient for a combination of irrigaged *ragi* and *cholam* (coarse cereals for consumption), irrigated Cambodia cotton for sale, dryland fodder and dry crops. Tenancy relations were either: (i) fixed rents in money or cotton, the tenant meeting all cultivation costs; (ii) the tenant as the landowner's *working partner* sharing labor, expenses and produce equally after a fixed deduction of land rent; (iii) or the landowner contributing half the bullocks with produce divided in proportion to the landowner's contribution after a fixed deduction for land rent. In all cases, land revenue was usually paid to the state by the landowner. These tenancy contracts demonstrate a spectrum of relations between land and labor markets, with the ideal tenant as "working partner" combining both.

Despite the decline in tenancy relations in the countryside, the notion of working partners echoes partnerships between labor and capital in Tiruppur knitwear many years later.[36]

The spatial separation of work and home in Gounder farming also echoes Tiruppur's present. Instead of attempting to consolidate fragmented agricultural holdings, each *tóttam* farm contained a "dwelling in which the farmer or a permanent laborer lives."[37] Gounder farmers stayed out in the fields during the cotton season, when "the cultivator and permanent coolies watch the crop during the night [in] turns."[38] This need to be close to the place of production rings familiar to the Gounder industrialist in Tiruppur today, who keeps a furnished room or suite so that he can sleep in the factory during the export season.

Another aspect of Gounder farming relevant to the present rests on gender relations in production and reproduction. Gopalaratnam, writing on Madathupalayam village, marks the crucial role of the *Goundachi-amma*, the mother of the Gounder farm household: "[H]is wife manages the household and works in the fields. A small vegetable garden and a cow or a buffalo are looked after by her. She gathers the harvest, disposes of the vegetables, milk, butter and ghee at the shandy nearby or . . . at her own house. With the money realized, and supplementing, at will, the income which her husband gets from the crops he raises, she maintains the whole family." The mother of the Gounder household was key not only in unwaged, reproductive labor but also in marketing household products. Moreover, she seems to have controlled family earnings to secure commodities necessary to reproduce the family. This implication that women held the purse-strings of rural Gounder households recurs in the gendered self-perceptions of Gounder men today, specifically in the ways self-made men speak of accessing family savings from their mothers.

Finally, along with the deepening commercialization of agriculture in Coimbatore District, the two village studies also reveal deepening local demand as well as indebtedness. Despite the expansion of irrigated Cambodia cotton in the 1930s, 60 percent of agricultural produce in Perumanallur was sold *within* the village. Moreover, while no family had saved to any extent, almost all were indebted to some extent. This was not forced commercialization, where farmers were compelled into cash cropping in order to pay off debts.[39] Indeed, detailed budget studies reveal the depth of local demand and rural households' reliance on commodities for production.

For instance, the budget of a Gounder farmer with ten acres of *tóttam* and twelve of dryland shows that most expenses were for farming, followed by food, life-cycle ceremonies and interest payments on loans. These loans, in turn, were for the *son's* marriage (as brideprice), "inherited encumbrances" (parents' debt), litigation (probably over land) and land improvement. This was credit not only for consumption but, more importantly, for property, production and marriage. Gendered, familial obligations were part of the deepening of a home market.

A 1930s study of farm household budgets in Avinashi, on the outskirts of Tiruppur, reveals the composition of the debt of different types of Gounder farmers: a proprietor, a share-tenant farmer and a cash-tenant farmer.[40] While all faced mounting debts, the cash-rent tenant and proprietor were relatively better off because they had diversified their activities through livestock, as was common among *ryots* of the area.[41] By the 1940s, medium and large farmers rode out rising indebtedness, unlike many smallholders and tenant farmers, as government debt relief under the Madras Agriculturalists' Relief Act seems to have supported the former. Moreover, land sales picked up after the surge in land prices after 1942, after which the sale of land accounted for about 58 percent of debt recoveries. This confirmed a process of consolidation among larger Gounder farmers, alongside forms of mutualism between Gounder *pankáḷis*, or agnates whom I call "brothers," at varying economic levels. Indebted smallholders with rich "brothers" fared much better than without these kin connections to draw upon. By the 1950s, sons of Gounder farm families had begun dividing family property and separating residence, practices which continued with the institution of land ceiling legislation in 1961. The fixture of fifteen acres as the maximum owned land provided legal architecture to the separation of property, but forms of mutualism continued to persist between brothers.[42] Fraternal relations between men were key to smallholders staying afloat, as they would later prove to be in Tiruppur.

What were the emergent characteristics of 1930s production politics that could become elements of a usable past? The central legacy was the Gounder farmer's participant supervisory skills at controlling differentiated labor arrangements to his advantage. This politics of work based on caste, class and gender difference allowed the landowner to exploit workers through familial idioms in the case of fellow Gounder men, through customary caste rights backed by indenture and ritual power in the case of Madaris, and through casualized and insecure spot-market relations in the case of women. Managing differentiated labor arrangements as a participant-supervisor constitutes the particular advantage that Gounders refer to as their propensity to "toil." Moreover, gender difference and the possibility of class mobility for Gounder male permanent workers may have attenuated conflict in agrarian labor relations, lending to the "labor peace" in the historical record. Several broader features of the Gounder farming system were also part of a shared structural legacy that could be indexed as the context of Gounder toil. These features include the particular character of working partners; the spatiality of work and residence; an ideology of reliance on mother and of gendered relations of production and reproduction; reliance on credit for purposes of property and production; and the attenuation of indebtedness and class differentiation by Gounder fraternity. Each has its parallel in Tiruppur today, as will become clearer in the following chapter, for "Gounder toil" to call forth in making use of the past.

IV. Agrarian Transition and Regional Industrialization, 1880–1970

[Tiruppur was] easily the fastest growing town in Tamil Nadu in the first half of the twentieth century.[43]

While Gounder farming took a particular form in the period of intensification and commercialization in the 1930s, a key feature of the regional economy since early in the twentieth century has been the density of intersectoral linkages built on agrarian commercialization and regional industry. These linkages allowed a regional agrarian transition in which agricultural change supported the growth of specialist towns, centered on specific commodities and caste monopolies, and of which Tiruppur is the most dramatic case. The analytic of agrarian transition roots the dynamics of these towns in ongoing processes of rural change. As early as the 1910s, agents of Coimbatore's spinning mills complained about *ryots* mixing grades of cotton in small cotton gins started by farmers alongside their newly electrified tube-wells.[44] These sentiments betray a process of rural diversification under way outside the purview of state and large capital. This section begins the analysis of this regional agrarian transition with the cotton trade, which fueled Coimbatore's textile mills as they began to rule the regional economy after the 1930s. The mills were also a hotbed of communist and labor union activism that was crucial in shaping regional politics. Alongside but linked to regional industry, agricultural specialization and diversification enabled the downstream processing and marketing of agricultural commodities in dispersed small towns. In this sense, Kongunad's towns were a consequence of processes of geographical—both agrarian and spatial—specialization. I conclude with Tiruppur's particular history of industrialization and labor unionism as products of these regional processes.

Cotton across Country and City, 1890s–1930s

By the late nineteenth century, Tiruppur had emerged as an important railhead on the main line across Madras Presidency, connecting Madras city with industrial Coimbatore City, and on to the plantations of the Nilgiri Hills. With the intensification of cotton farming, Tiruppur became an entrepôt in the cotton trade, opening up opportunities for a variety of processing activities. The spread of Cambodia cotton was initially pushed by large textile and cotton interests in Coimbatore District, such as the House of Binny, one of the major British textile groups in South India.[45] The successful spread of Cambodia coupled with the draw of new cotton gins provided steam to the rapid growth in cotton farming. Production finance for growing cotton came not from urban merchants but from a range of village moneylenders, landlords, rich peasants and grocers, so that cotton production remained outside the direct control of mercantile interests in contrast to the groundnut market.[46] This is why the thriving commercial economy of agrarian Coimbatore was so different from the dry plains of Arcot,

for instance, where merchants' capital dominated the regional economy.

Cotton trading had long been within the sphere of farm household
activity, with Gounder women managing the marketing of raw cotton
kapas at *cantais* with their own production finance.[47] The Kongunad
cotton market was highly speculative, and profits were made on the
timing of cotton sales. Gounder farm households were therefore loath
to entrust cotton marketing to merchants. Indeed, before 1890 there
was no cotton market in Kongunad. *Kapas* were either taken by bullock cart to markets in the southern cotton tracts of Madras Presidency
or cotton was ginned, pressed and transported by train to Madras.
After Binny's successful spreading of Cambodia cotton, and with a
surge in the growth of Bombay's mills during World War I, Bombay
merchants came down to Kongunad to secure their supplies of cotton.
The thirty merchants who came to Kongunad in 1916 are said to have
gone to villagers with bags of rupees, giving loans to anyone who would
agree to grow Cambodia cotton. Cotton quickly took over a third of
sown area, doubling in acreage over 25 years. When the Bombay merchants chose the small ginning town of Tiruppur as their regional
headquarters, they helped establish it as the primary cotton market in
South India by the 1930s. From a small rail junction of 6,000 people
in 1900, Tiruppur became a bustling entrepôt of 18,000 by 1931, en
route to becoming a trade and industrial town of 52,000 by 1951.[48]

The cotton market at Tiruppur took on a speculative character early
on, in part due to the character of supply—cotton was susceptible to
the vagaries of nature and easily substitutable in Gounder farms—and
in part due to impermanent ties to Bombay buyers. The Bombay cotton merchants used Kongunad to top off their quotas after requisition
from Maharashtra and Gujarat. Purchases in Bombay were made
within the short period of fifteen days, when a large number of suppliers competed furiously for orders and fortunes were made and lost
overnight. Despite their initial push into Kongunad with generous
credit to farmers, Bombay merchants did not seek permanent ties in
Tiruppur. They did not subsequently extend much credit, or use
forward contracts, but prized Tiruppur's flexibility as a spot market.
Even after the Bombay mills went into long-term decline in the early

1920s, as cotton began coming to Tiruppur not only from its hinterland but from all parts of India, and as the cotton trade became more tightly linked to Coimbatore's textile industry, the market retained its character as a speculative spot market.

However, Kongunad's cotton farmers stayed clear of mortgaging their crops or relinquishing control over the timing of sale. The Madras government was perpetually frustrated in trying to educate farmers on the virtues of the market, as information on the market is said to have reached villages on a weekly, if not daily, basis. Consequently, a 1919 survey shows that a third of the cotton sold in Tiruppur was brought to market by cultivators themselves.[49]

During the 1920s, as the Tiruppur cotton market grew, the role of commission agents became key in monitoring fluctuations of the cotton market and in securing the appropriate time of sale. These agents forged strong ties with particular groups of farmers, allowing them to store cotton in exchange for more discretion over the terms of exchange. This did not mean farmers were losing ground in market power; agents had often come out of farm backgrounds and often continued to work on the instructions of cultivators. Ginners were another key category of intermediary in the cotton commodity chain, as dispersed rural cotton gins converted *kapas* into lint for a comission. Farmers were able to use this service as a way of increasing the value added on their commodities as they continued to be the owners of the lint until final sale on the Tiruppur market.

This process of "thickening" in markets for producer goods and services—by which I mean the elaboration of institutions and social relations mediating producers and consumers—required as its converse a deepened reliance on credit. The premier creditor caste of South India, Nattukkottai Chettiars of coastal Tamil Nadu (who had built their fortunes by financing the plantation economies of South and South East Asia), were quick to move into Coimbatore and Tiruppur to seize the opportunities driven by the expansion of Cambodia cotton farming, ginning and marketing. The credit market had already drawn in Multani and Marwari bankers from North India, as well as joint-stock companies that were otherwise loath to lend in agricultural markets. A final agent in the credit market were *nidhis* or local cooperative banks that emerged out of savings funds and lent short-term capital against stocks of cotton deposited in urban warehouses. No less than 125 *nidhis* sprang up by 1930 in the district in response to the volatile and speculative nature of the Tiruppur cotton market.

As I have mentioned, this structure of credit swirling around Tiruppur's cotton commodity chain was quickly rationalized through the effects of the Depression. The liberal credit of the late 1920s washed up by the late 1930s: fifteen bazaar banking firms in Tiruppur closed shop during this period, as did most *nidhis*. The Bombay merchants picked up and left when their position as market intermediaries was threatened both by the fall in the price of cotton and by labor troubles in the Bombay mills. Their hold as buyers in the Tiruppur cotton trade had already slipped to a small number of ginning factory owners and cotton-brokers who had risen up from the ranks of commission agents. By the late 1930s, the Depression had rationalized the market to the extent that two cotton brokers and twelve gin owners dominated the Tiruppur cotton market. This small group of mercantile interests bought most of the cotton and, in the absence of the range of creditors, credit was entirely in the hands of joint-stock banks.

After the Depression, several farm households took the opportunity to diversify into the textile industry. The downturn in the local cotton trade, the Bombay mills and foreign trade combined to open opportunities for investment in Coimbatore's spinning mills. The large Kamma Naidu families who started the major mill groups of Coimbatore began through substantial transfers of capital from agriculture. However, other farmers who rode out the Depression used opportunities to invest idle capital not only in mills but also in cotton ginning, trading and finance. By the late 1940s, cultivators sold as much as half their cotton directly in the market, and Gounder cultivators, ginners and their cooperatives sold directly to textile mills. Despite the emergence of other market towns dealing in cotton, Tiruppur remained preeminent in South India, and Gounder farmers were key in keeping it so.[50]

These shifts in post-Depression Kongunad cotton had their parallels in other agricultural markets in South India, where circuits of capital became more strongly tied to local demand rather than to exports. However, because the power of diversifying rural households over the Tiruppur cotton market increased through the Depression years, the market was not disrupted as in other parts of the presidency. While elsewhere the government stepped in to strong-arm the re-regulation of markets, this did not happen in the Tiruppur cotton market. The tide was certainly turning to the urban sphere, but rural households were a part of these new fortunes. With the collapse of *nidhis* and bazaar banking institutions, room was created for the entry of formal banks. The banks of the 1940s lent primarily to urban industry and to retail trading. Industry and the towns, however, continued to be joined to the countryside through the increased migration of rural people to the towns and mills of Coimbatore.

The Great Depression was a milestone in urbanization both through the pull of industrial, commercial and urban growth, and by the push of rural distress and entitlement failure among the rural poor. The state's failure to support rural livelihoods left many in the countryside pauperized and vulnerable to catastrophes like the influenza epidemic of 1918–19, as well as to the secular decline in foodgrains production after 1921. The shift from foodgrains to cash crops meant that the price of coarse cereals shot up in the 1910s, so that landless and land-poor households had to bear the brunt of the sharp decline in foodgrain production in the late 1910s. Entitlement failure among the rural poor further compelled distress migration to towns. Collapse in local demand coupled with the decline in export of Madras handkerchiefs and *lungis* to East Africa and the Malay Peninsula brought crisis to several forms of household industry controlled by left hand weaver and trader castes.[51]

One consequence of this shock was the cleaner separation of dispersed weaving from mercantile interests, with impoverished weavers joining peasants in flocking to the cities for industrial employment. Yet, pauperized as they were, decentralized handlooms retained some resilience and continued to provide a local market for Coimbatore's spinning mills. By the 1930s, the regional economy was dominated by the process of modern industry emerging from Coimbatore City.[52]

Modern Industry in Coimbatore City, 1920–1950

After a few false starts, the first successful textile mills of Coimbatore City were begun by European houses: Messrs Binnys, Harveys, Stanes, and so on. Whether they engaged only in spinning yarn or also in weaving cloth, textile mills held vast economies of scale, and Europeans' access to capital provided an unchallenged edge. The first major Indian concern, Kaleeswarar Mills, was begun by a Nattukkottai Chettiar with access to substantial banking capital. Indian mills were initially smaller and less profitable than their European counterparts. In the 1920s, three large landholding agrarian families engaged in cotton farming and trading moved into the spinning mill industry. These were Kamma Naidus, affiliates of an agrarian caste from Andhra who had recently migrated to western Tamil Nadu who would become the leading industrialists and public patrons of the city of Coimbatore. The new Pykara hydroelectric works in the hills above Coimbatore provided the literal spark to Coimbatore's textile mill boom in the 1930s, but there is some debate as to sources of new capital. Chris Baker argues that the Depression left a lot of money capital idle in cotton trading and financing, and that this idle capital was productively reinvested in new Indian-owned mills. On the demand side, it is clearer that the regional handloom sector—another mainstay of the regional economy, peopled by left castes such as Devanga Chettiars and Sengutha Mudaliars—provided a local market in addition to the export trade. What is key is that the cultivator's ability to diversify down the cotton commodity chain allowed capital and expertise to flow through trade to the post-Depression textile mill boom. In contrast to Coimbatore, Nadar cotton farmers in the southern districts of Madras Presidency did not respond through rural diversification, nor did the region go through a similar agrarian transition.[53]

The boom in Coimbatore's textile mills also brought the colonial state into the economy in new ways: in industrial licensing, provision of inputs on quota, arbitration in labor disputes and control over exports. In these capacities, the state had to walk a fine line between the interests of spinning mills and decentralized handlooms. This process of state negotiation reflected what would become central to nationalist

debates on economic policy posed in terms of Nehruvian commitments to heavy industrialization and self-sufficiency in capital goods
vs Gandhian commitments to rural employment, democracy and
appropriate technology.[54] Modern industry in Coimbatore District
steered between these poles, as Coimbatore's textile mills specialized
in spinning yarn, leaving weaving the province of decentralized looms.
In contrast to Bombay's composite mills, which engaged in spinning
and weaving, tariff protection for woven cloth was never a key concern
for Coimbatore's textile elite. As the textile boom peaked in 1935 and
tailed off in 1938, some Gounders and Naidus started small spinning
mills, through relatively easy access to energy, capital, and markets in
decentralized weaving and exports. Finally, specialization in spinning
entailed much less skilled labor than in composite mills, and rural
migrants pushed by agrarian distress provided a pool of cheap, compliant labor.

The pattern of industrial investment in Coimbatore's mills followed the classic form of initial capital proving itself safe, moderately
profitable and with low barriers to entry, followed by a rush of secondary investors linked through personal contacts and guarantees.
The resulting industrial structure by the late 1930s was a confluence
of small industries crowded together at varying levels of productivity
and profitability. This mill-building boom ended by the late 1930s, as
the dramatic increase in capacity over the decade meant that yarn
supply far outstripped demand. Rather than cutting the price of yarn,
the Coimbatore millowners turned to stronger lobbying against the
state through the rhetoric of unfair Japanese competition. Those that
could shifted to higher counts of yarn as a way of retaining a price advantage, and indeed it was the larger European and Naidu firms begun
in the initial period that fared best. Most mills intensified work by
moving to shift systems that kept the machines running as long as possible.

The rationalization of the labor process meant burdens on skilled
labor were acutely increased: workers supervising a spinning frame
now had to supervise two. Wages were cut to such an extent that Coimbatore had the lowest wages of South Indian mills, which as a whole
had lower wages than the mill centers of the North and West. Harveys,

one of the main mill groups, cut wages on the grounds that the price of food had fallen during the Depression. One consequence of this regressive attitude to labor was an increase in strikes and communist mobilization, particularly in the ranks of skilled workers and supervisors. The important point is that a rural labor force that was known for its docility and "spirit of compromise" was quite quickly mobilized into a period of sustained labor struggle in the towns after the late 1930s. Bouts of compromise and agitation became par for the course in industrial Coimbatore.[55]

This period of industrial restructuring and union militancy had an important consequence in the form of state intervention in the economy. Against the rising currents of the nationalist movement and with the Communist Party of India banned and forced underground, the government set up arbitration mechanisms for resolving industrial disputes. The state sought to standardize and raise wages and to rationalize the inefficient and corrupt management of mills. The industry was spared strong rationalization by the opening up of new markets in East Asia, freed from Japanese control during Japan's war in Manchuria after 1938. World War II also brought new markets, particularly for colonial military requisition, and the Coimbatore mills were buoyant once more. Conditions of profitability and work in the textile mills became much more heterogeneous in the 1940s, with wages constantly trailing inflation. Wartime took the mills through another boom and bust cycle, and by the late 1940s the industry was faced with a combination of low profits, labor militancy, shrinking and volatile markets, and antiquated technology.[56]

Coimbatore's entrepreneurs responded to the fragility and volatility of textiles by spreading their risks from the 1930s. Early diversification of investment was in services and retail, particularly small bus and lorry fleets, then cinema houses and printing presses, in addition to investment in urban land, agriculture and trade. The structure of the mill industry prompted this kind of portfolio investment that altered the morphology of the city. At the helm of urban life were the few Naidu families who had started the first Indian mills and had since kept their families tightly involved in textile. As patrons of urbanity, these Naidus endowed a series of important public institutions, including colleges, hospitals and a textile research institute.[57]

An important shift in the city and its productive activities took place through the textile mills of the Naidus. Several skilled workers left the mills to start small foundries, machine shops and repair works. In this, the Naidu owners often encouraged and monetarily supported their ex-Workers, partly on the notion that these ancillary units could provide various services for the mills. The trajectories of these skilled workers were key to Coimbatore's shift from a textile town to light industries. One important element of this diversification was the development of irrigation pump manufacture, which found a ready market in the electrification of groundwater-driven farming in rural Coimbatore District. Industrial diversification in Coimbatore City began through strong rural linkages. One of the Naidu pioneers, the owner of the PSG Group, began with a small workshop manufacturing and repairing ploughs and other agricultural equipment. With the advance of modern industry, the stage was set for light industry that was qualitatively different from earlier artisanal production, but with persisting rural linkages through the provision of producer goods to farmers.[58]

Coimbatore was fast becoming the biggest and most diversified industrial town in the South. Some of the new concerns were in retailing consumer goods such as soaps, detergents and tea; in wholesaling of industrial goods such as cement; and in services, principally printing and the cinema industry. Coimbatore would become a center for consumer durables, such as food processors and other home appliances. Early on, Coimbatore Mill owners joined bankers in investing in film-making in the late 1930s. Coimbatore City revealed in microcosm what industrialization in Tamil Nadu, and most of India, revealed at large: that the advent of modern factory manufacture did not drive out small-scale and petty production, but pushed these activities into the unregulated or informal sector. Indeed economically active populations in the latter far overshadowed factory employment. In the wake of wartime shortages, the combination of putting-out industry and state-subsidized grain through the Public Distribution System, in place in 1943, drew substantial rural populations into the sphere of urban work. I turn next to the ways in which dispersed urbanization and industry in Kongunad grew out of interactions with the countryside.[59]

Geographical Specialization and Kongunad Towns, 1870–1970

What did the draw to Kongunad's towns look like spatially, and how did the space economy of urbanization and industry change over time? In a fascinating cartography of phases of urbanization in Tamil Nadu between 1871 and 1951, Baker maps relations between towns and their developmental functions across four periods of urbanization. In the first period (1871–91), governmental functions such as district or taluk headquarters and railway junctions were the main spur to growing towns. During the second period (1891–1911), cash cropping of cotton and groundnut in particular encouraged the growth of market towns. By the third period (1911–31), the commodity entrepôts of the earlier period grew most strongly in Coimbatore District, while temple towns of the river valleys were in decline. The final period (1931–51) saw the rise to dominance of industrial towns, particularly in Kongunad.[60] What is useful in this periodization is the concentration of urban industry and of an impoverished working class in what was also the heartland of agrarian capitalism, Coimbatore District. This was far from fortuitous.

R. Rukmini has made an important contribution in situating Coimbatore's specialist towns in the geography of agrarian transition. Regional industry has built on the commercialization of agriculture through strong intersectoral linkages, in a pattern of urbanization through the "thickening of the countryside" rather than through the transformation of established towns.[61] Rukmini shows empirically that a combination of "spatial specialization" and "crop concentration" in the process of agrarian commercialization creates the possibility of specialist agro-based towns. The underlying mechanism for agro-based urbanization is economic development along the division of labor, as the drive to integrate into marketing or processing down the commodity chain has a stronger chance of being located in the same region if the region already specializes in and has a concentration of a particular crop. A central clue as to how these rural towns were formed, in this explanation, lies in "the nature of the peasantry" engaged early on in intensive and extensive farming, marketing and agro-processing.[62]

A second clue to dispersed rural urbanization lies in the way regional industrialization was a diversified, yet interlinked process. Coimbatore District experienced sustained urban growth from 1920 to 1970 in a process of intensification across several towns, along with extensive urbanization and ancilliarization from the main centers. However the crucial period connecting processes of agrarian and industrial change was the 1920s and 1930s, the same period in which a new production politics was forged in Gounder farming. Contemporaneously, the division of labor in agriculture was driving processes of spatial specialization and crop concentration, so that Palladam and Udumalpettai Taluks came to be specialized in cotton farming, while Pollachi Taluk became specialized in groundnuts. Agricultural specialization in combination with existing transportation and communication routes helped make market towns in these taluks. The missing ingredient is *how* changes in Gounder agriculture created conditions for the progressive Gounder peasant to create the necessary intersectoral linkages, the topic of the following chapter.[63]

When agricultural commodity and credit markets collapsed during the Depression, Tiruppur grew spectacularly, at rates of 117 percent, much higher than other Kongunad towns or Coimbatore City. Rural distress and incipient urban industry helped make Tiruppur the fastest growing town in the Madras Presidency. The rationalization of the market and shift in urban power to a small group of gin owners also marked Tiruppur's transformation from cotton entrepôt to manufacturing town with abundant supplies of cheap labor. There is much debate surrounding why the effects of the Depression on agriculture, trade and finance prompted investment in industry in Coimbatore District alone. Rukmini intuitively identifies a regional "resilience" in Coimbatore, based in production flexibility and "the nature of the peasantry," with its dispersed savings and its "enterprising nature, market orientation [and] substantial trading interests."[64]

By the late twentieth century, the "nature" of this peasantry, a product of colonial processes and ideologies, had become common sense not just for social scientists, but also for inhabitants of Tiruppur. I follow the important insight that the peasant question, while not an explanation of everything of consequence in Coimbatore's economy, is central in forging a kind of agrarian flexible specialization. The next chapter traces the continuities across agriculture and industry through the histories and self-presentations of Tiruppur's Gounders. Before doing so, it remains to explicate the character of industry and unionism in Tiruppur in its transition from cotton marketing to manufacturing town.

Industry and Unionism in Tiruppur, 1910s–1940s

Modern industry in Tiruppur drew working people from its rural hinterland in different ways. While rural women found work in gins under conditions of severe insecurity, Gounder men had had access to relatively privileged forms of work in textile mills. This gender- and caste-differentiated landscape of job security had important implications for the trajectories of workers. However, modern industry also brought traditions of unionism that were fundamentally conservative, but which also held an undercurrent of radicalism. These processes imparted a particular character to Tiruppur's industrial geography.

With Tiruppur's growing importance as an entrepôt in the cotton trade, the town became a focus of class conflict between farmers, middlemen, merchants and buyers over control of cotton, particularly with the formation of a regulated cotton market.[65] Subsequently, Tiruppur became a center of cotton pressing and ginning. Some of the largest European textile concerns in Madras Presidency established ginning subsidiaries in town. The House of Binny, a pioneering European industrial house in South India, established the Tiruppur Press Co. Ltd in 1881 and pressed 8,500 bales of cotton a year through the 1880s. In 1912, Messrs Binny & Co. added ginning to its operations in Tiruppur.[66] Other European concerns, in particular Harvey & Co. and Kearny & Co., also chose Tiruppur for ginning operations because of its cotton market and easy access to Coimbatore's mills. In 1931 Tiruppur had six cotton presses, eighteen ginning factories and the railway station was taken over by the large quantities of cotton that moved through it.[67]

The town also had five banian factories, two of which were mechanized, though the banian trade was still small, earning Rs 800 from exports each month. Banian manufacture was overshadowed by petty industry in nearby villages, such as the brass and bell-metal vessel production from Anupappálayam village three miles from town, which hired 15,000 workers, obtained material from as far as Madras and exported vessels of half a lakh each month all over the princely state of Mysore and Madras Presidency.[68]

By the 1940s Tiruppur's distinction was firm as the most important cotton-ginning center in Madras Presidency, producing processed cotton for Coimbatore as well as for Lancashire and Tokyo. By 1943 Tiruppur boasted of twenty-four cotton gins and five presses, hiring an average of 2,333 workers per day. The first gins were owned by Bombay merchants, but had since been bought or leased out by locals. Coimbatore mill interests owned over half the ginning factories in Tiruppur in the early 1940s. Finally, unlike most gins in India, which dealt with the vagaries of the trade through the pooling of factories, Tiruppur was peculiar for the absence of pooling arrangements.[69]

Cotton came to Tiruppur from the adjacent towns of Avinashi and Palladam as well as from adjacent villages. The dealers who brought cotton to the factories would engage primarily female workers to clean the cotton for ginning, and most of these workers were not registered on the employers' books. Factory records showed inflated absentee rates of 10 percent to 25 percent because workers were routinely marked absent when they were not needed. Work was entirely casual.[70] Employment was also predominantly female, even among gin-feeders and seed carriers. Women and men earned differentiated payments, in daily wages and piece rates respectively, although women foremen employed to oversee female workers were paid a fixed weekly wage. These workers were hired from agriculture during the slack season, and the colonial report explains female discrimination in labor markets as necessitated by the seasonality of cotton.[71]

Gin workers' wages were fixed by the Cotton Merchants' Association of Tiruppur in 1944, after the *kaláci* or manual transport workers' strike in a prominent gin. This strike was a watershed in activism among seasonal workers in Tiruppur's gins. The *kalácis* are reported to have refused to watch factory premises at night, as this was not in their labor contract. When seven were dismissed, the rest called a factory-wide strike. The Labour Conciliation Officer from Coimbatore was brought to mediate, and ultimately the factory stopped both piece rates and direct employment of *kalácis*. Since then, *kalácis* received weekly group payment, according to standardized rates for different strains of cotton.[72]

While this colonial document argues that the poor, particularly women, are pushed to take to low-paid jobs in gins, it lauds Tiruppur workers for their thrift. While painting working-class suffering with a noble brush, it also suggests how families got by. Workers sought credit from private moneylenders or from their villages, and rural families continued to seek to mitigate uncertainty through the diversification of their income streams into a range of occupations: "In a family, the father may work, for instance, as a paddy boiler in a rice mill, the daughter in one of the cotton gins, and the son as a mill hand in one of the textile mils. The family pools all the earnings and somehow ekes out a livelihood. There are also instances of parents staying at home to look after their small agricultural holdings while sons and daughters take to factory work."[73] Agrarian households crept into industrial work and made their mark on its character by pooling earnings from several kinds of work. Rural women found waged work early in the history of modern industry in South India, in gins and in petty agricultural trade.[74] Farm families were unlikely to dispose of their agricultural holdings unless, as the life histories in Chapter 5 suggest, they were forced to through debts in the village. Instead, farm families near Tiruppur could seek work in any of 25 cotton gins, 12 rice mills and 3 textile mills in 1943.[75]

The textile mills of Coimbatore had taken off in the 1930s with steady electricity from the Pykara Water Works in the Nilgiri Hills. While Bombay's composite mills stagnated, Coimbatore's spinning mills grew, offering the lowest wage rates of South Indian spinning mill centers to its predominantly rural workforce.[76] The spinning mill gates continue to carry memories of workers' meetings as well as violent clashes between colonial police and communist organizers.[77] Union processions still begin or end by paying homage at the mill gates. The memories of prominent unionists provide a partial view into the history of unionism in Tiruppur.

While looking for old Mill workers in one of the oldest working-class colonies in Tiruppur, I stumbled upon Tyagi P. Ramasamy in his modest apartment.[78] Ramasamy was a communist in nationalist clothing, and one of the first labor union organizers in Tiruppur. He began speaking with an uncanny sense of his place in history:

> I am now 78. I was born on April 12, 1919, at the same time as the Punjab massacre at Jallianwallah Bagh, on April 13. At the same time, in the Soviet Union, the revolutionary government was caught in a World War. In order to help the military, the people of that country decided to work for free on one Sunday; that was April 13. That has not happened anywhere else in the world. Because that happened right at the time I was born, it is just *there* in my memory. First point.[79]

With this stunning introduction, P. Ramasamy builds up to the history of unionism in Tiruppur, with detours through the Gandhian khadi activism of the nationalist movement.[80] In the activism of this period Kumaran, the son of a Chettiar khadi merchant, was beaten to death by a policeman for holding up the Congress flag at the head of a procession. Tyagi Kumaran has since been the mythic hero of Tiruppur who continues to be resurrected for a multitude of purposes. The symbolic power of raising the flag linked Kumaran to a wider cause, but the symbol was used for alternative purposes as well. Decades after Kumaran's martyrdom, a young CPI activist and Asher Mill worker, Palanisamy, is said to have shouted "Victory to the Red Flag! May the Struggle Continue!" before being shot in custody by the police in 1941. Palanisamy is immortalized through the same idiom of martyrdom as Kumaran, despite quite different circumstances underlying his murder. Nationalist idioms could be used for quite different causes.[81]

Ramasamy worked as a "sider" in Dhanalakshmi Mill, the first mill to open in Tiruppur in 1933. The first labor union in Tiruppur was started in 1934 by two members of the Justice Party, one of whom was also Municipal Chairman; these men were, for all intents and purposes, allied with Mill owners.[82] Ramasamy claims his dismissal from Dhanalakshmi Mill sparked the first strike. While the Congress Party could not make its mark on Tiruppur's workers, neither could the

Justicites.[83] When the communists started organizing in Tiruppur, however, their movement spread like wildfire. Ramasamy says he was the link between Communist Party activity in Coimbatore and Tiruppur, and he described his movements between these spheres as extremely dangerous, with severe police repression of communist activists. Despite these circumstances, Ramasamy led the formation of unions among workers in different sections of Tiruppur—including dyeing workers, Mill workers, printing workers and municipal health workers.[84] By the early 1940s, about 90 percent of workers were unionized in sectors in which the union was active.[85] To put it differently, this was the period in which the CPI managed to bring in various smaller unions in Tiruppur under its mantle. This was also the period in which the CPI and the Indian National Congress (Congress) joined forces, for the communists had to become a secret faction inside Congress, until 1945, when the ban on the CPI was removed. Despite the thin presence of Congress in Tiruppur, histories of worker and nationalist agitation were combined, with intertwined icons and idioms. Confrontation with the police inevitably centered on the flag, whether tricolor for Congress or red, particularly at the May Day meeting in 1941. Symbols, rather than shopfloor organizing, marked this moment of communist unionism in Tiruppur and Coimbatore District more generally, as the party fought for recognition of the CPI general workers union, the All-India Trade Union Congress (AITUC), against the hostility of the colonial police.[86]

Alongside the fight for recognition, workers from Tiruppur's mills were involved in one of the most important struggles for Indian industrial labor at the time. The War Allowance Struggle of 1941 linked Indian textile mills, with centers of activism in Bombay and Kanpur in West and North India. Tiruppur's role in this national struggle for a living wage in the face of war shortage is now part of local lore. A strike of this magnitude—thirty-nine days—was a first in the history of Tiruppur's working class. In Ramasamy's words, "all other mill workers gained from the Tiruppur mill workers' struggle."[87] At the end of the strike, 100 people were jailed and 200 lost their jobs, but all mill workers had won 12.5 percent War Allowance. I want to point out three features of the strike from Ramasamy's narrative.

First, when owners attempted to break the strike as they had earlier with scabs from other towns, fifty workers attacked and destroyed the Dhanalakshmi and SRC Mill gates. The mill gates, recall, remain powerful symbols of industrial capital. Heads of the unions were arrested, but the authorities were confused as to who among the crowd was involved in the attack. To think of this differently, there was some kind of reciprocity within the crowd that prevented the police from arresting all but the most visible leaders.

Second, Ramasamy found through the course of the strike the importance of workers' relief. Workers "struck without getting disappointed," but their endurance had an important basis. The union appointed volunteers from each ward to collect contributions of money and food from surrounding villages to support worker families. In effect, agrarian connections fueled union struggle in town. However, the union held out its vision in remarkably global terms. An early piece of propaganda was a notice put up by Tiruppur communists, which read: "We were defeated in the Smalensk struggle, but the Soviet Union had a glorious victory. We have won the War Allowance!"[88] The union was reliant on affiliations to surrounding villages while scripting its role in a global communist movement.[89]

Third, another consequence of the strike was that as workers who lost their jobs went to various other lines of work, they passed on union propaganda and helped form unions in other worksites such as *kaláci* (manual transport), rice mills, gins, and so on.[90] Unionization spread like wildfire through the itinerant movements of Tiruppur's workers. Palaniappan, another union organizer from this period recounted the many ways in which new workers were drawn into the movement. Palaniappan was from Vanjipalayam, famous for rice trading and, from 1936, for rice mills run on oil engines.[91] With electricity readily available in Tiruppur, most of these mills shifted to the town in the 1940s. Like many boys from Vanjipalayam, Palaniappan followed the rice mills to Tiruppur in 1938, and went to work for a Muslim from his village. After suffering health problems, Palaniappan switched to sack trading, where he was employed as a petty trader for a shop.[92] He then met Ramasamy and other founders of the regional communist movement, and they began a sack workers' union in 1943. Palaniappan soon left his work and, with a substantial pay cut, became a full-time labor organizer. At the height of communist activism in Tiruppur, a hundred CPI leaders emerged from Tiruppur's mills. Many were women workers from the reeling department, and Palaniappan insisted that they were very active, in contrast to the unions of today.[93]

The same period saw the organization of *kaláckárars*, manual laborers who transport for merchants for a share of the latter's earnings. When these *kaláckárars* won a modest wage increase, their employees, *kai-vandi kaláckárars*, or hand-cart transporters, demanded higher wage payments as well. Ramasamy intervened to settle the first agreement between fractions of labor. Subsequently, the *kaláckárars* union became a very popular force in Tiruppur. Workers in this union played a role in organizing workers in rice mills and ginning factories. In 1942, 10,000 women workers in cotton ginning became members of the communist union and obtained raises. Unions were formed for construction workers and for workers in grocery, cloth stores and printing workshops. Stitching workers unionized in order to get scarce thread provided on quota to members, and weavers followed suit.

Occasionally, the union played a defensive role in protecting consumers and preventing violence. When crowds gathered in front of cloth and food stores in the face of shortages, "red-shirt volunteers stood in front of the stores to make sure that a fair price was given . . . [and] owners of the godowns thanked" Ramasamy for preventing riots.[94] What is important is that communist volunteers acted to prevent both sellers and working-class buyers from gaining the upper hand, and the idiom of this mediation was *fairness*, a point I return to.[95]

The union made some inroads organizing farm workers and sharecroppers, but communist mobilization in the countryside never took off because party commitments lay predominantly in the cities. When I pressed Palaniappan about this, he snapped, "Hey! What was there to struggle for in agriculture?"[96] Indeed, since the communist movement was dominated by landholding Gounders, with little, if any, representation from Dalits, there was little incentive to take up the cause of rural inequality.

Yet, early communist action in Tiruppur was not always blind to agrarian questions. When a large landlord on the urban periphery,

K.R.E. Gounder, was hoarding grain during a drought, red-shirt volunteers took over his farm in his absence and occupied it for two days, promising to distribute the grain by the third unless the government intervened.[97] The District Collector sent the relevant government officials to procure the grain for consumption, and the volunteers disbanded. The landlord, in turn, had the support of some young men of the *valayar* caste of fishermen, but when Ramasamy sent messages to their parents, they left town as well. The union had succeeded in encouraging flight from their patron in order to facilitate fair access to the hoard. With both sides of the conflict neutralized, the resolution betrays the conservatism in Ramasamy's unionism. When K.R.E. returned, he was grateful to Ramasamy for managing the situation and, in the latter's words, they became friends. This way of negotiating with black marketers in the face of scarcity, usually of food or cloth, recurs in Ramasamy's memoirs.[98]

Palaniappan was deeply critical of Ramasamy's class compromises, but in my opinion his brand of orthodox Marxism misses a crucial point. Unions were defensive in order to protect workers' rights against the stability of markets and the conditions of production. Ramasamy narrates this incident immediately after meditating on the disastrous Bengal Famine of 1943–4, after which a group of leaders in Tiruppur, including him, sent a relief package. The environs of Tiruppur faced several drought years beginning with monsoon failure in 1945 and intensifying between 1947 and 1953. Union actions to preserve working peoples' entitlements to food constitute, in the exact sense, what E. P. Thompson called the "moral economy of the crowd," of popular struggle to prevent drought turning into famine.[99] This commitment to secure entitlements underlay the conservatism that would remain constitutive of unionism in Tiruppur. Hence, even with the emergence of a more militant union consciousness, union practice never willfully threatened the conditions of accumulation, in marked contrast to the neighboring state of Kerala.[100] Unionism in Tiruppur remained fundamentally defensive and conservative.

This defensive unionism also helped forge a particular kind of public culture in Tiruppur, which sought fairness on the market. Tiruppur had the first fair-price shops in Tamil Nadu, and the union won permission to ration ¼ bag of rice per week for each Mill worker.[101] The

Dhanalakshmi Mill also had the first cooperative society with reasonably priced commodities for workers.[102] The union tried to intervene in workers' consumption by discouraging them from drinking away their wages rather than saving. Furthermore, the union made a list of moneylenders who charged usurious interest rates and told them to lower their rates and to collect through the union office. The union also provided interest-free loans to workers to pay off debts, and, Ramasamy comments, workers' *families* grew much closer to unions as a consequence. Before this public role of unions came into being, workers were beaten by moneylenders when they could not repay debts, but these practices stopped with the growing public presence of red shirt volunteers in urban life. Not surprisingly, residents in Tiruppur's neighborhoods had mixed feelings about this public role of unions. The women of Anaikkadu demonstrated this very tangibly when the local landlord tried to refuse the entry of communists by saying Anaikkadu was his inheritance. The women of Anaikkadu came out into the streets and gave buttermilk, lime juice and water to the CPI procession as it came through. Soon after this the union bought a home and set up shop. The women of the neighborhood had trumped the power of the landlord.[103]

This section has explored how, by the 1940s, a multifaceted industrial history had sedimented into Tiruppur's landscape, imparting it a specific character centered on an idiom of *fairness*. By the time the knitting industry took root, the industrial geography was dominated by three spinning mills and numerous cotton gins. The latter provided seasonal work, particularly for rural women, drawing rural people into the insecure rhythms of capitalist work. Spinning mills provided the most sought-after jobs, which Gounder men were poised to access. The ramparts and gates of these mills and cotton gins still outline this older work history in Tiruppur. However, I have tried to suggest that the more important sedimentation in Tiruppur's industrial culture came through a rich history of unionism and popular struggle.

While this unionism was essentially conservative, it spread through Tiruppur, across spheres of production and reproduction, drawing working-class families, and particularly women, into the protection of entitlements to food, cloth, fair prices and cheap credit. While a fractious and contradictory idiom of *fairness* spread across the division of labor, across workplaces, neighborhoods and homes, an incipient labor unionism was emerging in fits and starts from within the social fabric. Radicalism was tempered by conserving the entitlements of working-class households, so that unionism in Tiruppur always claimed to be pragmatic. The Luddite destruction of knitting machines in neighboring Travancore in this period did not find favor in Tiruppur's culture of labor activism. This pragmatic unionism was an important legacy for participants in the early knitwear industry.

V. Conclusion: Geographical Specialization and the Politics of Work in Coimbatore's Regional Capitalism

The countryside remade the town in its own image.[104]

Industrial towns in Tamil Nadu responded to meager rural demand by turning to government contracts and public-sector employment. In the wake of agricultural decline, and in its efforts to placate the powerful Mill owners, the state used limited welfare to redistribute resources in towns. In turn, the flood of rural poor seeking cheap state-subsidized food and able to work for low wages fueled small service and artisanal industry, in sectors such as handloom, tanning, beedi-rolling and matches. In this expansion of unregulated work, shaped by the state's reluctance to address rural poverty directly, the town was drawn into the social inequalities of the countryside.[105]

There are two key ways in which agrarian questions shaped Tiruppur's industrial trajectory. First, a production politics forged in Gounder farms in the 1930s honed the farmer's skills in participant supervision and control of caste- and gender-differentiated labor arrangements. Second, regional agricultural specialization and intersectoral linkages prompted by a diversifying peasantry created the conditions for dispersed, commodity-specific towns. These legacies came together in a particular landscape of agro-industrial flexible specialization across town and country.

Tiruppur's richly sedimented industrial geography has also been shaped by a vibrant history of unionism and popular struggle. Communist unionism in Tiruppur was always under check through a conservative undertow expressed in the idiom of fairness. Hence, labor militancy was tempered by pragmatic concerns centered on maintaining working-class entitlements rather than throwing caution to the wind. Through the broad-based efforts of labor organizers, this conservatism became part of a public culture, which, in valorizing fairness, focused working class politics on the sphere of exchange rather than on the workplace. Gounders would come to this work regime with a very different relationship to work, derived from a confluence of colonial knowledge and social transformation in rural Kongunad.

The countryside also made its presence felt through the emergence of the most important social movement in modern Tamil Nadu, the Dravidian Movement, which went through three broad phases before gaining political power: through an alliance of elite "non-Brahmins" under the Justice Party, a broad-based backward caste alliance under the Non-Brahmin Movement, and mass anti-Hindi linguistic nationalism.[106] The Dravidian Movement signaled the decline of the power of rural elites in the valleys and a shift in power to mobile backward castes. The Dravidian political parties subsequently developed strong connections with rural working classes, and especially with rural women, a legacy of the feminism of the radical phase of Dravidian politics.

Gounders were precisely the kind of backward caste who could have been participants in the Dravidian Movement. However, the radical second phase of the Non-Brahmin Movement did not make major inroads in rural Coimbatore. In part this had to do with political compromises made between Gounder elites and the Congress Party. With the expansion of franchise under the Government of India Act of 1935, the colonial state granted the vote for the somewhat inconsequential legislative assemblies to lesser landholders, to expand the electorate by a factor of between 4 and 5. This made it all the more important for the Congress Party to gain rural support in Coimbatore. Both Congress and elite Gounders concurred over a mutual silence on issues of land reform, and Congress campaigned using rural disenchantment over issues of irrigation and land taxation against the Justice Party.[107] Gounders also kept clear from Gandhians in Congress, with their paternalism towards the "uplift of Harijans." Gounders emerged as key power brokers in the late 1930s, invaluable to Congress gaining power in Madras in 1937.[108] Regional politics in Coimbatore was at this point oriented away from Tamil nationalism and certainly from the radical anti-caste Dravidian Movement that would sweep the rest of Tamil Nadu to create the conditions for radical populism.

In contrast, as Coimbatore industrialized through strong rural–urban linkages, it also became a heartland of a pragmatic Communist politics. Coimbatore did not develop the kind of grassroots radicalism and pro-women ideology of Keralite communism, which pushed for radical land redistribution, women's empowerment, and mass literacy. Communism in Coimbatore was neither elite and Brahmin-led as in Madras city, nor radical as in neighboring Kerala. Agrarian development without extreme polarities, centered on the ideology of the Gounder small farmer, mirrored the conservatism of Communist unionism in Coimbatore's urban centers. In these many ways, the politics of the regional agrarian question had left its trace in industry. The following chapter asks how Tiruppur's self-made men have used traces of the agrarian past in remaking the industrial present.

CHAPTER 5

Can the Subaltern Accumulate Capital? Toil in Transition, 1950–1984

I. Introduction: How Peasant-Workers Made an Agrarian Transition

They are never afraid of working. Gounders are very industrious people.[1]

Most owners here aren't big owners. Most still go to work in their companies. If you tried to find rich owners you won't find a majority in banian companies. Maybe those who came after 1984 were the kind who sold their lands and came in with a lot of capital. But these companies couldn't stand, and these were rich owners. A banian company cannot run if labour and owner are on opposite sides: if they don't respect each other. Both have to work together in order for a company to grow. These Gounder farmers are used to working the *Vaṇṇa, Nácuva, Cakkilian* castes by scolding them and extracting their labor . . . in the same way, in banian companies the owners have to scold the workers and extract work from them. You didn't need to enter with large capital. You just had to work and manage work and the office and quality all at once. Big men couldn't stand. Only small people from modest backgrounds have succeeded.[2]

What is to be made of these Gounder self-presentations, and how can they reveal a usable past? This chapter explores how Gounder peasant-workers used colonial and agrarian legacies to transform Tiruppur's knitwear industry and their place in it. I first detail the character of Tiruppur knitwear forged by an older guard of owners and labor organizers. I then show how Gounders of agrarian origins came in multifarious ways from the countryside, drawing various resources into their different trajectories as peasant-workers, then as knitwear workers, often as communist labor unionists, and finally as small-scale industry owners. Through a stylized narrative of moments in agrarian and industrial transition, I show how these Gounders renovate an agrarian past, while also calling into critique their self-presentations of mobility, and industrial success.

This social and cultural historical geography of Tiruppur speaks to and reconstructs understandings of agrarian transition in two ways.[3] First, I detail a specific form of agrarian transition under the auspices of peasant-workers, unlikely agents of regional industrialization, let alone globalization. Second, I demonstrate how Gounder men used a culturally and historically specific labor theory of value to translate and renovate elements of their agrarian past to reorganize industrial work. Combining these questions of transition and translation, I ask *how* this trajectory of uneven development is rendered culturally and materially.

In using life histories to understand political economy, I am guided by the injunction that experience is only intelligible as narrative.[4] Making narratives is not simply a matter of individual rationality because narratives are always caught in currents of dominant ideologies. People use metaphors and metonyms not entirely of their own making.[5] Hence, I ask two questions as a critical realist: (1) what practices lay behind the metonym of toil, which took Chapter 4 back to 1930s agriculture, and (2) how was this metonym *used* in forging control over work and social labor in the industrial present?—the topic of this chapter. As an important caveat, caste and gender affiliation do not guarantee for all Gounder men the capacity to effect successful transitions, but my archive of life histories is weak in showing ways in which workers did not make it as owners. I refer the reader back to the counterfactuals in Chapter 3 for the difference and causal significance of *Gounder ex-Worker* narratives and trajectories from those of others.

In asking the rhetorical question that is the title of this chapter, I am not arguing *that* the subaltern can accumulate capital, in addition to riding horses and so on.[6] Capitalism proceeds through the production and subsumption of various forms of subalternity, but what is surprising about Tiruppur's self-made men is the way in which they claim subalternity in order to become capitalists.[7] The point, therefore, is not that Tiruppur's Gounder men are truly subaltern in a metaphysical sense, but rather to understand how they renovate singular histories and practices to use capitalist opportunity and to reap its unintended consequences. Tiruppur's self-made men fan the flames of the rhetorical question—"can the subaltern accumulate capital?"—to attempt to legitimate capital as toil. The important question is: how does toil translate into capital and for whom?

There are two main arguments in this chapter. Section II explores the character of knitwear in its early phase, when capital was entirely in the hands of business communities, including Muslims, Iyers, Chettiars and Mudaliars. As was the case regionally, industry in Tiruppur was characterized by an idiom of fairness concerned primarily with the sphere of exchange rather than with the politics of production. Using memories from old guard owners, a union organizer and a non-Gounder worker, I frame the industry to which Gounder peasant-workers came to work.

Section III turns to seven moments in the making of Gounder peasant-workers' transitions to fraternal capital: their preparation through agrarian backgrounds, their work and difference as peasant-workers, labor militancy as the opportunity for industrial decentralization, class mobility and the making of bosses, state intervention to creditworthy "peasant" owners, their interpellation as a new class through Gounder toil in the labor process, and the making of a tenuous fraternity of decentralized capital. These analytical moments do not fit neat historical periodization, and are marked with approximate dates, and sometimes only with start dates as certain moments continue to the present. I try to convey internal difference and contingency in the construction of each analytical moment. Memories slow down the historicism of successive moments by attending to the ways in which people translate particular struggles and aspirations in the wake of social change. Finally, in the practice of toil, the agrarian question becomes a usable past in making an exclusionary and exploitative present.

II. The Character of Industry and Unionism under the Old Guard, 1920s–1940s

Cotton hosiery was produced in Calcutta at the turn of the last century and made its first appearance in the Madras Presidency in the 1910s. Sowerimuthu Chettiar and Sowdi Chettiar knitted socks in Coimbatore for sale in Bombay and Bengal. In the 1920s, these pioneers purchased manual flatbed knitting machines from Calcutta and Kerala to manufacture banians, that is, undershirts. When these banians failed to be as popular as the tubular banians of Calcutta, Sowerimuthu Chettiar switched to manual circular machines. Soon Sowdi Chettiar's brother-in-law Pethi Chetty and daughter C. Chellammal joined the business. They would later find their home in Tiruppur. What is surprising is that only at this earliest stage was a woman a prominent owner, and she continues to be remembered as a *gettikári*, "tough woman," who ventured to the bank, and even to Madras, on her own. [8]

Following these pioneers of the Chettiar community, the first banian factories in Tiruppur were started by Muslims: M. Abdul Raguman Sahib's Azad Knitting Co. of 1925 and M.G. Abdul Sardar Sahib and M.G. Gulam Khadar Sahib's partnership Baby Knitting Co. of 1926. Star Babu Bhai was another pioneering Muslim owner whose Star Knitting Co. began in 1931, when electricity came to Tiruppur. [9] Knitwear in Tiruppur from the 1930s through the 1950s was peopled by a handful of Muslim, Mudaliar, Chettiar and Iyer entrepreneurs who sought to impart a particular moral content to industry. They also tried to integrate as much as possible of the labor process under one roof. Rajendra Knitting, begun by Pethi Chetty and Chellammal, was typical of these companies in combining knitting and garment stitching with calendaring and bleaching in large cement tanks, all in the same premises. Old-guard owners convey their expertise in technical and market terms rather than in terms of work practice. This is not to say that they did not know the labor process thoroughly but that they saw their activities as owners as markedly different from those of workers. Work and business meant different things.

This section traces the moral character of industry, primarily through two pioneering owners, a Communist labor leader, and an old worker who would later watch some of his Gounder comrades become millionaires. This set of lives provides a decidedly partial window into industry and unionism under the old guard, but it resonates with the argument about work and unionism in Tiruppur in the last chapter.

Old Guard Capital in Knitwear, 1920s–1950s

There were only about thirty-four companies in Tiruppur in the early 1940s. The first major impetus to mechanize was driven by access to the key raw material, yarn. World War II yarn shortages and wartime requisition prompted new state policy of yarn provision on government quota on the basis of knitting machines owned, and there was a scramble for imported knitting machines.[10] Early owners prided themselves on adopting new technologies and techniques not only for the advancement of their own companies but for Tiruppur as a whole.

Star Babu Bhai narrated his life history with remarkable coherence at the age of ninety, after making me a glass of home-made soda water. He told me how he came to Tiruppur in the 1920s to his *maccán's* company, Baby Knitting "when *current* [electricity] came," where he spent a period as a paid apprentice. Star Bhai then started a company in 1932, for which he bought a stitching machine and a German circular knitting machine, a first in Tiruppur, from his father-in-law for the sum of Rs 500.

> First I only had one man to turn the machine—Tiger Knitting[11]—I did all the rest, all-in-all. I did the yarn rewinding even. I made 300 dozens manually then. Three-four people would turn the machines by hand, Gounders. After breaking off from my *maccán* . . . *current* came and we worked night and day, stopping the motor once a week. Still, I would do bleaching myself. I was the first to do manual calendaring. Then I was the first to do steam callendaring. I was sending V-neck banians to Bombay [in the 1930s]. I was the one to bring "fine" banians to Tiruppur. After that everyone started doing it.[12]

Star Bhai emphasizes details about machines and markets, but he also knew the labor process inside out and performed several functions himself. Unlike the working-class owners to come, pioneers like Star Bhai used family and community connections only in starting firms, not to build chains of dependent units. Star Bhai's memories focus on his role as a local innovator and adopter of various new techniques. As a pioneer in the thin "fine" banians, that allowed Tiruppur to establish its presence in the national market, he stakes claim to Tiruppur's boom. He also emphasizes his commitment to transparency rather than to guarding his insights as trade secrets, again putting Tiruppur's industry above his personal gain:

> I showed the machines to everyone. My castefellows,[13] my uncle, my *maccán* . . . I showed them all the work. I'd say, only if you show everyone the work the industry will become strong. Just like that, I helped 15–20 factories by giving them addresses, arranging the purchase of machines, giving addresses of *parties*. Even my son doesn't believe it now. "Would anyone do that?" he asks. I thought the industry would grow only if there were many factories. My hand is in 25–30 factories. Of people who work-ed for me and became owners, there are about 50 in Tiruppur. Then many factories grew, one seeing the other, seeing another. Now, without know-ing anything, someone who's studied till the 3rd class goes to America to get an order: Gounders.[14]

Whether or not he privileged his "castefellows," Star Bhai claims to have helped several new owners through advice on markets and machines, rather than by advancing capital. What is important, par-ticularly in marking his distance from the new Gounder owners, is Star Bhai's emphasis on his technical expertise.

Workers enter Star Bhai's vision not through their command of the labor process, but in a communalized claim to leave from work. Star Bhai goes as far as to imply that workers held the cards fighting the logic of the motor, but the effects of labor organizing are visible in the edges of the frame: "Workers had one day of leave per month. If you turned on the motor, you had to keep it running for a month. I had 40 workers in Star Knitting. Then they asked for leave once a week; Maximum[15] said '*Amávácai, Amávácai*.' The Factory Party [Mill workers union?] was strong then. We used to keep giving leave. What-ever [workers] said would happen. What [owners] said would not happen. There was a period like that, 30 years ago."[16] Star Bhai sees labor organizing as a plea for the Hindu holiday of *Amávácai*, the new moon, from a Muslim boss. Similarly, he describes his difference as a *Muslim* owner through his non-reliance on credit, particularly in the form of loans for fixed capital, as opposed to bank-mediated credit through bill discounting.[17] Star Bhai's notion of correct business practice was subject to negotiation against concerns with Muslim piety, which he links to a wariness of credit. His industrial practice would remain fundamentally different from Gounder strategies of decentralization, which *required* a freer flow of credit to smooth commodity flows across networked units. Business, for this owner of the old guard, remained a slow and personalized system of exchange, not all of it monetized. Babu Bhai narrated an incident in which his worker declined a wage for secure access to food. The moral of the story was that the worker knew all too well that he could rely on bonds of friendship and non-monetized exchange between elite families in Tiruppur through his boss in order to secure food, and this was enough.[18]

Star Bhai's narrative conveys a specific structure of feeling, combining technical ingenuity, fairness and transparency in business, and communal attachment, with its related claim to Muslim piety. Other old guard owners share various of these elements. Both Star Bhai and Sundaram Iyer combined mechanical knack, almost never through formal training, with mercantile connections. These capacities brought owners of business communities not only to fraternize along caste and religious lines, but also form occasional partnerships. Between 1948 and 1961, the number of knitwear companies rose to 200, including the first Gounder companies.[19]

The most important personality to emerge from the old guard was S.A. Khadar, founder of SIHMA in 1956. Khadar came from a family of timber merchants who had migrated to Tiruppur from Pollachi, and had involvements with Congress nationalists in the early 1940s. When the timber business folded up, Khadar engaged in trade before acquiring an old knitting machine from a cousin in Calcutta. With an initial investment of less than five thousand rupees, he started a knitting workshop to make a living alongside his political activism.[20]

Khadar's workers were mainly boys from surrounding villages, mainly Gounders but also Dalits.[21] He also held an annual function to "expose the trade" to provide public recognition to prompt and efficient workers and stockists. These annual functions brought together not only people in the trade but also key political friends, large farmers, financiers and businessmen, including prominent Chettiars and Gounders. These meetings began by hoisting the flag of the new Republic of India, followed by speeches and prizes, like the political meetings that Khadar had organized for many years as a Congress Party member. Publicizing the industry was, he would later tell his family, an extension of his political work as a nationalist: he saw it as his duty to national development to bring jobs to people in this semi-arid agrarian region.[22]

Messrs Khadar Knitting Co. celebrated its tenth anniversary in 1956 by releasing at the annual function a monograph on the development of the KKC Group. This firm history provides another window into the character of industry under the old guard. The pamphlet begins with a Muslim invocation and a commitment to transparency. S.A. Khadar wanted his business practices to have a public face, in marked contrast to the guarded nature of business knowledge in Tiruppur today. This firm history reveals how the key spokesman for the early decades of Tiruppur knitwear envisioned and amplified a vision of industry centered on fairness in exchange.[23]

The firm history explains how the two subsidiary units in S.A. Khadar's group were born in the inhospitable climate of state control of yarn during World War II. The second unit was begun when Khadar's friend, the mill owner Soundappa Chettiar, provided him a substantial amount of capital to help the initial stagnant unit. The new unit was split into a distinct factory for reasons of physical space. The third factory was a fabrication or cloth production section of a larger spinning mill in Travancore, Kerala, which was exempt from yarn control because of its integrated production system. This acquisition was a way around yarn control, as yarn was made into cloth in Travancore, then sent to Tiruppur for banian production. In both cases, expansion and the multiplication of units was driven by market considerations in the provision of money capital and yarn, and by constraints of physical space. This is an important contrast to the kind of expansion by multiplication of units that would take place in decades to come for reasons of *labor control.*

The opening of KKC's second unit was an occasion for pomp and circumstance, with invited speakers including the former Speaker of the Madras Legislative Assembly, J. Sivashanmuham Pillai, and the Chief Minister of Tamil Nadu, K. Kamaraj Nadar. These were public leaders and upwardly mobile political representatives of non-Brahmin castes. Khadar's public respect to them, and his gestural donation to Pillai's fund to feed and lodge Harijans[24] in Chennai are important for the use of a public opportunity to stake claim to the politics of non-Brahminism and democratization in Tamil Nadu. This broader political role of the industrialist is a primary subtext in the history of the KKC Group: industry "needs steadfast policy" provided by the *vartahar* or businessman, whose "aim is . . . of providing public service rather [than of only making] profit."[25]

Workers and their work enter obliquely into this vision of industry, and when they did it was in the same paternalistic way as the Harijan question.[26] Working-class audiences were clearly important for Khadar's views, for instance in securing labor for the unit at Travancore. Yet, Khadar's concerns centered not on the labor process but on fair remuneration in the sphere of exchange. Khadar acknowledged in public that workers who had been with his group for five years were due certain entitlements, such as health insurance and medical care. As a benevolent patron, he also extended "appropriate bonuses not just at the end of the year but . . . to Hindus at Deepavali, to Mussalmans at Ramzan, to Christians at Christmas . . . [and] at a worker's marriage or other important occasions."[27] Against the rationalist discourse of communist party organizing, Khadar's appeal to workers' differentiated religious affiliations was ammunition for anti-communist politics.

The main theme in Khadar's vision is that fair conduct as businessmen requires maintaining market standards. Fairness in the market would be rewarded by due profit.[28] The theory of value implicit in this notion of good business is that the market decides due values of things and metes out rewards of its own accord. Profit then flows back to the entrepreneur as he computes the costs, just as long as all is fairly exchanged. The history of the KKC Group concludes with a long list of stockists and agents provided "a special year-end commission . . . for their efforts."[29] The last page of the history charts sales, yarn purchased and wages/salaries paid annually from 1951 to 1956, as part of Khadar's commitment to transparency and fair business.[30] Khadar's market-centered understanding of industry held the customer supreme, and the history of his group provided an opportunity to publicize his commitment to transparency and to build "mutual respect" between him and his customers. When encouraging his young workers not to smoke by providing a small bonus for shaking the habit, he admonished that this may "spoil *customers'* minds and bodies" (my emphasis).[31] This statement provides a window into a notion of valuation in which the physical attributes of labor are imbued in the product.

I draw this insight from Richard Biernacki's comparative social history of labor in England and Germany, in which he argues that Marx's key insight was to bring the German notion of *Arbeitskraft* or laborpower—labor capacity as performative and transformative in the production of value, which resonated with the quotidian work practices of German weavers—into English political economy debates. The latter were based on the notion that labor was alienated from workers and embodied in things exchanging on the market, a notion of valuation that resonated with the everyday practices of English weavers. This discursive differentiation was part of the cultural process through which experiences of labor diverged in technically identical industries across two different social formations.[32] A similar divergence within the same social formation appears between the older owners and upstart Gounders of working-class origins. Old guard owners saw knitwear as another business, so that even while putting labor and machines to work, their sights were set on fair exchange. Gounders would draw from their agrarian histories a different sensibility as working owners who saw work as exploitative in Marx's sense of value deriving from transformative practice in the labor process. The older elite would not notice their Gounder ex-Workers starting tiny stitching sections and dismantling the industrial structure from within until it was too late. By then the rug was pulled from under their feet. The next sub-sections turn to the character of unionism and work under the old guard.

Early Labor Unionism in Tiruppur, 1940s

G. Velusamy was one of the labour organizers who initiated the union-ization of knitwear workers in Tiruppur. As a spinning Mill worker, Velusamy participated in the early labor movement's fight for the most basic rights in spinning mills, including the right not to be beaten at work. When the spinning Mill workers' union struck for a War Allow-ance, a "living wage" supplement to keep up with wartime inflation, banian workers from Tiruppur came to their support. This first show of class action came even before banian company workers had won the eight-hour day in Tiruppur. Velusamy began narrating his story insisting that, until the mid 1940s, both workers and manufacturers in Tiruppur knitwear were Muslim. "One gave the wage the other did the work." This communal rendition is similar to that of owners of his time, but is strikingly different from the worker's narrative in the next sub-section.[33]

Everything changed at independence, when the banian industry started growing, drawing workers from Tiruppur's rural hinterland. Velusamy represents this transformation, in his words, "as a Commu-nist should," in a detailed list of factors that made Tiruppur's industry: the railways, good water from the Noyil River, small children, low wages, yarn from Coimbatore, machines from Punjab, and a growing home market for banians in post-1947 India. What is especially inte-resting in this order of things is the last element: changes in local con-sumption that accompanied rural working people's shift from country to city:

> Many people didn't know how to wear clothes then . . . when they first went to the mill to work. They didn't know how to wear a banian. Only in the 1940s when they went to the mill they would buy *khadi* cloth and get a banian stitched. In 1938 Asher Mill was started and villagers came and joined it. Asher was fully people from villages . . . They ate like in villages . . . They would come on foot, upto fifteen miles. Nobody knew how to drink tea. They started giving tea in a couple of places, and we became familiar with it in the mills. Then they stopped it. We struck. Then they said no, you have to pay eight annas for tea. When the habit was formed we had to drink it and then we had to pay . . . When they

came to Tiruppur they started cutting their hair. Before that they had *kutumis*, but they had to cut them. If you cut the *kutumi* it takes away strength, lowers the rank of our caste . . . So they wouldn't cut it at first, but the ones who went to the mills started to. Then they came to mills and became familiar with different things. There was a general social transformation from the old culture after independence. As society changed, people started wearing banians; the banian-wearing culture started. Spider started holding exhibition stalls in Coimbatore, Madurai and advertising in big cities.[34]

Distancing himself from these changes, Velusamy described the ways in which these first industrial workers from the countryside had to change their bodily habits.[35] Despite being a self-described rationalist, Velusamy was nostalgic for caste status lost through the cutting of the *kutumi*.[36] Moreover, Velusamy suggests that as rural workers were habituated to industrial work and to new patterns of consumption, as in wearing banians, they had to renegotiate their place in local configurations of power and status. The worker drawn into wider social transformations visible to the communist is clearly gendered as the worker whose sweat makes the banians that he can wear, as advertised by early companies such as Spider. There is certainly a utopian element in this rational masculine worker, shorn of his caste, if not gender, making mass consumer commodities that he might also consume.[37] When the first workers from the countryside, unaccustomed to industry and urban life, proved a challenge to early union organizers, the latter sought to draw them in through foreign icons and sports.[38] "We couldn't have a union with these small children [workers.] So I arranged a celebration for *Poo Pongal* [festival] at the banks of Noyil River. People used to come to the river. So we put up Stalin's photo, Lenin's photo and all that . . . and had a girl's race with 1 *paun* as the prize. That's when we started the union."[39] The CPI comrades drew young men and boys into the fledgling union not by appealing to their sense of exploitation, but by organizing sports events along the river as part of a festival. Once they had signed up, a wider repertoire of organizational tactics could be used to keep workers involved, but this was not Velusamy's concern. Indeed, Velusamy was imprisoned in 1948, while the ban on the CPI was still in effect, so he could not have much knowledge of day-to-day union relations with rank-and-file workers. After several years and many escape attempts, he was released from prison and went to Bombay to work until the ban on the party was revoked in 1951. On his return to Tiruppur, Velusamy found the industry changed in ways far beyond his experience. He found "the man who used to cut banians and clean the floor is now an owner."[40] Some of these Gounder workers-turned-owners supported Velusamy's return as a local communist leader. However, Velusamy never spoke concretely of labor politics in his life history. On the contrary, he held a strong sense of owners' right to market share and to fair competition. Like the old guard of company owners, this union leader's vision centered on fair access to markets, fair prices and the right kind of policy to maintain these goals. Removed from their shared vision was the politics of production.[41] A gulf separated owners and labor leader from workers' everyday experiences in the labor process. I turn next to how a very old worker remembered his years in the early period of industry.

Memories of a non-Gounder Worker, 1930s–1960s

The recollections of Abdul Rashid, an old Muslim worker, were at considerable variance with the views of bosses and union leaders. Rashid remembered neither the communal politics of work that recurs in elite narratives nor the organized class-consciousness assumed by the labor leader. The narrative strategy employed by Rashid is far more personalized and tentative about generalization, in direct contrast to the Velusamy's objectivist account. Rashid stresses caste and communal diversity among workers who nonetheless came together through the act of work:

> I came to Baby Knitting in Khadarpet when I was very young. There were only 7–8 companies. Owners were Muslim and Hindu. I worked on knitting machines. In those days they did bleaching in their own companies. They would do all the things [in the same place.] There were 10 to 40 people in each company. Workers were from inside Tiruppur: Chettiars, Gounders, Muslims . . . all were there. Now it's changed. Then we were all like *annan—tambi* [older brother—younger brother.] In the place I worked, only 4–5 Muslims were there, the rest were Goundammar, Chettiar, Mudaliar. We were many *jadis* [castes or communities] then . . . and we became friends.[42]

Rather than being communalized and politically fractured, Rashid felt cameraderie among the all-male workforce of his time. He also emphasized that workers did all the work, even bleaching, within the company, in contrast to today's disintegrated workplaces. Factories had as many as forty workers skilled in all aspects of knitwear production. While Abdul Rashid had the same knack with machines as some of the early entrepreneurs, without access to family money or business networks, he remained a worker. In traveling all over the South as a Ludhiana Punjab Machine Works knitting machine fitter from 1952 to 1994 or so, his narrative suffered a similar break between past and present as the union leader, Velusamy. Lines blurred between Communist, Congress and industry leaders as he rattled off names from memory. He joined the Muslim League because "we need a party," implying "they"—Gounders—had captured the party that represented workers. While he became an itinerant machine fitter, however, Rashid also noted the phenomena that some of his fellow workers of the Gounder caste had become owners.[43]

> By 1960, companies became big. Like Maximum[44] Govindasamy . . . we used to work at the same time. I knew him, Maximum. Now he's a big rich owner. They were like me once . . . Gounders. Not many Muslims grew that way. Gounders mostly . . . You need help from people. *Máman, maccán* [men related through marriage], gold that can be put in the bank to buy a company: like that they grew. We can't get money on interest. We have rules: don't take money on interest or trouble anyone. They take interest; they do whatever they want. We have rules; they don't. We shouldn't harm anyone, take interest, have affairs, drink alcohol. That's why we're going the way we do. If Muslims had money they could have companies. S.A. Khadar did, his thambi had BBC Akbar, they all had companies.[45]

Rashid's friend Govindasamy passed him by to become a leading owner whose company is now a key landmark in Tiruppur. Rashid had therefore to confront at a personal level the class mobility that destabilizes a stable "subalternity." Rashid's narrative strategy in doing so is to communalize the historical process and to explain class mobility in moral terms. Hence, Gounder success turns on their caste morality, as Muslim failure turns on Islamic piety. Yet, rather than seeing the hold of Muslim piety as absolute, Rashid sees the power of money in

making successes out of elite Muslims like Khadar. Rashid also sees
how his Gounder co-workers could break the hold of the old guard
elite through peculiar forms of mutual assistance among Gounders. By
piercing through the salience of caste and community as constitutive
of self-made men, Rashid revisits the Gounder workers of his past as
different from others: they had "help" but not "rules." Rashid's narrative challenges elite accounts which do not explain the class mobility
that would fundamentally transform the town and its work.[46] Gounders
had access to resources other workers like Rashid did not. Section III
details the steps by which Gounder workers became the town's leading
owners.

III. Agrarian Transition in Tiruppur

This section works through the steps in the interlinked transformations in class, space and place through uses of the agrarian past.
Through multiple lives, I chart the agrarian transition in Tiruppur
through seven moments: first, their agrarian and family backgrounds
as preparation for transition; second, their work histories as rural
workers in the knitwear industry; third, the militancy of workers in the
wake of industrial decentralization; fourth, processes of class mobility
and of "raising" self-made men through dedicated production; fifth,
state intervention through institutional credit to nascent small-scale
industrial owners; sixth, the interpellation of toiling Gounder owners
at work by a shared agrarian past; and seventh, the tenuous hegemony
of fraternal capital thus constituted by the 1970s. Through life historic
and survey evidence, I show how these moments transform the geography of work substantially from its form under the old guard.

1. Moment of Preparation:
Gounder Family Backgrounds, 1930s–

Muthusamy Gounder spoke in rich detail about rural life while sitting
amidst knitting machines in his son's fabrication unit. He began by
telling me of the relative lack of *pana-palakkam*, or "money habits,"
in the peasant agriculture of his childhood of the 1930s near Vanjipalayam, rice-trading village on the main railway line to Madras.[47] Though
they had "no need to buy things"—they never had enough cash to buy
rice, let alone to save—"everyone had to work." In detailing work,

Muthusamy counted women's cooking alongside agriculture as part of the nexus of productive and reproductive work in the peasant household. While they could not buy rice that came by train from the paddy-growing districts to be milled in Vanjipalayam, the rice mills provided the household its first non-farm waged work. Women were employed in drying and carrying rice to the godowns and warehouses, and men would work in the godowns at night. As his siblings married, his sisters left for their husbands' households while his brothers left "to do their own work," outside this semi-subsistence farming. Two brothers bought a bullock cart together and hired out transport services, while another ran a *malihaikkadai,* or petty grocery store.[48]

Muthusamy came to Tiruppur to work at Dhanalakshmi Mills at the age of sixteen as a "sider." In two years he was made *maistry* or foreman who watched over twenty machines, or about fifty workers. He then brought his parents to town to live with him. Seven years later, in 1940, he started a *malihaikkadai,* grocery shop, for which he had to employ an accountant to keep his records and pay sales tax, as he had no formal education. After marrying in 1943 he brought his wife to his new home in the expanding working and middle-class neighborhoods on the north side of the tracks. In 1960 Muthusamy started a power-loom unit,[49] for which he bought *kádu,* dryland, on the north side of the tracks. He ran twelve looms until the unit closed in 1987, by which time he had been president of the Powerloom Association for twenty years. In parallel, he also began a knitting fabrication company in 1975 while his son was in engineering college.[50]

Muthusamy looked back at the agrarian transition he described with a sense of inevitability. "In the *kádu* [dryland farm in the village] they could neither remain well nor eat well. So they came little by little, one after the other, to [non-farm] work . . . there were soon no people to work in agriculture." Part of their quest was for regular wages, which is what industrial work in Muthusamy's day could offer. Wages were so low that families barely survived on coarse cereals and were far from being able to afford the rice that was so important to the economy of Vanjipalayam. It was therefore necessary for agrarian families to maintain rural ties as long as possible. At the same time, increased rural–urban migration created a shortage of agricultural labor.[51] With nobody left in Muthusamy's family to *páduppadu,* to suffer or to tough it out, he was shorn of his agrarian roots. I have used Muthusamy's story to demonstrate a range of non-farm work as rural families diversified their incomes. Muthusamy concluded by dramatizing the draw early rural migrants like him felt, despite breaking with rural life, in an expanding sense of possibility: "If [we] stayed in the *kádu* we'd never be able to *know*."[52]

Gounders came in multifarious ways from the countryside, but familial work and business backgrounds of today's Gounder owners of working-class origins diverged from other routes in significant ways, as Table 18 in Appendix 2 begins to explore. These early Gounder entrants were least likely to be involved in agricultural trade and rural industry. *Gounder ex-Workers* (in italics, as a "route to capital," from Chapter 3) in the domestic association represent the early phase of transition, in which rural families had engaged in some petty trade, work in spinning mills and cotton gins and urban coolie work before coming to work in Tiruppur knitwear. Significantly, family backgrounds in traditional and non-traditional textile sectors, both important elements of the regional economy, were *least* important to the most successful class fraction, *Gounder ex-Workers*.[53] The separation between agrarian and artisanal work, a product of an older division of right and left castes, left its trace in Gounder trajectories.

The survey indices are historical markers: rural diversification into rural industry became more important once the peasant-worker transition opened up opportunities for Gounder farm families to invest in urban industry. Hence, later entrants such as *Gounder* exporters represent the subsequent transitions of well-off rural households, *and* were much more likely to have had families involved in rural industry.

Entrants through the *Gounder* route, who did not work in the industry and remained domestic producers, tended to come from families with backgrounds in small grocery shops, trade and moneylending, work in businesses and unrelated professions. These owners, like *Southerns* and *Northerns* in domestic production, were likely to have family already owning hosiery units on their entry into the ranks of ownership.

Finally, *Gounder ex-Workers* were likely to have had family members involved in some capacity in Tiruppur knitwear prior to their entry as workers. There was a remote chance that their families were involved in agricultural trade and industry. However, it was far likelier for these early Gounder entrants of modest origins that their families had diversified into rural powerlooms or had sought employment in spinning mills, cotton gins and urban *coolie* work, or manual labor of some sort, from which work in hosiery was only a short step. This was the route that Muthusamy had taken, and his son would become a fabrication company owner following his father's cue.

2. Moment of Work: The Difference of Rural Workers, 1950s–1960s

In the days when I was a worker, there was no such thing as time. We would work from morning to night. We were paid daily wages. Sometime later, time came. In the beginning we worked as much as we could. Then, after 1955, time arrived. These unions became strong and union leaders and politicians decided on an 8-hour day. There were clocks and bells to announce the beginning of the work shift at 8, and we would come five minutes early outside. Again at 12:00 the bell would go off for lunch, and again at 1:00 to resume work. Again at 5:00 the bell would come on at the end. When I went to work in 1948 first this system wasn't there. The 8-hour day came much earlier to mills and to other big factories, but to this sort of banian work it came late. People didn't understand this sort of 8-hour day in the beginning. There wasn't that much development. Even if the union leaders knew, the average worker didn't understand it. They'd say, "What's the guy saying something about working 8-hours . . . We've got to work between bells?!" They didn't know they had the *right* to an 8-hour day.[54]

These reflections of Velusamy Gounder who worked in the industry in the 1950s and is now a prominent company owner suggest that early peasant-workers came with different senses of time and work. Rural workers had to become accustomed to the strictures of factory work and the importance of rights "they didn't know they had." Velusamy's suggestion of a "lack" of development behind workers' experiences was perhaps intended for the benefit of this foreign researcher. His memories nonetheless convey the shock with which people with different sensibilities met the temporal discipline of industrial work and found new ways of acting within it. This story is familiar from E.P. Thompson's classic account of the discipline of the clock in English industrialization: "The first generation of factory workers were taught by their masters the importance of time; the second generation formed their short-time committees in the ten-hour movement; the third generation struck for overtime or time-and-a-half. They had accepted the categories of their employers and learned to fight back within them. They had learned their lesson, that time is money, only too well."[55] Gounder workers learned this lesson quite differently than Thompson assumed. Rather than learning that they were dominated by the law of value, they learned how to work in ways that would turn their labor-time into capital. This would require an alternate theory of value which could challenge existing norms at work. In Section II, I argued that the politics of work in the early phase of the knitwear industry was centered on an elite preoccupation with exchange and fairness. The first unions grew by broadening labor's rights in the idiom of fairness in the market. Neither capital nor organized labor represented its interests in terms of day-to-day practices in the labor process. In this section, I focus only on work experiences of Gounder men in this early phase of the 1960s and 1970s, when their quotidian practices began to mark the difference of their work as toil. Tommy Kandasamy's memories come to this point by arguing that rural workers retained a different sense of the space and time of work:

> We came to work for Muslim owners from a 10–20 miles radius. Then Chettiars and Mudaliars started about 30–40 companies. 3–4 people from each surrounding village would come to town. Four of us would come, but wouldn't go back at night to the village. One person would go and bring food while the other three would sleep in the company. We'd take shifts to go back to the village. At 2 *Anas* cycle rent, we couldn't all go. All the ones who have come to the fore have come from more than 15 kms away. If you look at older families from Tiruppur, with grandparents, known people, comfortable homes . . . these people have not come to the fore . . . because they would keep looking at their watch to see when 5:00 comes. When it was five, he'd take his shirt and cover his head and go. He'd go and talk about MGR or Shivaji or Lenin or Stalin— film and politics all night—and then he'd come slowly in the morning,

not even by 8. The workers [from the countryside] would not talk back to the owner. [They] would do all sorts of things . . . stand by the threshold, get water. The town worker would say "no, that's not my job" and go. The rural worker would run and get water. [The town worker] wouldn't get a chance to become familiar [*paḻakkam*.] Workers who listened, the owner would give them any work . . . he'd get O.C.[56] work from them. "Take this cheque to Chettiar's or Gaurava Mudaliar's." I could go into many places and meet people. I could meet agents from all over the country. They would remember me, my face. I'd go and check their orders. This familiarity—going and giving a cheque at the yarn shop, getting a tea for the agent—this, precisely, was capital for me. I only put in Rs 1,500 [as initial capital when he started a unit], which is no capital. These relationships were my capital, my "background." I didn't look at how much I was getting in wages. I did all I could. I never made demands. I worked very hard. Gounders will *toil*. No other caste would stand against this. We suffered more, *toiled* more.[57]

Taken literally, Kandasamy concludes by emphasizing that toiling to the point of suffering is a caste attribute of Gounders. As a metonym, however, the detail Kandasamy uses to bolster his claim speaks of the particular work practices of these migrant workers. Workers like Kandasamy were structurally insecure due to their distance from familial spheres of reproduction. They were forced to collaborate with owners in securing their means of reproduction, in contrast to urban workers. This vulnerability compelled them to take on all sorts of unpaid labors, unlike town workers who would look at the clock and leave. As workers from the countryside, they would have found "unfree labor" around the specified job contract not unlike agrarian work.[58] As rural people, they also carried a more fluid conception of work that traversed production and reproduction, and which relied on power in the guise of familiarity.

On the other hand, compulsion created its opportunities. These migrant workers could use the range of extra-contractual work practices as a way of both learning about the industry and as a way of cementing relationships with people in other locations in the division of labor. Through familiarity, Kandasamy built his "background" or reputation, which retrospectively he could see as a resource to cash in later.[59] What can be surmised is that peasant-workers profited at least as much from social relations as from savings, if not more. While building their backgrounds across knitwear companies, Gounders were also refashioning themselves differently from other workers. Propertied proletarians viewed their options and contexts quite differently from other workers, in ways that could use the petty-bourgeoise possibilities that capitalism offers.

Gounder workers were poised to become multi-skilled through their work careers in stitching, machine fitting, and packing, as all activities were under one roof. Giraffe Nalasamy, for instance, came from the countryside with his two brothers in the early 1950s after the major drought of 1952–3. He joined Star Bhai's company in 1955 while his two younger brothers went to school. For the first three months, he worked without a wage, *palakkartukku,* "to become familiar," in a period of informal apprenticeship. Nalasamy worked for three companies—owned by a Muslim, a Chettiar and a Mudaliar—over a period of six years, where he did stitching, machinery fitting and packing. "Workers of that time learnt all the work. Today's workers don't know anything but the job: if they come to sweep, they only know how to sweep," he said frustratedly. In explicitly contrasting his past with the present, Nalasamy argued that workers like him in the 1950s could pick up a range of skills. Part of this had to do with the fact that in his day and unlike today, "all work was in one place," and part of it had to do with the openness of work contracts for workers like him, encompassing a range of activities as suited production.[60]

The spatial organization of work and the openness of work contracts fueled opportunities for Gounder workers like Nalasamy to become multi-skilled. The survey comparisons speak to what was different about the social relations of work for *Gounder ex-Workers* like Nalasamy. Tables 19 and 20 in Appendix 2, and Table 21 in the text sort through work histories of ex-Worker owners, predominantly *Gounder ex-Workers* and *Other ex-Workers,* but also of a few *Northern* ex-Workers who were employed either as accountants or contractors.

Table 19, Appendix 2, shows that on average *Gounder ex-Worker* exporters entered the industry as workers in the mid 1960s, and, along with *Gounder ex-Worker* domestic owners, worked until the late 1970s, by which time *Gounder ex-Workers* would consolidate their

Table 21: Job Mobility through the Division of Labor

Route	Helper	Sing. Tailor	Stitch	Iron	Cut	Check	Fabric	Acct	Cont
Domestic									
Gounder									
ex-Worker	−55%	−1%	26%	−1%	17%	0%	−1%	1%	12%
Other									
ex-Worker	−35%	3%	16%	−3%	0%	0%	10%	−6%	23%
50% of									
Northerns	0%	0%	0%	0%	0%	0%	0%	−17%	17%
Export									
Gounder									
ex-Worker	−58%	0%	0%	0%	17%	0%	0%	−33%	75%
Other									
ex-Worker	−40%	0%	0%	0%	20%	0%	0%	0%	0%
10% of									
Northerns	0%	0%	0%	0%	0%	0%	0%	0%	0%

Notes: (1) This table was constructed by taking the change in percentages of workers across the range of jobs above at "entry" and "exit" of their work careers. The change in percentages reflect where careers have changed most dramatically, providing an indicator of routes of mobility in the division of labor. Where percents don't change much, there has not been much mobility; where the change is strongly negative, more workers have "entered," and where it is strongly positive, more workers have "exited." The first row, for instance, shows Gounders in domestic production entered predominantly as helpers and ended their work careers as skilled laborers in stitching or, secondarily, in cutting.

(2) The job classifications are standard in Tiruppur and are explained with respect to the division of labor in Chapter 2. "Cont" is the prized work of contractors; "Acct" is accounts; "Fabric" is short for fabrication of knitted cloth; "Sing. Tailor" is single-needle stitching while "Stitch" is garment stitching, which along with "Cut" or cutting, is the labor intensive heart of the production process. "Stitch," "Cut" and "Fabric" comprise skilled labor, with "Iron" next and "Check" and "Helper" last. "Check" or checking is a phase that came in with exports; it is entirely female so it is understandable that none of these men began or ended in this section. "Accounts" is the only section requiring formal education.

hold on Tiruppur knitwear. *Other ex-Worker* exporters only came in as workers on average around 1984, when export production was well under way, and after the structural opening for working-class owners was already made. Gounders also began working at relatively younger ages than other owners who emerged from the working class. Furthermore, Gounders of working class origins, and *Other ex-Worker* domestic owners, worked for a substantial number of years before becoming owners. Moreover, all of them held, on average, one or two jobs, which means that they had much more job security than do workers of today. The bosses of *Gounder ex-Workers* were about as likely to have been their relatives as not, but very likely to have been castefellows, unlike *Other ex-Workers. Gounder ex-Workers* were also much more likely to have been recruited through relatives, while *Other ex-Workers* tended to have been recruited through friends. In both cases, recruitment was informal, through relationships with workers inside knitwear firms.[61]

Of workers who would become owners, early entrants until 1970 were predominantly Gounders. These workers tended to be recruited through relatives employed in companies owned by their castefellows, and they went on to have stable work careers. Table 20, Appendix 2, shows that less than half of Gounder domestic owners and most Gounder exporters said they could save from their wage earnings.[62] Gounders were generally low paid, but saw a slow and steady increase in their wages, which could enable small savings. Finally, a significant percentage of Gounders in domestic production, 20 percent, were members of labor unions for an average of thirteen years.

Wage information does not say much about the character of mobility, which is better gleaned by looking at the entry and exit points of work careers through the division of labor. Using data on initial and final jobs of ex-Workers, Table 21 charts changes in percentages of workers entering and exiting different parts of the division of labor. When read horizontally as arrays, these percentages provide an indicator of the extent to which particular sections in the division of labor were "net" entry or exit points, and hence indicate routes of mobility, to the extent that averages can reveal dynamic processes. For instance, *Gounder ex-Workers* in both associations stand out for drawing in workers as helpers, at the bottom of the hierarchy of jobs. On the other hand, *Gounder ex-Workers* among domestic owners emerged from their work careers primarily as skilled workers in garment stitching and, secondly, in cutting. Alternatively, most *Gounder ex-Workers* among exporters emerged as contractors and secondarily through stitching. Of all workers *Gounder ex-Worker* exporters saw the most dramatic class mobility in their tenure as workers. This mobility allowed the most successful of them, who now fill the exporters association, TEA, to be contractors before spinning-off into bosses. Many *Gounder ex-Workers*, particularly those still in domestic and merchant production, ended their work careers as skilled labor in precisely the sections where manual labor and its control is key: cutting, and most importantly, garment stitching. What is more, this class mobility through cutting and stitching came precisely in the period in which time-rated wages were being replaced by piece rates.

3. Moment of Militancy and Decentralization, 1960s–1970s

While Coimbatore District was a center of communist unionism emerging from the textile industry, the CPI in Coimbatore District was peopled largely by Gounders.[63] Communists gave voice to the concerns of upwardly mobile backward castes such as Gounders through a vocabulary which represented their concerns in caste- and gender-neutral terms. Union militancy and industrial decentralization were dialectically intertwined. An earlier wave of union mobilization that had built the entitlements of the first generation of Gounder workers, met a capitalist offensive in the institution of piece rates, and this, in turn, prompted new forms of worker militancy to defend the erosion of workers' entitlements.

Gentex Palanisamy was one of the "first batch" of Gounders who took over from the old guard in the 1960s. Palanisamy's reflections on his involvement in communist party unions from 1958 to 1965, a good four years after he became a small owner, suggest a period of class conciliation. "When I was a worker," he said, "strikes would not come because unions wouldn't tell workers to strike. Problems wouldn't come. There was automatic wage increase." General strikes increased only after the departure of the old CPI leaders, P. Ramasamy and Velusamy, referred to at length in the last and this chapter.[64]

When Velusamy was around, on festivals Tiruppur would be red. Now you can't see the leader. Now the leader has phones and scolds owners on the phone. Then there were rules. There were wages even if there was no work, and laborers would make cases for all problems. Now there are direct "compromises" settled by unions, and if the laborer gets Rs 5,000 from the company, Rs 2000 is kept by the union, Rs 500 for expenses. Velusamy would make sure that the worker can get back to work. He wouldn't get a settlement and send the worker home. [65]

Palanisamy valued the modest union leader in a time when unions kept workers at work. "Then a worker could put in 8–10 years *service*, now 8–10 days *service*. There's no *service* now."[66]

This labor peace would gradually be undermined with the phased arrival of piece rates. Indeed, oral and archival evidence does not indicate that the shift from wage payment by time to by the piece took place en-masse. Before piece rates were codified through Taylorist time-motion studies and institutionalized through collective bargaining, the spread of piece rates was sporadic. Workers and union organizers speak of a long period during which workers had to be convinced that piece rates were in their interests. Kongu Velusamy's memories explain piece work as one part of an evolving history of class struggle, in which owners used decentralization as a way of buying out labor from under the mantle of unionism:

> After 1960, piece work arrived, because production wasn't that fast with time wages. So owners started giving orders on contract, and workers could work as many hours as they wanted to . . . Workers now worked as much as their strength would take them. Workers liked piece-rates, but unions didn't . . . There was a three-day strike in 1964, then there were strikes in 1974 and 1984. There are difficulties during strikes, which change people of all sorts. Owners consider their problems during strikes and decide not to have one unit but to split it up into three or four. They split the firm for industrial peace. This happened after every strike. After the 1964 strike, stitching units became numerous. After the 1974 strike, people started giving rolls of cloth out to cutting-stitching-finishing sections more. After 1984, people started giving out orders, where the sub-contractor had to buy the yarn and get the fabric knitted and produce the whole garment on contract.[67]

In the early stages of this process, union organizers Punyamurthy and Mohan Kumar explain piece rates as not just a way owners dealt with strike periods, but the way in which they could continue to strip away the rights won through years of labor organization. Owners claimed that piece rates "included" the rights that knitwear workers by the 1960s had: Employee Sickness Insurance (ESI), Provident Fund (PF), Annual Bonus, Gratuity, No-Work Allowance, and so on. Piece rates also became a way of lowering the general wage.[68]

> As new workers were hired, rates were lowered bit-by-bit. Workers thought time-rated work is less because you only get paid for a fixed amount of time. With piece rates, you can go at 7 a.m. and work until 8 p.m. So with piece rates workers could save. Owners used few workers to increase productivity. Unions did not accept this, but non-union workers were the majority. Then owners started using them and slowly eroding the privileges of workers. By taking even existing liberties . . . there was a change to more than 70 percent piece rated workers without any liberties. Finally, unions said okay you can keep workers as time-rated, piece-rated or contract. As rates, you can fix what you want, but as workers, all the needed liberties must be given. Instead of asking for all rights back at once, we have been asking for them slowly, step by step.[69]

In this rendition, workers cannot see that they are being exploited more through piece rates, because they would rather earn more. Alternatively, rural workers may have been unused to the discipline of time-rated work, preferring the flexibility of piece rates. Mohan Kumar adds a sharp rejoinder to the presumption that workers actually desired piece rates: "One reason was to increase productivity, but the real reason piece rates were brought in was to remove workers' rights and benefits. They will say workers prefer it. Workers suffer and prefer it. That's not just is it? To say they don't want their rights isn't just."[70]

Workers' preference for piece rates seemed to confound E.P. Thompson's notion of time discipline. If workers had realized that time is money, capital had fought back with the rhetoric that time is power. Piece rates seemed to cede power over labortime to workers, offering the appearance of more money without technical change or union action. The communist labor leader Mohan Kumar's point is that workers soon felt conflicted, however, by appearing to make more money and have more power while bearing the burden of more intense exploitation with fewer rights.

The main negotiator from the domestic owners' association, SIHMA, who sat across the bargaining table from Mohan Kumar in the intense period of negotiation over the new regime of wage payment, had somewhat different insights into the changing politics of work. Srinivasan's view was that owners brought in piece rates as late as 1972, because of the limitations of increasing the rate of exploitation within the working day.[71] "Piece rate came in 1972. Work was limited in time-bound shift. We wanted more production . . . we wanted to induce labor to give more. They [owners] wanted to work more than 8 hours. [Workers would do] in 12 hours what they used to do in an 8-hour shift. We wanted to induce labor to give more . . . to double the quantity."[72] Work effort was low, from the perspective of this owner, as the working day was already extended to what is still called "1.5 shifts," a twelve-hour day, without overtime wages. Piece rates also provided a way for owners to indiscriminately terminate labor contracts: "At the end they could fire labor. They could say 'you take this money and get out.' " Yet, in Srinivasan's view, piece rates "ultimately helped CITU," the Congress of Trade Unions, the militant labor union of the CPI-M. This owner and SIHMA representative thought that unions slowly resumed organizing workers behind the simple truth that "as per government law, in whichever way you pay labor, they are entitled to gratuity, earned leave, maternity leave, ESI, and so on." CITU would subsequently begin to educate its workers so that they would not, for instance, accept that the Deepavali bonus is "included" in the piece rate. In effect, these shifts allowed the militant communist union to speak to the problems of intensified exploitation and the breakdown of workers' entitlements.[73]

By the mid 1970s, piece rates were the new norm of production relations in Tiruppur. L.M.K. Balu, for instance, told me of a unit of his that was giving time-rated wages as late as 1978. Workers struck at this unit because, in the owner's view, "they felt they'd get higher wages as piece-rated workers . . . So we got fresh workers and restarted on piece rate."[74] In the early 1960s this situation would have been unimaginable. These memories of owners, ex-Workers and unionists collectively reveal a time of rising workers' entitlements subsequently eroded across the board in the shift to piece rates and contracting.

To see how certain Gounder workers were poised to become petty owners during the first strains of industrial decentralization, I turn to the contrasting recollections of a non-Gounder ex-Worker from the 1960s. Arumugam was a jovial man I met ironing clothes on his street cart in northern Tiruppur. A Vannar or "washerman" by caste, he said his father had agricultural land which was lost "on a caste basis" through loans to powerful Gounders in his native village. In 1962, he began work in Tiruppur at Jippy Knitting, a Gounder company, where he began as an apprentice in ironing. Arumugam, like the old worker Rashid, said that there were all kinds of owners and workers in knitwear, and no overt casteism. "It wouldn't come out. Everyone would become familiar in the same way." When he joined Jippy, there were 100 workers in one place and he earned Rs 5.25 a day.[75] "Now they've ripped it apart into sections. Because they had to give ESI, PF [benefits] and so on, certain owners gave their work to 4–5 sections, with 15 or 25 workers [each], because they'd have to show numbers to the labor office, isn't it? The change was after 1967."[76] Arumugam then shifted to TM Knitting, another Gounder-owned company, where he earned Rs 9–10 per shift for an eight-hour shift. In his next job, in Taipei Knitting, owned by a Chettiar, he was paid a piece rate of Rs 1 per dozen. The explanation given by the owner was that these were collar shirts, not plain banians as in Jippy and TM, so the work had to be piece rated. Arumugam couldn't save anything as a knitwear worker, but while he had regular work all year in the beginning of his career, by the end he said most work was temporary. For this reason, Arumugam decided to return to his traditional caste occupation of washing, with his new skills in ironing. He explained his decision in terms of the transformations in knitwear work that passed him by:

> They'd give contracts to trustworthy workers, of whichever caste, those who know the work. Owners gave all responsibility to the contractor. It's good profit for the owner. Nobody gets [benefits.] The owner says he has no relationship [to workers]. They kept workers temporary for ten years even . . . Actually, if someone supports you . . . through support, that's

how they came [to be owners.] If you are just within a company and are just a worker you cannot do it. Only if someone says in the bank that he knows the worker so put something down, only then can he rise up. Not from one's own toil. There was work for one to nine months. If there was [regular] work there may have been a chance. You can't be a laborer and come to the front. If someone supports at the bank, one can . . . There's no casteism here. Any caste can know the work and do it. [SC: Then how did Gounders rise?] Yes, they have inheritance. They can manage with inheritance and "background." They didn't just do it themselves and rise. Either they have land, or means, or someone gives it to them. It didn't work for me so I said okay, I'll do my own work.[77]

While the employer offensive through industrial decentralization forced Arumugam to return to self-employment, he could see how Gounder workers could use decentralization to their advantage to rise into the ranks of small owners. Arumugam explains Gounder success in materialist terms, cutting through the ideology of self-made men to the social relations which enabled Gounder workers to "rise." I turn next to the ways in which new owners were nurtured through the transition.

4. Moment of Class Mobility: Nurturing the "Seeds of the Earth,"[78] 1950s–

". . . *suyasámbátiyáttil capital develop-panni* . . ." [. . . having developed capital through self-management . . .][79]

This turning point in Gentex Palanisamy's story of class mobility from worker to petty owner is remarkable for explaining initial capital through self-fashioning. In the next three moments, I explore the broader processes and contextual conditions that link this masculinist appeal to individual agency to fraternal relations between "seeds of the earth" in an emergent mode of power over social labor.

Palanisamy Gounder was part of the "first batch" of Gounders who took over the industry "about thirty years ago." In the late 1940s, Palanisamy and a worker of the Naidu caste started a partnership powertable unit with a few stitching machines. They would get cut-pieces and stitch them into garments on contract for other firms. Palanisamy brought Rs 10,000 as initial capital: Rs 5,000 from his father's land sale and petty agricultural trade, and Rs 5,000 from his own savings as a banian company worker. His former employer, Star Bhai, gave him support, but only in the form of blessings. When the initial powertable unit grew into a larger company engaged in the entire manufacture of a garment, Palanisamy broke off from the partnership. Firm splitting was common among the first generation of workers-turned-owners, as partners routinely broke off to form their own concerns. However, new firms were most often not proprietorships but partnerships with closer family members and landowning kin who would join as "sleeping partners," who would contribute capital for a profit share but would not be involved in day-to-day production.[80]

Through this process of firm expansion and splitting through kin and caste connections, support given to new entrants changed dramatically from the passive blessings of old guard owners like Star Bhai. Palanisamy was reticent in describing how he actively supported others, particularly people from his village, as he felt some of the recipients of his support have since become big owners and would think he was taking credit for their success. To disrupt the narratives of self-made men in such a way would be unthinkable: it would betray the caste and gender exclusions that constitute this secular individualism. Having said this, Palanisamy proceeded to drop hints: "One of the main people in Tiruppur is one of our men . . . Even LMK [a prominent owner] has put together work for many families, their relatives."[81] Palanisamy emphasized that though these new owners were all Gounders with land, they came *without* selling land. "They were given help in starting a unit and then [the supporter] would leave after the unit grew: he split off." Palanisamy helped start about five units in this way. Palanisamy's narrative strategy is important: temporary silences are a claim to masculinity *as* self-making, but the slips about "our men" mean all masculinities are not the same. Some men have relied on others, and the hierarchies of masculinity rely on the patron not revealing his patronage. This homosocial structure, moreover, mirrors the dependent chains of "sister concerns" that facilitate subcontracting and dedicated production. Finally, when men like Palanisamy speak of supporting others, they often use the language of *valarcci*, "growing" or "raising" bosses, in the same idiom of raising crops or livestock. With this productive, biological metaphor, the making of bosses seems more a matter of nature than of power and gender.

Through my first year of research, I presumed that support for Gounder class mobility would come through interlinked ties of family, kinship and patronage. The life stories I collected, however, confound simple formulation. Part of this is intrinsic to the veiled secrecy of support. For instance, L.M.K. Balasubramaniam, or Balu, the man Palanisamy referred to as an owner who supported many others, claimed that he neither received much support nor offered much in turn. Of the forty-two Gounder males who came from his village to Tiruppur knitwear, six came before him, but he said he himself never searched for his relatives' help. This was an ambiguous response. What Balu said unambiguously was that people did not come to be owners by saving money from agriculture, but primarily through "our toil" and "bank support," which I turn to in the next sections. Balu's own story of self-making, however, hinges on relations between brothers.[82]

Balu's home village had suffered from severe drought, forcing his father to sell land early on and shift first to petty trade, then to tenancy and subsequently to plantation labor in the Nilgiri Hills. When he was twelve, Balu and his brothers went back to their village, in reach of opportunities at Tiruppur, and his father followed after their mother's death. The first two brothers joined banian companies in succession in the late 1950s while they sent Balu to school. The father then bought a bullock cart and engaged in transport and petty trade between town and country. Balu's two elder brothers worked from 1956 to 1967, by which time they had become accomplished stitchers. By 1967, the brothers had saved some money and had put Balu through SSLC, the equivalent of 12th grade. Balu bought waste or cut pieces, and his brothers stitched them into babies' jetties, or underwear, at fifty dozens per day. Their initial capital in 1967 was Rs 3,000, for one powerlock and one flatlock stitching machine. The capital was entirely from the brothers' savings, augmented by the sale of one brother's marriage jewelry. In addition to the brothers, three boys were hired as helpers. In the subsequent growth of their business, they bought urban land as security for bank credit. Neither agricultural land nor agrarian ties had directly enabled the formation of Balu's initial capital, but work skills, brotherhood and marriage were key.[83]

As Table 22 shows, Gounders were most likely to have family in knitwear on their entry to the ranks of ownership. Both *Gounder* and *Southern* domestic owners started with little initial capital, and indeed several would have started when entry requirements were low. *Gounder ex-Workers* stand out in the export sector as well for bringing in much less initial capital than others, particularly in contrast to *Other ex-Workers*. Proprietorships were rare for most concerns, with the exception of *Northerns* in the domestic sector. Finally, *Gounder ex-Workers* stand out among exporters and domestic owners for how little capital they brought into firms that were predominantly partnerships.

Comparing information on sources of initial capital, Table 23 reveals that *Gounder ex-Workers* secured capital across family, non-farm work and agriculture, while *Gounders* gained stronger support from the farm. *Other ex-Workers* secured capital from family and work. What is surprising is that Gounders are not the highest in terms of family capital, and that their sources of capital were the most

Table 22: Initial Conditions: Capital, Family, Proprietorship

Route	Family in Knitwear	Initial Capital (1000 Rs)	Proprietor	Own Capital
Domestic (SIHMA)				
Gounder ex-Worker	73%	159	21%	81
Gounder	61%	578	13%	94
Other ex-Worker	28%	236	24%	107
Southern	57%	159	42%	131
Northern	36%	1251	73%	822
Export (TEA)				
Gounder ex-Worker	91%	103	9%	47
Gounder	75%	501	38%	258
Other ex-Worker	40%	2080	20%	1366
Southern	38%	411	14%	369
Northern	50%	1571	33%	344

Table 23: Sources of Initial Capital

Route	Family	Farm	Non-farm work	Chit Fund	Bank	Dowry	Land State	Other
Domestic (SIHMA)								
Gder ex-Worker	49%	17%	49%	16%	7%	22%	6%	0%
Gounder	35%	45%	50%	0%	20%	10%	0%	0%
Other ex-Worker	47%	7%	47%	13%	10%	10%	3%	3%
Southern	77%	0%	36%	0%	9%	14%	0%	0%
Northern	18%	0%	55%	0%	18%	0%	0%	9%
Export (TEA)								
Gder ex-Worker	55%	18%	36%	9%	0%	0%	9%	0%
Gounder	13%	25%	75%	13%	13%	0%	13%	0%
Other ex-Worker	80%	0%	40%	0%	20%	0%	0%	0%
Southern	88%	0%	50%	0%	25%	0%	0%	0%
Northern	67%	0%	33%	0%	0%	0%	0%	0%

Note: A "chit fund" is a kind of informal credit union; "dowry" is from the owner's marriage only; "farm" and "family" can be double-counted, but "family" is not included if family members are partners with separate asset and profit shares.

diversified across farm, family and non-farm work, and to a lesser extent from chit funds,[84] marriage dowries,[85] and land sales. Bank credit was key to securing working capital once the business got going. In very few cases were term loans sought from banks for plant and machinery at inception.

Many Gounders, like Uranium Ramasamy, cobbled together initial capital through a combination of savings from knitwear work, and from family and agrarian savings.[86] Often, this was built on prior diversification of income streams in their rural households. These first peasant-workers were not drawn to becoming bosses in any significant degree by support from their kin or ex-boss in the industry. When they became bosses, *Gounder ex-Worker* owners modified the context of class mobility so as to attempt to control who would become owners and how.

However, particularly in the early phase, Gounder men often say they accessed family savings through their *mother*. Marriage dowries were not yet an important mechanism through which men accessed family finance, and indeed Muthusamy, from the first sub-section above, argued that the institution of dowry had only recently replaced traditional practices of brideprice. Muthusamy said, "in my marriage they [his family] gave Rs 125 in *pari paṇam*" or brideprice, half of which went to expenses of the wedding, while Rs 35 went directly to his wife. Gounder families of the bride would demand this *pari paṇam* from the groom's family. While it is difficult to date this transition from brideprice to dowry precisely, it is important that some part of this brideprice may actually have been held by the new bride, perhaps as the seed for the savings fund of the *Goundachi amma*, the mother of the Gounder household. Hence, when *Gounder ex-Workers* said they accessed money through their mothers, it is still not clear what kind of discretionary power Gounder mothers had over the purse-strings, but it seems that sons could make the strongest claims on these family savings.[87]

Lenin Knitting Kaliappan came to Tiruppur after a severe drought in his village in the early 1970s pushed those who could leave to pow-erloom work in the town of Somanur or to Tiruppur's banian com-panies. He came to Tiruppur at the age of twenty-one while his elder brother and mother engaged in petty agricultural trade in rice. Kaliap-pan was too old to be taken on as a helper in stitching, so he got to know (*paḷakkam*) the work on his lunch breaks. In the short span of a year, by 1971, he teamed up with two co-worker friends to start a stitching unit. He brought in Rs 2,500 which his mother gave him from her savings from agricultural trade. Importantly, Kaliappan did not ack-nowledge his brother's role in securing this initial capital. A week after starting a company, there was a three-month general strike which the fledgling unit could not withstand, so Kaliappan went to his sister, and sold her gold jewelry for Rs 300 to keep running. He seems, in this narrative, to be able to acquire his sister's jewelry relatively easily. The new small unit did stitching jobwork for older Muslim companies in the neighborhood of Khadarpet. Kaliappan's partners were dissatis-fied and wanted to leave the partnership a year later because they "had more experience" as workers and could make more money in wages. This is a rare glimpse, in the narratives of self-made-men, into the re-verse flow of petty owners who decided to return to waged work. Kaliappan had a different strategy in mind: "Again I went back to my mother. She had saved sacks from agricultural trade, so we sold several for Rs 3000." Mother's savings again came to the rescue and Kaliappan became a proprietor.[88]

Sometimes mother's support came in the form of her gold jewelry, perhaps from her marriage. P.P. Natarajan got Rs 2,000 from his mother's gold to augment his savings and loans from his village, in making Rs 15,000 initial capital.[89] Blue Sundaram's father stayed on in agriculture and even bought land after he and his siblings came to Tiruppur for work. Despite keeping agricultural land, however, none of the sons ever used the land as collateral for loans "because father is still alive." Sundaram and his siblings first came to stay at his *mother's* house, which she had from her father. His maternal grandfather was also responsible for his first recruitment to knitwear work. When I asked Sundaram about his work career, he said he didn't save, but then added that his mother did. Like many old workers and ex-Workers, he describes being spartan: "We never spent, even on tea." In the context of constrained worker consumption, the *Goundachi amma* continued to be able to secure some part of her sons' earnings and save for the family's future. When Manickam and his brother decided to start a unit in 1972, their initial capital of Rs 600 came from "mother's savings."[90]

When Fine Line Chandrasekhar stopped working, he started a unit in partnership with his *taimáman*, or maternal uncle, who put in 50 percent of the initial capital.[91] The *taimáman*, preferred marital match for a girl, is a key relationship for married women to maintain access to their father's property.[92] The relationship is just as important for men to prevent the dissipation of inheritance, and to use the opportunity of marriage to build firm alliances. For instance, I witnessed a lavish puberty ritual conducted by one of the top Gounder exporters for his sister's daughter. In effect, this owner was linking the prestige of his wealth and productive capacity to the potential alliances his female kin could command. As the *taimáman*, this exporter was using his sister's continued dependence on him for post-marital financial and ritual resources as a means of controlling potential husbands for her daughter. The latter would also allow possible mergers with other knitwear families or perhaps the acquisition of rival production chains. Lavish rituals in this sense represent much more than simply conspicuous consumption, but are part of intricate links between gendered family politics across networks of property and production.[93]

Marriage dowries became increasingly important to the initial capital that young Gounder grooms brought into knitwear companies after the export boom of the late 1980s. My unmarried Gounder friends would tell me how precise dowry giving has become. They could expect several *pauns*, gold sovereigns, a car and perhaps even a building in town, as befits their value as businessmen whom potential fathers-in-law might want to cement ties with. Many young men speak of "*máman-maccán* support," transfers from father-in-law (or maternal uncle) to son-in-law (or brother-in-law), a euphemism for dowry. The traffic in firms leaves in its wake the ties that bind, and Gounder men would often use the formation of firms as a vehicle for cementing marriages, conserving resources given to daughters and reeling-in wayward sons.[94]

Familial relationships are not guarantees for nurturing bosses, however, nor were wayward men easily reeled in. Crown Rangasamy came to work for his *taimáman*'s company at the age of fifteen. As the owner's sister's *son*, however, he is an inessential male relative in that these men are not *pankáḷis*, or male shareholders in family property. The *taimáman* does not have the same rights over his nephew as his niece, nor does his nephew have any resources to gain from him by virtue of kinship. Rangasamy began as a helper and received no wage for fifteen years, while housed and fed by his uncle. It was only after being a power-table contractor for seven years that he could save from his earnings in order to start a partnership company. The *taimáman* did not play a significant role in nurturing his nephew's class mobility. More dramatically, in several accounts, familial relations lead to intensified struggles over property, particularly between *pankáḷis*, who I call "brothers."[95]

As a final case of intertwined family and kin dynamics in the making and unmaking of self-made men, A. Duraisamy received support from his ex-boss to start New Saturn Knitting in 1969, to which he brought Rs 1,000 initial capital from his father's work as a *kaláskárar*.[96] When he married K. Saraswati in 1974, she brought Rs 12,000—which their manager today calls "*tāi sottu*," or mother's inheritance—which they invested in a new partnership company called Dint. Their share in Dint was in the name of Duraisamy's "brother," Ramasamy, who was initially a working partner who did not bring in any capital of his own. Duraisamy said: "New Saturn even paid for Ramasamy's marriage," but Ramasamy proved to be an errant "brother." In the late 1980s he demanded a quarter of the firm's assets when he decided to spin off into his own firm. Duraisamy and Saraswati now rue the day they wrote his name on the company deed. Dint closed in 1988. While Gounders could draw on extensive notions of brotherhood, these were no guarantees of trustworthy ties. Fictive fraternity could be made and broken for entirely instrumental reasons.

Meanwhile, Saraswati's father had diversified their family concerns from farming into bleaching in the early 1970s. When her elder brother and another "brother" started Yummy Garments in the late 1980s, they sought her support as a third partner. She brought in Rs 30,000 as a "sleeping partner" in Yummy, which she said was from her husband, Duraisamy, in all probability from the closure of Dint. In effect, the brothers sought to use Saraswati to access their brother-in-law's capital, but by the early 1990s they were "released" from the partnership. Devaraj, Duraisamy's "brother," was put in charge of Cute, but he also proved to be an errant "brother" when he made off with Rs 1.5 million to start his own unit. Finally, Duraisamy was "released" from his partnership in New Calcutta in 1994 and he now controls Cute with his wife Saraswati as the "main manager."[97]

Mechanisms for making and unmaking companies were remarkably similar for Gounders between the 1970s and into the 1990s. There are some peculiarities in the story of Duraisamy and Saraswati, however, not least that it is exceptionally rare for a Gounder woman to seize to this extent the opportunities provided by her pivotal role in forging property alliances and transfers. This is a rare instance in which one of the women who enables several self-made men actually enters center stage. Secondly, their story was different from other Gounders in that neither of them could sell or pledge ancestral agricultural land. His father didn't have any, and her father's land was converted into a bleaching company which is now a dying unit controlled by her brother. While there were several mechanisms to effect an agrarian transition, Gounders' use of land in accessing credit for working capital was a key way of amortizing initial capital to enable the process of productive reinvestment to take hold. In this, the allotment-holding proletarian found favor in the policies of newly nationalized banks.[98]

There were a variety of ways in which self made men were nurtured and raised by their ex-bosses, co-workers, family and kin. The processes of making self-made men, and their sister concerns, are gendered in multiple ways. Many new owners in Tiruppur continued to struggle on the margins, and many slid back down into wage work, where, certainly in the 1970s, income was steady. On the other hand, the mark of arrival was introduction to the bank.

5. Moment of State Intervention: The State Bank of India and the Creditworthy Peasant, 1960s–1970s

The bank [State Bank of India (SBI)] liberalized its terms in the 1970s in order to promote small scale industrial units. 1969 onwards, [SBI decided nationally that] loans should be need-based, not security-based. This involved a certain amount of risk. We had to see the person. We had to see his background. A person who has come from the laborers stage to start a unit by himself, he should be an enterprising man. He will not give false promises and he will not go back on his word. After 1972, lots of Gounder community people started coming, once they got loans from banks. Upto Rs 25,000 the bank said you do not need to be security-oriented.[99]

Before 1960, SBI was lending to the rich. 1970s brought many borrowers from hosiery.[100]

It has become commonplace that state intervention in industrialization in Tiruppur has been circumspect. To paraphrase S. Neelakantan, an economist from Western Tamil Nadu familiar with these environs, Gounders have succeeded *despite* the state and it is this success under inhospitable conditions that highlights the central role of the entrepreneur.[101] Indeed, the state's primary role has been in protecting specific commodities for the SSI sector, defined in investment in plant and machinery, and in providing a range of subsidies that are sometimes more populist than developmental.[102] What I discuss here is state action of a more interventionist nature, central to agrarian transition and industrial restructuring in Tiruppur. While the logic of small-scale populism allowed most "small-scale industries" to either set up front companies or to sacrifice efficiency in lines in which economies of scale prevail, this populism has in fact been generative of small firms in Tiruppur knitwear through the provision of credit. In other sectors and regions, small-scale populism has allowed larger capital to make incursions into the SSI sector. In Tiruppur, state intervention in the supply of credit, particularly working capital to pay for production in advance of final garment production and sale, allowed industrial dispersal, class mobility, and a profusion of owner-operators.

The key agent in opening access to working capital was the State Bank of India (SBI). This section is an institutional biography of SBI's activities in Tiruppur constructed through recollections of staff members from the 1960s and 1970s who saw how the bank provided credit to encourage small-scale industrialists. SBI established a branch office in Tiruppur in 1923, when the mainstay of the town was the cotton trade.[103] Until the early 1960s, bank business was centered on government accounts, pensions and a few large private accounts. Messrs Dhanalakshmi Mills, one of the main spinning mills, was the biggest account holder to whom money was advanced; most private borrowers were cotton merchants. Cash credit advances were given on a "lock and key" basis, where the key of the locked godown, warehouse, was kept as collateral. All advances were fully secured, with limits of Rs 5 to 10 lakhs.[104]

The Small Scale Industrial Development Officer from SBI Madras, Thimmaiah, came to Tiruppur in 1964 and had a daylong meeting in the owners' association, SIHMA, then under the leadership of the Muslim patriarch S.A. Khadar. The following year, SBI started a pilot scheme with the account of two knitting companies: Khadar's own KKC and Sundaram Iyer's Olympic, both owned by non-Gounder old guard patriarchs. Khadar's son narrated to me how his father "prodded SBI" into shifting out of its rigid lock-and-key model into a new system of credit provision.[105]

Earlier, banks only gave credit on receipt of the dispatch bill—that is, the lorry receipt or railway pass which confirmed that the goods were sent to the buyer. After the commodities were in transit, the bank would discount the bill and pay the knitwear owner 90 percent. In effect, the bank would purchase the documents concerning the trans-action (the dispatch memo, invoice from the buyer, railway or lorry pass and demand note), send the documents to the buyer's city, secure the money from the buyer in a given period and finally collect interest from the proceeds. This was called "Documents Purchased."

Under the new system, the bank provided two instruments that allowed credit provision in *advance* of commodity production. "Bills Receivable Limit" would allow a knitwear owner to deposit the buyer's promise of payment in a certain period of time, at which point the bank would discount the promissory note and provide the owner 90 percent for use in securing the means of production. When the buyer finally paid the bank, the additional 10 percent would be credit-ed to the owner's account. A second instrument called "Mandi type loans" advanced 75 percent of stocks in the factory as credit.[106] The new instruments caused a stir among new owners, and at the same time ownership of units started rising much more sharply in the late 1960s, as Figure 8 in Appendix 2 shows.

"Everybody wanted SBI because of its new items," said Zintex Sri-nivasan. In the view of Khadar's son, what was new was that "receipts were enough to build a non-security-based trust."[107] SBI also started giving term loans to buy machines, with either building documents or personal guarantees. Only by the early 1970s, when the amounts of term loans grew larger and there were more defaults, did SBI start asking for collateral security. At this time, Gounders started using their agricultural land deeds for loans in large numbers. Consequently, loan amounts grew from about Rs 30,000 to more than Rs 100,000.[108] The bank was ready to provide support for an agrarian transition already under way.

Murthy, an SBI clerk since 1964, recollects the "sub agent" or branch manager encouraging people to take advances around 1970–2. Industrialists were required to demonstrate that they had 15–25 percent of the loan in hand as working capital or machinery. "Rural land could be used as collateral security . . . and a third party with securities could stand guarantor," but primary securities were often urban land and buildings. Murthy recalls that, around 1970, the loan limits sanctioned by SBI headquarters for Tiruppur was sorely underutilized, so the bank actively sought people to borrow more.[109] Meera Karthikeyan, a major figure among exporters, recalls how SBI pushed him to borrow more than he had originally bargained for.[110] Palanisamy, a staff member in the early 1970s, stressed that more important for security for small loans was "background"—"[Field officers would] know from experience, through gathering information about family background. In good units [owners] would introduce some *parties* [or potential owners] saying 'this fellow is doing well.' If an important customer introduced someone, we blindly gave the loan. 50 percent we go by that only. People would come with the background of such a person. Either they would have worked under them, or they would have known them through some relatives . . . distant relatives."[111] Personal connections with established owners was key, and if these were connections through work as well as distant kinship, they served to reinforce the potential client's "background." Gounders' expansive notions of kinship served "brothers" particularly well under these circumstances. Only for loans over Rs 25,000 was collateral security necessary, and in these cases Gounders often used agricultural land. When I asked how field officers valued rural land when it was used as security, Palanisamy said field officers "would just go to the village and ask and they would simply say. Generally village people wouldn't lie, at least in those days." As the land market developed early in Coimbatore District, it would have been commonplace in villages in the vicinity of Tiruppur to have had some land transactions that could be referred to in valuing land. There was still a remarkable faith in this SBI officer's vision in a kind of rustic honesty that would have prevented collusion by villagers in inflating land values for the purposes of businesses they may have been investing in as "sleeping partners." This was not that important, in his words, because the decision to provide credit was based "90 percent on the person, not the collateral security."[112]

According to a staff member posted to SBI Tiruppur since 1964, by the late 1970s the bank was handling 80 percent of knitwear owners' accounts despite ten other banks in town. Raghavan remembered that security was "either agricultural land, about 60 percent, or factory or house in town." When they used agricultural land, "they would just say at what value" and the bank lawyer would look over the deeds to decide whether the property "belongs without encumbrance . . . Field officers and the common knowledge of bank officials judged whether the land value was right." On the question of defaults, it seems that SBI was particularly lenient and only in the "few cases of chronic defaulters was security seized, sold and the case was sealed . . . Usually some amount was generated and slowly paid off." Other banks seem to have caught up with these particularly liberal practices towards small industrialists only by the 1980s.[113]

A second turning point, in the recollections of Murthy, was a shift from gradual growth in lending in the mid 1970s to sudden growth in the early 1980s, after the Emergency, Indira Gandhi's shortlived experiment with totalitarianism. "People were afraid of losing their black money during the Emergency, so after that SBI lending shot up. All needs of industry were taken care of by SBI and other banks after this point, including very-short-term loans. SBI has never had any losses in Tiruppur."[114] The Emergency was the final jolt through which modern banking took hold of the knitwear industry in mutual dependence, to provide the volume of credit to allow the industry to grow through production networks. While this institutional biography provides a window into the kinds of resources that new owners could use, the carrot of credit is insufficient to explain the way broader relations could interpellate Gounder advantage in production. For this, I descend into the black box of "Gounder toil" in stitching sections at the heart of the division of labor, where self-made men were made.

6. Moment of Toil: Interpellating Place and Class at Work, 1960s–1970s

Because we came from agricultural families, I have [the ability to] toil.[115]

In the morning I'd go to the bank. In the afternoon I'd watch cutting. I could cut and iron, my two brothers could stitch and another brother could also cut. Two of my brothers would wake up at 6 a.m. and start stitching and they would work until 1 p.m. Then they'd have lunch and rest and come back to work until midnight. Since 1967 when we started and at least until each of us got married, we'd all work from 6 a.m. to 12 p.m. daily . . . even on Sundays . . . The reason for our development is bank support and our toil.[116]

Gounder workers did not make a smooth transition from worker to owner. Many worked in their own firms for about five to eight years. Neither did these men rely on family labor to warrant a simple notion of familial self-exploitation in their firms. Gounder owners tended to work alongside their hired hands, and it is in their relationship to hired labor in the labor process that the social basis of their toil lies. A leader of the Gounder community put it to me in particularly euphemistic terms: "the Gounder community has a knack of extracting work in a mutually beneficial manner."[117] What everyday practices on the shopfloor lay behind this "knack"?

A.C.T. Selvaraj, an articulate Naidu industrialist who has watched the rise of Gounders from his midst, explained their advantage through their daily work practice of being "close to labor in order to take advantage of the rights of labor . . . They could extract more work without paying attention to workers' rights." Selvaraj explained how Gounder workplaces of the 1960s and 1970s were different in that "the owners' table was close to the cutting section. Profit was counted in the cutting section and all problems were seen visibly there. Owners would watch each lot and calculate on the cutting table."[118] Arrow Muthusamy spoke of this as Gounder owners' skill in *ner párvai*, or direct supervision, in which *ner* carries implications of frankness and apparent equality, and he spoke of this as drawing from their prior *éduppádu*, or engagement, with connotations of devotion and immersion, in agriculture.[119] Gounder owners were marked by an everyday closeness and involvement with workers, and with a reputation for being able to control work directly. The space of work brought classes into proximity.

In part, this was a calculated move. Gounders were less educated, as Table 24 in Appendix 2 shows. They often hired a *kanakkupillai* or accountant to take care of the books while they took care of the practical task of manufacturing banians. On the shopfloor, the Gounder self-made man could use his practical knowledge in production. I found on several occasions that these working-class owners were the hardest to convince of an interview until it was clear that I wanted to know their histories of work experience rather than formal mastery of business administration.[120] On the other hand, I also met slick accountants, as the man in the Preface who implied that I should forget the uneducated boss: "What would he know, he's only studied till the 3rd [grade.]"

These Gounder owners had finished their careers as workers in stitching or cutting, or as contractors of power table sections, and had typically become multi-skilled in the central production tasks of garment manufacture. They entered the division of labor primarily as owners of *taiyal nilayangal*, stitching sections. The early 1970s saw a profusion of "independent" stitching sections, which bought cut pieces and produced garments. These units were profoundly frustrating for the industrial elite, like one of Tiruppur's textile magnates, Soundappa Chettiar:

> [By 1972,] a large number of small units appeared with a few knitting machines and began to sell knitted fabrics. These *pseudo-manufacturers* are mostly traders [who] get the yarn knitted from knitting units, have the fabric bleached at a bleaching unit and get it tailored from a tailoring unit according to their own standard. These pseudo-manufacturers have no stake in business . . . [They are] not responsible for statutory obligations such as factory license, E.S.I., P.F. and gratuity. The composite units represent the industry in the *real* sense.[121]

Though he was wrong that it was knitting rather than stitching that was going on in these "small units," this Mill owner was disturbed by decentralization because it had begun to upset his idea of industry. Far from being mere traders, these "pseudo-manufacturers" marked a transition to a modern form of subcontracting based on tighter control of labor power in both the detail and social division of labor. Gounder owners of working origins had moved beyond the exchange-centered visions of the old guard, to decentralize and deepen structures of exploitation.

There is a danger in explaining Gounder toil through the self-presentation of ex-Workers, as their fetishism of labor as the basis for capital is seductively similar to Marx's labor theory of value. In taking apart this fetishism of individual agency, I turn to the concept of interpellation to explain how shared historical, spatial and structural relations are instantiated, maintained and transformed in practice.

My argument is that Gounder worker-peasants were interpellated through ongoing acts of toil as a class fraction with particular advantages in the division of labor. This ongoing process of interpellation was located in new spatial practices of disintegrated and networked work in stitching sections, through which Gounder peasant-workers made space in the division of labor to draw in and make bosses of their male kin and castefellows. Class mobility and the making of bosses allowed Gounder men to link power over the labor process to power over social labor in a new politics of work. Consequently, they remade industrial work while remaking themselves as a new class fraction, which I call the Gounder fraternity of decentralized capital.

The crucial point in stressing *acts* of toil is that the sign "toil" functions indexically. Brusquely put, linguistic anthropologists drawing from pragmatic and materialist traditions of semiotics, particularly from the philosopher C.S. Peirce's distinctions between icon, index and symbol, argue that while referential signs such as symbols name or describe in arbitrary ways defined by changeable conventions, non-referential signs are linked to objects in less arbitrary ways. Hence, icons work by resembling that which they represent, as statues resemble particular people. Indexical signs are the least arbitrary of signs, pointing toward the objects or relations through which they have been produced. In order for indexical signs to work, participants must implicitly understand their context of production and use. This shared context, as Alaina Lemon clarifies, "is not limited to the 'real-time' here and now but can include knowledge about the past, about social hierarchies, or about cultural and generic associations."[122] *Acts* of Gounder toil in the division of labor allow specific agrarian structural and historic relations to *interpellate* the production of place and class.

While engaged in these new spatial practices at work, these Gounder men were renovating an older history of agrarian work. Indeed, the centrality of manual labor in stitching and the need for participant supervision and labor control were familiar to Gounders of modest agrarian roots. Gounders could draw on an agrarian work politics forged in the 1930s, hinged on the farmer's participant supervision of differentiated labor arrangements. Remembered through a colonial lens as a propensity of their caste to toil, Gounders could renovate this shared agrarian past in the industrial present. The elite failures explored in Chapter 3, including the aristocratic *Kaniyalar* Gounders, the older guard of industrialists, and large Indian textile houses, can be seen as failures in part because they did not carry these advantages of toil. In contrast, Gounders could secure more absolute surplus value through the sweating of labor *and* more relative surplus value through organizational innovation, to turn their toil into capital.

The hermeneutics of interpellation can only be understood ethnographically, with attention to the ways in which subjects are recruited differently by also making room for acts of misrecognition.[123] In other words, self-made Gounder men can hinge their retrospective narratives of success on *their toil*, naturalizing the sign as marking *their* difference precisely because they are the privileged subjects whose specific historically constituted capacities are hailed in everday acts at work. As an indexical sign in the labor process, toil works specifically for Gounder men who implicitly relate to the context of its production and use. Today's flexible proletariat do not, for the most part, recognize themselves as *ulaippalis* or toilers in this respect. On the rare occasions that non-Gounders stake claims to being able to turn their toil into capital, they know that toil is *not quite* their advantage, and yet some non-Gounder workers have used the structural openings in Tiruppur's industry to forge their routes of class mobility. This *misrecognition* is key to the dialectics of toil, as it both hails all workers to realize the value of their labors, while valorizing the specific labors of successful Gounder owners. Precisely because toil recruits subjects selectively, it becomes the linguistic means for reworking social and spatial difference.[124]

By the late 1960s and early 1970s, Gounder industrialists had remade the industry through two means. First, in order to forge their hegemony over the cluster, a small group of Gounder owners attempted a putsch in SIHMA. Second, and in a more gradual manner, Gounder owners elaborated the process of industrial decentralization and contracting through fraternal networks of linked sister concerns. Contracting, in turn, met the increased requirements for labor supervision and control necessitated by the production of "fine" or 40s count banians that extended and consolidated Tiruppur's reach over the all-India market.

7. Moment of Fraternal Hegemony, 1967–1981

In 1967–8, S.A. Khadar was president of SIHMA. Gounders had the feeling that our community is dominant; we should have a Gounder as leader. 2–3 people joined together and changed him. The government wanted to implement minimum wages. Khadar said the times are changing; we should do it. One group wanted to avoid the government legislation because this is a small cottage industry. Many agreed. One was a registered communist, but even though he was a communist he also preferred a Hindu. Non-Gounders didn't want a Muslim.[125]

The words of this company owner with close involvements in SIHMA reflect the ways in which economic and communal concerns were intertwined. Through a short and quick takeover, a group of prominent Gounders replaced the founding president, S.A. Khadar, with a young man whom they hoped to control as a pawn. Instead, Mohan Kandasamy remains the leader of SIHMA to this day, thirty years later and with a political career that far outshines the performance of his now defunct company. There are many versions of this coup, but what is clear is that at some point S.A. Khadar turned in his resignation in part because of his willingness to accept a State Government Order to pay workers an extra day's wage for each six days worked.[126]

For the decade of the 1970s, SIHMA ruled industrial relations in Tiruppur and managed to discipline militant unions into a new order of class conciliation. The steering committee of SIHMA, composed in the 1950s of Muslims, Chettiars, Mudaliars and a few Gounders, had by the 1970s been replaced entirely by Gounders. This paralleled the emergence of Gounders in all prominent public positions in local politics and associations such as the Rotary and Lions' Clubs, almost to the exclusion of all other communities ever since. Recall from the walk through the town in Chapter 1 that older monuments of Tiruppur have been forgotten with the installation, at the most important intersection in town, of the dazzling silver statue of Palanisamy Gounder,

"Tiruppur *Tandai*" or "Father of Tiruppur." By the 1970s, Gounders had become the upstart elite.

How did "the mother of associations," SIHMA, become the seat of Gounder power over social labor, tightening it's hold over the working class? Figure 8 in Appendix 2 shows changing SIHMA membership from 1956 to 1994. A cursory glance shows a sudden spike between 1971 and 1975/6. A closer look at the lists of dues payments in SIHMA from the early 1970s reveals that a total of ninety-six firms paid dues only for the period of this spike, between 1972 and 1975. In other words, a large number of new firms joined SIHMA while older firms left, and many firms stopped paying dues altogether in the mid 1970s.[127]

One major reason for starting phantom firms was the provision of yarn to the knitwear sector by quotas disbursed through SIHMA. Several owners multiplied the names of their companies overnight in order to access yarn. Another reason was the threat of interstate excise duty, which applied only over a certain volume of business. Both these forms of state control over the small-scale sector tended to multiply numbers of spurious firms. The dispensation of yarn quota centralized the power of SIHMA for a short but crucial period. SIHMA also continued its lobbying functions called for by the subsidy-based system of small-scale industrial policy. In this respect, SIHMA was extending functions established in its first years of existence.

What was new about SIHMA in the 1970s was its ability to build its dominance over social labor in parallel with the deepening of a decentralized organization of work. SIHMA established a mode of regulation of labor unions by institutionalizing piece rates, which could be adjusted only through collective bargaining after the threat of general strike was demonstrated. What is more, these new norms in industrial relations came at precisely the time when Tiruppur began to produce a new variety of "fine banians," made of fine counts of thread, which deepened Tiruppur's hold over the all-India market. Fine banians intensified the labor supervision requirements in stitching. Work was increasingly fragmented and directly controlled, particularly with highly variable and unregulated piece rates in cutting and stitching.

Under the invitation of SIHMA, the Madras Productivity Council sent representatives to Tiruppur to conduct a series of Taylorist time-motion studies in order to fix piece rates for various categories of workers working on different categories of yarn. Unions were drawn reluctantly into the process of instituting these piece rates, although they claimed ex-post that their representatives were absent at the time of the time-motion studies and therefore the 1972 Report of the Madras Productivity Council was biased in favor of owners. The unions remained resolute in their opposition to variable piece rates as opposed to uniform wages. When the dispute was referred to the Industrial Tribunal in Madras, adjudication was in favor of the Productivity Council, and SIHMA found its dominance over the new regime of variable wages institutionalized. A Labor Tribunal decision in 1976 further sealed the Council's findings. Unions continued to fight these institutionalized workloads as inordinately high and unsupportable of a living wage.[128]

An outspoken communist active in labor union politics in the early 1970s decried none less than the old guard union leader Velusamy, whose life I explored early in this chapter, for selling out the working class. In Palaniappan's view, Velusamy had deliberately failed to seize opportunities to protect the working class: first, in the implementation of minimum wage legislation, the very issue which prompted the Gounder takeover from the leader who was ready to accept it, S.A. Khadar; and second, in agreeing to the entry of the Productivity Council and the institution of variable piece rates. With the split in the communist unions at the national level in 1970, following the division of the Communist Party in India (CPI) in 1964, the Congress of Indian Trade Unions (CITU) emerged as the competing communist union of the breakaway Communist Party of India-Marxist (CPI-M), with dissenting unionists like Palaniappan at the helm.[129]

CITU remained the radical arm of labor politics through its early years in the 1970s, where it quickly gained ground to rival its parent AITUC, the union of the CPI, by the mid 1970s. A series of general strikes in the first half of the 1970s reflects the rise of this radical section of the labor movement. In parallel, however, the industrial form was progressively decentralized through the contracting of garment stitching.[130] Often loyal or "familial" workers would be kept in charge of garment sections and were given contracts for work by the owners, who could then say they *owned the machines but not the work.* "Where unions were strong, owners gave the union leader the contract," said Palaniappan, and piece rates were disguised as "shift rates" while leaving workloads inordinately high. Union strength dropped from 100 percent under the undivided communist union to less than 60 percent with the spread of contracting in the 1970s. Moreover, while unions forced SIHMA to negotiate through strikes in 1972 and 1973, a sixty-day general strike in 1974 was a dismal failure due to the withdrawal of support from the older communist union of the undivided party, AITUC.[131]

The politics of work in the 1970s was transformed by the spread of contracting, as the new Gounder owners split off from partnerships across multiple sister concerns. Gounder owners continue to nurture other self made men through the transition to ownership. For instance, Uranium Ramasamy mused about how he had "put together" companies for several "good workers" who worked for him for five or six years. Ramasamy's categories blurred between ex-Worker, loyal worker, good worker, relative and castefellow: Gounder fraternity traversed this ground. So did lines of effective control, as these relations in many occasions formed networks of dependent firms. When I asked Uranium Ramasamy about whether he would invest in the firms he "supported," he replied "I get some money from them and put some [of mine in.] One can get money in all sorts of ways, one can do work, but it's difficult to get the right man. I had to make the right man ready." In other words, repayment was not a problem; the problem was in making the right dependent male bosses. Fraternity, in this context, is decidedly unequal and illiberal, and carries no necessary connection with liberty and equality. Greetings of "elder brother," "younger brother," "brother-in-law," "son-in-law," "maternal uncle" or "father-in-law," are all indicators of actual or potential exchanges of marriageable women or property. In the absence of a strongly paternalist state, fraternity slips more easily into relations of authority and violence, in a horizontal patriarchal form that belies its own apparently egalitarian practice of masculinity.[132] Particular care had to be taken with errant "brothers" with whom there might be potential conflict over property.[133]

The expansion of sister concerns in the 1970s became the Gounder strategy for using fraternal networks to control a web of worksites. In this way, contracting allowed Gounder toil to be writ large over social labor. Only as the center of gravity began to tilt toward export production in the early 1980s did fissures begin to appear in the politics of work. For one thing, it became harder to maintain confrontation and dominance over labor unions when the threat of strikes in the seasonal export sector proved much more expensive, a point which I return to. Here, I want to remain with early critiques of toil from workers and from the first large exporter who shook the style of industrial relations in Tiruppur.

Gounder toil is so much a part of the story of Tiruppur's development that it is difficult to find stories from the 1970s that do not in some way reference it. However, there are instances in which the reference does lay bare its class contradictions. I begin a discussion of the changes in labor politics through the period of industrial restructuring detailed in previous sections with an incident of precisely this nature.

Zippy Nalasamy was a Gounder who epitomized the magic of the self-made man. He was absolutely destitute as a child, but worked his way through the ranks to become an owner in the early 1970s. Nalasamy's story is so dramatic that, once an owner, he was courted by SIHMA to join its steering committee as a personification of the toiling Gounder owner who could not possibly follow labor legislation. He explained to me that because he was a worker-turned-owner, the more privileged Gounders in SIHMA at the time "wanted to know details about work and workloads, the difficulties of workers and how to negotiate with them." Nalasamy had at that time just opened his first "sister concern," Zippy Knitting, in 1974, seven years after opening his first company. He was still a communist, and was close to the union leadership since his active days in the union. When he opened Zippy, Nalasamy decided to pay workers differently from his first unit, on the grounds that the fledgling Zippy would not be able to withstand the same wage rates as the first unit. The union would not accept this. He claims the union said, "We know it's not just, but then why did you pay your first union more?" Nalasamy responded curtly, "You're no communist," and locked out his workers for three months.[134]

A series of posters, unsanctioned by the labor unions, sprang up all around the main streets to the bus station, portraying "Nalasamy the Worker" next to "Nalasamy the Owner": on one side as a thin, monkeyish, emaciated *tolilali*, or worker, and on the other as a fat, cigarette-smoking *mudalali*, or owner. It read "*Andre ní, Indre ní*," or "You then, You now," using the impolite form of "you" nonetheless.[135] This was a spontaneous critique of "Gounder toil" from the crowd, and a damning one.[136]

This kind of protest, unsanctioned by labor unions and away from specific workplace conflicts, is rare to find in the personal archives and memories of Tiruppur's past. What appears in the archives is a range of tactics employed in day-to-day workplace struggles, before the routinization of class struggle in formal collective bargaining procedures. The threat of strikes punctuated the early 1970s, and the SIHMA files on Labor Disputes reveal letter after letter written between 1973 and 1975 by exasperated bosses to the Deputy Commissioner of Labour (DCL), the Labour Officer, or the Sub-Inspector of Police. The letters typically confirm firm-level strikes, decry workers' demands as "extravagant" for small-scale industry, and request arbitration and police protection for property. The letters also reveal a range of tactics employed in labor struggle outside the formal process of negotiation. For instance, on one occasion, the SIHMA President and General Secretary both complained to the DCL that workers led by union leaders "shouted very ugly, very uncivil and unprintable slogans against the President and other office bearers . . . the slogans were very personal and included the family members."[137] Abusing the owner's family meant calling into question the morality of self-made-men, and emasculating them by revealing their vulnerability to representations of "their" women. The targeting of family is also an attack on the individualism of self-made men as well as of the owner myth that Tiruppur is "one big family."

More common were firm-level wildcat strikes, in the form of "stay-out" and "stay-in" strikes, which persisted in this period of transition to institutionalized collective bargaining.[138] On two occasions, frustrated owners describe workers as *gheraoing* or surrounding and restricting the movement of owners and staff:

> The workers are resorting to some sort of objection of movements of the partners and other loyal workers. Actually the partners are being *gheraoed*. Now one of the partners who went inside the factory this morning is not able to come out of the factory because the workers are objecting him. He has not taken his morning *tiffen* yet.[139]
>
> "[W]orkers are *gheraoing* Sri N.R. Viswanathan clerk and Mr M. Mohamed Alli office boy . . . The above two staffs could not go out even for urine and other routine works. Till this time they have not allowed the two staffs to take their tiffen or meals.[140]

These types of techniques of restricting the bodily movements of adversaries have had wide currency in Indian labor movements. While the *gherao* is an old and important form of nonviolent action in India, labor leaders often used the specifically Gandhian technique of controlling one's *own* body to provoke moral obligation from the adversary, most often in the form of *unnáviridam* or hunger strike.[141] On another occasion, workers prevented the owner and his allies from entering a factory, planting red flags in front of his home. Again, workers flout the separation of work and home, owner and his family. What I want to demonstrate is the multiplicity of local forms of unroutinized protest drawn from broader techniques under the mantle of labor unionism. At times, SIHMA would explain its own actions in similar idioms, as in calling a one-day lockout by hosiery owners a "token *hartal*" or strike.[142]

A range of workers' tactics were part of a vibrant labor unionism in the early 1970s, and, as I have suggested, these tactics persisted through the years of successive general strikes in 1969, 1970, 1972, 1974 and 1975. This was the period in which SIHMA and labor union leaders forged collective bargaining procedures. In the second half of the 1970s, until 1981, however, it seemed that SIHMA and the labor unions had achieved a kind of "labor peace," or that the routinization of class conciliation had effectively stemmed labor militancy. There

were no general strikes through this period. The deepening of contracting through "sister concerns" had played a major role in under-
mining labor militancy. There are rumors that the union leaders of the
1970s had been bought out—or that the SIHMA leader had an
"understanding" with labor leaders of the CPI union (AITUC) and
the union of the regional Tamil nationalist party, the Dravida Munnetra
Kazhagam (DMK). The evidence is mixed; it seems more likely that
the DMK leader had made such an alliance, as he is now a part of a knitwear empire himself and had in 1998 arranged a marriage between his
family and that of the SIHMA leader.

The turn toward conciliation and routinization of class struggle in
Tiruppur must be seen in the context of the break in the Communist
Party of India in the late 1960s into "right" (CPI) and "left" (CPM)
communist parties. In Tiruppur, the united communist labor union,
AITUC, which claimed to have achieved 100 percent unionization in
the 1950s and 1960s, had to contend with a competing offshoot of the
new CPM, CITU, which had only 150 members in 1969. Key union
activists from AITUC had defected to CITU, which took a harder line
in conciliation than AITUC. The strongest criticism of AITUC and
the DMK union in the 1970s came from this fledgling CITU. The
1972 general strike of forty-two days was settled by the former unions
without a wage increase, to the dismay of CITU activists, who only had
about 15 percent of the unionized working class behind them. By
1974, CITU had quickly gained membership to match AITUC, while
the DMK union was left in the lurch. A key CITU activist from this
period described DMK union leaders as "union capitalists" who were
openly taking bribes. CITU didn't accept the agreement that came out
of the sixty-day strike in 1974, but signed it reluctantly despite meager
gains to labor. A CITU leader active at the time described it as a "be-
trayal to workers" who lost their faith for the next seven years. Therefore, there were strong currents of unionism in the mid 1970s, with a
radical component represented by CITU, but these currents were in
tension with the deepening of contracting in the same period. There
were only "individual company settlements" after 1974, not general
strikes. The CITU leader saw 1975–81 as a period of defensiveness, of

"rebuilding the union," as the Gounder fraternity had quelled labor activism for the while.[143]

A pivotal series of incidents shocked these myriad forms of protest and transformed industrial relations for both SIHMA owners and labor unions, with the arrival in Tiruppur of a strange character. If one personality could mark the shift the tenor of class struggle as Tiruppur's center of gravity moved toward export production, it was Antonio Verona, a mysterious Italian from Milano, rumored to have had Mafia ties, who eventually died in Ethiopia after being barred from entering all European countries. Antonio Verona came to Tiruppur in 1979 through Calcutta exporters who had begun sourcing from Tiruppur. In a few years, he practically took over a stagnant unit, run by an ailing *Gounder ex-Worker* with an incapable son. Verona told the bankrupt owner of City knitting, "You're the owner on paper. I decide how to do things." The owner had a somewhat mysterious heart attack soon after this. In the meantime, Verona had City build a huge 10,000 square foot factory "fully integrated" with processing, though completely contracted internally. Verona knew that if contracting could harness toil to big capital, Tiruppur could go global.[144] "Before Antonio," said Chad Green, an American settled in Tiruppur who worked for Verona for a while, "an average company exported a case a day, while Antonio did 7,000 dozens/day." Verona was the first high-volume foreign buyer from Tiruppur and his account at SBI of Rs 2.5 million per year was bigger than anyone else's, as SBI staff still concur. Verona sent one shipment of eleven containers to Europe and by the time it reached the shores of Italy all the garments had "Made in USA" tags. There remained no trace of India on the identity of the goods. By the early 1980s Verona could be found in his lavish home lounging by the poolside with his Tamil secretary-lover. As a representative of the global, Verona had ruptured the boundaries of local production, but it was when he went after organized labor that the Gounder fraternity took notice.[145]

The normal course of industrial relations around 1980 was that unions would use the threat of strike at the festival of Deepavali in October, when workers were due their Deepavali bonus. SIHMA, the domestic owners' association, had by this time begun to take on a hard line on labor. In 1981, SIHMA tried to arrange with union leaders to

have the strike in April instead, "with the idea that if you starve the
workers in April, they won't strike at Deepavali." April was, however,
at the tail end of the export season, and time had become expensive for
exporters, a marginal presence in the domestic owners' association.
Mohan Kandasamy, the head of SIHMA, called the strike. Verona
moved fast. He had an advertisement drafted immediately for the
Tamil dailies, which began by describing how he came to Tiruppur
and struggled to feed 3,000 families. He then had two choices of para-
graphs to finish the story. "(A) This has all been discussed with the
union leaders and all my factories will run with a 25 percent increase,
less than the 50 percent asked for by unions, more than the 10 percent
offered by SIHMA; or (B) This has all been discussed with the union
leaders and they, the unions, will have to support 3,000 families from
now on." He called the union leaders to his office and said, "No negotiations: A or B." According to Chad Green, "They didn't know what
hit them. At 9 a.m. the next morning, the papers had A on them."
Later, with a crowd of Gounder owners assembled in a Gounder marriage hall, Mohan Kandasamy of SIHMA came to plead with Verona,
now at his poolside, but it was too late. "Antonio had opened up
Tiruppur."[146] Industrial relations would never be the same, and SIHMA
would give way to a new class of owners who would concede to unions,
at least on paper. More importantly, a new class of Gounder exporters
could now begin to consolidate their power in a new owners association, the TEA, while deepening a gendered form of class domination
behind the veneer of routinized collective bargaining procedures.

IV. Conclusion: Gounder Toil and
Fraternal Capital

By the early 1970s, Gounder men had forged their class mobility by
elaborating a fraternal form of decentralized control over networks of
sister concerns, and by institutionalizing their hold on Tiruppur
through SIHMA. As the toiling fraternity circulated in and between
workplaces, working alongside their workers while maintaining networks of "brothers," they performed Gounder masculinity and camaraderie in the ongoing work of regulating social labor. In this practice
of work discipline, an ideology of individualism stands in tension with

its exclusionary social and cultural conditions of possibility.[147] In historicizing the toil of self-made Gounder men, I have sought to show how their self-presentations are the product of the ongoing interpellation of the industrial present by an agrarian past. In doing so, I have shown how an entrepreneurial caste has learnt to deploy its alleged caste character, to turn subaltern knowledge to capitalist advantage.

Gounder toil was a specific resource that Gounder men could recall, through their shared agrarian and colonial histories. The counterfactuals in Chapter 3 support this argument that in fact toil made the difference that access to capital, labor, markets and political influence alone could not provide. Yet, this synergy also required the right timing, the right kind of policy with respect to subsidized credit, and the right turn in local class struggle. While Gounder toil could become an instrument of power over social labor through the deepening of hierarchical producer subcontracting, Gounder toil was not enough to contain the twists and turns of capitalist development. A strange Italian intruder "opened up" Tiruppur to high-volume production for export by harnessing the combination of sweated labor and organizational innovation that made the whole town work. The voice of organized labor grew strong, but would subsequently be disciplined.

The recollections of a non-Gounder rank-and-file worker speak directly to the tensions of Gounder toil: to class mobility and its constitutive exclusions. Disco Ravi has been a cutting worker from the age of twelve to twenty-eight and is a staunch member of CITU. I asked him about whether it's true that many workers think they'll become owners. He responded, "That kind of thought is there; even I have it." I asked if he had friends who've gone from worker to owner. "Oh, many, there are many," he replied, adding, ". . . owners to a certain extent: First they went on a cycle, then a scooter and now a [motor] bike; to that extent. Some are even in the party." Ravi's optimism about becoming an owner was soon tempered by his views on those who have, through caste and gender exclusion. "They only try to suppress other men. Suppose a Gounder boy goes to work they'll give him preference . . . he's 'our boy,' '*mappilai's* boy,' 'sister's boy,' let him have his own section. Give him some extra. If I do it they'll say, 'give the guy Rs 0.25;' for him they'll say 'okay, give him Rs 0.50.'

I keep going down; his wage keeps going up. Most of the big company owners are Gounders. 'We must look after our men.' Their only aim is to look after Gounders. Whether they're big or small, they support each other."[148]

Ravi is cognizant of the possibilities and exclusions of Tiruppur's self-made men. He is cognizant, that is, of casteism, though his words index gender directly and in specific ways. The problem for Ravi is that not all men can be nurtured to become owners, but many continue to hope that they might. Gounder toil encapsulates the dialectical tensions of Tiruppur's modernity. By transforming the structure of work from within, Gounders of modest origins open a route for continued class mobility through toil while challenging an ascriptive notion of caste as determinative of occupation and social location.[149] As a specific labor theory of value, toil also provokes a challenge to capitalism by summing up the specific demands of the exploited to the fruits of labor and the dignity of work. Toil opens progressive possibilities while foreclosing them through the constitutive exclusions of capital in working class clothing. To critically interrogate Ravi's thoughts from the perspective of today's differentiated workforce, what is striking are the very different gendered interpellations in the views of other workers who cannot imagine their toil becoming capital. While the practice of fraternal capital became more tenuous in Tiruppur's transition to export production in the 1980s, a seemingly unified fraternal hegemony unraveled into multiple gender politics at play in the dynamics of work.

CHAPTER 6

Gender Fetishisms and Shifting Hegemonies, 1974–1996

I. Introduction: Fraternal Capital and the Feminization of Labor

Gender appeared as an analytic for scholars concerned with Tiruppur precisely in the transition to exports, as the knitwear labor market shifted from an entirely male preserve to a highly differentiated workforce.[1] There are decidedly unsubtle reasons why experts and participants equate gender with the entry of working women and their specific concerns. The problems of working women, however, have to be seen as part of a transition in the gendering of work from the fraternal discipline of an entirely male workforce to a new mode of regulation of an increasing diversity of workers, wage levels, skill classifications, types of security, exposures to violence, and forms of sexualization. I call the emergent form of power over social labor a subtle and insidious form of gendered hegemony. Gender does not stalk around with male and female written on its forehead. Gender fetishisms are potent precisely because of the way in which they harness sexed bodies to broader projects of differentiation.[2] In doing so, gender becomes a powerful sealant for multiple dimensions of social inequality. The difficulty that feminists have long addressed is in the way gender structures and discourses limit radical rearticulations of sexed bodies to notions of difference that challenge rather than deepen social inequality. Consequently, many, including feminist geographers, have sought to chart the concrete ways in which spatially and temporally overlapping sex/gender structures work to maintain inequality across a range of linked, unequal practical contexts, of family, work, market, government, and labor and civic organization.[3]

This chapter charts a path through overlapping, gendered spatial structures in Tiruppur's transition to exports, to show how capital accumulation shifts from a fraternal hegemony in which Gounder toil is a source of class mobility, to a gendered hegemony based on the routinization of work and the deepening of class antagonisms in more pernicious forms.[4] I use the term gendered hegemony, not because of rising numbers of women workers, nor just because of deepening gender divisions of labor, but because, as I demonstrate, new articulations of sexed bodies to notions of difference mark gender explicitly. Disco Ravi, my last interlocutor in Chapter 5, could be read to say that nobody was supposed to notice the masculinism, as opposed to the casteism, of fraternal capital.

This shift from fraternal to gendered hegemony, moreover, derives from very different geographies. Whereas fraternal hegemony emerged through a geography of movement from country to city, gendered hegemony resonates with much wider circuits of power and knowledge. The late-twentieth-century global discourse of the "feminization of labor," operating through transnational media, scholarship, advocacy, production and other networks, had assumed a natural connection between dexterous, docile, Asian/Latin American female bodies, on the one hand, and cheap labor for footloose global capital, on the other.[5] The groundbreaking feminist critiques of Third World industrialization fought these fetishisms as untrue, while recognizing their generation of new forms of postcolonial peripherality. The acceptance of feminization as a real thing, whether to be defended or opposed, relies on linking sexed bodies to global differentiation, so that export-based peripheral capitalism can seem to *require* disciplined female labor. Subsequent work has asked how feminization works as a powerful, productive fiction to violate the entitlements of a variety of groups of people rendered marginal and perpetually insecure by contemporary capitalism. However, these differentiated labor markets also work as niche markets in sexual violence and pleasure, to undermine the phenomenal grounds for labor solidarity based on romantic, masculinist conceptions of male breadwinners with sound family values as the vanguard of labor militancy. The effects of feminization reverberate through global relations of production and consumption, altering expectations for labor, capital, consumers and intermediaries in multiple and indeterminate ways.

Hence, rather than write on these themes with a defeatism that fetishizes the abject Third World woman worker, hunched over the production of First World commodities, I begin by questioning shifting hegemonies in the transition of exports. I then turn to new articulations of working bodies and difference in the 1984 strike, the height of Tiruppur's history of working class struggle. This 127-day strike revealed in public the fissures in fraternal hegemony, while gendered pedagogy in union street theater shows the complicity of organized labor with an emergent gender regime at work. Indeed, the workplaces and work experiences of the 1990s show the underside of export growth in a realm of heightened sexual violence, and limited agency, in the context of fragmented exploitation. This contradictory work regime, moreover, has spawned a variety of gender fetishisms that claim to speak for working women by upholding very different conceptions of conjugality and sexual morality. Relating multiple notions of femininity back to hegemonic masculinities, I return to the remaking of Gounder toil in a period of strong consolidation of capital under the aegis of TEA. As a last reminder of the importance of gender performance and its many foibles, I reflect on the story of an important heist that played the fraternity and won, through globalization by fraud. The gendered spatial structures that work through these narratives do not articulate as seamlessly as does Gounder toil in making fraternal capital in the 1970s. The multiple femininities produced by Tiruppur's gendered accumulation are not forged through common sensibilities with respect to Gounder toil. Instead, gendered hegemony pushes the class dynamics latent in fraternal capital, intensifying export-led accumulation while fragmenting lived experience and deepening inequality. I conclude by situating this account of shifting gendered hegemonies in a broader terrain of gender and accumulation in provincial Indian capitalism.

II. Fraternal Discipline in the Transition
to Exports, 1974–1984

No sooner than Gounders had forged their caste domination of the town than tensions of export production become more acute for their fraternity of capital. Indeed, Gounder control in SIHMA, the association of local producers, was challenged for the second time by an ascendant class-fraction of Gounder exporters who formed the rival association, TEA, begun in 1980 by the nephew of the SIHMA leader. But the new association was more than an expression of tensions between *máman* and nephew. The ascendant class of exporters was unlike the Gounder owners who had achieved the upper hand with organized labor through piece rates and contracting. Exporters could not afford overt confrontation with labor because of the risks associated with time and quality in the fast world of fashion garments.

These Gounder exporters also did away with many of the trappings of their fathers and fathers-in-law in SIHMA. They seldom wore a starched *vécti* and *kaddar* shirt to work; most wear Western office attire, and the head of TEA often wears sunglasses indoors. These men fancy themselves as urbane, which is why, when I asked one man about caste, he snapped back, "We in Tiruppur are a cosmopolitan people." Most importantly, these men do not spend time on the shopfloor with workers; they are much more hierarchical in their approach to staff, and retreat into their tinted, airconditioned offices, safely out of view of their laborers. I return to the continuing forms of personal involvement in production networks, but my first point is that TEA exporters represent a form of class consolidation from within the fraternity of Gounder capital accompanied by new forms of Gounder masculinity. As this apex class fraction of export-oriented capitalists has emerged from the fraternal hegemony of Gounder domestic owners to now rule the roost, they have done so by fashioning a cosmopolitan masculinity with Gounder characteristics.

These cosmopolitan Gounder exporters supervised the feminization of labor along the lines of wider attempts to equate cheap labor with docile and dexterous women workers. While the pioneering scholars of gender and industry since the 1970s saw the entry of women workers as a complement to transnational capital's search for cheap labor, more recent ethnographic research asks how discourses of femininity and masculinity are used in the politics of production, in managerial attempts to discipline workers.[6] In Tiruppur, new sections of the labor process in emerging export firms of the late 1970s and early 1980s began to be coded as unskilled and feminine, marking older sections of work as the domain of masculine privilege. Through this equation of gender and skill, women were sought for knitwear work with the presumption that they would accept gender segmented labor markets, and in this respect Tiruppur's owners were responding to broader expectations about feminization as a cost-effective strategy for global production.

Through such a logic, L. Nataraj of Complex Exports claimed to be the first to "bring in ladies" to the industry in 1975, as checkers and helpers. Nataraj is a non-Gounder from a traditional South Indian business caste, and his father had started a knitting company in Kerala in the 1950s, which failed because of labor militancy. After finishing SSLC, or high school, Nataraj worked as a quality control manager in a spinning mill before starting Glad Knitting in 1970 with his sister as a partner. Glad has since become a major brand in the Indian national market. By 1975, Nataraj owned two units, Glad and Complex, and he said the units were "almost 100 percent women: 200 women in two units." Though he continued to employ men in cutting and stitching, Nataraj decided not to concentrate in "labor intensive" areas. He also said that, as a non-Gounder, he had to minimize trouble with labor by employing women. Nataraj stands in for owners for whom Gounder toil could not be an instrument for labor control, but who could nonetheless circumvent the advantage of toil through an ideology of women workers as more controllable. Important in Nataraj's rhetoric is the way "labor intensive" is not defined literally by the intensity of work, for which piece-rated manual labor in stitching or cutting would certainly qualify, but rather is used to reference lower skill designations and lower wages. These structural aspects of low-end jobs are coded as feminine, in contrast to masculine jobs with machines and regular wages, as should befit a family-oriented breadwinner.[7]

Women, Dalits and migrants from poorer southern districts of Tamil Nadu were drawn into the workforce increasingly by the late 1970s and 1980s. In the early 1980s, women were employed in export production in one of the eight large export companies in town. These new rural migrants knew little about Tiruppur's vibrant labor history, nor were they incorporated into its labor union culture. In the view of Palaniappan, the outspoken communist activist from the 1970s referred to in Chapter 5, new types of workers and new types of labor contracts, particularly piece rates and task rates, were part of an owner offensive against organized labor. What is clear is that the entry of workers under new conditions of vulnerability was not so much a concerted strategy by capital as a process of adjustment begun by a few exporters seeking ways around the expectations of Tiruppur's unionized, male, non-Dalit workforce. Importantly, Palaniappan's frame showed no trace of resistance from this unionized, male, non-Dalit labor to the entry of women and Dalits.[8]

Indeed, women were not, for the most part, brought to the knitwear industry to substitute male labor. Most were employed in new sections of the production process particular to exports, like checking and finishing.[9] Rather than meeting resistance from male workers whose jobs would have been replaced, women found tacit acceptance in the reservation of low-paid jobs for feminine, unskilled work. Dalits, in a sense, paved the way for this process, as they were already employed in the most physically degrading work of bleaching while standing inside a vat of bleach under the sweltering sun, as described in Chapter 2. While Dalits are coded as hypermasculine bodies not worth protecting, women are coded as bodies to protect too much, at low wages that do not threaten the links between male workers and the masculinity of breadwinner wages.[10] The process of feminization in Tiruppur began through rigid masculine and feminine sections of the labor process as defined through ranges of skill and labor intensity, with the complicity of labor unions.

By the mid 1980s, both Krishnaswami and Cawthorne found a strong gender division of labor in place in Tiruppur. They found women employed primarily in checking sections of export firms, where they were treated as temporary hires and paid a time-rated wage. While noting the shift to piece rates in several sections which were exclusively male, particularly in cutting and ironing, Krishnaswami found that the subordination of female workers did not require the decentralization of incentives through piece rates.[11] Skill definition is only partly defined by the position in the labor process, but more importantly a product of collective mobilization over what work in the division of labor gets defined as skilled, semi-skilled, or unskilled. Jobs classified as skilled included knitting machine attendants, cutters and garment stitchers; these were entitled to the highest pay and were for the most part monopolized by men. Young boys in knitwear firms were considered to be apprentices in the process of acquiring skills while young girls were temporary, unskilled labor. Job definitions were rigidified through Taylorist time-motion studies conducted by the Madras Productivity Council of the Tamil Nadu state government at a time when the workforce was entirely male. New sections of production like checking and trimming were classified as semi-skilled and coded feminine. Moreover, union acceptance of job descriptions set down by the Productivity Council, along with the unregulated nature of production, made it infeasible for disputes over official classification to actually change wage scales.[12]

In fact, notions of skill, labor intensity and gender could be flexible as required by changing accumulation strategies. For instance, garment stitching allowed some room for the entry of women as far back as the mid 1980s, despite the association of stitching with the masculine work of tailoring. The dominance of men in single-needle tailoring in India is the reason only men engage in extremely vulnerable Singer tailoring work described in Chapter 2. Only after the 127-day struggle of 1984, when many owners laid off workers and hired new ones, were women hired in limited numbers in a range of masculine, skilled jobs, particularly in domestic units.[13] However, women stitchers continued to earn less than men in the same jobs because of the persisting idea of a lack of fit between women workers and masculine work.

The fraternal workplaces of the 1970s had condensed the experience of masculine work with the production of garments for men, principally the common man's banian. Unmarked male workers could envision wearing the fruit of their labors, and indeed they could imagine transitioning to the ranks of petty ownership of banian companies. As the conditions for class mobility began to become more circumscribed, and as the products of Tiruppur's labor became more ambiguously gendered, the politics of work began to shift to a new articulation of gender at work, linking sexed bodies to difference and differentiation in new ways.

When Muthusamy narrated key shifts in his thirty-years of work experience, central to his early days was an ability to go directly to his owner to negotiate the terms of his labor contract. In contrast, since the 1984 strike and the deepening of piece rates and contracting, workers have not been able to question the arbitrary terms of employment either at work or at the union.[14] To really grasp how feminization emerged from shifts in class struggle, I turn to the major strike in the history of Tiruppur knitwear, when the fraternal hegemony of self-made Gounder men would give way to a deeper form of gendered hegemony.

III. Gendered Militancy, the 1984 Strike

The Gounder fraternity of capital could not possibly forge consent through an ideology of toil once the industry began to expand and draw in entirely new sets of workers including women, migrants and Dalits. While toil was useful in forging Gounder fraternal hegemony, institutionalized in the owners' association SIHMA, this hegemony was called into question in the period of intensified class struggle in the early 1980s as Tiruppur's center of gravity shifted toward exports. However, the breakdown of consent was part of the process of making a deeper form of gendered hegemony over a heterogeneous, fragmented order of work. A close look at class struggle in the period of transition in the early 1980s reveals gendered meanings in unreflective use, interpellating subjects, workplaces, families and sites of politics in new ways.

The 127-day struggle of 1984 was the longest and most intense working-class action in the history of Tiruppur.[15] The object of the strike was *panjappadi*, or Dearness Allowance (DA), a bonus to the wage which is meant to substitute for inflation-indexed raise, or what in other contexts is known as a Living Wage.[16] Known as the *Panjappadi Poráttam,* or "DA Struggle," all labor unions participated in this general strike under the direction of CITU, affiliated with the CPM. The strike was a turning point also in the way in which owners represented the collective interest of capital. The first act was a strike in 1981 which lasted forty-nine days, in which unions demanded the payment of ESI, Provident Fund (a pension scheme) as well as revision of workloads. A group of exporters of the nascent TEA signed an agreement to end the 1981 strike *without* SIHMA. This was a slap in the face of the Gounder fraternity of capital, and one it would not forget.

In 1984, when labor unions struck for DA, political winds were in their favor. After months of striking, labor unions won a Government Order in May 1984, granting workers the right to receive DA. SIHMA, however, refused flatly. When some companies complied with the government order and resumed work with DA, prominent owners from SIHMA actually *took to the streets* to prevent the implementation of the legal rights of labor. An employers' procession through the streets of Tiruppur was an unprecedented act. The cover of *SIHMA Bulletin,* the magazine of the owners' association, shows these Gounders in their trademark starched white shirts and *véctis* marching down Kumaran Road with a will. These representatives of the Gounder fraternity then demonstrated outside working companies, and, in the recollections of a labor activist, tried to forcibly stop such companies from working. When workers tried to obstruct these owners, the police intervened and twenty-one owners were arrested and jailed in Coimbatore city. SIHMA called a one-day *bund,* a lockout against the legally-won rights of labor. When these twenty-one owners were released the following day, they were garlanded and "felicitated" by SIHMA, and their group portrait made another cover of *SIHMA Bulletin.* This was the first and last collective public display of Gounder fraternity as capital on the streets of Tiruppur. Between the two covers of *SIHMA Bulletin,* hegemony was on display as failure, despite tacit support from the repressive arm of the state. What neither these Gounder owners nor their labor union adversaries bargained for explicitly was that fraternal hegemony was already giving way to a different type of gendered hegemony which did not require the overt display of capitalist power as Gounder masculinity.[17]

Even before the government order came through, the key negotiator for SIHMA who had worked closely with the unions since 1967 suggested to the owners' association that the unions had mobilized a large section of the working class to the cause of DA and they would not back down easily. Srinivasan suggested instead that they begin by granting DA for time rated or salaried workers, who represented about 15 percent of the working class, allowing piece-rated workers the option of switching back to lower time-rates. He claims that union leaders agreed with his plan until the arrival of a government order to grant DA to all workers, including those on piece rates. Srinivasan was a non-Gounder and was accused by certain SIHMA Gounders of being a representative of the labor unions. He was edged out of his position in SIHMA and his position was granted to Chairman Velusamy, another Gounder in office in perpetuity. Chairman Velusamy has since also become the leader of the dyers' association in order to dampen conflicts between knitwear and dyeing companies. With Srinivasan out of the way, class antagonisms only deepened, and the strike moved decisively in favor of the labor unions.[18]

However, rather than an unqualified victory for labor, I argue that this period marked a more subtle and pernicious turn in the gender politics of work. Despite launching a period of institutionalized collective bargaining, unions were being drawn into a lived hegemony, in Raymond Williams's sense, that would work through internalized meanings of work and precisely by eliding formal rules.[19] To see this process of hegemonic revision in the making, I turn to a particular telling of the strike through CITU street theater, as it represents the way in which meanings of class and gender, could circulate differently through Tiruppur's spaces of work, family and public politics. Central to the lived hegemony portrayed by the play is the way in which gender mediates capitalist control over fractured, insecure working-class households.

Panjappadi Poráttam, the play, was enacted forty times during the strike in 1984. The purpose of this guerilla theater was to educate working people and to maintain their support for a strike that became very difficult for working-class families to endure. The play was a threadbare production, enacted on street corners and back alleys: anywhere and anyhow. A handful of committed CPM and CITU activists took part in the play, and kept improvising it in each subsequent performance, adding bits and pieces of news from the strike as it progressed. The final production, of which a recording was made, is therefore a history of the strike from the vantage point of committed union organizers and their working-class supporters who stayed through the difficulties of four months of unemployment. However, *Panjappadi Poráttam* is also a class morality play expressing timeless differences between worker and owner *families*. Without the means to analyze audience response, I focus on the internal circulation of signs in the story, to ask how it is meant to function as a pedagogic device intended to instill new gendered values in working-class families. This aspect of the text as a moral narrative purveyed through imagined geographies of work and family shows how gender interpellates union militancy, making space for organized labor's tacit support of an emergent kind of hegemony.

The play works through six distinct locales: a tea-shop, the owners' association office, a workplace, the home of a worker, the home of an owner, and the door of a marriage hall. What is striking is the separation of spaces of worker and owner experience in a town that has by this time been fundamentally reworked by owners of working-class origins.

Early in the play, the tea-shop is marked as the place where workers associate between shifts, where they learn about their right to DA and the importance of union organization to achieve this right. This is the site of independent working-class consciousness, where the working-class audience is meant to see their allies and receive lessons on the issues at stake in the real strike. Here, the actors intend to fulfill their pedagogic functions as labor organizers.

The owners' association office is the mirror image of the tea-shop, as the site of capitalist class consciousness. Unlike the rational realization of exploitation at the tea-shop, conversations at the owners' association are fraught with contradictions and doomed to narrative failure. Workers are meant to see that there is no logic to capital, only naked power. In this sense, both sites of organized class interest represent intentions overtly.

The workplace is enacted literally as a collection of skills, as the actors mime various elements in the labor process. Mime renders work iconically, but it also signifies a generalized worker, shorn of caste, gender, and history. Representing work without culturally specific meanings, the actors present labor as entirely rationalized and deskilled. Hence, when conflict appears at the workplace, it is over the terms of labor contracts expressed in generic terms. What is more, the fragmentation of work through piece rates makes negotiations between owner and the piece-rated worker obsolete. When a cutting master is chided for being late, he retorts sarcastically that it's his business as he's paid by the piece. The sarcasm is worth giving pause to, as it indicates that the working-class audience is meant to see through the hypocrisy of owners professing to decentralize control over the labor process, while continuing to expect timeliness. Furthermore, in a series of scenes, workers keep returning for unsettled wages, which the owner keeps refusing pending wage negotiations in Madras. The key problem is that owners do not respect labor law. Conflicts are set up in ways that require the organized forces of labor and capital to negotiate elsewhere than on the shopfloor, to prevent owners from flouting institutionalized rules. The lesson to learn is that institutionalized collective bargaining is the proper recourse for worker militancy.

The narrative shifts to homes of worker and owner as a respite from class struggle, to reveal the human and familial lives of classes. These are also the arenas in which the organizer-actors slip from intentional instruction to index that which is taken for granted outside the circumscribed zones of work and labor politics. Where intentional pedagogy ends, the work of interpellation begins, in representing classes as *families.*

Back at the tea-shop, in a moment of foreshadowing, workers discussing their troubles see in the newspaper a story of a woman who kills herself because she could not provide a dowry. She is pitied without analysis, because this sentiment should be transparent. A singer speaks of comrades' difficulties, driving home through juxtaposition the importance of seeing labor conflict in the broader context of problems in poor families. For this scene to be effective, both actors and audience must assume that workers ought to be able to earn enough to pay for daughters' dowries.

Contrasting households of classes allow the actors to speak about class antagonisms in the realm of consumption and health more generally. A coughing worker finds no food at home, as he has not been paid in a while. In contrast, the owner phones his doctor because his son eats too much "Horlicks, Bournvita and icecream." A worker nearby chides, "Your boy can't even go through the door now!" The different bodily maladies of classes could not be more pronounced.

The owners' association leader is portrayed as a buffoon. When he does not know what to do with black money, he decides that since they've built several buildings, bought farms, and integrated into spinning mills, they might as well invest in the film industry, a well-known place to launder ill-gotten gains.

Meanwhile, the class differences between owner and worker *families* become increasingly marked. The worker's daughter, Janaki, played by a man, starts going to work secretly at a ginning factory. The owner's daughter is bored of watching videos at home, and someone suggests that marriage should keep her occupied. With this difference between owner and worker daughters set, the issue of DA, arrives on stage in conversations between workers at the tea stall.

The owners' association is caught unaware by workers' demands. Luckily for the leader, he can just pick up the phone and call a disembodied "Brain" to tell him what to do. The Brain tells him not to acknowledge DA, so the leader does not. The owners' association members are confused by their leader, since it is logical for them to pay DA. The leader's perpetual response, like a broken record, is "How can we pay DA, this is a cottage industry!" One frustrated association member interjects, "When I ask you what DA is, you say cottage industry. When I say cottage industry, you repeat cottage industry. Get lost!" The confused leader awaits advice from the Brain he doesn't seem to have, a metaphor for anarchy at the heart of collective capital. Hence, when the owners go to negotiate in Madras without the Brain, they are struck by how strong the united interests of workers are. To further highlight their disarray, a prankster comes into the owners' association periodically with various bits of mockery. He ridicules the notion that this is a cottage industry and confronts the leader on slandering workers in the newspaper. At each turn, when he becomes dangerously frank, he shrugs his shoulder and exclaims "That's not what I'm saying; it's what the people are saying outside!" Like Lear's fool, the prankster can speak truth to power because he is with the audience. In instructing capital of its folly, he instructs the working-class audience of their right to DA.

In a final act of lunacy, the owners consider how they might spirit out their machines to work outside town avoiding workers who have been guarding the streets to prevent capital flight. The owners decide, quite literally, to fly off with the machines! Needless to say, it doesn't work. This only spurs the prankster to mock the leader more, asking whose brain the Brain really is, and capping it with his refrain, "That's not what I'm saying; it's what the people are saying outside." The owners are routed, but what is important is that the play must go on.

Back home, the worker tells his son, between coughing fits, that he will take out a loan to marry off his daughter Janaki. Simultaneously, the owner holds a lavish wedding for his daughter at a local marriage hall. The worker cannot find his daughter the next day, and he recalls her distress the night before. She had said, "It's because of me that you have such difficulties. Why is there this urgency to marry me off?" Just then a man runs up, shouting that Janaki has committed suicide on the railway tracks.

The class tragedy of the failed working-class father and sacrificed daughter is treated as necessary costs of class struggle while the union fights for the right to DA. What is key to this union narrative is the way in which a gendered, familial narrative interpellates, or unintentionally scripts, the way in which these costs should be borne. In contrast to the workplace, tea stall and owners' association, the home and family are outside the scope of internal critique. There is no jester to point out gendered contradictions in scripting the two daughters' marital and bodily fates. This narrative, moreover, is quite different from the gendered narratives of Gounder self-made men explored in Chapter 5, which center on the masculine individual, assisted by his mother and by "brothers." The unit of working-class travails is now the family, and its dynamics center on fathers and dependent daughters.[20] Whereas marriage payments were relatively unimportant *vis-à-vis* a range of other material processes in the making of self-made men, both owner and worker fathers in the play measure their worth in their ability to marry off their daughters. Janaki stands for the sexual inadequacy of an unmarried girl who must be married off to ensure working-class reproduction. However, Janaki can also not be the breadwinner worker whose rights are being fought for, and when she decides to work on the sly, it is in traditional women's work, ginning. Anxieties about Janaki's sexuality conceal a deeper acceptance of gender difference and inequality across spheres of work, family, and labor union.

Panjappadi Poráttam was the first public representation of new gendered idioms to explain class conflict, consciousness, and action in Tiruppur. In the context of its audience, a workforce in the process of becoming increasingly feminized and insecure, this street theater marks the incorporation of trade unionism into the gendered hegemony of capital. Capital no longer required the visible authority of owners on the street because gendered meanings of work would seem to allow a more subtle and pernicious lived hegemony to cohere. From the rule of "brothers," Tiruppur's primary gender myth was tilting toward a rule over "daughters," from egalitarian masculinity to dependent femininity.

There has never been a strike on the scale of the 1984 strike again. Instead the rights of workers have been systematically eroded in the transition to export production. The same period has seen the consolidation of a class fraction of exporters and the new owners' association, TEA. These exporters have since been unwilling to risk strikes of the same magnitude when time is of the essence in producing for seasonal export markets. Despite being the sons and nephews of the Gounder fraternity of capital, the major exporters in Tiruppur have refused to be as antagonistic to labor unions in quite the same way.

The new offensive of capital, since the shift to export and particularly after the 1984 strike, has been effected through widespread contracting which allows owners to pass off "labor problems" to contractors. In retrospect, gendered idioms describing working-class experience in the play *Panjappadi Poráttam* are the more important didactic function than simply the details of the fight for DA. The significant absence of "toil" as a source of value, the portrayal of the workplace as de-skilled and routinized, and the starkly differentiated life choices of classes, mark a despotic hegemony that does not speak of class mobility at all. Indeed, what is key to this hegemony are fathers' responsibilities and daughters' sexual subordination across class. Tiruppur's otherwise dedicated communist organizers are instructed to be impervious to deepening sexual divisions of labor and charged sexual politics.

As a consequence, the new sex/gender regime has allowed a growing divergence between formal, institutionalized rules and differentiated work experiences. Difference has been mobilized to subvert labor rights under a veneer of formal obligation. I turn next to changing practices in the new gendered hegemony of capital, and to new representations of femininity and masculinity produced by the dynamics of accumulation.

IV. Sex/Gender/Violence: Differentiated Labors and Multiple Feminisms, 1984–1998

"It's not just that ladies wages are different. The inner problem is that men who work the same job get differentiated wages just as ladies' wages are highly differentiated."[21] This regional leader of the CPI-M, Mohan Kumar, explains the labor market discrimination of women workers as part of the differentiation of all labor contracts. Implicit in the order of things, gender interpellates the differentiation of "men" from "ladies," their forms of work and remuneration. What remains second-nature to Kumar is the way in which a discourse of feminization has become productive of difference. This section explores how gendered hegemony over social labor has come to differentiate sexed bodies, and how this process of differentiation is understood from multiple positions in the division of labor.

By the 1990s, the gender division of labor identified by scholars in the mid 1980s had become slightly permeable. Women had made strong incursions into stitching sections, and slight incursions into cutting, but most women workers remained consigned to the least paid, least skilled work in garment checking. Women also continued to receive lower wages in stitching and cutting, "even less than men," in the words of Muthusamy, a male cutting master. "If a man makes Rs 75, a woman makes Rs 55-50-60, or so." Muthusamy explained this discrepancy through the docility of women and their lack of union involvement: "When men don't go, how would women."[22] What is significant is that both women's wages and their lack of unionization are seen as phenomena that are not distinct to women, and yet women workers are marked as different by being structurally dependent on men. Muthusamy provides a window into Tiruppur's version of feminization, which combines the dependent feminine idiom in the play *Panjappadi Poráttam* with a more widely legible attribution of docility to women workers.

Gendered hegemony also operates through the new products of export work, and the ways in which products are linked to notions of struggle for workers' rights. Banians were easily marked as masculine commodities, marketed to absorb the sweat of the common man, and within the purchasing power of the average banian worker. Fraternal hegemony was built on a sort of Fordist conception of masculine breadwinners who could consume the fruit of their labors. Export fashion garments, on the other hand, are more ambiguously gendered; they are out of working-class consumers' reach; and they do not provide today's differentiated, insecure workforce a sense of shared gendering through consumption. Instead, "fashion" allows export garments to conceal the operation of gender in deepening exploitation. Exporters often explained differentiated wage payments as determined by the fashion of the garment rather than by the specific labor involved. Similarly, workers often said they were paid "fashion-*pórtta*-rate," or piece rates "appropriate to" particular fashions, even if their actual labors remained the same. This attribution to fashion effectively makes wage determination entirely up to the whim of the owner, or more precisely to his power to pass on competitive pressures to workers. As I argue in Chapter 2, this labor market flexibility forces accommodation to the dubious business practices of global garment sourcing companies from Europe and North America.[23]

Differentiated labor arrangements, explained as effects of fashion, allow a dramatic divergence between labor rights won through three-yearly general agreements between organized labor and capital since the 1984 strike. The agreements have usually been pushed by the threat of strikes, but most labor unions, particularly the less militant AITUC, have preferred conciliation. Most owners do not prepare for annual general strikes around the Deepavali festival as an eventuality, as they did in the 1970s and 1980s. Moreover, most owners do not follow the general agreements, although the latter exert some pressure on the band within which wages vary, as I argue in Chapter 2. The leader of CITU held that the struggle of labor unions since 1984 has been to regain the rights stripped of labor through the shift to piece rates. "So now piece rated workers receive bonus, gratuity, festival allowances: benefits that were once held and lost in between."[24]

Cutting master Muthusamy, with thirty years of work experience, found his take-home pay increase when his wage was changed from time to piece rates after the 1984 strike, but he no longer had the range of benefits he had when on time-wages. Muthusamy remained pessimistic about rank-and-file workers' ability to contest the rules of the game: "There was a major struggle . . . and they won DA, travel allowance, marriage allowance for girls and so on. Some companies follow it and a lot of companies don't. They signed the Agreement and they agreed to it but they don't give to workers. If a worker goes to the labor union and reports that they don't get paid according to the Agreement, they ask 'Who's reporting this' and for some reason or the other the worker is laid off. This happens a lot. The Agreement is between labor unions and owners."[25] Among the rights that Muthusamy counts as won but not provided is "marriage allowances for girls," in which companies pay a portion for the marriages of their unmarried female workers. This is one major occasion that labor unions have fought and secured a "right" for women, by making the employer partial provider of "their girl's" dowry. Again, the idioms of *Panjappadi Poráttam* are recognizable in this paternalistic control of Tiruppur's working "daughters."

Muthusamy is joined in this critique of labor unions by women workers who do not have the luxury of attending union meetings or are afraid of the consequences when they can. Rajeshwari worked between 1985 and 1995, from the age of twelve to twenty-two, initially in domestic companies. She started as a helper for Rs 5, and though she occasionally approached her owner to discuss her labor contract, she said she had no time to go to the labor union. Rajeshwari and other young women like her say that work provides a way out of the watchful eyes of parents, while union membership provides no direct benefit, but instead the opprobrium of family and community.[26]

Responding to critiques of the notion of patriarchy and to elitist presumptions of Third World feminist resistance, Gillian Rose proposes a feminist geography sensitive to "paradoxical spaces" that are not counter-hegemonic, but "are spaces imagined to articulate a troubled relation to hegemonic discourses of masculinism."[27] Paradoxical space is a useful metaphor in mapping how people work around the brittle edges of gendered hegemony. In Poompuhar Nagar and surrounding workers colonies, women in neighboring homes share childcare and other services between intermittent labor contracts. Valarmati is one such middle-aged woman who has worked in ginning companies from the age of twelve, alongside her mother, before coming to knitwear companies. She says work in Tiruppur is entirely impermanent and particularly insecure for women: "They can always throw us out. We are like slaves! There's no unity [*otrumai*] among women at work; no women leaders." Valarmati has had various maladies from work, for which she takes periods of rest from companies. She has eye problems from the oil guns used to clean stains in checking, and she says the heat can be unbearable in companies. A visit to a private doctor costs Rs 40; she adds with a laugh, "with or without *úci* [injection]." Her husband left her twenty years earlier, but she reckons she would be worse off if he was around to waste her hard-earned wages on drink and *cít*, gambling. Valarmati has private debts of Rs 5,000, with a monthly interest of 6 percent. Valarmati resolutely refuses the existence of a collective women's consciousness across fractured workplaces and families. In doing so, she claims an outsider status to the fetishism of the abject, but resistant, Third World woman. Valarmati is proud and unwilling to be the dependant woman scripted in *Panjappadi Poráttam*. What remains to be studied concretely are practices of care-giving and reproductive work that Valarmati relies on within her neighborhood during periods of respite from waged work. These space-times of unpaid reproductive work, compounded by Valarmati's health expenses and private loans, provide ongoing forms of primitive accumulation for capital. However, Valarmati does not give up on the politics of an insider in Tiruppur's gendered hegemony in continuing to call for women leaders.[28]

Valarmati says her life is better than that of her twenty-year-old neighbor, Geetha, whose father is still asleep drunk. Geetha assents, adding "He doesn't even bring home 5 paisa." She has also been working in the knitwear industry for eight years, first as a helper, then in stitching. Geetha's mother of forty worked irregularly in checking, while her father of fifty was a tailor who "drinks his wages." During the season, Geetha often works *vidi-night* or all-night shifts, in addition to working 1.5 shifts during the days. As a young woman, Geetha has faced all kinds of sexual harassment on the job. She says that one in ten women get harassed on the *vidi-night* shift, but it's half their fault; she insinuates that many young women have loose morals, unlike her. Then she adds that women like her cannot go to the owner because the charge of sexual impropriety would be turned against them. Instead, they opt to quit. Mobility is the only response young women can use against sexual harassment. Gendered hegemony forces this speeding of the mobility of women's labor through the ongoing threat of sexual violence.

Geetha was also working for her dowry of three gold *pauns*, or eight-gram coins, for which she needed Rs 20,000. As she spoke to me, her father walked in and said "women have become costly," a cruel reminder of the ways in which masculine power colludes across home and work in devaluing working daughters. Geetha's family is supported by her wages and her mother's, and part of their wages go to repaying outstanding loans of Rs 10,000 for her elder sister's marriage. These women's exploitation at work is compounded by extraction from moneylenders and marriages. Geetha refuses to give her earnings to her father, rather than her mother. She and her mother know they are the real breadwinners whose wages might secretly be saved. All the same, her father demands Rs 20 each morning as his right. Behind this right is the threat of domestic violence. If Geetha has some autonomy as a wage worker, it comes at a high price.

Particularly for unmarried women, the risk of moral failure through alleged sexual impropriety, backed by the threat of sexual violence, makes life in Tiruppur something like walking a tightrope. One way in which women attempt to externalize these risks is by misrecognizing gendered hegemony; that is, by recognizing the discourse of domination while seeing it as "*not quite* about me." By decrying the aggressive feminine sexuality of the *veḷiāḷ, or* "outsider," Tiruppur's Tamil working women attempt to maintain their sexual propriety by casting aspersions on an internal enemy. Valarmati, Geetha, her mother and grandmother speak together about how *veḷi pombḷe*, outsider women, are truly degenerate women who offer even cheaper labor than they do. "They don't eat properly," said the grandmother, adding double entendre by raising her pitch and acting more coy, "They waste money on flowers for their hair." The old lady then mimicked them walking with swaying hips in fancy saris, with flowers and bangles "like going to the temple . . . these beggars!"

The temple, it is implied, is a brothel. The prime target as outsider women are Malayalis from the neighboring state of Kerala, who "even come to Tiruppur to live alone after marriage." Ironically, these Keralite women have often been enabled to enter higher-level secretarial and supervisory jobs because of their education, a product of Kerala's more woman-friendly developmental trajectory. For women like Valarmati and Geetha, the transgressive sexuality of Keralite women is a form of negative consciousness, through which they attempt to displace the moral and physical risks of gendered class domination. What is clear is that these women, who face the threat of sexual violence tangibly, neither consent to nor resist gendered hegemony very easily. Moreover, by recognizing multiple femininities, they hold the possibility of breaking the fetishism of femininity more generally.

A different window into the experience of gendered hegemony comes from Bhuvana, who I describe in Chapter 2 as one of the few women I encountered who runs her own small business. A thirty-eight-year-old housewife, Bhuvana runs Lata Collars, specialized in collar separation, or the taking apart of shirt collars knitted manually and bundled off for separation. What is so interesting about this small owner is the way in which her conception of work supports her moral commitment to housewifery. Bhuvana gets bundles of collars from knitwear companies and subcontracts the separation to other housewives. She tried to give to "decent families," whose husbands preferred women to stay at home because of the stigma somewhat well-off families associated with company work. While at first glance this seems a wholesale adoption of dominant idioms of domesticity, it is important to recognize that this kind of work provides an opportunity for older women and women with small children to engage in waged work while also tending to children and to unpaid domestic care-work. Unlike working class women, Bhuvana also spoke of her freedoms in consumption. She was excited to tell me how she first spends her earnings on clothes, then on "fancy items," and then on the beauty parlor, of which there are now several in Tiruppur. Sexualization is both domination and pleasure, and not just for women in Bhuvana's class.[29]

Women working in banian companies are certainly cognizant of the way notions of sexual attraction and beauty structure their ability to negotiate the terms of work. Kamakshi, a young woman, spoke matter-of-factly about how "nice looking and young girls are preferred in checking," and how "wages are based on how women look, and on how light their skin is."[30] In the same breath, she and her friends also talked about their friendships at work as ways of escaping parental authority, as well as of providing support under conditions that are more easily shared with peers. Working women often spoke of their desire to dress up, buy flowers, and gossip with their girlfriends on the way to work. Work provides avenues for camaraderie, even through the difficulties that permeate insecure livelihoods.

One artifact of this contradictory process has been the emergence of Valentine's Day as another local festival. In one company, a worker distributed sweets because he had a "love marriage" with a woman he had met working in the company. In another company, workers protested to their owner to distribute sweets because he had just had a love marriage. A friend of mine, moreover, told me somewhat coyly that he and his girlfriend were going to cut the cake at the (Hallmark) "card shop" that Valentine's Day. Tiruppur's gendered hegemony has brought questions of sex, gender, and romantic love to centerstage in social life. While these questions are strongly circumscribed by conventional understandings of marriage and sexual propriety, and while the commodification of desire opens new opportunities for capital accumulation, some working class people do find new freedoms in the loosening of mores. While some working women misrecognize the gendered hegemony that shapes their possibilities, they continue to hold to a form of "double consciousness" in the paradoxical spaces of Tiruppur's fractured homes and workplaces. In concluding this section, I turn to two elite feminisms in Tiruppur, and one subaltern alternative that points to a different feminism outside the elitist binary of abjection and resistance.

Mrs George is a powerful woman who has been through personal tragedy and continues to have an important place in Tiruppur's elite culture. Her husband was a doctor who treated several of the main families in Tiruppur, and he had the reputation of an older generation of doctor who would visit even when his regular patients were well, just to check on their everyday health. When he died prematurely in a car accident, Mrs George had already had a women's hostel built by the YMCA, with rooms sponsored by local industrialists. At the felicitation to the SIHMA leader in the ceremonial opening of the hostel, the leader acknowledged his patronage of the hostel as part of his broader mandate to take care of the working daughters of Tiruppur. In order to gain admission to the hostel, working women must have a signature from their father or husband, so as to prevent impropriety. Most importantly, the hostel allows Mrs George to claim the position of protector of "the girls," as an ally of capital in its search for mid-level women workers in secretarial and supervisory positions. This is a feminism of capital scripted into Tiruppur's gendered hegemony, which tries to recuperate the hapless daughter in *Panjappadi Poráttam* in order to get her to work.

A second kind of elite feminism is represented by Tamilmani, a political activist who has been involved in radical communist, anti-caste and *Drávida Kaḻagam* (DK) politics for many years alongside her "ex-Brahmin" husband. Tamilmani identified with strands of the Dravidian Movement, a mass anti-caste and anti-Brahmin movement which had transformed large parts of South India, paving the way for the early emergence of sub-nationalist parties in Tamil Nadu.[31] Coimbatore District was exceptional in not becoming a major focal point because it was, until lately, a stronghold of Congress and Communist Party activism. Quite simply, Tamilmani's political roots lay in other parts of Tamil Nadu. Though she had a *cuyamariyátai kalyáṉam* or "self-respect marriage" many years earlier, she had since begun to wear the *táli* that she once saw as the yoke of women's oppression. While Tamilmani did not know the history of Tiruppur and its toiling Gounders, she could critique continuing Gounder caste dominance and Dalit subservience, and she derided elite leaders like Mrs George for going to Dalit communities just to "clean the nose of a baby and then leave." Tamilmani presented herself as a more responsible woman leader in Tiruppur, because of her sensitivity to caste domination. However, when it came to speaking for women workers, she relied entirely on elite convention in deriding their sexual immorality. This is the feminism of a section of the progressive political elite, maintained through polite distance from teeming masses.

In contrast to these elite feminisms, Palaniammal, a boisterous Dalit woman who ran a mobile tea stall frequented by Singer tailors and other company workers, spoke passionately about how some people have been turning the charge of impropriety into opportunity. Palaniammal began by telling me that many women retain part of their wages for household goods, but added that this isn't very surprising. What is surprising, she continued, is that though divorce is rare, couples often separate and maintain separate households with other partners in each other's vicinity, even when they continue to see their legal spouses each day. Working-class communities keep this information from employers, lest owners brand these women as immoral and therefore compliant in multiple ways.

> Women think, "Why divorce, what will we get out of it. So let him manage and I'll manage." They won't get any inheritance. She might say "Give me something for the household if you like or marry some other woman if you please." In the old days, men would say, "Just give me your signature, I'm off to live with another woman . . . I'll get some more jewels and 10 pauns [gold as dowry.]" Now there are no expectations. If they desire to, they stay married; if not, they earn and eat for themselves. Since there are companies, one can work day and night. If there is desire for someone, they might live together for a long time. Now you can have a companion and live by yourselves and people will say you have a companion and you're managing and getting by.[32]

Palaniammal restores a sense of dignity to Tiruppur's working-class communities by pointing to the ways in which people improvise around the edges of gendered hegemony to create new kinds of conjugal relations in the absence of sanction for divorce, particularly from sexually charged export workplaces. However, Palaniammal is defensive in that she does not claim a direct challenge to dowry either, and she includes working-class women and men in a shared space outside dominant mores of feminine propriety, where different kinds of sex/gender relations are afforded social sanction. While not fully articulated as counter-hegemonic, or indeed feminist, these practices signify on-going resolve in reworking meanings of domesticity, sexuality, and care in working-class communities. Raymond Williams cautions that sources of working-class radicalism are located in multiple struggles that may not seem immediately "political" or "economic."[33] Informal working class divorce points to the possibility of new ways in which gender and class rearticulate sexed bodies to alternative, progressive notions of difference.

V. The Return of Toil: Fieldwork and the Consolidation of Capital in the 1990s

For innovative responses from working people maneuvering around the edges of gendered hegemony, there are innovative responses from capital that reassert fraternal capital. On one occasion, as I sat in a small T-shirt printing workshop on the outskirts of town, a stylish man zoomed up the dirt road in his Mercedes and came in to meet the print-ing owner. He chatted up the owner for a while and drank some tea before finally looked over at me questioningly. I said I was from Los Angeles, California, to which he responded nonchalantly "Oh, Los Angeles. I was just there, but I only stay in Beverly Hills." As he gave me an imposing business card, I learned that this man was a partner in an export firm and often travelled around the world. I asked him why on earth a big-shot like him would have to come to check up on his order to a little printing unit on the outskirts of town, rather than sending his quality control manager. He pointed to the printing owner and said, "My *maccán* here will not print my batch of garments unless I come here and sit with him and make sure he does it. It's fieldwork. Fieldwork is key."

This fieldwork implies not only the active personal presence of owners in the division of labor in order to discipline subcontractors

and ensure networked production, but also the continued performance of Gounder masculinity across networks of firms. Rather than
seeing this as a lack of professionalism or of trust in a professional class
of production managers, as outsiders often say about Tiruppur, fieldwork can be seen as Gounder toil in another guise. This personal
grease, necessary to ensure that subcontractors actually deliver the
goods, remains the monopoly of Gounder fraternal networks.

On several occasions, while collecting survey data, I encountered
Gounder owners involved in inter-firm contracts visiting each other's
units and spending time with each other with little immediate reason
except to bond as fellow Gounder men. Older Gounder men enact
their masculinity through a particular style of attire: starched white
vécti and white *kaddar* shirt, complemented by a bodily comportment
that exudes a kind of aggressive masculine confidence, through raised
vécti and direct speech. These forms of embodiment recall stereotyped
images of sturdy Gounder farmers, as depicted in the film *Cinna
Gounder.* Among the newer generation of big exporters, these forms of
address are less important as markers of Gounder masculinity and
capital. The exporter who frequents Beverly Hills, for instance, was
dressed in a bright colored "safari suit," his sunglasses and cell phone
prominently placed in a shirt pocket. This internationalist self-fashioning is meant to assert a cosmopolitan masculinity, both at home
and farther afield. Like the head of TEA, who also fancies himself as
a sort of dandy in bright silk shirts and trapezpoidal sunglasses, these
men portray a masculinist class power that claims to be beyond caste.
Their Gounderness is saved for the domestic sphere and for extravagant
rituals like marriages and puberty ceremonies. In other words, the
image of the worldly Gounder exporter, free of caste, is predicated on
a changing geography of work and home in Gounder elite lives as well,
in which the home and family become the repository for Gounder
caste and culture.

The cosmopolitanism of this class of exports has become possible
through the rise of a class fraction of exporters at the apex of the division of labor, towering above networks of fraternal owners. This consolidation of capital, institutionalized in TEA, relies on the fieldwork
of small owners and the everyday operation of gendered hegemony
over social labor. To understand how Tiruppur's exporters made their

mark in exports, I briefly retrace the way in which Tiruppur's knitwear industry went global.

In the late 1970s and early 1980s, most exports were carried out through export houses from Bombay, New Delhi and Calcutta. This North Indian trading capital exported from Tiruppur in two ways. First, Calcutta-based trading houses exported knitted cloth, not garments, primarily to Bangladesh for low-end T-shirt production through cheaper labor than in South India. Vimal Chandmal said he was one of a handful of people like him in Tiruppur, along with ten in Calcutta, exporting to Bangladesh.[34] Second, garment export houses, primarily from Delhi and Bombay, sourced from a number of Tiruppur producers since the late 1970s. Zigzag Ltd is a Bombay-based export house which tried its hand at production with a large factory with a hundred stitching machines, which failed after three years in 1994 because they couldn't "control laborers," and because contractors absconded during Deepavali, when workers make their annual demand for a festival bonus. The North Indians who stuck it out and continued to have a presence in production in Tiruppur in the 1980s and 1990s did so primarily on a mercantile model, with characteristics I have explored closely in Chapter 3.

Five Bombay merchant houses dominated the export knitwear trade from Tiruppur in the early 1980s, before the existence of export quotas under the Multi Fiber Agreement. When quota restrictions for knitwear came into existence, these merchant houses continued to get the largest shares based on the quota category of "past performance."[35] Foreign buyers were reluctant to come to Tiruppur without a Western-style hotel, and preferred to deal with Bombay suppliers. By the late 1980s, buyers came to stay in nearby Coimbatore, and by the 1990s they began staying in Tiruppur's new fancy hotels, particularly the one built by a family of elite *Kániyálar* Gounders who could not make inroads in production. When foreign buyers started coming to Tiruppur, the town's direct exporters pulled the rug out from under the Bombay merchants by undercutting their prices. While the Bombay houses kept their margins fairly fixed, Tiruppur exporters took orders at any cost, and even for a loss in the hope of sustained contacts with foreign buyers. The result was not only a shift toward Tiruppur owners, but also the fueling of fierce competition based not on quality and technical change but on undercutting prices. [36]

The ascendant class of direct exporters from Tiruppur, represented by TEA, had by the late 1980s recaptured much of the export share formerly in the hands of North Indian merchant exporters. Consequently, these Gounder exporters consolidated their class power over social labor and forged strong ties with national state institutions. The elite strata in control of TEA has risen from the familial and fraternal relations of decentralized capital, which is why there has been no major resistance from small owners to the consolidation of capital. The simultaneous dominance over unions through gendered hegemony meant that the burden of price-cutting could be passed down to the feminized proletariat with little resistance. Finally, this export capitalism has shorn itself of its agrarian past and has roped the state and international institutions into an aggressive form of export-oriented deve-lopment that subordinates rural and urban livelihoods and environments to the accumulation of capital.

The main symbol of class consolidation, and of dominance of the rural and urban environs, for this apex class of exporters, has been the New Tiruppur Area Development Corporation (NTADC), formed in 1995. As discussed in Chapter 2, NTADC proposed to fund a massive overhaul of the rural–urban production system through a privatized system of water distribution, sewage and effluent treatment and a new model township on the main highway. NTADC is, moreover, to be financed through a combination of loans, aid, money raised on US capital markets and forced land purchase from peasants on the north side of town for resale by TEA as plots in New Tiruppur. The last element points to one of the most controversial elements of the NTADC: the Model Township requires 500 acres of rural land to be "procured" from peasants at farmland prices, to be then resold by TEA as urban plots. Communist and farmers' movement leaders in late 1998 were arguing that the state should handle the sale of public land and that farmers should get a fair price. This last element drives home quite powerfully that the politics of agrarian transition continues to rear its head as the leading exporters of TEA seek to transform the rural environs to resolve the environmental consequences of industrialization in town. The consolidation of capital has come with changed relations with the countryside rather than a sharp break with the agrarian past.

Finally, the Gounder fraternity of yesteryear has far from slipped backstage. The SIHMA Business Delegation from India to China conducted a tour of Shaoxing, Guanzhou and Hong Kong in April 2003. This group of forty-five was led by the leader of SIHMA, and overwhelmingly comprised Gounder owners of older companies or groups, including some of the men who participated in the street protest during the 1984 strike. The trip is a proactive measure to address increasing Chinese competition with the phasing out of garment export quotas under the World Trade Organization's 1995 Agreement on Textile and Clothing. The official website includes general statements, the itinerary, key products from Tiruppur, and an array of photographs of delegates, each looking deadpan into the camera. This visual document of Gounder men of modest means preparing for China announces that the fraternity continues to make itself known on a global stage.[37]

In letting its industrial culture be known more widely, not just to the stray ethnographer, Tiruppur makes its mixture of gender and class legible also to a few intrepid foreign buyers. Antonio Verona was one such man who, in the early 1980s, could become an active participant changing production politics as Tiruppur shifted to exports. By the late 1990s, once Tiruppur had made it's name in global garment production, the stage was set for a very different kind of interface between a global buyer and the fraternity of capital.

VI. Globalization by Fraud, or Playing the Fraternity

I met Mr Doha early in my research in Tiruppur, in 1996. He said he was a Bangladeshi settled in New Jersey who had come to Tiruppur as a representative of a US apparel company along with his assistant, a white American called Lisa. I must admit I was suspicious early on. Mr Doha spoke with an affected twang that barely concealed a strong Bengali accent, as if he was trying very concertedly to sound *foreign*. Every once in a while, he would fish out a picture from his wallet, of himself posing with his Porsche in front of his New Jersey home, and he provided me, and anyone else, with a long list of cellular phone numbers at which he could be reached in the US. If this was his evidence, I knew I had a story. Little did I know what it would be.

Once, while I tried to get an interview with him, Mr Doha, who never asked to be called by his first name, Syed, asked me to come with him on his routine. We were driven around town, first to a black-market shop to get him and Lisa imported toothbrushes, then to a company which was trying to secure an order from him. Mr Doha looked squarely at the young owner and asked if they employ child labor, and the man said "no," looking back just as squarely. Mr Doha turned to me and said he would never stand for child labor in his products. He knew I was a researcher, and he knew how to present himself as the kind face of corporate responsibility.

Through the tinted windows of his car, Mr Doha recounted how impossible it would be to get around without a vehicle, but he feared he was too popular to walk around in Tiruppur. He laughed as he confessed to me that he couldn't even open the car window without being mobbed, and that if he ran for mayor, he would probably be elected. The exporter in the front seat, sitting with the driver, laughed appreciatively. Mr Doha certainly knew the importance of performance.

That afternoon, we ate in the restaurant of the Velan Hotel, where Mr Doha was running a large tab entertaining all sorts of men who sought to work with him on various projects. When he talked, the table came to a hush. He spoke of the new venture he wanted to launch in the Maldives, in which many of the men at the table seemed to consider a lucrative investment opportunity. He also joked about his first trip to Madras, when he claimed to rent out the entire top floor of the Connemara Hotel in order to wine and dine notable politicians, bureaucrats and businessmen. The question was not whether he was ready for the Maldives, but whether the Maldives was ready for Mr Doha.

The next time I saw Mr Doha was at a party at his home, a cottage offered rent-free by influential people in Tiruppur. The scene was like E.M. Forster's (1924) famously sarcastic rendition of the colonial "Bridge Party," which was intended to bridge the cultures of Britain and India. British women were far in the interior of the house with the most important British officers, British subalterns and Indian officers spilling out onto the verandah, and most invited Indian women farther out in the gardens. I walked in and out of this postcolonial bridge party, imagining gradations of racialized authority extending to the street outside. Lisa had left the inner sanctum of the house only once, giggling after being dressed in a sari. Mr Doha carried his own bottle of Johnny Walker Black Label, Duty Free, as he swaggered in and out of Lisa's airconditioned room, making small talk with some of the men in the house in his peculiar foreign accent. My younger friends, eager to get contracts, were consigned to the outer section of the compound, but within reach of flowing alcohol and sizzling meat, compliments of Velan Hotel.

When I returned to India less than a year later, the first person I mentioned the name Doha to, in Chennai, told me never to repeat it unless I wanted trouble. Mr Doha, it appeared, had absconded with large sums of money, leaving many men in Tiruppur in the lurch. He had played their homosociality down to alcohol and the lure of a white woman and global markets, and he had extorted from all of them successfully. Mr Doha's fraudulence proves by example that forms of gendering can be legible to wider circuits of accumulation. Indeed, Mr Doha's effectiveness in performing a legible masculinity to a range of exporters in Tiruppur was key to globalization by fraud. Rumor has it that Mr Doha now lives large on an unnamed island with Lisa. Needless to say, his cell phones were not taking my calls in 1998.

A disgusted exporter said to me, "He was just an employee of some company. He wasn't even an owner." The trace of toil persists, even after the fraternity has been played to the hilt.

VII. Conclusion: Gendered Hegemony, Difference and Accumulation

Ranajit Guha has argued that the difference of the colonial state in India from the metropolitan bourgeois state was precisely that hegemony, power backed by the consent of subjects rather than by everyday corporeal force, prevailed in the latter but not in the former. By "dominance without hegemony," Guha means "it was not possible for [the colonial] state to assimilate the civil society of the colonized to itself."[38]

Even with a less restrictive definition of hegemony that admits the periodic use of violence alongside provisional consent, the Gounder fraternity of capital could not forge consent through the promise of mobility once the industry began to expand and draw in new workers under much more insecure terms. If Gounder toil was meant to be a tool for forging a fraternal hegemony, its promise was nearly exhausted by the 1980s, with exports and the revival of labor militancy. The breakdown of consent presented an opportunity for capital to forge a more despotic, gendered hegemony over a heterogeneous, fragmented workforce. This hegemony through difference and periodic sexual violence allows an inordinate separation between institutionalized routines of class conciliation in the form of tri-annual general agreements between capital and labor, and workplace realities. Moreover, the rule of difference has allowed a class of exporters to rise above the Gounder fraternity of capital to dominate the cluster as a whole.

In explaining relations between gender and accumulation in up-wardly-mobile backward castes, like the Gounders of western Tamil Nadu, Barbara Harriss-White proposes that they organize accumulation through a *social*, as opposed to statist, corporatism. In social corporatism, capital, labor and the local state are brought together in the interests of capital not through the mediation of state organs, but through social institutions; included in the latter, are gender relations through which the "male control of sexuality shap[es] the key social structures of accumulation in ways which both cut across class *and* define the capitalist class."[39] Certainly, Tiruppur's fraternal capital has attempted to consolidate its class power through particular caste and gender relations. However, "male control of sexuality" is an extremely tenuous and negotiated cultural process, which takes multiple forms and has multiple consequences. Certainly, Tiruppur's Gounders have transformed relations between men from vertical relations of authority to horizontal relations of fraternity along the way to consolidate their class power.[40] However, gender regimes have linked sexed bodies to processes of differentiation in varying ways. Fraternal hegemony help-ed crystallize the trajectories of Gounder men, but it could not be im-mune to alternative gender regimes and discourses, nor to new forms of capital accumulation and proletarianization.

Fraternal hegemony only proved to be a stepping stone to a deeper form of gendered hegemony which would hold not only the working class but also a mass of small toiling owners in thrall to an industry ruled by an apex class of exporters. As Tiruppur shifted its focus to export production, a powerful gender discourse of feminization became a new lever of social transformation, shaping expectations of owners and workers in new ways. This global discourse presumes that Third World women are naturally linked to new forms of local and global differentiation. Locally, feminization meant a redefinition of skill in binary gender terms in order to further fragment the political power of labor. Globally, feminization placed Tiruppur's workers in a broader map of global inequalities in the price of labor and, more fundamentally, in value of human life, so that it would seem necessary for footloose global capital to seek the cheapest feminized labor in postcolonial landscapes of the global South. The consequent extreme devaluation of women's livelihoods in this discourse of feminization took its own particular cultural form, as the play *Panjappadi Poráttam* demonstrates, in a new paternalism over Tiruppur's working daughters. This paternalism is a new ideological apparatus that seeks consent for new forms of sexual violence in the everyday work and movements of women across home and work in Tiruppur in the 1990s. I have found the analytic of interpellation useful to understand the power of gender in these processes, because it shifts from the volitional language of "male control of sexuality" to the multifaceted, unintentional productivity of sex/gender regimes in fragmenting and controlling a despotic order of everyday violence at work.

This shift in the hegemony of capital has also been able to differentiate struggles over working people's entitlements so that the latter are experienced and fought out in entirely different arenas. Today's unions have been forced into retreat, in a desperate fight to regain the rights of workers in production lost through decades of decentralization and contracting. Hence, a deepening of inequality through difference is experienced as a multiplicity of struggles. Environmental entitlements to clean water, women's sexual violence across work and home, and the effects of divorce on employability are seen as separable from labor unionism. While labor unions retreat to idioms of struggle harking to a masculinist unionism centered on the rights of male breadwinners, gendered hegemony creates its own gender fetishisms and forms of feminism. Most working people engage in a range of tactics which do not threaten the fundamental axes of gendered hegemony.[41] Fragmentation in working-class experience has, however, created opportunities that, while not challenging dominant mores of caste masculinity and capital, make possible new articulations of sexed bodies with notions of difference, as in forms of informal divorce. These are tactics in a paradoxical space tenuously tied to capitalist control, laden with both new burdens and opportunities, and the most marginal of opportunities make profound claims on a just future.

Selvi, a women's labor leader in CITU, inhabits such a paradoxical space, marginal to the possibilities of Gounder toil, while rendered semi-autonomous by growing class polarization. Selvi spoke to me tentatively after her work hours. She said that her owners did not know about her union activism when she was hired, but now that they do, they did not give her leave that easily. Once, when she was fired, the union helped her get her job back, so she feels some responsibility to CITU. However, Selvi continues to find it difficult to attend evening meetings, at the union "because people talk if a woman goes to the union; men don't have that problem." Selvi lives with a double consciousness: on the one hand, cognizant of the ways masculinist power relations limit her mobility across work, home and labor union; on the other hand, resolute in fighting through the terms of labor organizing for the diversity of Tiruppur's working-class concerns.[42]

CHAPTER 7

Conclusion: Globalizing the *Mofussils*

It is not enough to know the *ensemble* of relations as they exist at any given time as a given system. They must be known genetically, in the movement of their formation. For each individual is the synthesis not only of existing relations, but of the history of these relations. He is a précis of all the past.—Antonio Gramsci[1]

Mofussil (s., also used adjectively) "The provinces,"—the country stations and districts, as contra-distinguished from "the Presidency;" or, relatively, the rural localities of a district as contra-distinguished from the *sudder* or chief station, which is the residence of the district authorities. Thus if, in Calcutta, one talks of the *Mofussils*, he means anywhere in Bengal out of Calcutta; if one at Benares talks of going into the *Mofussils*, he means going anywhere in the Benares division or district (as the case might be) out of the city and station of Benares. And so over India. The word (Hind. from Ar.) *mufassal* means properly "separate, detailed, particular," and hence "provincial," as *mufassal 'adalat*, a "provincial court of justice." This indicates the way in which the word came to have the meaning attached to it.—Sir Henry Yule, *Hobson Jobson*, p. 570.

Through the lives of old guard owners like Star Babu Bhai, Gounder self-made men like Uranium Ramasamy and Lenin Kaliappan, and cosmopolitan Gounder exporters of today; through older communists like Ramasamy, younger radical CITU activists like Durairaj, and marginal women labor organizers like Selvi; through the struggles of male workers, like Disco Ravi and Dastan Bannatic Kings, who can imagine being owners, and of women workers, like Geetha and Valarmati, who fight sexual violence at work and home while remaking relations of care and community; from strange foreign intruders like Antonio Verona to the fraudulent Mr Doha; I have tried to explain the industrial present in Tiruppur genetically, as an ensemble always in the making. The variability, creativity and volatility in these intertwined stories constitute the lived experience of class struggle.

In analyzing this ensemble of relations genetically, I have asked how histories of practice and practices of recollection animate accumulation, keeping in mind accumulation in Marx's twin senses as the accumulation of capital and surplus labor. I have tried to see relations coalesce around provisional hegemonies, whether of the old guard or of fraternal capital or of today's exporters, always through a mixture of consent and coersion. Moreover, I have tried to ask how these hegemonies draw on singular histories and politics of place, to transform social and spatial relations. In particular, I show how agrarian histories of Gounder toil become instruments in decentralizing the geography of industrial work. Finally, I have tried to see these shifting hegemonies over the anarchic development of capitalism by bringing a decentered Marxism in relation to subaltern self-presentations. Globalization in the *Mofussils* requires this Janus-faced critique in order to question the ties that bind the globalization of capital to the conditions of subaltern inequality.

In writing an ethnography of capital as toil, I have explored the conditions through which certain Gounder men have forged their class mobility while remaking a geography of work. In explaining transition, I asked how self-made men renovate colonial and agrarian meanings and practices in the everyday politics of control of social labor. In doing so, I have also had to bring the question of transition in relation to the politics of translation. To not do so would be to see toil as simply a Gounder version of a universal labor theory of value rather than, as Diane Elson puts it, of a historically and culturally grounded value theory of labor. In other words, I try to understand this fetishism as it really works in the self-fashioning of subaltern men as working capitalists.[2]

Finally, I have sought to show how the remaking of industrial work has brought changing gender regimes into play in articulating sexed bodies to broader processes of differentiation. Through the mediation of gender in processes of accumulation, fraternal capital has been both made and unmade, as capitalism is provincialized in the *Moffusils*.

In bringing this ethnography to a close, I revisit some general themes that brought me to write it. First, I return to agrarian studies and the cultural political economy of agrarian transition. I ask what the broader significance is of Tiruppur's capitalism and its heroic entrepreneurs who have emerged from the poorer end of a differentiating peasantry. What is to be made of them, that is, when one takes their self-presentations seriously and critically. I then ask how this particular regional account of transition from peasant-workers to fraternal capital sheds light on gender and the development of capitalism in provincial India. I ask how the transition from fraternal to gendered hegemony in provincial India speaks to the way in which gender mediates the twin processes of accumulation of capital and surplus labor, by linking multiple layers of governance to the conditions of reproduction, and neglect, of laborpower.

The Agrarian Question Comes to Town

What is most important about the agrarian question in the environs of Tiruppur is that it does not conform to the notion that diversifying rich peasants are the most likely "carrier class" of agrarian transition and industrialization in India. The Gounder peasantry of western Tamil Nadu has taken a non-linear route in that it was undergoing a process of class differentiation throughout the first half of the twentieth century, and it was certain young men from the poorer end of this differentiating peasantry who would become Tiruppur's fraternal capital.[3] What is to be made of this anomaly to orthodox Marxist expectations?

I have tried to argue that the notion of a vanguard class of agrarian transition does quite some injustice to the multiple internal routes and contestations through which capitalism is made. Moreover, because capitalism has always to mix consent with coercion, the everyday understandings of its participants must be part of the explanation of agrarian transition. However, Tiruppur also questions the social historian's conceit of writing "history from below," as the subaltern hero of Tiruppur's boom replicates a masculinist bourgeois liberal ideology

rather than a proletarian critique of capitalism. In other words, Gounder toil can be taken at face value as entrepreneurial utopianism. I have
tried to take these self-presentations seriously, and critically, to show
how they are part of local histories and practices of control over social
labor that are rooted in the regional agrarian question.

In reframing the central question in this way, I suggest that Tiruppur speaks directly to three key elements of the agrarian question in
contemporary India: a deepening of economic divergence between
prosperous regions in the north, west and south from the east and center; the rising political and economic clout of rural capitalists in certain
prosperous regions; and the fragmentation of labor militancy and the
proliferation of localized forms of labor control and work organization.

First, spatial divergence in the Indian economy has been seen in
large measure due to more or less unequal agrarian structures and their
effects in promoting quite different types of regional development.
Largely unreconstructed farming systems in northern and eastern
India, for instance, do not promote intersectoral linkages and vibrant
agrarian capitalism as in southern and western states like Gujarat, Punjab and Tamil Nadu. Regional divergence in the Indian space economy
calls for broadening the notion of agriculture's contribution to industrialization from the savings contribution of agriculture to include the
expansion of non-farm employment and rural industry.[4] I have sought
to demonstrate through Tiruppur how peasant-workers have also
reworked agrarian social relations—concerning ways of working and
controlling work—in controlling the detail and social divisions of
labor in industrial work. Agrarian transitions are material and cultural
processes, as they provide material resources as well as histories of
meaning and practice through which non-agricultural work regimes
are made. Economistic accounts of agrarian transition miss this entirely.

Second, the rising power of rural capitalists in certain highly com-
mercialized regions has supported broad-based agrarian populist
movements. Interpretations of these movements remain diverse but
what is clear is that the new farmers' movements and their contend-
ers—movements of Dalits, Adivasis, women and environmental activists in particular—attest to the persistence of classic peasant politics
of land, labor and the fetishism of rural culture. It is important to

remember, however, that Gounder farmers were the first of the new style of mobilizational politics, but Tiruppur Gounders have been conspicuously unsupportive of the new agrarian interest. Indeed, while they have used agrarian social relations to rule the industrial roost in Tiruppur, Gounder capitalists are uninterested in the rural movements of "their" countryside. In their new scheme to rationalize water use and pollution, and in acquiring rural land for New Tiruppur, Gounder exporters at the helm of TEA have become something much more akin to the stereotypical "urban biased" industrial class. What Tiruppur demonstrates is the contingent and fragile nature of agrarian politics, and of shifting class struggles and alliances across town and country. What gendered hegemony does is revive questions concerning the social reproduction of laborpower, and the outstanding political question is whether and how these concerns will be represented by organized labor.[5]

Finally, many studies of recent changes in rural India note the casualization of work, the reworking of patron–client relations, the decline in non-negotiable labor contracts, new forms of piece-rated labor, the "stickiness downwards" of rural wage rates, and the fragmentation and segmentation of rural labor markets which maintain differential wages even for the same tasks across neighboring villages. Tiruppur demonstrates how the fragmentation of work can use resources from the local past to articulate with global production networks.[6]

Tiruppur speaks to the intersection of these three aspects of the agrarian question in India. Agrarian transitions can be local and material as well as cultural. Rural politics are contingent and constituted by contradictory class politics, and the new farmers' movements are a far cry from the timeless defense of agrarian "tradition." Finally, the fragmentation of work, supposedly a hallmark of "Post-Fordism" and "flexible accumulation," can be made through tools hewn from local agrarian histories, as from the flexible *thottam* farms of 1930s agrarian Coimbatore, to hook into late-twentieth-century globalization. In both the sense of an agrarian legacy in contemporary industry, and in the sense of an analytic that can get at the multiple determinations through which the globalization of capital remakes provincial India, the agrarian question has come to town. I turn next to Tiruppur's significance to debates on the cultural and political economy of development in provincial India.

Gender and the Accumulation of Capital and Labor in *the Moffusils*

The historian Sanjay Subrahmanyam has suggested that while scholarship has sufficiently critiqued and pluralized the notion of Indian tradition, there is still much work to be done in pluralizing Indian modernities. To the extent that some Weberians have sought to take on the task, they have remained preoccupied with caste as India's difference. While some political scientists have thought comparatively, they have often resorted to civilizational terms, "echoing the most banal constructions of Orientalism." Instead of these approaches, Subrahmanyam suggests a form of comparison, perhaps across Asian geographies, that can get at differences in institutional trajectories "without necessarily reducing these to simple differences in the immanent natures of civilizations."[7] I have tried to make a case for a different developmental trajectory through attention to the dialectics of culture and economy, and to the social and cultural construction of place.

Moreover, I have sought to link questions of transition and translation. What is different about Tiruppur's fraternal capital is undoubtedly its ability to turn something specific called Gounder toil into global capital. In translating their particular life histories as accounts of practice, I have tried to link their value theory of labor to Indian agrarian and development studies.

I conclude by situating Tiruppur in an important debate initiated by Michael Kalecki and revived by Harriss-White's recent book on provincial India, which centers on "intermediate classes" and, relatedly, on India's "intermediate regime." In Kalecki's view, intermediate classes—like peasants, small producers, family businesses and the self-employed—do not carry a contradiction between capital and labor. In the context of an incomplete land reform, a weak national bourgeoisie and geopolitical non-alignment with respect to US and Soviet imperialism of the 1950s, these intermediate classes form the backbone of

India's "intermediate regime." K.N. Raj explained the intermediate regime as resting somewhere between the capitalist state that served the interests of capital, and the socialist state that represented the interests of peasants and workers. An important corrective came from Pranab Bardhan, who framed the Indian state more precisely as an uneasy alliance of a heterogeneous set of dominant classes, which perpetuates a system of patronage and subsidies that accrue to relatively affluent communities and relatively developed regions. What is important about this reframing is that politics ultimately prevents the heterogeneous coalition of dominant classes from consolidating their interests in the form of a capitalist developmental state. What, then, accounts for accumulation led by precisely such intermediate classes—of which the Gounders of western Tamil Nadu are but one example—from underneath this clumsy edifice?[8]

Bardhan returns twenty years after the Kalecki–Raj formulation of the problem, in the wake of the 1991 economic reforms, to ask: "Is the 'intermediate regime' finally being taken over by full-blooded capitalists, the 'caged tigers' of yesteryear?" While acknowledging limited change in the context of gradual liberalization—particularly in diversification of the industrial structure and in the narrowing gap between elites in the dominant coalition, for instance through processes of rural diversification into small industry—Bardhan remains skeptical of unleashed tigers in the absence of fundamental political economic reform:

> All these changes and realignments in the composition and attitudes of the dominant coalition do not mean that the political resistance to far-reaching reforms is likely to wither away. The affluent classes will not easily give up the lion's share of State subsidies . . . Political heavyweights will not easily give up on their lucrative deals with sections of private capital in exchange of brokered State favours. Unionized workers will aggressively oppose attempts to reorganize and restructure ailing or uncompetitive units in the industrial and financial sector . . . The small propertied interests will resist encroachment on their market niches . . .[9]

While this is fair analysis of the limitations of national social transformation without deeper reforms in entitlements, what slips through the cracks of Bardhan's macro-level vision is precisely the wave of accumulation led by small propertied interests in provincial India that Tiruppur is but one crest of. While this accumulation may not as yet fundamentally alter the intermediate regime, it has important implications for the geography of poverty and development. Tiruppur demonstrates how small property has become the main local player without being bled by parasitic local state institutions. Moreover, Tiruppur's labor movement has been key, as I have argued, to the processes of industrial restructuring and to the politics of accommodation through which the majority of the local working class is held in conditions of near-perpetual insecurity.

Gender has been central to working-class insecurity and local governance of economic development, by linking ideologies of differential embodiment to broader projects of social differentiation. Both fraternal capital and gendered hegemony rely on articulations of sexed and caste bodies to social exclusion. I want to also suggest that sex/gender regimes are also ideological tools for linking regional government with the differential reproduction of laborpower. Hence, working-class women fight a variety of struggles across work and home, against a multiplicity of forms of violence and neglect, with limited means of scaling the many walls of institutionalized political action. On the other hand, fraternal capitalists can link caste, masculinity and politics, so that some of them can go global through new political articulations with tiers of government and multilateral institutions. Both processes of accumulation of capital and surplus labor therefore rely on gender relations in linking power to the reproduction of class.

The accumulation of capital in Tiruppur, I have suggested, involves a politics of work rooted in local configurations of capital, labor and state, with an intermediate class in the lead. The practical moorings of this production form allow one to see how this uneasy alliance keeps the majority of working people impoverished and insecure. The accumulation of surplus labor through gendered hegemony has, moreover, brought questions concerning sexuality, gendered violence and the reproduction of laborpower into public view. While fraternal capital took gender and kinship dynamics out of the agrarian family into the control of social labor, gendered hegemony questions the specific ways in which the feminization of poverty works in this corner of the *Moffusils*. While capital uses difference to dominate all workers, gendered hegemony makes space for emergent activism to question work more fundamentally, across home and family, production and reproduction.

Gounder toil encapsulates the dialectical tensions of Tiruppur's capitalist modernity. Far from a Kaleckian vision in which class antagonisms are submerged, this intermediate class has made them increasingly pronounced and increasingly provincialized, or mediated by local histories of caste and gender exclusion. Hence, as Gounder capitalists have made this baroque industrial form, the production of place has been intertwined with the production of a gendered form of class domination, which secures the conditions for the accumulation of capital alongside the accumulation of a reserve army of labor. The politics of place and class in Tiruppur are twin sides of the same coin that is fundamentally brittle, fraught with the gender, class and caste contradictions of its construction. In this contradictory capitalist geography, there remains something radical in the way in which countless lives are transformed each day, some in the most surprising ways. Tiruppur reminds us that even a most awkward of classes, peasant-workers, might yet be agents in provincializing the globalization of capital.

Gounders in the Third Italy

As a consequence of the research that has been asking whether Tiruppur can follow the lead of the Third Italy, the United Nations Industrial Development Organization (UNIDO) and the National Small Industries Corporation (NSIC) sponsored seven exporters and the secretary of TEA to take a trip out to the Third Italy in 1997 to learn how things should really be done. They were taken to Modena, Carpi, Prato and Bologna in order to encourage them to engage in joint ventures, integrated marketing and so on: what the industrial districts literature calls "joint action." Their responses reveal many things about themselves.

In short, the Tiruppur exporters were incredulous. "They don't know small factories," said one. Knitwear firms in Modena, the global center of knitwear production, combine all elements of production. They are large, highly capital-intensive factories that are fully integrated horizontally into all the processes in knitwear production. Moreover, they only employ about five to ten people, half of whom are family members of the owner. There are much fewer factories in these districts, not thousands upon thousands as in Tiruppur, so coordination problems are quite different if not fewer. The strangest thing to the Tiruppur exporters was that they never saw anyone stitching. They never saw the heart of the production process. When the Gounders pressed them, the Italians would just shrug their shoulders and say it was too hard to get to stitching sections. As it happens, stitching in Modena, the heart of global knitwear production, is invisible because it is entirely given out to women in households. The Tiruppur exporters, when they realized this, found it to be a much more hierarchical form of subcontracting than they were used to. One exasperated

Gounder said to me: "Owners may be preventing household stitching from rising." To prevent workers from rising is to prevent a boss from being made through his toil: this was an alien concept to the TEA exporter of modest origins. In the shock experienced by a self-made Gounder man lies a singular past through which peasant workers like him have made a fraternal form of contracting that holds some opportunity for class mobility. In the face of the Third Italy, Tiruppur's particular geography of power, memory and exploitation comes into sharp relief.

Official Data on Industry in Tiruppur, 1996–1998

Given the bewildering diversity of production activities carried out in Tiruppur's workplaces, it is reasonable to expect that agencies maintain records with different motivations and categories. Consider first the evidence from the District Industries Centre (DIC), Coimbatore, which provides Small Scale Industry (SSI) certification to companies within a given turnover limit for domestic manufacturers to access various concessions. Data collected from firms registering as SSIs in Table 1 indicate spatial concentration of firms in the category of "hosiery and garments" in Tiruppur Block, and this concentration has become more prominent over the decade in the DIC records since 1986. Of 8,555 SSI's in this category, 6,355 are in Tiruppur Block. Note that Coimbatore Corporation has a large total number of SSIs, but they are diversified over a range of sectors, unlike Tiruppur. A memo of the DIC from May 1997 identifies the total number of registered units engaged in hosiery and related activities in Tiruppur as 7010, of which 5515 are "hosiery garment" units while 576 are producers of hosiery cloth. The memo also reports a mere twenty-two export-oriented units, a gross underestimate from the most cursory observation of export firms. The Deputy Inspector of Factories, Tiruppur, provides a different view of industry through employment in registered factories, not just SSIs. Table 2 shows that Hosiery and Garments accounts for about half of working factories and more than a third of employment. Indeed, the Cotton Textiles sector employs more than Hosiery and Garments. Table 3 on decadal change since Cawthorne (1986) finds a decline in cotton ginning and an expansion in spinning mills as well as, quite dramatically, the powerloom sector.

Table 1: Spatial and Sectoral Concentration
of Small Scale Industries Across Selected Blocks and
Coimbatore Corporation of Coimbatore District

Small Scale Industries	Cbe	Avn	Pol	Udm	Tir	Pld	Total
Food products	233	37	126	52	85	77	862
Beverages & tobacco products	25	2	29	1	14	6	119
Cotton textiles	456	341	62	167	644	876	3785
Wool, silk, synthetics	21	1	0	4	8	6	63
Jute, hemp	11	0	2	1	3	1	26
A. Hosiery & Garments	995	156	269	114	**6355**	122	8555
Wood products	194	17	55	8	53	12	445
Paper products, printing	569	46	65	26	123	20	1053
Leather products	120	13	7	22	43	11	352
Rubber & plastic products	868	8	21	4	59	10	1211
Chemical products	312	13	70	17	30	12	629
Non-metallic mineral prodn.	224	12	54	20	40	19	619
Basic metal industries	610	40	9	10	9	22	1094
Metal products	1096	27	42	26	48	27	1823
Machinery and parts	1925	30	144	91	136	124	3329
Electrical machinery	975	20	17	7	8	23	1353
Transport equipment	177	2	1	4	1	0	248
Misc. manufacturing	536	4	10	12	23	27	696
Construction	9	0	0	0	0	1	16
Activities allied to construction	1	0	0	0	0	0	1
Storage and warehousing	1	0	0	0	0	0	4
Medical and health services	6	0	0	0	0	0	7
Personal service	38	1	2	2	1	0	51
Data processing	42	1	1	1	7	1	61
Repair services	617	37	32	49	109	17	1225
Colour film processing	14	0	1		0	0	15
I. Total	10075	804	1020	638	7799	1414	27640

Source: Schedules on "Blockwise and Codewise Classification Lists of SSI Units in Respect of Coimbatore District, 1996," District Industries Center, Coimbatore.

Block abbreviations are: Coimbatore Corporation (Cbe), Avinashi Block (Avn), Pollachi South (Pol), Udumalpet Block (Udm), Tiruppur Block (Tir) and Palladam Block (Pld).

Table 2: Investment and Employment in
Small Scale Industries Related to Knitwear Production
in Tiruppur, 28 May 1997

Product	No. Units Registered	Investment in Land & Building (Million Rs)	Investment in Plant & Machinery (Million Rs)	Employment
Hosiery Garments	5515	156.0	376.7	74822
Hosiery Coth	576	103.4	197.1	3945
Bleaching	70	9.3	9.4	821
Dyeing	171	32.4	52.9	1903
Calendaring	74	16.7	170.1	572
Screen Printing	258	32.4	34.1	2829
Embroidering	12	4.6	16.3	92
Mercerising	3	1.6	0.4	33
Raising	5	1.1	1.5	32
Curing	6	1.9	3.7	44
Other Allied Units				
a. Labels	14	1.1	0.4	74
b. Elastic tape	45	3.0	6.7	193
c. Kaja button	22	1.7	3.5	46
d. Readymades	175	1.5	1.1	642
e. Sewing	9	0.7	0.9	126
f. Tailoring	33	1.9	0.5	231
Total	7010	386.0	869.0	86721
Export Oriented Units (of above)	22	17.4	146.4	316

Source: Letter from Thiru. V. Rangaswamy, G.M. of the District Industries Centre, Coimbatore, to Thiru Mukesh Gulati, Consultant, United Nations Industrial Development Organization; filed as Memo No. 12972/D8/97, dated 28-5-97.

Table 3: Working Factories and Employment in the Private Sector, Tiruppur Division, 1996

Activity	Number of Working Factories	Average Number of Workers	Total Labor-time (Man-days/yr)
Food Products Manufacture	114	3179	746567
Cotton Ginning	107	3475	812088
Powerloom weaving	54	1395	313951
Cotton spinning mills	205	14182	4292885
Cotton composite mills	130	9578	3245627
Non-manual bleaching/dyeing	68	1368	1803718
Total cotton textiles manufacture	576	30293	10568716
Knitted cotton textiles	854	25051	2573518
Floor rugs, garments, textile goods	122	1224	270767
Total textile products (w/apparel)	991	26573	2986285
Industrial machinery for food & textile, and light engineering	19	4265	1250524
Total Private Sector	1904	71412	17554572

Source: "Statement II: No. of Working Factories and Employment in Working Factories—Private Sector, Tiruppur Division," 1996, at the Office of the Deputy Inspector of Factories, Tiruppur.

Table 4: Decadal Change in Factory Employment, Tiruppur Division, 1996

Industry	Employment, 1986	Employment, 1996	Decadal Change
Ginning	6860	3475	-49%
Spinning	9360	23627	152%
Dyeing/Bleaching	950	1368	44%
Powerloom	40	1395	3388%
Knitting	9970	26573	167%

Source: "Statement II" 1996, at the Office of the Deputy Inspector of Factories, Tiruppur, and Cawthorne (1990), Table 5, p.27, derived from same source in 1986. "Knitting" in this table refers to "Total textile products with apparel" in Table II.

Table 5: Distribution of Factories by Employment, Tiruppur Division, 1996. (No. of factories across ranges of workers employed)

Industry	<10 workers	10– 19	20– 49	50– 99	100– 499	500– 599	>1000
Rice & Oil Milling	22	38	17	30	10	1	0
Cotton Textiles	47	137	207	96	34	4	0
Knitting	130	310	497	37	7	0	0
Wood Products	5	6	3	0	0	0	0
Paper & Printing	4	15	6	1	1	0	0
Chemicals	3	7	1	2	0	0	0
Rubber, Plastics	0	9	3	5	0	0	0
Basic Metals/Alloys	10	25	14	3	2	2	0
Metal Products/ Parts	1	11	8	0	4	0	0
Machinery/ Equipment	9	4	13	7	10	2	1
Repair Services	2		8	7	2	1	0
Total	238	624	782	192	71	10	1

Source: "Statement III,"1996, at the Office of the Deputy Inspector of Factories, Tiruppur.

Indices of Transition

Table 18: Familial Sources of Income Prior to Entry into Knitwear Cluster

Route Trade	Agricultural Industry	Rural loom	Hand-loom	Power-mill	Cotton Work	Mill Work	Gin
Domestic (SIHMA)							
Gounder							
Ex-Worker	12%	9%	1%	6%	0%	15%	16%
Gounder	23%	14%	0%	9%	0%	27%	0%
Other							
ex-Worker	32%	6%	19%	16%	3%	6%	3%
Southern	26%	11%	15%	7%	0%	4%	0%
Northern	27%	27%	0%	9%	0%	0%	0%
Export (TEA)							
Gounder							
ex-Worker	0%	8%	0%	17%	0%	17%	0%
Gounder	25%	38%	0%	13%	0%	13%	0%
Other							
ex-Worker	17%	0%	33%	0%	0%	17%	0%
Southern	25%	25%	0%	0%	13%	0%	0%
Northern	20%	0%	0%	10%	30%	0%	0%

Route	Urban Coolie	Small Shop	Trade, Money-lending	Work in Business	Other Profes-sions	Hosiery Work	Hosiery-related Owner
Domestic (SIHMA)							
Gounder							
ex-Worker	12%	4%	1%	3%	7%	38%	4%
Gounder	5%	27%	18%	23%	18%	0%	23%
Other							
ex-Worker	10%	16%	26%	16%	26%	6%	10%
Southern	7%	26%	41%	19%	19%	0%	26%
Northern	0%	9%	45%	45%	9%	0%	27%

Export (TEA)

Gounder							
ex-worker	8%	8%	0%	8%	0%	17%	17%
Gounder	0%	25%	38%	63%	38%	0%	13%
Other							
ex-worker	0%	17%	17%	0%	67%	0%	0%
Southern	0%	13%	38%	25%	13%	0%	13%
Northern	0%	0%	90%	0%	0%	0%	10%

Notes: "Entry" means as worker and/or owner. "Rural Industry" implies agro-processing of various sorts, particularly rice milling, oil milling, cotton ginning and dairy. "Handloom" includes hand spinning and weaving, the traditional occupations of Devanga Chettiars and Senguntha Mudaliars in western Tamil Nadu. "Powerloom" includes other non-traditional small textile-related activities, especially tailoring, and these are usually owner-operators. "Cotton Mill" refers to owners of large spinning mills as well as owners of cotton gins and sizing units. "Mill Work" refers to work in spinning mills, while "Gin Work" refers to work in cotton gins; the first are predominantly men, the second women. "Urban coolie" refers to a range of unskilled manual labor in town, including *kalasi* and construction. "Small shop" refers to ownership of tiny grocery stores, vegetable sales, petty services such as a bicycle shop, etc. "Trade, Money lending" refers to larger non-agro-based trading in yarn and cloth, sometimes also engaged in putting-out to weavers and often combined with moneylending and real estate. "Work in business" refers to apprenticeship or employment in non-trade, non-agri-based businesses including services such as bus and truck lines which were often ways of acquiring necessary entrepreneurial skills. "Unrelated Professions" include a range of occupations (medical, engineering, banking, etc) as well as government jobs. "Hosiery Work" is work of family members before the respondent's entry into Tiruppur knitwear; "Hosiery-related owner" refers to ownership of knitwear and allied concerns by such family members.

Table 19: Work History Characteristics

Route	Av Start	Av. Age	Yrs of	No. of	Boss Relative	Boss Same	Recruiter		
							Relative	Friend	Other
Domestic (SIHMA)									
Gounder ex-Worker	1970	18	8	2	43%	75%	60%	22%	1%
Other ex-Worker	1975	21	9	2	23%	55%	33%	47%	13%
50% of Northerns	1984	20	4	1	80%	80%	100%	0%	0%
Export (TEA)									
Gounder ex-Worker	1966	16	11	1	50%	75%	78%	11%	11%
Other ex-Worker	1987	21	4	1	20%	20%	40%	60%	0%
10% of Northerns	1987	26	3	1	0%	0%	0%	100%	0%

Note: "Boss Relative" refers to whether the boss was a relative of the worker. Recruitment in these cases is informal and was usually introduction and recommendation to the boss by another employee, either Relative or Friend; Other refers mainly to hire without any prior connections.

Table 20: Wages, Savings and Unionism in Work Histories

Route	Initial Daily Wage	Final Daily Wage	Wage Increase	Could Save	Savings, 1000 Rs	Union Members	Yrs in Union
Domestic (SIHMA)							
Gounder ex-Worker	8.42	44.08	424%	45%	27.52	20%	13
Other ex-Worker	15.77	56.82	260%	52%	32.29	7%	3
50% of Northerns	46.15	47.69	3.30%	50%	45.00	0%	0
Export (TEA)							
Gounder ex-Worker	10.87	40.96	276%	85%	18.83	0%	0
Other ex-Worker	16.58	111.54	573%	40%	100.00	0%	0
10% of Northerns	–	–	–	0%	0.00	0%	0

Note: These are nominal wages, which only show divergence in orders of magnitude across work careers. 50% and 10% of *Northerns* in SIHMA and TEA, respectively, had work careers in knitwear.

Table 24: Levels of Education

Route	Primary	Middle	SSLC/PUC (Secondary)	College	Professional at Degree
Domestic (SIHMA)					
Gounder ex-Worker	16%	26%	34%	17%	0%
Gounder	4%	0%	61%	30%	0%
Other ex-Worker	13%	3%	52%	29%	0%
Southern	0%	4%	54%	42%	0%
Northern	0%	0%	36%	64%	0%
Export (TEA)					
Gounder ex-Worker	25%	8%	33%	25%	0%
Gounder	0%	0%	63%	38%	0%
Other ex-Worker	0%	17%	50%	33%	0%
Southern	0%	0%	33%	67%	0%
Northern	0%	0%	20%	70%	10%

Figure 8: SIHMA Members, 1956–1994

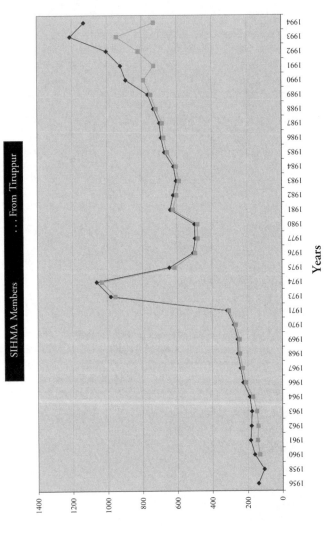

Source: *Āndarrikkaigaḷ* Annual Reports, SIHMA

Notes

Chapter 1: A Worker Path to Capital?

1. Krishnaswami's (1989) arguments concerning labor sweating and informality are compatible, to some extent, with Cawthorne's (1990, 1993) argument about "amboebic capitalism" reliant on absolute surplus value. When Cawthorne (1995) reframes her research as a "low road" to industrial flexibility based on cheap labor and market access rather than innovation, she does not make enough of organizational innovation. It must also be said that Cawthorne does not collect any information in Tamil, nor does her work mirror Krishnaswami's ethnographic closeness to the labor process, and this has important analytical costs.

2. Note that knitwear production is reserved under state policy in the "small scale sector," defined in 1996 by investment in plant and machinery at Rs 6-7.5 million ($200K).

3. Swaminathan and Jeyaranjan (1994, 1999) are very careful about simply transferring the Third Italy as a model, but instead use the opportunity to argue for the importance of treating informal sector dynamics on its own terms in multiple respects, including informal processes of worker skilling and the extreme gendering of inequality.

4. This internationalist reading of *Capital* is from Harvey (2000), who accepts Brenner's (1976, 1986) argument concerning the exceptional conditions for transition to capitalism in the British countryside, while seeing these conditions as also linked to processes of "originary" accumulation on a world scale.

5. Harvey (2000), p. 38.

6. Gillian Hart (2002:224) has made the astute observation that Mao's mobilization of the peasantry may have provided the basis for "spectacularly and distinctively 'non-Western' trajectories of industrial accumulation later in the century."

7. Henri Lefebvre's (1991) provocation remains fundamental to radical

geographic thought, in that a truly social understanding of the production of space must move beyond the dichotomy of physical, container-space and mental, cognitive space. Lefebvre argues that social spaces of particular epochs carry specific contradictions. Without an understanding of the social space produced, and undermined, through capitalism's anarchic developmentalism, Lefebvre faults traditional Marxists for assuming that a seizure of state power can transform practice. Beheading the king does not remove the spaces we live in.

8. Hart (2001) argues that post-leftists share with neoliberals the conflation of two senses of development in their critiques of the role of the state in capitalist development. On the one hand are discourses and practices of intervention in the postcolony carried out under the sign of "development" since the era of decolonization. On the other hand are processes of capitalist development.

9. Cooper, Holt and Scott (2000) draw inspiration from C.L.R. James's (1938) classic on San Domingo's "Black Jacobins" as forgotten participants in the French Revolution, to call into question understandings of Enlightenment rationality, market economy and political liberalism as totalizing universalist rhetorics that thinly veil the extension of colonial rule. Cooper (1997) retains the same sense of partiality and struggle in arguing that development discourse emerged not from the well-intentioned brows of European colonizers in the sunset of empire, but from the pressures of multiple forms and sites of collective working-class struggle.

10. Coronil (1997) provides a decentered analysis of subaltern capitalist modernity by de-linking relations between capitalism and democracy, capitalism and nature, and capitalism and bounded national spatiality.

11. Thanks to Sunil Agnani for this formulation, at a presentation in the English Department, University of Michigan, January 27, 2003.

12. Coronil's (1997) analysis de-fetishizes a particular type of peripherality forged through a colonial transition and rentier postcoloniality that tends toward a functional disarticulation between enriched and impoverished sectors of the social economy (see deJanvry 1981). This characterization of peripherality emerges from a particular episteme centered on the Latin American radical nationalisms of ECLA structuralism and dependency theory, which Coronil questions through a postcolonial critique of Venezuelan populism.

13. Pranab Bardhan cautions against "anarcho-communitarianism," in reference to authors like Sachs (1992) and Escobar (1995), as noted in

Corbridge and Harriss (2000:194.) Similarly subaltern studies historiographies of work in India, principally Chakrabarty (1989) and Prakash (1990a) have been critiqued by Subrahmanyam (1996) for presuming traditional obstacles to capitalist modernity. However, these revisionist histories make more important contributions in showing how the expectations of colonial political economy are confounded by subaltern pasts and illiberal practices in colonial labor regimes. In both cases, subaltern power/knowledge cannot be explained away through the universal categories of colonial bureaucrats or metropolitan Marxists.

14. Kohli (1990).
15. See *India Today*, March 31, 1994, p.88.
16. Tyabji (1989) is a historical explanation of state populism in making small-scale industries policy.
17. Corbridge and Harriss (2000) call Hindu nationalism and economic liberalization "elite revolts," a formulation that is more compelling than Barrington Moore's (1966) provocative prediction of the possibility of Hindu fascism. On the pogrom in Gujarat, see Prashad (2003). Much of my analysis of Indian development is drawn from Corbridge and Harriss (2000), and Harriss-White (2003).
18. For an exploration of competing claims in early Indian development, see Corbridge and Harriss (2000). For shifts in the light of Cold War geopolitics and global development discourse, see Gupta (1998), Chapter 1.
19. On the postcolonial Indian state as a coalition of dominant classes responsible for slow transformation in productivity, see Bardhan (1984a). On the changing politicization of caste under colonialism as a form of indirect rule, see Dirks (2001), p.15 and *passim*.
20. This elaboration of Antonio Gramsci in India is in Chatterjee (1986), elaborated in light of Indian development politics by Corbridge and Harriss (2000).
21. Corbridge and Harriss (2000), Chapter 2.
22. Barbara Harriss-White (2003) has championed a "field economics," inspired by Polly Hill's pioneering work in West Africa to characterize this "India of the 88%" largely misunderstood through the presumptions of metropolitan and corporate India. See especially p. 91 and p.15 on the effects of liberalization.
23. Holmström (1998) summarizes Piore and Sabel's notion of flexible specialization as "Networks of small, relatively autonomous decision-making units (small firms or departments of a large decentralized

company), closely interdependent, each with equipment and skills to perform a limited range of tasks, but open to experiment and innovation. Flexible technologies rather than single-purpose machines . . . A high level of trust between entrepreneurs, even when they compete . . . Some basis for trust between employers, or managers, and workers . . . [who] are used to solving new problems and constantly learning new skills" (p. 27).

24. This argument in its earlier iterations (Piore and Sabel, 1984; Pyke *et al.*, 1990; Rasmussen *et al.*, 1992) has been subject to criticism of the underlying processes at work (Sayer and Walker, 1992; Gertler, 1992; Amin and Robins, 1990; Hart, 1997). In his response to the growing debate on decentralized alternatives for the Third World after the decline of import-substitution industrialization, Holmström (1998) draws on the dichotomy of "high" and "low" roads to flexibility. This distinction, from Pyke *et al.* (1991) contrasts a high road based on efficiency enhancement and innovation, to a low road based on sweated, insecure labor. Holmström does not admit of ways in which innovation and sweating, or absolute and relative surplus value combine. In contrast, many have observed unfree labor relations in the heart of capitalist agriculture (Brass, 1986, Hart, 1986, Wells, 1996; Watts, 1994), and unskilled, politically subordinate labor in electronics sub-assembly in the *maquiladoras* of the US–Mexican border (Shaiken, 1994). For collective efficiency, see Schmitz (1989).

25. Alfred Marshall ([1890], 1986) was concerned with efficiency gains through the clustering of skilled labor, specialized machinery, suppliers, services and specialist trade knowledge. The resulting economies external to firms were pecuniary, but also more than pecuniary, through, for instance, exchange of knowledge, development of skills through labor mobility, buyer–supplier interaction and other non-pecuniary or "real" externalities. The new industrial district studies extend real externalities to planning functions for collective capital. Joint action—the neologism for collective capitalist planning—involves cooperation over ensuring the conditions of profitability and in creating milieux of innovation. See the discussion in Nadvi (1996.) Nadvi and Schmitz (1998) use the term "clusters" so as not to assume the exceptional social relations implied by "industrial districts." Saxenian's (1994) ethnography of firm networks in Silicon Valley explores the mix of institutional practices that create its regional advantage.

26. Holmström (1993) is a major advocate of flexible specialization in

India, through an epochal argument that Fordism is dying and it is incumbent on Indian workers to use craft traditions to make the "Emilian model" their own, and doing so requires dismantling ties of ethnicity and kinship between Indian entrepreneurs and craftsmen that deter the formation of "trust." Since small firms are disadvantaged in terms of technology and access to markets, Holmström suggests that decentralization within large firms and multinationals might be the way to think of flexible specialization in India (pp.32-4). With this, flexible specialization becomes more squarely a strategy for corporate dominance with some support for a labor aristocracy of skilled workers.

27. Knorringa (1998) finds the interfirm division of labor compensates for vertical disintegration of production processes into specialized stage firms in Agra's footwear cluster. Tewari (1996), on Ludhiana's light engineering industry, also finds roving specialized labor gangs who tinker with and adapt machinery to a variety of tasks in the manner of what Storper and Salais (1997) call a "district labor market," which have in fact been typical of several early industrial transitions, as in the US Midwest (see Page and Walker, 1991). Nadvi's (1992) research on small-firm clusters in Pakistani Punjab finds process-specialized firms to be "autonomous" in that they were not tied or dependent but could contract with several firms. Horizontal inter-firm relations might be in the form of "capacity contracting" in which firms share production orders (Nadvi, 1992; Knorringa, 1998), pool strategies in marketing (Holmström 1998) and lobby the state for resources (Tewari 1998b). Tewari argues that Ludhiana's industrial associations' negotiations with the local state government on the issue of electric power shortages have been successful precisely because of strong horizontal cooperation.

28. Nadvi and Schmitz note that relations of association and skill-acquisition often emerged in a mixed, indeed "communal," space of domesticity, residence and production, a point of departure for a gendered critique of production/reproduction and "community" (Nadvi and Schmitz, 1998, p. 100). For comparative scholarship rethinking Weberian notions of Asian business from the 1950s and 1960s, see Rutten (1995), Upadhya and Rutten (1997) and Upadhya (1997). Cluster theorists also often invoke Granovetter's (1985) language of embeddedness as the basis for trust, which grounds stable economic action; this is strongly critiqued in Hart (1998).

29. Tewari (1998a, 1998b).

30. Cawthorne (1990), pp.121–2.

31. Storper and Salais (1997) use a practice-theoretic political economy to speak in terms of conventions of "identity" and "participation."

32. The classical agrarian theorists theorized the ways in which peasant households persist and differentiate, the difference of agrarian capitalist development from non-agricultural industry, the ways in which agrarian capitalism deepens a home market for manufactures, and the political influences and wider implications of the transition to capitalism in agriculture. See Kautsky ([1899], 1988); Lenin ([1899, 1908], 1974); and Chayanov ([1924], 1966).

33. Byres (1991, 1995). On the English transition, also see Dobb (1963) on the role of *kulaks* or rich peasants, and Brenner (1978) on "improving landlords;" on Latin America, deJanvry (1981); on the northern USA, and petty commodity production more generally Banaji (1977), Bernstein (1977, 1988), Gibbon and Neocosmos (1985), Freidmann (1978.) On the importance of petty private property rights and social services in the form of public infrastructure and cooperative organizations in Taiwan and South Korea, see Bardhan (1986b), and on the "garrison state" taking the place of the improving landlord, see Apthorpe (1979).

34. For the classic account of the social history of the permanent settlement, see Ranajit Guha (1963).

35. I have benefited from revisionist agrarian studies that draws on feminism, social history and cultural studies to ask *how* non-modern or non-capitalist practices, meanings and power relations recombine at the heart of capitalist social formations. See, for instance, Agarwal, 1994; Berry, 1989, 1993; Carney and Watts, 1990; Guyer and Peters, 1987; Hart, 1986, 1991, 1992, 2002; Mackintosh, 1989; Moore, 1993; Roseberry, 1989; Watts, 1992, 1994; Wells, 1996; Wolf, 1992. Hart's work on East Asia and South Africa speaks precisely to grounded understandings of rural diversification and industrialization, and to intersecting struggles over resources across multiple institutional arenas and scales of analysis. A good critique of the cultural difference of Asian capital and labor is Rutten (1994); on the agrarian origins of industrial flexibility in the Third Italy, see Paloscia (1991); on intersectoral linkages and industrialization in Taiwan, see Orru (1991), and for Chinese rural industrialization Hart, 1997; Oi, 1992; Bowles and Dong, 1994.

36. Srivastava (1995).

37. This is Hart's (1986) formulation. On the classic framing of interlinked markets, see Krishna Bharadwaj (1985); on the persistence of "precapitalist" relations see Bhaduri (1973, 1983); critics argued that accumulation might proceed alongside forced commerce, either through

the exclusion of small peasants from the former or through seasonal labor tying (Bhalla, 1976; Bardhan and Rudra, 1981); Bhaduri's (1983) response specifies regional class configurations that explain, for instance, the divergence between eastern and western India; Bardhan (1984b) draws on the Bardhan–Rudra survey to show that tied-labor contracts are more common in tight labor markets and are therefore not simply a form of unemployment insurance, but are evidence of "extra-economic" or "social and politico-legal" compulsion; Rudra (1992: 269) also shies away from seeing labor-tying as involuntary, but he questions Bardhan's economism in explaining these illiberal relations in monetary terms, arguing that *begar* in Maharashtra, *sagari* in Rajasthan, *holeya* in South Kanara, and *kamia* and *jan* elsewhere are cases of bonded labor that persist for reasons of social power; Breman's (1993) ethnography of *hali* labor relations in Gujarat has been useful in demonstrating the adaptation of "bonded labor," but *hali* is then posed as a case of consensual, unequal labor. Brass (1990) takes to task the voluntarism in the notions of exchange and of the resolution of problems of uncertainty and risk in Bardhan, Rudra and Breman, arguing that unfree labor relations represent both a cheapening and a disciplining of labor. Reflecting on these Indian debates in comparative context, Hart (1986) shows how these "multi-stranded arrangements" become instruments of social control and capital accumulation. For village studies that relate local power relations to the persistence of unfreedom, see V.K. Ramachandran (1990), J. Harriss (1982), and Athreya, Djurfeldt and Lindberg (1990); these village studies put "unfreedom" back in their contexts of agrarian class relations.

38. An early analysis of differential caste and gender effects of agrarian commercialization is T.S. Epstein's (1962) comparison of a dryland and wetland village in South India. The irrigated village, with strong economic development, reproduced the subjection of Dalit labor and unpaid women's labor in enabling male participation in broader economic activities; the dry village, with weak local development, showed tremendous economic diversification, weakened hereditary Dalit labor, and more independent sources of income for women. These divergent gender/ caste outcomes do not conform to a Leninist notion of economic growth *leading to* the dissolution of noncapitalist forms of social control. On the wider operation of gender, see Harriss-White (1995) on agro-commerce in Coimbatore District and Breman (1994) on informal labor in Gujarat. Kapadia's (1994, 1995) ethnography in Tamil Nadu critiques some of the central themes of the agrarian labor market

debates in India. Here, mutuality between workers of the same caste maintains labor market segmentation and fragmentation, so that what appears to be a form of domination may instead be a nascent form of subaltern assertion at work and home. However, exclusionary sororal gang labor of this sort has fueled competition between fractions of labor rather than strengthening their class solidarity. Kapadia's insights point to a complex understanding of local hegemony in which subaltern agency is indeterminate, and often contributes to subordination across domestic and work spheres.

39. See Dirks (1996), Reiniche (1996), and Chris Fuller's Introduction and other articles in Fuller (1996).

40. The orthodox interpretation of forced collectivization as necessary for "primitive socialist accumulation" to fund Soviet industrialization was fundamentally questioned by the debate between Alec Nove and James Millar following the revisionist data of A.A. Barsov. Ellman's (1975) stocktaking shows that the intersectoral terms-of-trade could be interpreted in a variety of ways depending upon how sectors are defined, and that if in fact the "industrial" sector is disaggregated into state and proletarian sectors, the evidence shows that industrial proletariat bore the brunt of Soviet industrialization; as rapid inflation and falling real wages allowed the state to redistribute resources toward industrial production.

41. Karshenas (1995) provides an elegant tracing of the debates on intersectoral terms-of-trade; on "urban bias" see Lipton (1977) and the critique by Byres (1979); on differentiation of struggle by crop and region, see Mitra (1977); Mellor's (1976) model of foodgrains-based agricultural growth in India was inspired by Teng-hui Lee's (1971) on Taiwan.

42. For research on the "lifestyles" of *patidar* capitalists in Gujarat, see Rutten (1995). For the Kamma Naidus of Andhra Pradesh in the remaking of Visakhapatnam, see Upadhya (1997). On the footloose proletariat of Gujarat, see Breman (1994), and in a more popular version with photographs of labor regimes across Western India, see Breman and Das (2000). The argument on agrarian continuities draws from Breman's earlier work on the *hali* system, for which see Breman (1993).

43. Frankel (1972); Sharma (1973).

44. Srivastava (1995) provides an excellent general overview. On farmers' movements, see Nadkarni (1987), Alexander (1981), and Hasan (1989), among others.

45. Corbridge and Harris (2000).

46. Kannan (1988); Sen (1992); Heller (1995, 1999).
47. Haraway (1991).
48. Thus far, I learn from Sayer (1992) and Burawoy (1991) on method.

Chapter 2: Social Labor, or How a Town Works, 1996–1998

1. Cf. Sayer and Walker (1993).
2. This notion of social labor providing the elementary form of relative surplus value, simple cooperation, which is offered to capital as a gift, is from Marx [1867] (1967), p. 333.
3. The Apparel Export Promotion Council (AEPC), the quasi-governmental agency responsible for disbursing export quota entitlements and for monitoring knitwear exports in Tiruppur, defines two types of exporters: Manufacturing Exporters who have their own production units that are certified Small-Scale Industries (SSI's), and Merchant Exporters who may not be producers. The distinction is important only because exporters producing through certified SSI's are entitled to lower duties on imports of raw materials as a percent of their exports. However, as the Secretary of TEA warned me, "registration in AEPC is common even if they don't do exports because every supplier hopes to do exports." In other words, the distinction between exporters made by AEPC has little resonance with reality and indeed it runs up against common parlance and practice. Interview with TEA Secretary, March 3, 1997.
4. Note that Cawthorne (1993) does not note the distinction between "jobwork" and "contract" in local discourse, but the latter is somewhat akin to her notion of "inside-contracting." The distinction is important because "jobwork" emerges earlier in the history of knitwear in Tiruppur than the contracting of stitching or garment manufacture. Moreover, "contract" does not necessarily mean internal contracting, as some companies engage in external contracts also with their allied units or "sister concerns."
5. "Known people," *terincavanka*, are either *nammál*, "our people," or they are actual or fictive kin, usually from the same caste.
6. "Banian waste" is the term for taken-apart surplus knitted cloth, which then assumes a sponge-like character due to the springiness yarn acquires through knitting; there is regional demand for banian waste in light engineering and automobile servicing for cleaning oil and grease.

7. Some powerful direct exporters integrated backwards, into the spinning mill sector after the yarn price hikes of the early 1990s. The yarn price hikes were a consequence of export liberalization of cotton yarn, a boon for the big spinning Mill owners but anathema to local consumers of yarn. Government subsidies for investment in "mini-mills" were the way in which local entrepreneurs hoped to climb out of the price hike while releasing their dependence on the mill sector. For the most part, this solution has not proven profitable five years after a few big owners set up their own mills, despite accessing cheap, unorganized labor, as well as "backward area" subsidies from the state for locating in green-field sites.

8. Interviews with Cobalt Devaraj, February 2, 1997 and May 27, 1997.

9. Thanks to Richard Walker for pointing this out to me. Personal communication, June 1998.

10. Thanks to Sandra Comstock for reminding me to stress this point. Personal Communication, April 25, 2003.

11. Interview with Gopikrishnan, November 2, 1996.

12. Rotary printing requires massive capital investment in heavy machinery, and is therefore more likely to be part of a larger processing establishment. Table printing is a much more labor intensive procedure through which fabric is rolled out onto long tables and designs are transferred using screens and squeegees.

13. For calling my attention to this here and elsewhere, and in relation to the credit system, a point I cannot fully address with my information, thanks to Keith Breckenridge. Personal communication, April 24, 2003.

14. Wolf (1982), pp. 74–5.

15. Wolf (2001), pp. 60–1.

16. Ibid., p. 340.

17. Ibid., p. 384.

18. Burawoy (1982).

19. See Marx [1867] (1967), and also Walker (1989b).

20. Burawoy (1982).

21. Here, I am informed by Sayer and Walker (1993).

22. For an argument that domination under capitalism seems independent of work practice but in fact is a consequence of new forms of social interdependence that cannot be understood in terms of concrete or personified forms of domination alone, see Postone (1993). In other words, in the realm of doxa or taken-for-granted practice, workers participate in

their exploitation despite their best intentions. Social labor as the sociality engendered by deepening divisions of labor brings this doxic experience of workers into view.

23. Cawthorne (1993).
24. A simple correlation of numbers of fabrication machines against firm turnover is 0.21 for SIHMA owners and 0.15 for TEA owners.
25. Cawthorne (1993), p. 54.
26. Backward integration is minutely correlated with turnover (indices are 0.03 for SIHMA, 0.16 for TEA.) Forward integration is also only slightly correlated with turnover (indices are 0.15 for SIHMA, 0.19 for TEA.) As there is considerable room for confusion in defining vertical and horizontal integration, I use them heuristically following Sayer and Walker (1993:18): "Vertical can either mean work hierarchies or sequential steps in processing; horizontal usually refers to divides between commodity sectors or parallel processes on the shopfloor, but might as easily apply to different stages in the production cycle or to work in circulation. While it is hard to avoid use of these terms, they cannot be more than rough and ready pointers."
27. Cawthorne has gone through a change of heart in thinking through the causality. Cawthorne (1993:46) claims: "as ownership and capital become more concentrated, production is being decentralized into separate units. I use the metaphorical term amoebic capitalism to conceptualize this process." Cawthorne (1995:45) only mentions amoebic capitalism in passing, and argues more precisely that the concentration of capital has proceeded "without the centralization of the production processes." This is certainly borne out through the decade of the export boom following her research.
28. Cawthorne (1995), pp. 46–7.
29. I am in concurrence here with the careful delineation of practical "worlds of production" in Storper and Salais (1997).
30. I am grateful to Leland Davis and Marina Welker of the Anthropology and History Program at the University of Michigan, for pressing me to clarify this point. Welker asked how local uses and meanings shape practice, particularly as a multiplicity of use values are created in the process of making garments. Davis suggested foregrounding the local mediation of core/ periphery relations in exporting alongside a vibrant local market. My response is that these markets and their goods are strongly bifurcated: the home market is for underwear, low-quality garments, export rejects and various waste products, while export garments

are expensive fashion garments marked as qualitatively different and priced far out of local reach. Workers do not see production and consumption in the same things. April 17, 2001 seminar on "Agrarian Questions," University of Michigan, Ann Arbor.

31. This formulation relies on the argument in Storper and Salais (1997).
32. Ibid., p. 34.
33. Ibid., p. 28.
34. Ibid., p. 48.
35. American Apparel Manufacturers Association (1997), p. 32.
36. Harvey (1982).
37. My survey evidence shows 82 percent of SIHMA owners and 80 percent of TEA owners utilize formal bank credit.
38. Only 64 percent of North Indians in SIHMA and 25 percent of North Indians in TEA utilize institutional credit through their Tiruppur concerns.
39. 95 percent of SIHMA owners and 94 percent of TEA owners who accessed bank credit did so through the provision of collateral security.
40. Interview with Mohan and Eswaran, March 22, 1997.
41. Interview with Radha, June 9, 1997.
42. Thanks to Keith Breckenridge for pointing out here that Sargam Agarwal challenges a simple notion of access to capital as a source of power. Breckenridge suggests in response to this section that the credit system might conceal an "absence of capital accumulation," and my last respondent concurs. My response is that the credit system conceals the concentration of capital, rather than the fact of capital accumulation, which surely is vigorously under way given the rapidity of expansion through technical change, at least through the early 1990s. Only large exporters like Sargam Agarwal could feasibly leave Tiruppur in the lurch rather than sink deeper into debt, and in the latter case I agree with Breckenridge that for a large section of capital this diminishes the possibility of accumulation. Personal communication, Ann Arbor, April 24, 2003.
43. A. Sakthivel, TEA Bulletin, March 1994.
44. See Nadvi (1992, 1996), and Nadvi and Schmitz (1998).
45. http://www.indiaurbaninfo.com/app/wsnsa.dll/niua/infrasearch22.r?recno=3 (updated July 31, 2002. Last Accessed February 28, 2004).
46. Interviw with Srinivasan, February 26, 1998.
47. Interview at SIHMA, June 9, 1997.
48. One estimate was 70–75 percent (interview with Zintex Srinivasan,

February 26, 1998) while the secretary of TEA, claimed 80 percent (interview with TEA Secretary Subramaniam, March 3, 1997).

49. AEPC pamphlet (1997), interview with Sakthivel, January 30, 1997, observations at India Knitfair, 1997.

50. Of these associations, BCMA, THYMA and TSPOA represent their various sections of production in disputes; they do not take the lead in joint action the way SIHMA and TEA can. TDA, the dyers association, has gained prominence through struggles over the right to pollute groundwater and rivers, and TDA has been engaged in fierce battles in the courts and against the Pollution Board over these issues.

51. Advocate Nalasamy, March 3, 1998.

52. Arbitration Council of Tiruppur, "ACT Objectives and Working Mode," memo, 1997.

53. Interview with Sakthivel, January 30, 1997.

54. "Travel into the Future of Fashion," brochure from India Knit Fair, November 1997.

55. Interview with TEA Secretary, March 3, 1997.

56. Interview with Sakthivel, January 30, 1997.

57. Interview with Iron Lokanathan, November 6, 1996.

58. Group interview with women workers on top of RKG Knitting, November 23, 1996.

59. "Statement IX—Distribution of factories submitting returns according to number of hours per week for year 1996," Office of the Deputy Inspector of Factories, Tiruppur.

60. Checking workers get an average of Rs 40 per shift. Cutting "masters" get around Rs 80 per shift. Ironing and stitching workers can get around Rs 70 to 75, or as low as Rs 50. Singer tailors, who primarily stitch labels onto garments, can get up to Rs 90, but these are piece-rated workers whose wage can admit wide variance. Finally, helpers and "damage" workers get paid as little as Rs 15 for young girls to Rs 25–35 for most children and young women and to Rs 40 for older women (Group Interview with women workers in Poompuhar Nagar, February 15, 1998). Another group of male workers at the Communist union CITU revealed similar shift wages: Rs 70 for ironing, Rs 35 for checking ("all women"), Rs 40 for packing (Rs 25 for child labor), and Rs 70 for cutting. Interview with Iron Lokanathan, November 6, 1996.

61. As a contrast, the predominantly rural and female spinning Mill workers in one of the rural mills a Tiruppur exporter has started, near Dharapuram to the south of Tiruppur, get paid much less than the

wages the same employer would pay in Tiruppur. Older women in the "Blowroom" get paid Rs 20/day, women in "Carding" and "Drawing" get paid Rs 30/day and women machine tenders make as little as Rs 10/day. These are pathetic wages in comparison with Tiruppur. Observations at a mill in Dharapuram owned by Tiruppur knitwear owner, 1997.

62. Interview with Leelavathi, November 20, 1996.

63. Interview with Gizani Mohan, November 17, 1996.

64. Their main expense is house rent, of about Rs 300–400 per month for a thatched hut, with an advance of Rs 1000; they also have to buy water at Rs 0.50 per bucket, or about Rs 50 per month; one lady said a couple spends Rs 500, without including food. Group interview with women workers on top of RPG Knitting, November 23, 1996.

65. Rent is Rs 350 in "outer" (it would be Rs 800–1000 in town), water is Rs 150 (since he is outside municipal water limits, he gets it from water lorries), tea is Rs 300, family maintenance is Rs 750, kerosene is Rs 200, school for children is Rs 300, luxuries ("hotel" or eating out, cinema) are Rs 200 and "dress" is Rs 150, which all adds up to Rs 2400 per month. He added that often they have to take out loans at 10 percent monthly interest. Interview with Ravi, November 6, 1996.

66. Cawthorne (1990), p. 136.

67. To date, in 1998, incidentally, the Factories Inspectorate reports no fatal accidents and five non-fatal accidents in the whole knitting and knitwear sector. The numbers are silent in reporting hazardous working conditions in a fractured and disintegrated industrial form where most employees are not recorded on "muster rolls" or indeed kept on in the event of serious injury.

68. Cawthorne (1990), p. 125.

69. AAMA (1997), pp. 10–11.

70. Cawthorne (1990), p. 126.

71. I disagree with Cawthorne on workers' perceptions, as her work does not demonstrate an ethnographic commitment, let alone fluency in Tamil. Cawthorne (1990), p. 131.

72. Thanks to Keith Breckenridge for this reminder. Personal communication, Ann Arbor, April 24, 2003.

73. I am grateful to Marina Welker for this point, which has helped my larger argument. April 17, 2000 seminar on Agrarian Questions, Anthropology and History, University of Michigan, Ann Arbor.

74. Swaminathan and Jeyaranjan (1994), p. 13.

75. Aloysius, director of SAVE in Tiruppur, quoted in *Indian Express,* December 12, 1997.

76. For evidence that young boys in knitwear are considered to be "apprentices" in the process of skill acquisition while young girls are considered casual, unskilled labor, see Yamuna and Jaya (1993).

77. Interview with Bhuvana, March 2, 1997.

78. Interview with Maniammal, June 15, 1997

79. Interview with Mohammad Rafi, November 26, 1997.

80. As a contrast, a couple of bullock cart drivers told me they make Rs 5–7/bag or Rs 50–105 per trip, but if they don't find work, they lose Rs 50 for the bullock cart rent. As we talked, a fancy looking export firm employee came up on a two-wheeler and was unrelenting in his offer of Rs 40/trip, which the bullock cart driver acquiesced to in the end, turning to me and saying "I'll have to do it." Interview with two bullock cart drivers, November 20, 1996.

81. In its manufacturing units, Ginwin has thirty women in checking working for Rs 30–40 per shift, usually for 1.5 shifts/day. Ten cutting masters are paid Rs 130–50 per shift. Ironing men get Rs 70–100/shift. Flatlock stitchers get Rs 85/shift while overlock stitchers get Rs 55–60/shift. Large units often have power single-needle stitching machines for which men and women are employed on piece rates; men get Rs 130–165/shift while women get Rs 85–105/shift, a little more than half the male wage rate. A group of four workers is paid about Rs 800/day in a group contract for button work. Finally, three helpers are paid Rs 35/shift. Observations at Ginwin, February 17, 1998.

82. Interview with Mani and Duraisamy, January 28, 1997.

83. Interview with Gizani Mohan, November 17, 1996.

Chapter 3: Accumulation Strategies and Gounder Dominance, 1996–1998

1. Chari (2000a).

2. Marx (1967). Braverman (1974) reproduces this dichotomy of the embodied power of the capitalist inside the factory, and the abstract power of market competition without.

3. Combining Antonio Gramsci's theory of hegemony with workplace ethnography, Burawoy's insight is that relative surplus value implies worker consent to exploitation. See Gramcsi ([1929–1935] 1971), Burawoy (1979, 1985).

4. Burawoy distinguishes the politics of work and the politics of politics; see the critique in Walker (1989a). Harvey (1982) argues that the neglect of discipline across exchange and production has led Burawoy to explain the lack of labor process change through struggles at the point of production by taking recourse to the irresistible external force of competition.

5. Sayer and Walker (1992); Sabel and Zeitlin (1997); Hart (1997); and for the global agro-food system, Goodman and Watts (1997a).

6. I use the term "affiliation" following David Hollinger's (1995: 17) argument to go beyond the concerns of "identity" prevalent in multiculturalism debates: "[I] dentity is more psychological than social, and it can hide the extent to which the achievement of identity is a social process by which a person becomes affiliated with one or more acculturating cohorts . . . Affiliation is more performative, while identity suggests something that simply is. To be sure, one can construe the achievement of identity as an action, but 'affiliation' calls attention to the social dynamics of this action."

7. The choices are Gounder, Chettiar, Mudaliar, South Indian Muslim, Other South Indian and North Indian. Devanga Chettiars and Senguntha Mudaliars are from handloom weaver backgrounds, while other Chettiars and Mudaliars, and most South Indian Muslims are from trader-moneylender backgrounds.

8. An inherent ambiguity in the notion of ownership in Tiruppur derives from shared ownership across multiple firms and from ways in which machines are contracted out. Where the owner "owns the machines but not the work," he might not always count the machine capital as his own. What ownership means is not accounted for in this information.

9. SIHMA coefficients for stitching machines and machine capital against turnover are 0.38 and 0.36 respectively; TEA coefficients are 0.54 and 0.45.

10. SIHMA coefficients are 0.03 for backward integration, 0.15 for forward integration and 0.11 for horizontal integration. For TEA: 0.16 for backward, 0.19 for forward and 0.07 for horizontal integration.

11. These frequency spectra count numbers of firms with countable qualities within various bands: as for instance firms with no machines, 1–10 machines, 11–15 machines and so on. The spectrum provides a cross-sectional representation of differentiation between firms without saying anything of the causal mechanisms that account for any observable differentiation. In comparing numbers of machines owned, fabrication

machines pose a problem because there are major cost differentials between domestic and imported machines. Stitching machines are more or less uniform across the industry, as there has been a general shift to imported machines, particularly with a thriving second-hand machine market. It is therefore more meaningful to consider the spectra of stitching machines owned as an index of differentiation. Note that in the frequencies that follow, the convention followed is of "greater than" and "less than or equal to," so that each period includes only its upper bound.

12. The composition of machine capital by caste shows Gounders are evenly distributed on the domestic spectrum, with a higher concentration in the Rs 0.5–1 million range (69 percent). The exporter spectrum shows a stronger concentration of Gounders in the Rs 1–5 million range (58 percent) and in the three ranges greater than Rs 5 million together (58 percent). In both cases, there is no evidence of strong concentration of machine capital in the hands of Gounders. I will argue that it is more important for owners to control production networks than to own machine capital.

13. Considering the composition of the turnover spectrum, the central bell-shaped section of the domestic spectrum is dominated by Gounder and ex-worker affiliations. If the bell curve of domestic turnovers indicates a sort of "middle peasant" phenomenon, it is clear that Gounders and ex-workers are major players in this phenomenon. In the exporter spectrum, a clear majority of the largest turnovers in TEA correspond to Gounders.

14. Again, backward integration is investment in yarn spinning, forward integration is involvement in trade and marketing, and horizontal integration is in processing/accessorizing firms within the cluster.

15. Chari (2000) details the correlations between religious/ caste/ communal affiliation and forms of integration, and the results only confirm these patterns. Interestingly, Devanga Chettiars are strong among domestic owners who integrate backward, into yarn trading in this case. North Indian Marwaris are very strong in forward integration into marketing, which they often call their traditional expertise.

16. 34 percent of SIHMA and 40 percent of TEA.

17. The correlation is most strongly positive for Gounders (0.26) followed by Mudaliars (0.14), while North Indians are negative (–0.14), and Chettiars (–0.19) and Marwaris (–0.20) are even more so.

18. The quick response times and differentiated products that characterize

the export sector pose strong challenges for labor supervision and control. Lazerson (1995) argues of Modena knitwear that these challenges lend themselves to modern forms of putting-out.

19. 17 percent of SIHMA and 34 percent of TEA reported "labor problems;" after property, income tax and the investment ceiling for recognition as a SSI, "labor problems" is the fourth most important reason given by SIHMA owners for starting sister concerns; in TEA it is the second most important reason after property division. Correlation with caste/ community is weak, but again Gounders are the most positive (0.09), followed by North Indians (0.08) but not Marwaris (–0.02), or Chettiars (–0.08) or Muslims (–0.08).

20. I found it very difficult to collect systematic data on workers because few records are kept. Labor contracts of even long-term employees are periodically settled and few firms keep the muster rolls they are supposed to maintain by law. Unions, particularly CITU, have been fighting for regular records for some time. Under these conditions, I had to rely on the average number of workers as reported by owners.

21. Correlating with turnover, the coefficient for SIHMA is positive (0.29) and more so for TEA (0.32).

22. In a much rarer arrangement called "company lease," an entire unit is leased out, sometimes on the condition of regular jobwork for the owner's company. This, however, is not a form of external contracting, by local convention, but one of several kinds of jobwork relations between specialized units.

23. In SIHMA, correlation with internal contracting is –0.07 and external contracting is 0.04, while in TEA, correlation with internal contracting is a stronger 1.12 and external contracting is 0.1.

24. In SIHMA, correlations are weakly positive for Chettiars (0.16) and Marwaris (0.15), with Gounders slightly negative (–0.02.) The corresponding coefficients in TEA are weakly positive for Gounders (0.14) and weakly negative by the same magnitude for other South Indians and Marwaris (–0.14 each.)

25. See Chari (2000) for more exhaustive data on this.

26. Interview with Natarjan, son of Maximum Govindasamy, January 28, 1997.

27. Interview with Yellowbee Velusamy, November 20, 1996.

28. Interview with Mani and Duraisamy, Maximum contractors, January 28, 1997.

29. Note that composite units above are double-counted in both fabrication and stitching/manufacture.

30. Support takes the form of capital, machines, jobwork, bank recommendations, business contacts, advice and "other recommendations" such as for yarn credit. Supporters include relatives, business relations and prior employers.

31. This is an ethnographic insight, suggested from life histories and interviews, and from one interview in particular in which an enraged owner cut short our conversation because I had broached the topic.

32. Cf. Neelakantan (1996).

33. Srikumar and Gunasekar, both Gounders, spun off from one of the top direct export firms and started a business together after leaving their jobs as worker and manager respectively in the 1980s, combining their respective skills in production and business management. Without using the term *kaṭṭakkoottaḷi*, they described the same situation. Interview with A. Srikumar and P. Gunasekar, November 8, 1997.

34. "Presumably" because despite TEA's claim that all its members are direct exporters, several are merchant exporters or traders who put-out all production.

35. One dependent jobworker was provided yarn in the initial stages of his regular jobwork for an exporter, when he did small orders of 2–3 thousand pieces. When his orders grew to 5–6 thousand pieces, and his dependence on the exporter grew, he stopped getting yarn from the exporter and had to secure it himself. (Interview with Saraswathi Gajendran, November 10, 1997.)

36. One merchant exporter, Balan, who does merchant production for Bombay exporters showed me his order sheet, which said nothing about the Bombay exporter's contract with the foreign buyer. Costs were assessed solely according to the various tasks and wastes, with 13 percent of production costs as Balan's profit share. Along one side, Balan had pencilled in his anticipated costs, retaining his 13 percent. What is interesting is that he had adjusted the wages of Singer Tailors down in order to boost the share of the contract garment stitching section. As an owner who maintains a strong presence on the shopfloor, it remains important for Balan to secure the work of contract stitching in order to meet the export order. Informality and power ramify into relations between owners and different kinds of workers, particularly those in stitching. Interview with P.S. Knits Balan, November 5, 1997.

37. Interview with Yellowbee Velusamy, November 20, 1996.
38. Interviews with Kittu Gounder and Ramesh, February 19, 1998.
39. Interviews with K.M. Gounder, December 24, 1996 and his son Rajan, March 1, 1998. Rajan did not know the term *Kániyálar* which marked off his class of agrarian lords from the average Gounder peasant, but he admitted to me that his families had recognized their mistake of being too aristocratic and are trying to become more "entrepreneurial."
40. The *úr Gounder*, Kandasamy, February 23, 1998; D. Vanavarayar, "prince" of the Uttukuli zamindar's family, February 22, 1997; and "the Pope of the Gounders," the *Paḷaikkottai Pattakkarar*, ex-Minister Mandradiar, March 15, 1997.
41. Observations while living in Delight Knitting Co., October 27, 1997– March 3, 1998.
42. Interview with Kasim Bhai, November 21, 1997.
43. The Naidus of Coimbatore city were large agriculturists, many of whom made an opportune shift into the spinning mill industry when Indian capital took over the reins from British mills in the inter-war period. Sathyaraj is a product of precisely this lineage, and he epitomizes the industrialist who invests in public institutions. Coimbatore industrialists prize their public image. When I went to interview the patriarch of this industrial group, I was first presented his published biography.
44. Interview with Sathyaraj, February 1998.
45. Interview with TEA Subramaniam, March 3, 1998.
46. Interview with Kamaraj, February 23, 1998.
47. Interview with Zintex Srinivasan, February 26, 1998.

Chapter 4: Agrarian and Colonial Questions in Coimbatore's Capitalism, 1890–1970

1. V.I. Lenin (1974), p. 181, my emphasis.
2. The film *Cinna GavunTar* (Small Gounder) exemplifies several features of a frontier mythology in its hero, who is anything but small, down to a scene in which he lassos a wild young woman who he domesticates to be his wife.
3. Kongunad is a cultural-ecological-historical region in western Tamil Nadu which, in the estimation of Brenda Beck, is recalled in poetry from an old bardic tradition (Beck, 1972, pp. 19-40). Chris Baker uses the term for one of three socio-ecological regions along which he charts divergent developments in modern Tamil Nadu. Baker, 1984.

4. Nicholson (1887), p. 260.

5. Baker (1984), pp. 94–7. Baker's conception of Gounder society in the fourteenth century is drawn from Beck's (1972) anthropology of a Gounder village.

6. On the Permanent Settlement, see Guha (1963) Certain *poligars* in South India were able to convert their authority over men in the military system into regional power via revenue collection. See the hagiography of the *Poligar* of Uttukuli by Vadivelu (1915–28).

7. Munro and Buchanan had apparently seen this system in operation in the Baramahal and Ceded Districts, and Munro in particular felt it combined conservative and utilitarian theory, eliminating wasteful intermediaries and proving the beauty of Ricardian principles. The implementation of the *ryotwari* system was far more difficult in rice-growing areas, where it sparked peasant protest spearheaded by the *mirasidar* landlords.

8. Baker (1984), pp. 75–6, argues that local circumstance rather than nineteenth-century British reformist ideologies were more important in configuring colonial administration in Tamil Nadu.

9. Mines (1984).

10. Baker (1984) uses this distinction of valleys, plains and Kongunad to good effect in demonstrating regional divergence in colonial Tamil Nadu.

11. The distinction between "left" and "right" hand castes was a central theme in the anthropology of South India: Left hand castes comprised merchant-warrior-artisan castes while right hand castes were farmers and their agrarian dependants. In tandem with the vertical hierarchical ordering of castes, this horizontal distinction has been seen as crucial to "southern kinship." Furthermore, the functional distinction of agrarian from mercantile-artisanal-warrior castes differentiates the spatial dynamics of trade from the place-based dynamics of agriculture. Unlike peasant households in Europe that combined artisanal and farming activities, the functional distinction of left and right hand castes kept them apart. The left/ right distinction is also interesting as the left hand is associated with pollution while eating and transfers of things are carried out with the right hand. Beck's (1972) study has Kongu Vellala Gounders at the top of the right castes, entitled to or tied to those with rights to land. Their prestige structures were centered on kingly power over territory: "local political power and control of day-to-day labor and production activity." In contrast, left castes acquired prestige through

material wealth combined with "ritual purity and self-control." In other words, while right castes were concerned with power over land and people, left castes were more concerned with acquiring wealth and ritual status. Gounders, Beck found, were slow in diversifying out of farming into non-farm activities, but when they did, they *did not* restrict themselves to right occupations, as some had even switched to the traditional left occupation of weaving in order to access state support to handloom weavers.

12. Lancashire only turned to Madras for long-staple cotton during periods of crisis. Madras remained far behind Java and the Caribbean in sugar, North India in indigo, Java and North America in tobacco, and Latin America and the Caribbean in coffee.

13. Baker (1984), pp. 98–106.

14. Ibid., p. 131; Rukmini (1993), p. 15

15. Government of India (1903), p. 129. This 1901 Census subdivides Vellalas by four regional divisions, of which Kongu Vellalas are described by later texts, such as Baker (1984), as Gounders. Kongu Vellalas are further subdivided into "Sendalais (red-headed men), Padaitalais (leaders of armies), Vellikkai (the silver hands), Pavalamkatti (wearers of coral), Malaiyadi (foot of the hills), Tollakaadu (ears with big holes), Attangarais (river bank) and others . . . the members of which can never marry." I never encountered these distinctions while conducting research, about a century later. W. Francis, author of this section, goes on to claim that there are several groups of pretenders who claim to be Vellalas but in fact cannot marry "genuine" Vellalas. Francis also acknowledges tremendous difficulty in determining castes at a time when, in his view, intra-caste subdivisions are increasingly fragmented while inter-caste distinctions are increasingly less distinct. This might be a valuable insight about precisely the remaking of castes into a wider "middle caste" category called Vellala, which draws a range of communities into processes of development through the twentieth century. There continues to be some flexibility in the category "Gounder" today, but what is striking is that upwardly mobile Tiruppur Gounders claim their purity as Kongu Vellalas, the "original peasants" of Kongunad.

16. This only makes the task of excavating relations of colonial power/knowledge and what Nicholas Dirks (2001: 7) sees as the modern career of caste, through its ethnicization and consequent localization, all the more complicated. Elsewhere, Dirks (1996: 268–9) identifies the work of a specific ideological dualism of Brahmin/anti-Brahmin in

South India that has become common sense in a variety of political positions, even lending tacit support to new forms of contemporary Brahman hegemony in Tamil Nadu. The rise of backward caste power, such as the economic power of the Gounders of Tiruppur, disrupts this formula fundamentally, but it poses new challenges to rendering alternative historical anthropologies of caste.

17. The main crops were *kambu* (millet) and *colam* (sorghum), with some cash cropping of castor, *kollu* (horsegram), cotton and *ellu* (gingelly.) Through a kind of "semi-subsistence farming," small amounts of marketed crops were grown to pay revenue and capital costs for well irrigation.

18. Draught power was readily available through the older order of cattle raising and ranching. The *Pattagar of Pazhaikottai*, the "lineage heads" of the Gounders, raised prized Kangayam cattle. When I met the current *Pazhaikottai Pattagar* in 1996 in his decaying palace on the outskirts of Kangayam town, he had me taken first to see his magnificent Kangayam bulls. Cattle rearing on poorer lands complemented and spurred smallholder farming on better soils, a marked contrast to impoverished subsistence cultivation on poor lands in the plains. Baker (1984), pp. 200–3.

19. Evidence from 1931 shows 28 percent of the rural population in cultivation, 1.9 percent non-cultivating proprietors, 40.9 percent cultivating owners, 0.3 percent non-cultivating tenants, 7.6 percent cultivating tenants, and 49.3 percent agricultural laborers; see Zacharias (1950), pp. 94–5.

20. Baker argues that "as the economy became more markedly commercial, this was reflected in the type of crime. Murder was a local pastime and Coimbatore had for a long time led the province in this respect; by the 1930s many of the murders revolved around land. [A] local historian noted that the Gounder farmers were 'easily affected by land disputes. Even an inch of ground or a small water-course or the right to a palmyra tree or a tamarind tree standing on the edge [of a plot] would result in the chopping off a head' " (1984: 212.) The image of the violent Gounder, passionate about land, persists in popular representations of this caste of "violent entrepreneurs," as in the film *Cinna Gounder.*

21. Baker (1984), p. 214.

22. Ibid., pp. 205–7; Cederlöf (1997), p. 99.

23. Ayyar (1933), p. 172.

24. Baker (1984), p. 209.

25. Ibid., p. 210.
26. Both Perumanallur and Madathupalayam lie to the north of Tiruppur; both were Gounder-dominated *ryotwari* villages, in which *ryots* or smallholders were granted long-term leases of land by the colonial state. Literacy rates were low: 2 percent of adults in Perumanallur. Ganesamurthy (1935).
27. Ibid., p. 277.
28. Ibid.,Gopalaratnam (1931), p. 523.
29. Cederlöf (1997) argues that Gounder farmers intensified forms of indebted labor-tying of Madari leather workers in the 1930s. This was possible because Madaris were not politicized in the way that Paraiyars, the other major Tamil Dalit caste, were. Paraiyars took on the title "*Adi Dravida,*" or "Original Dravidians," as part of the Non-Brahmin Movement, and identification with broader currents of caste and class reform was mutually supported by their mobility as they left agrestic servitude as migrant labor for the expanding plantations of the Nilgiri Hills. Madaris, in contrast, remained phenomenally local and detached from circuits of "free labor." This was true of the village suburb of Nallur even in the 1990s, as all but Madaris found work in Tiruppur; as a contrast, most Dalit Christian men in Nallur village were employed in Tiruppur, my observations 1996–8.
30. Cederlöf (1997), p. 55.
31. Ayyar (1933), p. 173.
32. Zacharias (1950), pp. 44–5. Indeed electric pumps were the most significant form of mechanization in Coimbatore District, while tractors were much more commonly in use in other areas, as in South Arcot. The number of carts in use in Coimbatore was also much higher than other parts of the Presidency, because, the author explains, of "brisk trade immediately after harvest," which in Coimbatore's case was of commercial crops. Zacharias (1950), p. 49.
33. Most of the Gounders I interviewed in Tiruppur switched to electric pumpsets only in the late 1960s, with the earliest electrification in 1951. While the Pykara hydroelectric works was operational in the Nilgiri mountains near Coimbatore after 1929, electrification spread through the countryside in the 1930s and 1940s. It was only by the 1950s that rural electrification in the fields of Coimbatore District made pumpsets viable. Most of my Gounder respondents, all from nearby farms, said their wells were dug in their grandfathers' times, which I estimate to be around the 1930s. All used *kavalai* irrigation for

their wet-land or *tóttam* on the order of ten acres (with the average size about double for Gounder exporters of non-working-class origins.) Oil engines were rare: only two respondents' families had them, after 1968. Almost all Gounders I talked to also said their families had hired-in labor since their childhood. Here, Gounder ex-workers in the domestic association were least likely to have hired-in labor in their farms (68 percent). This was also the only group of Gounder owners who hired-out labor to other farmers as well. I only mention this to say that mechanization was slow: only after the 1950s, but reliance on hired-in labor alongside family labor was strong since around the 1930s. Interviews and survey research, 1996–8.

34. The evidence of Sir George Paddison, Government of India (1927), *Royal Commission on Agriculture in India, Vol III: Evidence taken in the Madras Presidency*, pp. 313–14.
35. Cederlöf (1997), p. 104.
36. Ganesamurthy (1935), p. 272.
37. Ibid., p. 275.
38. Gopalaratnam (1931), p. 525.
39. Bhaduri (1973).
40. Tenancy relations in cotton-cropping areas, as around Tiruppur, tended to be in cash rather than share payments. Cash tenancy meant that when the price of cotton was high, land values and rents rose dramatically, but when prices fell by more than half, land rents only fell about a third. Often, landlords were themselves indebted and their main interest was in charging the highest rents possible. The interlinking of land rental and cotton markets therefore provided a means for landlords to pass debts down to tenants. However, struggles over land and debt were played out increasingly in the courts. Ramachandra Chettiar, lawyer at the Coimbatore High Court argued, "Law is becoming more and more crowded. Within the last ten years, Coimbatore Bar has doubled and even small towns with Third-Class magistrate Courts get permanent lawyers." Government of India (1927), *Report of the Unemployment Committee, 1926–27: Vols II & III, Evidence.*
41. S.V. Duraisamy (1934).
42. Cederlöf (1997), pp. 108–10.
43. Baker (1984), p. 268.
44. Government of India, Committee on Cotton (1914), *Agricultural and Trade Conference, Madras.*
45. Baker (1984), p. 206

46. Harriss-White (1995), p. 81.
47. Ibid.
48. Baker (1984), p. 268.
49. Ibid., pp. 268–9.
50. Ibid., pp. 272–4.
51. See note 11 for the distinction between left and right hand castes.
52. Rukmini (1993), pp. 60, 73–6.
53. Baker (1984), Mahadevan (1992).
54. On this debate and its relevance to the evolution of Small Scale Industrial Policy, see Tyabji (1989).
55. Baker (1984), pp. 354–63; Murphy (1981).
56. Baker (1984), pp. 364–7.
57. Ibid., pp. 364–8.
58. Ibid., p. 370; Berna (1960), pp. 26–7, 70; Harriss (1983).
59. Baker (1984), pp. 417, 420; Rukmini (1993), p. 234.
60. Baker (1984), p. 385
61. This is a term that Rukmini draws from Bairoch (1988), whose argument was that urban centers like Liverpool, Birmingham and Manchester displaced the old county seats by emerging out of "over-grown industrial villages." The underlying mechanism was a process of capitalist industrialization that took root in the countryside in order to access water, coal and cheap labor, but which then built on strong inter-sectoral linkages to forge new spaces of urban manufacture, cited in Rukmini (1993), p. 7.
62. Rukmini (1993), p. 257.
63. Ibid.
64. Ibid., pp. 256–7.
65. Powerful cotton growers and sellers of Coimbatore district met in 1918 to form the Coimbatore Cotton Marketing Association and to attempt to establish a spatially distinct Regulated Cotton Market in Tiruppur administered by the Tiruppur municipality. The market was meant to remove middlemen and lower various charges the ryot paid in the process of selling to cotton commission agents. Opposition to the market— or more precisely to standardized prices and weights and measures— was led by these dealers, agents and middlemen, and the Municipal Council suggested a regulated market for all agricultural products including foodgrains. After the election of new Municipal Councillors in 1920, the regulated market was formed for all crops. "Except for providing space and accommodation where buyers and sellers can meet,

none of the original objects" remained in effect; it was a class stalemate, reflecting strong *and overlapping* claims made by sellers, middlemen, merchants and buyers. November 13, 1926, Evidence of Mr Rudolph D. Anstead, Director of Agriculture, Madras, Government of India (1927), *Royal Commission on Agriculture in India.*

66. de Souza (1969).

67. Ayyar (1933), p. 240.

68. Ibid., p. 239.

69. Ambedkar, B.P., for Government of India, Labour Investigation Committee (1946), *Report on Labour Conditions in the Cotton Ginning and Bailing Industry* (henceforth *Report on Ginning*).

70. The investigator notes, "the question of retirement and dismissals does not arise." *Report on Ginning*, p. 30.

71. *Report on Ginning*, pp. 29–30.

72. "Excepting this strike there have been no instances of labor trouble in Tiruppur for the last 15 years," reports the 1946 document. *Report on Ginning*, p. 35

73. *Report on Ginning*, p. 36

74. Women were engaged in petty agricultural trade in the weekly Tiruppur *cantai* (shandy or periodic market.) Interview with Palaniappan, April 24, 1997.

75. *Report on Ginning*, p. 36; contrast women's access to work in ginning with their exclusion from banian companies until the shift to exports; early companies were entirely male and older local units still are.

76. *Report on an Enquiry into Conditions of Labour in the Cotton Mill Industry in India*, S.R. Deshpande, Labour Investigation Committee, Government of India Press, Simla (1946).

77. The mill gates are the primary site of class struggle in C.A. Balan's classic autobiographical sketch *Túkkumarattin niḻalil*, "In the Shadow of the Gallows" (1979).

78. *Tyagi* means "one who sacrificed," a title held by prominent freedom fighters, not for those who were killed alone. Tyagi Ramasamy's autobiography *Enadu Ninaivugal* (My Memories) had just been released in 1996. Interview with P. Ramasamy, January 29, 1997.

79. Interview with P. Ramasamy, January 29, 1997.

80. The causal links with Gandhianism are weak, but Gandhi did have connections with P.D. Asher, the owner of Asher Mill, and stayed with Asher Seth before his Salt Satyagraha march to Vedaranyam. Not much

is made of this visit, except by the family of P.D. Asher, who display a photograph of Gandhi in the company of Asher in their home.

81. The book written in his homage has as its explicit purpose to document *tyagam* or martyrdom/suffering for new generations of labor unionists; in Tiruppur, an appeal to *tyagam* is a way of claiming Kumaran. (Rajamani, 1993). Ramasamy describes over several pages his escape from the same police inspector who beat Kumaran to death (Ramasamy, 1996). On one occasion, Gentex Palanisamy read out a speech he had delivered on the radio, in which he appealed to Kumaram's "fighting sprit" as a precursor to Gounder entrepreneurialism. Interview with Gentex Palanisamy, February 28, 1997.

82. The Justice Party, representing primarily landlord and mercantilist interests in alliance with the British colonial state, dominated the first phase of the non-Brahmin movement in South India until the 1930s. Madras Institute of Development Studies, MIDS (1988), p. 22.

83. When Congress leader Jawaharlal Nehru visited Tiruppur, he was hindered by the Justicites from speaking in town and had instead to appear in a cotton gin in Gandhinagar, on the outskirts of town. The Justice Party labor union disintegrated when the Municipal chairman was replaced in the next election by a Congress candidate, who, in turn, began a union which also lasted for only a short period. Ramasamy (1996), p. 6.

84. The municipal health workers' union was begun by Municipal Counsellors, and the Municipal Health Department Strike was the first strike in Tiruppur under the direction of the CPI. Ramasamy (1996), p. 20.

85. Interview with P. Ramasamy, January 21, 1997.

86. Ramasamy (1996), pp. 4–6, 21–4. "Police prohibited putting a flag in front of the union. As soon as the police took one flag, they would hoist another red flag. Finally, on May Day, the police came and took down the flag at the general meeting with force, but the unionists fought and made it compulsory." (p. 24.)

87. This claim is often made by locals. What is significant is that the millworkers of Coimbatore, the center of South Indian industry, did not spearhead this cause and Tiruppur did. The institutionalized power of millowners in Coimbatore, the South India Millowners Association (SIMA), told the three Tiruppur mills not to pay the War Allowance. Initially, Asher Mill agreed to give 15 percent but Ramasamy declined, hoping to hold out for 25 percent; Asher then went with Dhanalakshmi

and SRC to join SIMA's offensive against the working class and the Tiruppur millworkers came together in response.

88. "On June 22, 1941, Hitler attacked the Soviet Union and fought over Smalensk town." Ramasamy (1996), p. 30.

89. Ibid., pp. 28–31.

90. Ibid., p. 31.

91. On the railway line from the paddy-rich Cauvery delta region, Vanjipalayam became a rice trading center early on and still holds this distinction.

92. *Sákku viyábáram*, sack trade, involved going to villages and buying sacks to bring back and sell in town; Palaniappan was "employed" by a shop which would advance him money to buy and sell sacks in exchange for a share of his earnings.

93. Interview with Palaniappan, April 24, 1997.

94. *Thondar* or "volunteer" also means "party worker."

95. Ramasamy (1996), pp. 33–8. Palaniappan was deeply critical of this book for its near-exclusive focus on Ramasamy rather than on the various members of the union history it claims to represent; he saw it as vindication of Ramasamy's closeness to owners rather than workers. Indeed the book tends to laud the "courage of leaders" (p. 49) and it does suggest Ramasamy's closeness and ability to negotiate with big owners he fought against, as in the incident I have just detailed. Interview with Palaniappan.

96. Interview with Palaniappan.

97. KRE's family was one of the handful of large landlords near Tiruppur; they are *kaniyalar* (aristocratic) Gounders who never touch the plough nor eat meat.

98. Ramasamy (1996), pp. 39–49.

99. E.P. Thompson's (1993a), p. 303.

100. On one occasion, an owner challenged Ramasamy: "Does a Coimbatore Gounder [i.e. Ramasamy] threaten a Tiruppur Gounder?" In response, Ramasamy said: "We are all Gounders, but there are different classes." He was not, at least overtly, part of a Gounder caste compromise such as would develop in a later period, when Gounder owners ruled the industry in the 1970s. Ramasamy (1996), p. 40.

101. Food is rationed by the state's Public Distribution System at subsidized prices through fair price shops.

102. When the Rangavilas Mill in Peelamedu, near Coimbatore, gave food-grains from the owner's farm to millworkers and subtracted workers'

wages accordingly, the union called it *pannai atimai* (bonded labor for a big farmer) and refused to work for *tániyam* (a share of the crop, rather than wages)! Unions were fighting for full proletarianization and its requisite rights rather than for a return to agrestic "welfare." Ramasamy (1996), p. 51.

103. Ramasamy (1996), pp. 50–64; Palaniappan's Oral History; on the women of Anaikadu, Rajamani (1993), p. 43.

104. Baker (1984), p. 527.

105. Ibid.

106. The Indian states were linguistically defined and the issue of Hindi as a national language became a rallying cry for anti-North Indian hegemony over the South.

107. The Justice Party had been in the Madras Legislative Assembly during the period of "dyarchy," the period of supposed shared rule by colonial and "elected" arms of government.

108. Arnold (1974).

Chapter 5: Can the Subaltern Accumulate Capital? Toil in Transition, 1950–1984

1. Interview with Zintex Srinivasan, July 19, 1997.

2. Interview with New Saturn Nalasamy Gounder, March 12, 1997.

3. Chakrabarty (1997) makes a distinction between two ways of looking at empirical evidence: as either particular/ specific in instancing general phenomena, or as singular in expressing uniqueness. Chakrabarty asks that the tensions between singular and particular be written so as to shock the reader. Translation generates new particulars to reconstruct theory, as Burawoy (1991) argues, particularly when it shocks the theorist into recognizing the conditions of possibility of accepted theoretical positions. Contextual uniqueness and theoretical generality need not come at the expense of each other. Indeed, their combination is central to the craft of an ethnographic or cultural materialism.

4. Sabel and Zeitlin (1997) argue that there are two broadly divergent ways of understanding experience, either as apprehending an always-already narrativized world or as discreet, discontinuous episodes experienced first as chaos and subsequently narrativized in the process of making the world intelligible. The distinction is a matter for ivory-tower philosophy, as all subjects with provisional aims have to construct causal claims, and hence narratives, in order to act.

5. The distinction is important. A metonym is the use of a word for another associated with it, as the White House is a metonym for actions of the President of the USA. Metaphors require semantic correspondence alone, while metonyms require contiguous correspondence, or proximity in real-world discursive contexts. Since metonyms require salience in shared histories or practices, their use is much more restricted than metaphors. Unlike metaphors, metonyms require a realist ontology to work. Precise and naturalized references to toil in Tiruppur signal its metonymic aspect, as an index of shared histories and experiences in agrarian and industrial work. Metonymy is key to the way people conceptualize the complexity of everyday life; it finds its home best in slang, common gestures, and colloquial tautologies. Talk about toil is therefore only the tip of the iceberg, as part of a repertoire of enactments of toil, including gestures and comportments in the labor process in stitching, which enables an ongoing process of interpellation of a particular class fraction.

6. I refer to Gyan Prakash's (1992) response, "Can the Sublaltern Ride," following the debate between Prakash (1990) and O'Hanlon and Washbrook (1992). Both sides brought important issues to the table while also affirming quite strong disciplinary locations, but I am less convinced in defending intellectual positions, in riding particularly labelled horses, rather than in a more heterodox approach that can attend to detailing capitalist development and its inequalities as well as cultural difference. Hence my attempt to think of translation and transition as intertwined in a broadly Gramscian perspective.

7. Fred Cooper (1994:1529) says of Spivak (1998), Coronil (1994) and Mallon (1994) that "all these scholars want to complicate and enrich their subalterns but still keep them subaltern." My challenge is to explain how certain Gounder men in Tiruppur use constructions of their subalternity for very different ends.

8. B. Manthagini (1983). Most of the evidence is from the recollections of Soundappa Chettiar. There is one prominent woman owner today, but she only stepped foot in a company after being widowed and in order to prevent the company from being usurped by her brothers and brother-in-law.

9. Babu Bhai was known as "Star Bhai" after his company, Star Knitting; *bhai* meaning "brother" in Hindi is a generic term for Muslim men.

10. There were only imported machines to be had at the time. B. Manthagini

(1983): most of her evidence, as earlier noted, is from the recollections of Soundappa Chettiar.

11. His employee later became the owner of Tiger Knitting.

12. Interview with Star Babu Bhai, December 2 and 4, 1996.

13. Star Bhai's family and S.A. Khadar, who would be the leading Muslim owner, were Dakkini Urdu-speaking Muslims whom Khadar's son claimed were "Mughal stock" who migrated south. He contrasted them to "the local stock of converts" who were Tamil-speaking Muslims: either Lebbai priests and teachers, Markay merchants and sailors or Rowther traders. Interestingly, Muslim sects are specified with respect to traditional occupations in the manner of castes. Interview with Karim Bhai, July 23, 1997.

14. Interview with Star Bhai.

15. "Maximum" was Govindasamy, who would one day become the owner of Maximum Knitting Co., a very prominent banian company; to this day Maximum is the most important landmark and intersection on the north side of the railway tracks.

16. Interview with Star Bhai.

17. Bill discounting is discussed in Section V, Chapter 2.

18. Interview with Star Bhai.

19. The papers of S.A. Khadar: B. Manthagini (1983).

20. Karim Bhai describes Star Bhai, Baby Knitting, Chellamma and Khadar starting within four months of each other, despite the actual difference of 20 years. In this blurring of historical memory, S.A. Khadar becomes another founder of Tiruppur knitwear. Interview with Karim Bhai, July 18, 1997.

21. The employment of Madaris was a reflection of Star Bhai's Gandhianism, in his son's telling. In contrast, Dalits, like women, were excluded from Gounder firms of the 1960s and 1970s, up into the period of the export boom since the mid 1980s.

22. Interview with Karim Bhai

23. Khadar Knitting Group (1956). Henceforth KKG (1956), p. 1.

24. Harijan was Gandhi's neologism for ex-untouchables; Ambedkar, Dalit leader and primary architect of the Indian Constitution, criticized the term as paternalistic and as confining Dalit to the unequal universe of Hinduism, where they could never truly envision social justice; the term Dalit meaning "the oppressed," carries this charge.

25. *Vartahar* also means trader or merchant, as opposed to *urpattiálar* or manufacturer, KKG (1956), p. 4.

26. In response to yarn control, Khadar said "workers could work. . . . It is the first responsibility of workers to work, isn't it?" He then went on to say that by starting TKC and bringing more cloth to Tiruppur, "KKC and NHM could give continuous work to many workers . . . alleviating [their] difficult lives." The desire to exploit continuously is arguably a more desirable alternative than with no regard to the continuity of work, as is the condition of the flexible workforce today. I do not, therefore, dismiss Khadar's promise as merely euphemistic, as his nationalism did draw his concern into important questions about the reproduction of working class families without his necessarily "knowing the workers' mind." Ibid., pp. 4–5.

27. Ibid., p. 5.

28. "After adjusting demand in the market, however much profit comes, we do not raise the price." Ibid., p. 4.

29. The letters of S.A. Khadar demonstrate continued relations with these customers, confirming the importance of sustaining market networks. Much of the discussion in these letters centers on the extension of various kinds of price subsidies in exchange for access to retailers in the southern states. Papers of S.A. Khadar, courtesy of his family.

30. KKG (1956).

31. The employment of child labor, at least recognized in this injunction, remains silent in the rest of the narrative. The same evidence that might be used in safeguarding workers' health was quickly alienated from the laboring body to become a hazard for customers. Ibid., p. 5.

32. Biernacki (1995).

33. Interview with Velusamy, December 1 and 12, 1996.

34. Interview with Velusamy. The slip from the pronoun "they" to "we" is unintentional, but it signals Velusamy's distance at first from non-modern tastes in attire and his sudden entry into the narrative as a politicized worker who struck for tea.

35. Another couple who both worked as millworkers told me similar stories, but in highly personalized ways; interview with Muthusamy Gounder and his wife, March 10, 1997.

36. While the *kutumi* is a symbol of Brahmanism, in Brahmin stories of transition from *agraháram* (Brahmin section in the village) to government jobs and urban professions, the cutting of the *kutumi*, like shaving, is a way of remaking rather than discarding caste distinction.

37. I am grateful to Marina Welker for pushing me on how meanings of consumption of banians enter the process of transition from agrarian to

industrial work. I can only answer in a general way, and extremely tentatively, as it is only in company advertisements and the communist activist's narratives that consumption of banians enters these narratives. Most of the boys working in early knitwear workshops constituted an insignificant share of the market, but they could envision wearing the garments they made. Agrarian Questions Seminar, Anthropology and History, University of Michigan, Ann Arbor, April 17, 2001.

38. Interview with Velusamy
39. Ibid.
40. Ibid.
41. Based on ibid.
42. Interview with Abdul Rashid, March 1, 1997.
43. Ibid.
44. Cf. note 15.
45. Interview with Abdul Rashid, March 1, 1997.
46. Ibid.
47. His family of eight held ten acres in which they planted course cereals for their own consumption and some "America" cotton. Interview with Muthusamy Gounder, November 26, 1996.
48. Ibid.
49. Decentralized powerloom weaving was expanding in this period of restriction on weaving in mills and with expanded state support small-scale and cottage industry. Coimbatore's mills specialized in spinning yarn, so their expansion was aided by growing local demand for yarn from decentralized powerloom units.
50. Interview with Muthusamy Gounder, November 26, 1996.
51. A contentious point, as migrants were primarily Gounder males and least likely to be Madaris. There may have been a shortage of *kudiánava* Gounders, landless Gounder families who stayed with landed families and worked for them, but it is unlikely that Madari labor supply altered that much.
52. Interview with Muthusamy Gounder.
53. Other ex-worker family backgrounds, in contrast, were most often in traditional handloom or non-traditional powerloom textiles, trade of some sort, or, particularly among exporters, from unrelated professions. Again, the exceptions among Gounders were later entrants: Gounder exporters who had invested in powerloom units that dot the rural industrial landscape.
54. Kongu Knitting Velusamy Gounder, March 9, 1997; my emphasis.

55. E.P. Thompson (1993c), p. 390.
56. "O.C." is Tamil slang for "free" with a hint of hoodwinking or making an angle; the idiom is a colonial artifact of British East India Co. officers who would get various perks "on company"—O.C.
57. Interview with Tommy Kandasamy, June 11, 1997.
58. Unfreedom in this sense of open-ended or non-task-specific contracts with limited employers, rather than in the more restricted sense of bonded or indentured labor, has been noted to be pervasive in Indian rural economies; see fn. 37, Chapter 1.
59. Interview with Tommy Kandasamy. This notion of cashing in reputation sounds like the rational agent of Bourdieu (1977), who invests, in this case the opportunity cost of extra-contractual labortime, in cultural activity which can be reconverted into money capital. This cultural capital can be conceived of either as an entrance fee to engage in restricted practices or as a form of insurance, both of which are key for workers considering shifting from waged work to petty production.
60. Interview with Giraffe Nalasamy, June 11, 1997.
61. At first glance, the 50 percent of Northerns in SIHMA who were ex-workers seem to be an anomaly, as they were most likely to be related to their bosses and were recruited by them. These North Indian families, particularly Marwaris, usually hired family members as apprentices in business before setting them up as managers. However, Northerns in both associations only began to enter along this strategy around the mid to late 1980s.
62. Needless to say that while I collected wage information, I have been confounded by the multiplicity of routes, durations, forms of payment, etc. that each data point reflects. Adding to this not only the problems of stabilizing wages across years but also of accounting for the effects of business cycles on the labor market, I decided to simply compare the average expansion of wages as cues into economic mobility. On average, Gounders worked during the late 1960s and through the 1970s, while Other ex-worker domestic owners worked in the decade between 1975 and 1985. As Other ex-worker exporters only worked in the late 1980s, I am not as concerned with them. Shorter fluctuations aside, the industry was expanding over the 1970s and 1980s, as Tiruppur produced for the national market, so it is not surprising in Table 20 in Appendix 2 that Gounder wages were lower than Other ex-workers. Gounders typically began working for very low wages when the industry was stagnant. They began as helpers without any wages, in an initial period of

apprenticeship. Wages of all these workers had increased several-fold in the late 1960s and 1970s, after the institution of piece rates, described in the next section, and this expansion was greatest for Gounder ex-worker domestic owners.

63. The communist movement in Madras city was dominated by Brahmins in its early days. Unlike the rest of India, where the CPI has its strength in industrial labor and the CPI-M among agrarian labor and the rural poor, in Tamil Nadu the situation is reversed. The CPI led efforts to organize Dalit agrarian labor in the paddy fields of Thanjavur District, while the CPI-M has a strong following in industrial Madras and Coimbatore.

64. Interview with Gentex Palanisamy, February 28, 1997.

65. Ibid.

66. Ibid. The English word "service" is a Tamil idiom for sustained relations between owner and worker. Employers use it to bemoan dying loyalty from workers, while older workers use it in speaking of lost entitlements and job security. A union leader said to me, "If you have permanent workers, you can't fire them at your convenience and they are covered *service-aha* [or "as befits service"] by ESI, PF, gratuity and other legal entitlements." Interview with Mohan Kumar, December 13, 1996.

67. Kongu Knitting, Velusamy Gounder, March 9, 1997.

68. Interview with Punyamurthy, November 30, 1996.

69. Ibid.

70. Interview with Mohan Kumar, December 13, 1996.

71. Interview with Zintex Srinivasan, July 19, 1997.

72. Ibid.

73. Ibid.

74. Interview with L.M.K. Balasubramaniam (Balu), February 26, 1997.

75. Interview with Arumugam, May 17, 1997.

76. Ibid.

77. Ibid.

78. Cobalt Devaraj's term for Gounders of modest means becoming owners is certainly an agrarian metaphor, rather than the Western idiom "the salt of the earth." Cobalt, as he is called, is a fabrication owner and a CPM member who has paid his dues as a labor organizer. He has a close understanding of the dynamic role a petty bourgeois class can play in capitalist development and is an owner with close connections to militant labor organizing in Tiruppur.

79. Interview with Gentex Palanisamy, February 28, 1997.

80. Ibid.

81. My translation is clumsy: *tó̱ḻil* is industry as a form of production and also as experienced work, as is often forgotten in spoken English, so I continue to say work/industry where both meanings apply. I translate *pan̲n̲i kudukardu*, literally "making and giving," as "putting together," which implies that someone other than the owner of the company has arranged capital and other sorts of relationships to enable business.

82. Interview with L.M.K. Balasubramaniam, February 26, 1997.

83. Ibid.

84. Chit funds are rotating credit pools.

85. "Dowry" was a response that many would not admit readily, nor did I push the point after one incident in which asking the question was enough to expel me from the interview. This may be because dowries are a relatively new custom among Gounders and in South India in general. See Kapadia (1999) on the transition from "southern" to "northern" marriage practices in South Indian kinship, particularly in the shift from isogamy to anisogamy and, hence, dowry.

86. Uranium Ramasamy, March 18, 1997.

87. Interview with Muthusamy Gounder, November 26, 1996. There is an important set of questions around whether and how the mother of the agrarian household secured earnings from wage earners, to create a family savings fund for investment outside agriculture, but these questions lay outside my research in town. Chapter 4 demonstrated the significant of women's work and economic activity in agrarian and industrial Coimbatore as far back as the 1930s. Note in Table 18 that "gin work" is a significant share of familial earnings for Gounder ex-worker domestic owners, and Gounder women were early entrants into this sector. I am grateful to a questioner after my talk for the Institute for Development Alternatives at Katha-South Publishers, Chennai, February 1996, for asking me how the rural mother secured an agarian surplus, but this remains something I can only conjecture about.

88. Lenin Kaliappan, February 13, 1997.

89. Interview with P. P. Natarajan, SIHMA Survey No. 164.

90. Blue Sundaram, SIHMA Survey No. 31. Elan Manickam also said he gave his earnings to his mother (SIHMA Survey No. 81). Ragam Tex Sundaram said saving was possible when he received good wages, all of which went to his mother for family expenses. Implicit in this is that he

was an occasional depositor rather than controller of the savings fund, which could have been the mother (SIHMA Survey No. 82).

91. Interview with Fine Line Chandrasekhar, SIHMA Survey No. 38.

92. See Kapadia (1995).

93. Observations at puberty ritual for prominent Gounder owner's niece, December 6, 1996.

94. *Máman* also means maternal uncle, the preferred father-in-law for male ego (cross-cousin marriage being preferred in South Indian kinship) and preferred to *maccán* or brother-in-law (husband for ego's sister). *Máman-maccán* relations are differentiated from relations between *pankális* (literally shareholders) or patrilineal male kin as property relations in the former are mediated through women. The allusion is to the "traffic in women," from Gayle Rubin's (1975) [2000] classic essay.

95. Interview with Crown Ramasamy, SIHMA Survey No. 132.

96. Duraisamy was an ex-worker of Gizani Muthusamy and a partner of New Saturn Nalasamy, both Gounder ex-workers who I have written of in previous sections.

97. Interview with Yummy Garments Duraisamy and Saraswati, SIHMA Survey No. 135.

98. Ibid.

99. Interview with SBI Manager, Palanisamy, July 14, 1997.

100. Interview with SBI clerk, Murthy, February 25, 1998.

101. Indeed, for Neelakantan (1996), it seems that development is entirely fortuitous and the agents he describes were indeed self-made. To be fair to his own experience, Neelakantan told me in passionate terms the effect of the Non-Brahmin Movement on his own sense of possibility as a young man in Western Tamil Nadu. Though neither Periyar E.V. Ramasamy Naicker nor the movement had an overt influence in Tiruppur's political culture, it has worked discursively and behind the scenes, so to speak, to disprove and desanctify elements of Gounder caste affiliation. At the least, the fact that the entrepreneur here came from the working class demands a more complex analysis.

102. I have discussed the origins of this "small scale populism" as a kind of hijacking of Gandhian ideology in Chari (1998), following Tyabji's (1989) general discussion of SSI policy in India.

103. Initially known as the Bank of Madras, it then became the Imperial Bank of India and then the State Bank of India after 1955.

104. Interview with SBI Raghavan, April 24, 1997.

105. Interview with Karim Bhai, July 23, 1997.

106. Interview with Zintex Srinivasan

107. Interview with Karim Bhai, July 23, 1997.

108. Interview with Zintex Srinivasan, July 19, 1997.

109. Interview with SBI clerk, Murthy, February 25, 1998.

110. Interview with Meera Karthikeyan, December 5, 1996.

111. Interview with SBI Palanisamy, July 14, 1997.

112. Ibid.

113. Interview with Raghavan, April 24, 1997.

114. Interview with SBI clerk, Murthy, February 25, 1998.

115. Interview with Lenin Kaliappan, February 13, 1997. The translation is awkward because "*uḻaippu irukite enkitte*," is literally "I have toil."

116. Interview with LMK Balu, February 26, 1997

117. Chairman Velusamy, May 13, 1997.

118. A.C.T. Selvaraj, November 2, 1997.

119. Arrow Muthusamy, November 29, 1997.

120. I had to persist with the owner in the Preface, for him to trust that I wouldn't belittle his lack of formal education and would value his story of toil.

121. Soundappa Chettiar, in Mandakini (1983); my emphasis. "E.S.I., P.F. and gratuity" are workers' benefits.

122. Lemon (2000), p.25. I am grateful to Alaina Lemon for distinguishing in my work between people's narrative renditions of toil, and enactments of toil in which where the sign "toil" takes on its indexical character, allowing shared context to interpellate the present. Personal Communication, Fall Semester, Ann Arbor, 2000.

123. If interpellation is the way in which subjects are "hailed"—as Althusser's (1971) policeman hails a jaywalker—then the problem remains as to why the hermeneutic circle closes: why the jaywalker knows she is the one being hailed, or why, for that matter, the policeman knows whom to hail.

124. Eagleton (1991), pp. 142–6; thanks to Anand Pandian for starting me off in rethinking interpellation as an ongoing process, Berkeley, 1999. I am particularly grateful to Marina Welker of the Anthropology Department at the University of Michigan for asking "how the concept ['toil'] interpellates a caste- and gender-marked class fraction . . . Is toil used in a selective fashion (emplotted in a retrospective narrative of success), or is it rather indiscriminately used but only selectively operating due to misrecognition?" April 17, 2001, Agrarian Questions Seminar, Anthropology and History, University of Michigan, Ann Arbor.

125. Interview with Zintex Srinivasan, July 19, 1997.

126. Durairaj (pseudonym) (1996), "*Pórátta Kálattil Baṇian Toḷilaḷi*" ("The Banian Worker in a Field of Struggle"), unpublished tract by member of CITU, union of CPM.

127. SIHMA *Ándarikkaigaḷ*, or Annual Reports, Tiruppur.

128. Cawthorne (1990), pp. 212–14 on the council's studies and union resistance, and Appendix 7 on the report.

129. Interview with Palaniappan, April 24, 1997.

130. Palaniappan claims that the old union leader Velusamy learned about contracting through a 1961 Central Government Order to end contract work in all industries; in this rendition, Velusamy then explained it to the leadership of SIHMA as a way of increasing production. Interview with Palaniappan, April 24, 1997.

131. Ibid., although the numbers must be taken with a grain of salt, the decline is evident across interview evidence I have collected from the period. Also Durairaj (1996).

132. I am grateful to Joshua Barker and Julia Adams for these insights. In contrast to Adams' work on fraternal networks across elite French families as a democratizing challenge to the absolutist state, both Barker and I have been trying to understand fraternities that are not egalitarian. Barker's comments on the police in Indonesia, whose seemingly indiscriminate power is related to a failure of the state's monopoly on force, put it particularly succinctly: "What do the brothers do when daddy's not home!" March 21, 2001, Michigan Society of Fellows, University of Michigan, Ann Arbor.

133. Interview with Uranium Ramasamy, March 18, 1997.

134. Interview with Zippy Nalasamy, December 3, 1996

135. Ibid.

136. Thanks to Marina Welker for the caution in seeing this action as resistance; University of Michigan Anthropology and History Reading Group, October 20, 2000.

137. South India Hosiery Manufacturers Association File on "Labour Disputes for Increased Wages" (henceforth SIHMA Labour File): Letters 10 and 11.

138. SIHMA Labour File: Letters 16–22. Rick Fantasia (1988), p. 60, makes a similar argument about persisting work stoppages in the United States after Taft-Hartley, which some thought the marker of the end of class struggle through bureaucratized collective bargaining, p.60.

139. SIHMA Labour File: Letter to Sub Inspector of Police, dated November 1, 1973. *Tiffen* means snack.

140. SIHMA Labour File: Letter to Superintendent of Police, October 16, 1973.

141. Thanks to Ramachandra Guha for clarification on this, March 2001.

142. SIHMA Labour File: Letter from SIHMA to D.S.P., 17-10-1973

143. Interview with Palaniappan, April 24, 1997; Interview with Mohan Kumar, December 13, 1996.

144. Thanks to Leland Davis for asking me how a big owner could prosper without his own toil. The early 1980s were the period in which the organizational innovation of decentralized work bore fruit, and networks of small-firms, made by toil, could harness intense work to accumulation. Verona did precisely this, and in a sense he paved the way for the big exporters who now rule the town.

145. Interview with Chad Green, March 29, 1997.

146. Ibid.

147. Willis (1977), p. 188, argues in his study of how working class "lads" are tracked into working-class jobs through a mythos of masculinity, sexism and manual labor that "the problem is that real forms of cultural understanding are broken up and distorted by an omnipresent ideology of individualism . . . which actually has real currency only for middle class choice." I am interested in how this kind of ideology works for a class for which it has tremendous currency.

148. Interview with Disco Ravi, July 13, 1997.

149. Kapadia (1999) argues that my research on Tiruppur Gounders shows that the notion of being "self-made" is a critique of an "ascriptive" interpretation of caste, which modernizes caste in an exclusionary notion of individual agency. The problem with the notion of ascription is that it does not account for the ways in which castes were periodically reconstructed and manipulated. There is a sort of Brahmanical common sense which equates modernizing caste with demonstrating liberal qualities, English literacy and other metropolitan conceits. When a prominent Gounder snapped at my questions about caste and said: "We in Tiruppur are a cosmopolitan people; Gounders have no caste feeling," he affiliates with precisely such a Brahmanical interpretation of caste. A range of social forces from the Dravidian Movement, to Dalit activism, to postcolonial studies, speak of multiple ways in which caste has been used in decidedly modern struggles over entitlements.

Chapter 6: Gender Fetishisms and Shifting Hegemonies, 1974–1996

1. Cawthorne (1990) is the first to note gender-segmentation in Tiruppur, though gender in her analysis is binary sex classification.

2. Among others, Leslie Salzinger (2003: 157) makes this argument eloquently in her new book on masculinities and femininities in Ciudad Juarez, Mexico.

3. For classic formulations, see Benería and Roldán (1987) and Elson and Pearson (1986), and for reformulations, see Pearson (1998) and Iglesias Prieto (1997). I have drawn from gender critiques that do not make hasty assumptions about resistance, such as Carney and Watts (1990); and which think relationally about masculinities, as does Connell (1987, 1995) and, for India, Jackson (1999). I do not equate the retreat from the sovereign subject of class with a retreat from the political economy of accumulation and exploitation, but find very useful Haraway's (1991: 193) notion of objectivity as necessarily partial, located and embodied. On gender and migrant women's work as a lens into multiple spatial structures of production and social reproduction, see Hart (1992, 1993), and Mills (1999). Gilmore (2002), and various public comments by Ruth Wilson Gilmore, have provided powerful lessons on race and gender as modalities through which class is lived, through fatal or mutualist articulations of power and difference.

4. I am grateful to Frederick Cooper for noting this shift in my evidence, from a genesis phase of exploitation without dispossession, in the vein of Berry (1993), to an export phase based on routinization and deepened class antagonisms refracted through gender in new ways.

5. Again, Salzinger (2003), chapter 2, is an elegant explanation of the salience of this global discourse, hinging it to actual gendered expectations and work practices.

6. For instance, Salzinger (2003), Lee (2001), Wright (1997).

7. Interview with Complex Exports L. Nataraj, February 9, 1998.

8. Interview with Palaniappan, April 24, 1997.

9. Interview with Lenin Kaliappan, February 13, 1997.

10. On gendered struggles over the breadwinner wage in eighteenth-century England, see Clark (2000).

11. Cawthorne (1990), Krishnaswami (1989), p.1355.

12. Cawthorne (1990, 1993).

13. As in Giraffe Nalasamy's company, Giraffe Nalasamy, June 11, 1997.

14. Interview with Arrow Muthusamy, November 29, 1997.
15. I am grateful to Cobalt Devaraj and to CITU for a recording of *Panja-padi Porattam*, a testament to the perseverance and creativity of union organizers in Tiruppur even against the odds.
16. DA is an artifact of colonial industrial relations, and was introduced during the First World War in lieu of wage revision, as a temporary measure until the end of wartime inflation. Wages did not catch up with prices, and DA became the means by which organized labor fought for a living wage in formal sector industrial work in India. See Pavaskar (1985), p. 3.
17. Durairaj (1996).
18. Interview with Zintex Srinivasan, July 19, 1997.
19. In Williams's (1977: 110) notion of lived hegemony, class rule does not operate through abstract ideologies or formal institutions as through the saturation of everyday practice, where "the pressures and limits of a given form of domination are . . . experienced and in practice internalized."
20. I am grateful to Laura Brown for helping me rethink the changing units of toil, and their entailments. Personal Communication, May 14, 2003.
21. Interview with Mohan Kumar, December 13, 1996.
22. Interview with S. Muthusamy, May 16, 1997.
23. See Chapter 2, Section IV. I am grateful to Sandra Comstock for sharing her insights to sharpen this section. Personal Communication, April 25, 2003.
24. Interview with Punyamurthy, November 30, 1996.
25. Interview with S. Muthusamy, May 16, 1997.
26. Interview with Rajeshwari, February 15, 1998.
27. On critiques of patriarchy, see H. Moore (1994), Hart (1995), Kandiyoti (1998). For important critiques of elitist feminisms, see the work of Carolyn Steedman, particularly Steedman (1987), and from a postcolonial perspective, see Mohanty (1984) and Mahmood (1998). Rose (1993: 159) speaks of "being both prisoner and exile, both within and without . . . a space imagined in order to articulate a troubled relation to hegemonic discourses of masculinism," see also the discussion in Peet (1998), pp. 285–8.
28. Interview with Valarmati, February 15, 1998.
29. Interview with Bhuvana of Lata Collars, February 16, 1998.
30. Interview with Kamakshi, February 15, 1997.

31. For a general introduction to politics in Tamil Nadu, see Madras Institute of Development Studies (1988). See Pandian (1992) for insights into the decline of the progressive phase of the Dravidian Movement through the MGR phenomenon. Agrarian communist activism in parts of Tamil Nadu, like Thanjavur District, was rooted in highly polarized class and caste relations, and a militant history of mobilization centered on Dalit labor. Tamilmani and her husband come from this charged political landscape.

32. Interview with Palaniammal, May 10, 1997.

33. The sources of alternative, working-class hegemony, Williams (1977) argues, require "the practical connection of many different forms of struggle, including those not easily recognizable as and indeed not primarily 'political' and 'economic,' thus lead[ing] to a much more profound and more active sense of revolutionary activity," p. 111.

34. Interview with Vimal Chandmal, January 19, 1997.

35. Four ways in which export entitlements are distributed through the quota system are: 1. Past Performance Entitlement, 2. Manufacturer Exporters Entitlement, 3. Non-Quota Exporters Entitlement and 4. First Come First Served (FCFS). Apparel Export Promotion Council, 1995.

36. Interview with Murugesan, February 13, 1997.

37. http://www.textiledelegation.com/

38. Guha (1997), p. xii. This is not the place to debate whether Gramsci's notion of hegemony is meant to "assimilate" civil society.

39. Harriss-White (2003), p.104.

40. Thanks to Richard Walker for his thoughts on "vertical" and "horizontal" relations between men and the importance of the latter in the class consolidation of networked capitalists (Personal Communication, February 2, 2000.) More important, I would add, is the quality of relations between men and the way in which gender discourses are used in practice to forge fraternal intimacies while differentiating the labors of those who cannot partake in these intimacies.

41. The notion of tactics is from de Certeau (1988).

42. Interview with Selvi, February 14, 1997.

Chapter 7: Conclusion: Globalizing the *Mofussils*

1. Cited in Kiernan (1995), p. 1.

2. Elson (1979), p. 174. I am grateful to Fernando Coronil for getting me

to think against this fetishism while explaining its conditions of possibility.

3. For this reason, Harriss-White (2003) takes issue with my use of the term "peasant" at all. I persist in using it with reference to a long tradition of scholarship of this "awkward class," as fragile, institutionally complex, shaped by multiple broader processes and politics through pluriactivity and rural industrialization, migration, state making and social movements, all of which do away with Marx's unfortunate characterization of "potatoes in a sack."

4. See Karshenas (1995), but also Lenin [1899] (1974).

5. This is precisely what Gillian Hart (2002) has been arguing with respect to post-Apartheid South Africa.

6. See, for instance Srivastava (1995), Nadkarni (1987), Dreze and Mukherjee (1989), and J. Harriss (1992).

7. Subrahmanyam (1996), p. 45.

8. Kalecki (1972), K.N. Raj (1973), Bardhan (1984a).

9. Bardhan (1993), p. 351.

Glossary

Note that owners in Tiruppur tend to prefix their names with the name of their company, so that *Saturn Nalasamy* refers to a man called Nalasamy, owner of Saturn Knitting Company. "Samy," or god, is also a typical suffix of male Gounder names, which are usually synonyms of the favorite Tamil god, Murugan. Some definitions are based on the *Dictionary of Contemporary Tamil* (1992) from Cre-A.

Agraháram	Brahmin neighborhood.
Ál tévai	Person needed.
Amávácai	New moon day, auspicious day for Hindus.
Ana	Money, an Anna is approximately 4 Paisa (100 Paisa in a Rupee, 25 Paisa is often still called 4 Annas, and 50 Paise, 8 Annas).
Annan	Elder brother.
Banian	Undershirt, but also basic T-shirts. "Banian cloth" means knitted cloth; "collar banian" means a T-shirt with a collar.
Biradari	Fraternity (Hindi–Urdu word not used in Tamil Nadu).
Bund	Lockout or curfew.
Calendaring	Machine ironing of knitted fabric, usually after bleaching and dyeing to bring the fabric back into a manageable form for cutting into pieces for garment stitching.
Cantai	Periodic market; origin of the Engish word "shandy," meaning the same.
Chennai	The Tamil name for Madras City.
Chettiar	"Forward" caste whose traditional occupations were

	in trade, moneylending or weaving (the last as in *Devanga Chettiars*); the most prosperous Chettiars in Tiruppur were in cotton and yarn trades.
Cít	From "chit," a slip of paper, promissory note, receipt, lottery ticket; or a general reference to gambling.
Cottu	Inheritance.
Coolie	Wage; or a wage worker. Also used in Tiruppur by jobworkers or owners of dependent units to mean work for simple reproduction of the firm, in which profits are used in reproducing the operation of the firm and in paying the owner a living allowance which fluctuates with the fortunes of the firm.
Cuyamariyátai Kalyánam	"Self Respect marriage," an innovation of the Self-Respect Movement, which rendered marriage between man and woman contractual and non-religious, without the intervention of gods and priests.
Cross cousin	Father's sister's offspring or mother's brother's offspring. Cross cousins are preferred marriage partners. Non-cross-cousins are considered blood relatives and there is a taboo against marrying them; among males they are *pankális*.
Crore	10,000,000 (written 1,00,00,000 in India).
Dalit	Literally "the Oppressed;" alongside their political organization, Dalit has come to be the affirmative term for those referred to as "untouchables" and as "Harijans" or "Children of God" by Gandhians (a term rejected by politicized Dalits for its paternalistic Hinduism and for the more general reason that social justice cannot be willed through names alone).
Deepavali	The major Hindu festival in South India. "Deepavali bonus" is one of the key benefits sought and won by Tiruppur workers.
Drávida Kalagam	"Dravidian Party."
Éduppádu	Engagement, devotion, involvement, immersion.

Geṭṭikári	"Tough woman."
Godown	Warehouse.
Gounder	The dominant peasant caste in western Tamil Nadu.
Goundacci amma	The mother of the Gounder household.
Hartal	Strike.
Iyer	One of the main Tamil Brahmin castes, prominent among the old guard of Tiruppur's knitwear owners.
Játi	Caste as locally defined endogamous group (rather than in the scriptural or colonial historical terms of a fourfold structure holding over all Hindus).
Jetty	Underwear, plural jetties.
Kactakkooṭṭu	Literally "effort-share" arrangements, in which one partner provides capital while the working partner or *kactakkooṭṭáli* provides skilled labor in exchange for a profit-share.
Kádu	Dryland, "wasteland," forest, land far from civility.
Kai-vandi	Hand-pulled cart.
Kaláci	Manual transport and related jobs like headload carrier (*Kaláci* is the occupation, *Kaláckárar* is the worker).
Kaṇakkupiḷḷai	Accountant, who often serves as office secretary or manager.
Káṇiyáḷar	A category of Gounders who were something like agrarian lords, with large landholdings, and Brahminical affiliations such as Vaishnavism (worship of Vishnu), vegetarianism, and a disdain for manual labor: *Káṇiyáḷars* would not touch the plough.
Kapas	Measure of raw cotton.
Kaja	Button-hole.
Kavalai	Traditional draught-powered lift irrigation technology.
Khadi	Handloom woven cloth made of hand-spun thread;

this quintessential "village industry" became the symbol of Gandhian development as well as of national self-sufficiency and resistance to the mill-made cloth of Lancashire pushed duty-free on the Indian market. Also *Kaddar* in Tamil.

Kottaṭimai Indentured labor or sharecropping.

Kuṭiánavan Literally, "man who stays with," used to describe landless Gounder families who stayed with landed families and worked for them; also called *Kudiánava* Gounders.

Kuṭumi Small tuft of hair on an otherwise bald head.

Lakh 100,000 (written 1,00,000 in India).

Lápam Profit.

Maccán Brother-in-law, or a fictive "brother" who can marry into a man's family.

Madari The self-identifying category in the Telugu language used by the main Dalit caste of rural Coimbatore District; also known disparagingly in Tamil as *Chakkiliar*. Their traditional occupation was in leather crafts, and they came to become agrarian labor in semi-arid Gounder-owned farms of Coimbatore District because of their skill in manufacturing traditional well-irrigation technology: the *pari* or leather sack used to raise water from wells through *kavalai* or draught power.

Madras (1) Region under direct colonial rule through representatives of the crown, Madras Presidency (1857–1947) is distinguished from earlier Provinces, Agency Tracts and indirectly ruled Princely States, and was comprised of modern Tamil Nadu State with parts of Karnataka, Andhra Pradesh and Kerala, prior to the linguistic division of states in post-Independence India.

(2) Today's Chennai City.

Maḷḷihaikkadai Petty grocer's shop.

Máman	Mother's brother (*Taimáman*), or father-in-law (*Mámanár*), or a fictive elder brother who can marry into a man's family.
Máppiḻai	Son-in-law, also used as a fictive term for a man who can marry into the family.
Marwari	Mercantile caste from Rajasthan or Gujarat; the pre-eminent "business community" in India with strong familial control of business networks, and apprenticeship systems for kin to provide managerial control over these networks. Marwaris via Calcutta have been the primary North Indian business community among fractions of capital in Tiruppur.
Mécai	Moustache.
Moottai	A measure of volume.
Mudaliar	"Forward" caste, in modern bureaucratic parlance, traditionally in trade or weaving, *Senguntha Mudaliar* being the main subcaste of Mudaliar weavers.
Mudaláḻi	Owner, capitalist.
Mudalédu	Capital.
Naidu	Caste of Telugu-speaking agriculturalists, the largest of whom became the majority of textile mill owners in Coimbatore City; Naidu is the honorific of Naicker, who are common among peasants closer to Coimbatore City.
Naḻḻa Neram	"Good Timing," auspicious times for launching events or actions.
Namáz	Muslim prayer.
Ner	Direct.
O.C.	Tamil slang for "free" with a hint of hoodwinking or making an angle; the idiom is a colonial artifact of British East India Co. officers who would get various perks "on company"—O.C.—account.
Ooci	Injection.
Otrumai	Unity, solidarity based on shared interests.
Páduppadu	To suffer or to tough it out.

Paisa	100 Paisa make a Rupee.
Paḻakkam	Habit, custom; used to express a process of "becoming familiar" with people or customs, also used to express an initial period of informal apprenticeship or skilling at work.
Panjappadi	Dearness Allowance.
Pankáḻi	Literally "shareholder," patrilineal male who has a share in inheritance; I translate as "brother," within quotes, for any man of the same caste who cannot marry-in is a potential shareholder; "brothers" emphasizes fictive fraternity.
Pari	Leather bag used to draw water in the traditional *kavalai* system of irrigation.
Pari paṉam	Brideprice; literally the money to make a *pari*.
Párvai	Sight, or seeing.
Paṉam	Money.
Párty	Vernacular Tamil-English that means "person," usually in reference to a type of person, so businesspeople often speak of contacts in business as "parties."
Paun	A gold coin weighing 8 grams; common measure for gold.
Póráṭṭam	Struggle.
Pórtta	Appropriate or suitable to. "fashion-*pórtta*-rate" means. Wage rates that are seen to be appropriate to the fashion of the product.
Power Table	A table with a motor and a shaft running along the bottom from which several (6–8) stitching machines work in tandem. The Power Table is the unit of garment production, and it is particularly suited to contracting out batches of garments of particular specifications so that the contractor arranges and controls the labor for that batch.
Pombḻe	Woman, as an epithet or in informal, colloquial speech.
Pongal	Important festival for Hindus in Tamil Nadu.

Puḷiár	The Hindu god *Gaṇésá*.
Ryot	Farm smallholder, peasant.
Ryotwari	Form of colonial land tenure settlement, which claimed to secure the land rights of smallholders. Contrast to *Zamindari* settlement which secured the rights of larger landlords.
Salt Satyagraha	One of Gandhi's main campaigns, this rejection of imported salt and call to the production of Indian salt led Gandhi to several coastal salt production centers, including Vedaranyam in southern Madras Presidency.
SBI	The State Bank of India.
SIHMA	South Indian Hosiery Manufacturers Association: the local and merchant producers' association. (The latter makes garments for other companies that are final exporters.)
SSI	Small Scale Industry.
Sleeping Partner	Partner in a company who invests capital and receives a profit share but does not intervene in production.
Suyasámbádiyam	Self-management.
Tambi	Younger brother.
Tamil Nadu	State in South India, also called Madras; literally, the Tamil country.
Terincavanka	Known person.
TEA	Tiruppur Exporters' Association: direct exporters who contract with foreign buyers.
Tái	Mother.
Táimáman	Mother's brother; considered a woman's link to her father's property after marriage.
Táḷi	Thread tied around the bride's neck by the groom, signifying the moment of marriage in a South Indian Hindu marriage ceremony.
Taiyárippu	Manufacture.

Taiyal nilayam	Stitching section.
Tondar	Volunteer or "party worker."
Tóttam	Garden, well-irrigated farm.
Tólar	Comrade, the title for any CP member.
Tólil	Work, job, occupation.
Tólilali	Worker.
Tyágam	Martyrdom, suffering.
Tyági	Martyr, one who has suffered but may not be deceased.
Úr	Town.
Urpattiálar	Manufacturer.
Ulaippu	Toil, hard work.
Unnáviridam	Hunger strike.
Urimai	Rights and obligations.
Vactú	Vedic science of architecture used for building auspicious spaces.
Valarccí	To grow.
Vartahar	Businessman, trader, merchant.
Vécti	Wrap worn by men.
Vélai	Job.
Veli	Outside.
Veliál	Outsider.
Working partner	Partner in a company who works in production or as a shopfloor supervisor and typically receives a profit share but does not invest initial capital.

References

Agarwal, Bina, 1994, *A Field of One's Own: Gender and Land Rights in South Asia*, Cambridge: Cambridge University Press.

Alexander, K.C., 1981, *Peasant Organizations in South India*, Delhi: Indian Social Institute.

Althusser, Louis, 1971, "Ideology and Ideological State Apparatuses," *Lenin and Philosophy*, London: Verso.

Ambedkar, B.P. (for Government of India, Labour Investigation Committee), 1946, *Report on Labour Conditions in the Cotton Ginning and Bailing Industry*, Simla: Government of India Press.

American Apparel Manufacturers Association (AAMA), 1997, *The Dynamics of Sourcing*, Arlington, Virginia: American Apparel Manufacturers Association.

Amin, Ash and Kevin Robins 1990, "Industrial Districts and Regional Development: Limits and Possibilities," F. Pyke *et al.*, eds, *Industrial Districts and Inter-firm Cooperation in Italy*, Geneva: International Institute for Labor Studies.

Amin, Shahid, 1995, *Event, Metaphor, Memory: Chauri-Chaura 1922–1992*, Berkeley: University of California Press.

Apparel Export Promotion Council (AEPC), 1995, *Garment Export Entitlement Policy, 1994–1996*, New Delhi.

Apthorpe, R., 1979, "The Burden of Land Reform in Taiwan: An Asian Model Land Reform Re-analysed," *World Development*, vol. 7, nos 4 and 5.

Arnold, David, 1974, "The Gounders and the Congress: Political Recruitment in South India, 1920–1937," *South Asia*, vol. 4, pp. 1–20, October.

Athreya, Venkatesh, Goran Djurfeldt and Stefan Lindberg, 1990, *Barriers Broken*, New Delhi: Sage.

Ayyar, Krishnaswami, 1933, *Statistical Appendix and Supplement to the Revised District Manual (1898) for Coimbatore District* (edited by A.R. Cox), Madras: Government Press.

Bairoch, Paul, 1988, *Cities and Economic Development: From the Dawn of History to the Present*, Chicago: University of Chicago Press.

Baker, Christopher John, 1984, *An Indian Rural Economy, 1880–1955: The Tamilnadu Countryside*, Oxford: Clarendon Press.

Balan, C.A., 1979, *Túkkumarattin Niḷalil.* (In the Shadow of the Gallows) translated from the Malayalam by Saraswathy Menon, Chennai: Sangam Books.

Baliga, B.S., 1966, *Madras District Gazetteers: Coimbatore*, Madras: Director of Stationary and Printing on behalf of the Government of Madras.

Banaji, Jairus, 1977, "Capitalist Domination and the Small Peasantry: The Deccan Districts in the Late Nineteenth Century," *Economic and Political Weekly* (Bombay), Special Issue.

Bardhan, Pranab, 1984a, *The Political Economy of Development in India*, New Delhi: Oxford University Press.

———, 1984b, *Land, Labor and Rural Poverty: Essays in Development Economics*, New Delhi: Oxford University Press.

———, 1986, "Marxist Ideas in Development Economics: An Evaluation," John Roemer, ed., *Analytical Marxism*, New York: Cambridge University Press.

———, 1993, "The 'Intermediate Regime': Any Sign of Graduation?," P. Bardhan, M. Datta-Chaudhuri and T.N. Krishnan, eds, *Development and Change: Essays in Honour of K.N. Raj*, Bombay: Oxford University Press.

———, 1997, *The Role of Governance in Economic Development: A Political Economy Approach*, Paris: Development Centre of the Organization for Economic Cooperation and Development.

———, and Ashok Rudra, 1981, "Terms and Conditions of Labour Contracts in Agriculture: Results of a Survey in West Bengal, 1979," *Oxford Bulletin of Economics and Statistics*, 43(1), pp. 89–111.

Bayly, Christopher A., 1992, *Rulers, Townsmen and Bazaars: North Indian Society in the Age of British Expansion, 1770–1870*, Delhi: Oxford University Press.

Beck, Brenda E.F., 1972, *Peasant Society in Konku: A Study of Right and Left Subcastes in South India*, Vancouver: University of British Columbia Press.

Benería, Lourdes and Martha Roldán, 1987, *The Crossroads of Class and Gender*, Chicago: University of Chicago Press.

Berman, Marshall, 1982, *All That is Solid Melts into Air: The Experience of Modernity*, London: Penguin Books.

Berna, James, 1960, *Industrial Entrepreneurship in Madras State*, New York: Asia Publishing House.

Bernstein, Henry, 1977, "Notes on Capital and Peasantry," *Review of African Political Economy*, 10.

———, 1988, "Capitalism and Petty-Bourgeois Production: Class Relations and the Division of Labour," *Journal of Peasant Studies*, vol. 15, no. 2.

———, ed., 1996, *The Agrarian Question in South Africa*, London: Frank Cass.

———, and B.K. Campbell, eds, 1985, *Contradictions of Accumulation in Africa: Studies in Economy and State*, Beverley Hills: Sage.

Bernstein, Henry and Tom Brass, 1996, "Questioning the Agrarians: The Work of T.J. Byres," *Journal of Peasant Studies*, 24 (1–2), pp. 1–21.

Berry, Sara, 1985, *Fathers Work for their Sons*, Berkeley: University of California Press.

———, 1989, "Social Institutions and Access to Resources in African Agriculture," *Africa*, 59, 1: 41–55.

———, 1993, *No Condition is Permanent*, Madison: University of Wisconsin Press.

Bhaduri, Amit, 1973, "A Study in Agricultural Backwardness under Semi-Feudalism," *Economic Journal*, 83/329

———, 1983, *The Economic Structure of Backward Agriculture*, London: Academic Press.

Bhalla, Sheila, 1976, "New Relations of Production in Haryana Agriculture," *Economic and Political Weekly*, Review of Agriculture, March.

Bharadwaj, Krishna, 1985, "A View on Commercialisation in Indian Agriculture and the Development of Capitalism," *Journal of Peasant Studies*, 12, 4, July 1985, pp. 7–25, reprinted in Bharadwaj, K., 1995, *Accumulation, Exchange and Development: Essays on the Indian Economy*, New Delhi: Sage.

Bhaskar, Roy, 1994, *Plato, Etc.*, London: Verso.

Biernacki, Richard, 1995, *The Fabrication of Labor, Germany and Britain 1640–1914*, Berkeley and Los Angeles: University of California Press.

Binny and Co., 1969, Messrs, *The House of Binny*, Madras: Associated Printers Pvt. Ltd.

Bose, Sugata, ed., 1990, *South Asia and World Capitalism*, Delhi: Oxford University Press.

Bourdieu, Pierre, 1977, *Outline of a Theory of Practice*, Cambridge: Cambridge University Press.

Bowles, P. and X.Y. Dong, 1994, "Current Successes and Future Challenges in China's Economic Reform," *New Left Review*, 208, pp. 49–76.

Brass, Tom, 1986, "Unfree Labor and Capitalist Restructuring in the Agrarian Sector," *Journal of Peasant Studies*, 14, pp. 50–77.

———, 1990, "Class Struggle and the Deproletarianization of Agricultural Labour in Haryana (India)," *Journal of Peasant Studies*, 18/1.

———, 1994, "Introduction: The New Farmers Movements in India," *Journal of Peasant Studies*, 21, 3–4, pp. 3–26.

Braverman, Harry, 1974, *Labor and Monopoly Capital: The Degradation of Work in the Twentieth Century*, New York: Monthly Review Press.

Breman, Jan, 1993, *Beyond Patronage and Exploitation: Changing Agrarian Relations in South Gujarat*, Delhi: Oxford India Paperbacks.

———, 1994, *A Footloose Proletariat: Informal Sector Labour in the Rural and Urban Landscape of West India*, Cambridge: Cambridge University Press.

———, and Sudipto Mundle, eds, 1991, *Rural Transformation in Asia*, Delhi: Oxford University Press.

Breman, Jan and Arvind Das, 2000, *Down and Out: Labouring Under Global Capitalism*, New Delhi: Oxford University Press.

Brenner, Robert, 1976, "Agrarian Class Structure and Economic Development in Preindustrial Europe," *Past and Present* 70, pp. 30–70.

———, 1978, "Dobb on the Transition from Feudalism to Capitalism," *Cambridge Journal of Economics*, vol. 2.

———, 1986, "The Social Basis of Economic Development," John Roemer, ed., *Analytical Marxism*, New York: Cambridge University Press.

Brusco, Sebastiano, 1990, "The Idea of the Industrial District: Its Genesis," F. Pyke, G. Becattini and W. Segenberger, eds, *Industrial Districts and Inter-Firm Cooperation in Italy*, Geneva: International Institute for Labor Studies.

Burawoy, Michael, 1979, *Manufacturing Consent: Changes in the Labor Process under Monopoly Capitalism*, Chicago: University of Chicago Press.

————, 1985, *The Politics of Production: Factory Regimes Under Capitalism and Socialism*, London: Verso.

————, 1991, "The Extended Case Method," *Ethnography Unbound: Power and Resistance in the Modern Metropolis*, Berkeley: University of California.

————, 1996, "The State and Economic Involution: Russia through a China Lens," *World Development*, 24, June, pp. 1105–17.

Byres, T.J., 1979, "Of Neo-populist Pipe-dreams: Daedalus in the Third World and the Myth of Urban Bias," *Journal of Peasant Studies*, 6/2, pp. 210–44.

————, 1991, "The Agrarian Question and Differing Forms of Capitalist Agrarian Transition: An Essay with Reference to Asia," Jan Breman and Sudipto Mundle, eds, *Rural Transformation in Asia*, Delhi: Oxford University Press.

————, 1995, "Political Economy, Agrarian Question and Comparative Method," *Economic and Political Weekly*, vol. 30, no. 10, March 11, pp. 507–13.

Cadène, Philippe, and Denis Vidal, 1997, *Webs of Trade: Dynamics of Business Communities in Western India*, New Delhi: Manohar Publishers.

Cadène, Philippe and Mark Holmström, 1998, *Decentralized Production in India: Industrial Districts, Flexible Specialization and Employment*, New Delhi: Sage.

Carney, Judith and Michael Watts, 1990, "Manufacturing Dissent: Work, Gender and the Politics of Meaning in a Peasant Society," *Africa* 60, pp. 207–41.

Castells, Manuel, 1996, *The Rise of the Network Society*, Oxford: Blackwell.

Cawthorne, Pamela, 1990, "Amoebic Capitalism as a Form of Accumulation: the Case of the Cotton Knitwear Industry in a South Indian Town," Ph.D. dissertation, Milton Keynes, U.K.: The Open University.

————, 1993, "The Labour Process under Amoebic Capitalism: A Case Study of the Garment Industry in a South Indian Town," DPP Working Paper, Milton Keynes, U.K.: The Open University.

————, 1995, "Of Networks and Markets: The Rise and Rise of a South Indian Town, the Example of Tiruppur's Cotton Knitwear Industry," *World Development*, vol. 23, no. 1, pp. 43–57.

Cederlöf, Gunnel, 1997, *Bonds Lost: Subordination, Conflict and Mobilisation in Rural South India, c. 1900–1970*, New Delhi: Manohar Books.

Chakrabarty, Dipesh, 1989, *Rethinking Working-Class History, Bengal 1890–1940*, Princeton, N.J.: Princeton University Press.

———, 1997, "The Time of History and the Times of Gods," Lisa Lowe and David Lloyd, eds, *The Politics of Culture in the Shadow of Capital*, Durham, North Carolina: Duke University Press.

Chamberlain, Mary and Paul Thompson, eds, 1998, *Narrative and Genre*, London: Routledge.

Chandavarkar, Rajnarayan, 1994, *The Origins of Industrial Capitalism in India: Business Strategies and the Working Classes in Bombay: 1900–1940*, Cambridge: Cambridge University Press.

———, 1997, " 'The Making of the Working Class': E.P. Thompson and Indian History," *History Workshop Journal*, 43.

Chandra, N. C., 1992, "Bukharin's Alternative to Stalin: Industrialization without Forced Collectivisation," *Journal of Peasant Studies*, 20, 1.

Chari, Sharad, 1998, "The Agrarian Question and Industrialization in Tiruppur, South India: A Historical Geography of the Industrial Present," M. Goodman and M. Watts, eds, *Globalising Food: Agrarian Questions and Global Restructuring*, Routledge, pp. 79–105.

———, 2000a, "The Agrarian Origins of the Knitwear Industrial Cluster in Tiruppur, India," *World Development*, vol. 28, no. 3, March.

———, 2000b, "The Agrarian Question Comes to Town: Making Knitwear Work in Tiruppur, South India," Ph.D. Dissertation, Ann Arbor, Michigan: UMI Dissertation Services.

Chatterjee, Partha, 1986, *Nationalist Thought and the Colonial World: A Derivative Discourse?* London: Zed Press for the United Nations University.

Chayanov, A.V. [1966], 1986, *The Theory of Peasant Economy*, Manchester: Manchester University Press..

Clark, Anna, 2000, "The New Poor Law and the Breadwinner Wage: Contrasting Assumptions," *Journal of Social History*, Winter, pp. 261–81.

Connell, Robert, 1987, *Gender and Power*, Cambridge: Polity Press.

———, 1995, *Masculinities*, Cambridge: Polity Press.

Cooper, Frederick, 1994, "Conflict and Connection: Rethinking Colonial African History," *The American Historical Review*, vol. 99, issue 5, pp. 1516–45.

———, 1997, "Modernizing Bureaucrats, Backward Africans and the Development Concept," Frederick Cooper and Randall Packard, eds, *International Development and the Social Sciences: Essays on the History and Politics of Knowledge*, Berkeley: University of California Press, pp. 64–92.

———, 2001, "What Is the Concept of Globalization Good For? An African Historian's Perspective," *African Affairs* 100, 189–213.

———, Thomas Holt and Rebecca Scott, eds, 2000, *Beyond Slavery: Explorations of Race, Labor and Citizenship in Postemancipation Societies*, Chapel Hill: University of North Carolina Press.

Corbridge, Stuart and John Harriss, 2000, *Reinventing India: Liberalization, Hindu Nationalism and Popular Democracy*, Cambridge: Polity Press.

Coronil, Fernando, 1994, "Listening to the Subaltern: The Poetics of Neocolonial States," *Poetics Today*, 15.

———, 1997, *The Magical State: Nature, Money and Modernity in Venezuela*, Chicago: University of Chicago Press.

———, 2000, "Towards a Critique of Globalcentrism: Speculations on Capitalism's Nature," *Public Culture* 12, 2, Spring.

Daniel, E. Valentine, 1984, *Fluid Signs: Being a Person the Tamil Way*, Berkeley and Los Angeles: University of California Press.

de Certeau, Michel, 1988, *The Practice of Everyday Life*, Berkeley: University of California Press.

de Janvry, Alain, 1981, *The Agrarian Question and Reformism in Latin America*, Baltimore: Johns Hopkins University Press.

de Souza, Francis, 1969, *The House of Binny*, Madras: Associated Printers.

Deshpande, S.R. (for Government of India, Labour Investigation Committee), 1946, *Report on an Enquiry into Conditions of Labour in the Cotton Mill Industry in India*, Simla: Government of India Press.

Dirks, Nicholas B., 1996, "Recasting Tamil Society: The Politics of Caste and Race in Contemporary Southern India," C.J. Fuller, ed., *Caste Today*, Delhi: Oxford University Press.

———, 2001, *Castes of Mind: Colonialism and the Making of Modern India*. Princeton: Princeton University Press.

Dobb, Maurice, 1963 [1946], *Studies in the Development of Capitalism,* New York: International Publishers.

Dreze, Jean and A. Mukherjee, 1989, "Labour Contracts in Rural India: Theories and Evidence," Sukhomoy Chakravarty, ed., *The Balance Between Industry and Agriculture in Economic Development,* vol. 3, London: Macmillan.

Durairaj [pseudonym], 1996, *Pórátta Kálattil Baṇian Toḷilaḷi* (The Banian Worker in a Field of Struggle), unpublished tract in Tamil, CITU labor union, Tiruppur.

Duraisamy, S.V., April 1934, "Low Prices and the Plight of the Lowly Ryot," *The Madras Agricultural Journal,* 22/f, pp.137–47.

Eagleton, Terry, 1991, *Ideology: An Introduction,* London: Verso.

Ellman, Michael, 1975, "Did the Agricultural Surplus Provide the Resources for the Increase in Investment in the USSR during the First Five Year Plan,?" *Economic Journal,* 85, December.

Elson, Diane, 1979, "The Value Theory of Labour," *Value: The Representation of Labour in Capitalism,* London: CSE Books.

———— and Ruth Pearson, 1986 "Third World Manufacturing," *Waged Work,* edited by *Feminist Review,* London: Virago, pp. 67–92.

Epstein, T. Scarlet, 1962, *Economic Development and Social Change in South India,* Manchester: Manchester University Press.

Escobar, Arturo, 1995, *Encountering Development: The Making and Unmaking of the Third World,* Princeton: Princeton University Press.

Fantasia, Rick, 1988, *Cultures of Solidarity,* Berkeley: University of California Press.

Foucault, Michel, 1982, "The Subject and Power," P. Rabinow and R. Dreyfus, eds, *Beyond Structuralism and Hermeneutics,* Chicago: University of Chicago Press.

Forster, E.M., 1924, *A Passage to India,* New York, Harcourt.

Frankel, Francine, 1972, *India's Green Revolution: Economic Gains and Political Costs,* Bombay: Oxford University Press.

Freidmann, Harriet, 1978, "Simple Commodity Production and Wage Labour in the American Plains," *Journal of Peasant Studies,* vol. 6, no. 1, pp. 71–100.

Fuller, C.J., 1989, "Misconceiving the Grain Heap: A Critique of the Concept of the Indian Jajmani System," J. Parry and M. Bloch, eds,

Money and the Morality of Exchange, Cambridge: Cambridge University Press.

———, ed., 1996, *Caste Today*, Delhi: Oxford University Press.

Ganesamurthy, N., 1935, "Economic Survey of a South Indian Village—Perumanallur," *Madras Agricultural Journal*, 23, 7, July, pp. 269–80.

Gertler, Meric, 1992, "Flexibility Revisited: Districts, Nation-states and the Forces of Production," *Transactions: Institute of British Geographers* 17, pp. 259–78.

Gibbon, P. and M. Neocosmos, 1985, "Some Problems in the Political Economy of 'African Socialism,' " H. Bernstein and B. K. Campbell, eds, 1985, *Contradictions of Accumulation in Africa.*

Gilmore, Ruth Wilson, 2002, "Fatal Couplings of Power and Difference: Notes on Racism and Geography," *Professional Geography*, 54/1, pp. 15–24.

Goodman, David and Michael Watts, 1997a, "Agrarian Questions: Global Appetite, Local Metabolism: Nature, Culture and Industry in *Fin-De-Siècle* Agro-Food Systems," D. Goodman and R.M. Watts, ed. *Globalising Food*, London: Routledge, pp. 1–32.

———, eds, 1997b, *Globalising Food*, London: Routledge.

Gopalaratnam, P., 1931, "Rural Studies—Madathupalayam Village, Coimbatore District," *Madras Agricultural Journal*, 19, 12, December, pp. 522–9.

Goswami, O., 1990, "Sickness and Growth of India's Textile Industry," *Economic and Political Weekly*, vol. 25, no. 45, pp. 2496–2506.

Gough, Kathleen and H.P. Sharma, eds, 1973, *Imperialism and Revolution in South Asia*, New York: Monthly Review Press.

Government of India, 1903, *Census of India, 1901. Volume 1. India. Ethnographic Appendices.* Calcutta: Office of the Superintendent of Government Printing.

———, Committee on Cotton, 1914, *Agricultural and Trade Conference, Madras*, Simla: the Superintendent, Government Press.

———, 1927a, *Report of the Unemployment Committee, 1926–27: Vols II & III, Evidence*, Madras: Superintendent, Government Press.

———, 1927b, *Royal Commission on Agriculture in India, Vol. III: Evidence Taken in the Madras Presidency*, India: His Majesty's Stationary Office.

———, Ministry of Industry, Department of Small Scale Industries,

Development Commissioner, 1995, *Small Scale Industries: Incentives and Facilities for Development*, New Delhi: Ministry of Information and Broadcasting.

————, Ministry of Labour, Agricultural Labour Enquiry, 1955, *Report on Intensive Survey of Agricultural Labour: Employment, Underemployment, Wages and Standard of Living, Vol IV: South India*, Simla: the Manager, Government of India Press.

Government of Tamil Nadu, 1997, Department of Industries and Commerce, District Industries Centre, official letter no. 12972/DS/97.

————, 1997, Department of Industries and Commerce, District Industries Centre, Records of Registered Small Scale Industries.

Gramsci, Antonio [1929–35], 1971, *Selections from the Prison Notebooks of Antonio Gramsci*, New York: International Publishers.

Granovetter, Mark, 1985, "Economic Action and Social Structure: The Problem of Embeddedness," *American Journal of Sociology* 91, pp. 481–510.

Greenhalgh, Susan, 1988, "Families and Networks in Taiwan's Economic Development," in E. Winckler and S. Greenhalgh, eds, *Contending Approaches to the Economic Development of Taiwan*, Armonk, N.Y.: M. E. Sharpe

Guha, Ranajit, 1963, *A Rule of Property for Bengal: An Essay on the Idea of Permanent Settlement*, Paris: Mouton.

————, 1983a, *Elementary Aspects of Peasant Insurgency in Colonial India*, Delhi: Oxford University Press.

————, 1983b, "The Prose of Counter-Insurgency," R. Guha, ed., *Subaltern Studies II: Writings on South Asian History and Society*, pp. 1–42, Delhi: Oxford University Press.

————, 1997, *Dominance without Hegemony: History and Power in Colonial India*, Cambridge, Mass.: Harvard University Press.

Gupta, Akhil, 1998, *Postcolonial Developments: Agriculture in the Making of Modern India*, Durham, N.C.: Duke University Press.

Guyer, Jane and Pauline Peters, 1987, "Conceptualizing the Household: Issues of Theory and Policy in Africa," *Development and Change*, 18, pp. 197–214.

Haraway, Donna, 1991, "Situated Knowledges: The Science Question in Feminism and the Privilege of Partial Perspective," *Simians, Cyborgs and Women: The Reinvention of Nature*, New York: Routledge.

Harriss, John, 1982, *Capitalism and Peasant Farming: Agrarian Structure and Ideology in Northern Tamil Nadu*, Bombay: Oxford University Press.

———, 1983, "Two Theses on Small Industry—A Report from Coimbatore, South India," Discussion Paper no. 80, School of Development Studies, University of East Anglia, Norwich.

———, 1992, "Does the Depressor Still Work? Agrarian Structure and Development in India: A Review of Evidence and Argument," *Journal of Peasant Studies*, vol. 19, no. 2, Jan, pp. 189–227.

Harriss-White, Barbara, 1985, "Agricultural Markets and Intersectoral Resource Transfers: Cases from the Semi-Arid Tropics of Southeast India," ICRISAT, eds, *Proceedings of the International Workshop, 24–28 October 1983*, pp. 279–301, Patancheru, India: International Crops Research Institute for the Semi-Arid Tropics.

———, 1995, *A Political Economy of Agricultural Markets in South India: Masters of the Countryside*, New Delhi: Sage Publications.

———, 1999, *How India Works: The Character of the Local Economy*, Cambridge. Commonwealth Lectures, Development Studies at Oxford, Queen Elizabeth House.

———, 2003, *India Working: Essays on Economy and Society*, Cambridge: Cambridge University Press.

Hart, Gillian, 1986, "Interlocking Transactions: Obstacles, Precursors or Instruments of Agrarian Capitalism?," *Journal of Development Economics*, 23, pp. 177–203.

———, 1991, "Engendering Everyday Resistance: Gender, Patronage and Production Politics in Rural Malaysia," *Journal of Peasant Studies* 19, 1, pp. 93–121.

———, 1992, "Household Production Reconsidered: Gender, Labor Conflict and Technological Change in Malaysia's Muda Region," *World Development* 20, 6, pp. 809–203.

———, 1993, "Regional Growth Linkages in the Era of Liberalization: A Critique of the New Agrarian Optimism," W.E.P. Research Working Paper no.37, Geneva: International Labour Organization.

———, 1995, "Gender and Household Dynamics: Recent Theories of the Household and Their Implications," M.G. Quibria, ed., *Critical Issues in Asian Development*, Hong Kong: Oxford University Press.

———, 1996a, "The Agrarian Question and Industrial Dispersal in South Africa: Agro-Industrial Linkages through Asian Lenses,"

Henry Bernstein, ed., *The Agrarian Question in South Africa*, London: Frank Cass.

———, 1996b, "Global Connections: The Rise and Fall of a Taiwanese Production Network on the South African Periphery," Working Paper no. 6, Institute of International Stuides, University of California, Berkeley.

———, 1997, "Multiple Trajectories of Rural Industrialization: An Agrarian Critique of Industrial Restructuring and the New Institutionalism," D. Goodman and M. Watts, eds, *Globalising Food*, London: Routledge.

———, 1998, "Multiple Trajectories: A Critique of Industrial Restructuring and the New Institutionalism," *Antipode*, vol. 30, pp. 333+.

———, 2001, "Development Critiques in the 1990s: Cul de Sacs and Promising Paths," *Progress in Human Geography*, 25, pp. 649–58.

———, 2002, *Disabling Globalisation: Places of Power in Post-Apartheid South Africa*, Pietermaritzburg: University of Natal Press.

Harvey, David, 1982, *The Limits to Capital*, Chicago: University of Chicago Press.

———, 1985, *Consciousness and the Urban Experience*, Oxford: Oxford University Press.

———, 2000, *Spaces of Hope*, Berkeley: University of California Press.

Hasan, Zoya, 1989, *Dominance and Mobilisation: Rural Politics in Western Uttar Pradesh, 1930–1980*, New Delhi: Sage Publications.

Heller, Patrick, 1995, "From Class Struggle to Class Compromise: Redistribution and Growth in a South Indian State," *Journal of Development Studies*, 31/5, pp. 645–72.

———, 1999, *The Labor of Development: Workers and the Transformation of Capitalism in Kerala, India*, Ithaca: Cornell University Press.

Hollinger, David, 1995, *Postethnic America*, New York: Basic Books.

Holmes, Douglas, 1989, *Cultural Disenchantments: Worker Peasantries in Northeast Italy*, Princeton: Princeton University Press.

Holmström, Mark, 1993, "Flexible Specialization in India?," *Economic and Political Weekly*, Aug 28, pp. M82–M86.

———, 1998, "Introduction: Industrial Districts and Flexible Specialization—The Outlook for Smaller Firms in India," P. Cadène and M. Holmström, *Decentralized Production in India*, New Delhi: Sage.

Irschick, Eugene F., 1986, *Tamil Revivalism in the 1930s*, Madras: Cre-A Publishers.

Jackson, Cecille, 1999, "Men's Work, Masculinities and Gender Divisions of Labour," *Journal of Development Studies*, 36, 1, pp. 89–108.

James, C.L.R., 1963 [1938], *The Black Jacobins: Toussaint L'Overture and the San Domingo Revolution*, New York: Vintage.

Ka, Chih-Ming and Mark Selden, 1986, "Original Accumulation, Equity and Late Industrialization: The Cases of Socialist China and Capitalist Taiwan," *World Development*, 14, 10, pp. 1293–1310.

Kalecki, Michael, 1972, "Social and Economic Aspects of Intermediate Regimes," *Selected Essays on the Economic Growth of the Socialist and the Mixed Economy*, Cambridge: Cambridge University Press.

Kandiyoti, Deniz, 1998, "Gender, Power and Contestation: 'Rethinking Bargaining with Patriarchy,' " Cecile Jackson and Ruth Pearson, eds, *Feminist Visions of Development: Gender Analysis and Policy*, London: Routledge.

Kannan, Kappadath Parameswara, 1988, *Of Rural Proletarian Struggles: Mobilization and Organization of Rural Workers in South-west India*, Delhi: Oxford University Press.

Kapadia, Karin, 1995, *Siva and Her Sisters: Gender, Caste and Class in Rural South India*, Boulder, Co: Westview Press.

———, 1999, *The Violence of Development: The Politics of Identity, Gender, and Social Inequalities in India*, New Delhi: Kali for Women.

Karshenas, Massoud, 1995, *Industrialization and Agricultural Surplus*, Oxford: Oxford University Press.

Kautsky, Karl, 1988 [1899], *The Agrarian Question*, London: Zwan Publications.

Kaye, Harvey, 1995, *The British Marxist Historians*, New York: St Martin's Press.

Khadar, S.A., n.d., Personal Papers of S.A. Khadar, courtesy of his family, Tiruppur.

Khadar Knitting Company, Messrs, 1956, *Tiruppur K.K.C. Group Banian Toḷilcaḷaigaḷin Vaḷarci Varalaru* (The History of the Growth of Banian Factories in the Tiruppur K.K.C. Group), in Tamil, Tiruppur: Alponsa Printers.

Khanna, S., 1989, "Technical Change and Competetiveness in the Indian Textile Industry," *Economic and Political Weekly*, vol. 24, no. 34, pp. M103–M111, August.

Kiernan, Victor, 1995, *Imperialism and its Contradictions*, New York: Routledge.

Knorringa, P., 1998, "Barriers to Flexible Specialization in Agra's Footwear Industry," P. Cadène and M. Holmström, *Decentralized Production in India*, Delhi: Sage Publications.

Kohli, Atul, 1990, *Democracy and Discontent: India's Growing Crisis of Governability*, Cambridge: Cambridge University Press.

Krishna, C.S., 1992, "First Congress Ministry and Labour Struggles of Textile Mill Workers in Coimbatore, 1937–1939," *Economic and Political Weekly*, July 11), pp. 1497–1506.

Krishnaswami, C., 1989, "Dynamics of Capitalist Labour Process: Knitting Industry in Tamilnadu," *Economic and Political Weekly*, July 17, pp. 1353–9.

Lazerson, Mark, 1995, "A New Phoenix? Modern Putting-Out in the Modena Knitwear Industry" in *Administrative Science Quarterly*, 40.

———, 1997, "Entrepreneurship in Italy," C. Upadhya and M. Rutten, eds, *Small Business Entrepreneurs in Asia and Europe: Towards a Comparative Perspective*, New Delhi: Sage Publications.

Lee, Ching Kwan, 1998, *Gender and the South China Miracle: Two Worlds of Factory Women*, Berkeley and Los Angeles: University of California Press.

———, 2001, "Lost Between Histories: Labor Insurgency and Subjectivity in Reform China," Paper presented at the 53rd Annual Meeting of the Association of Asian Studies, March 22–25, 2001, Chicago.

Lee, Teng-hui, 1971, *Intersectoral Capital Flows in the Economic Development of Taiwan, 1895–1960*, Ithaca: Cornell University Press.

Lefebvre, Henri, 1991, *The Production of Space*, trans. Donald Nicholson-Smith, Oxford: Blackwell.

Lemon, Alaina, 2000, *Between Two Fires: Gypsy Performance and Romani Memory from Pushkin to Postsocialism*, Durham: Duke University Press.

Lenin, Vladimir I., 1974 [1899, 1908], *The Development of Capitalism in Russia*, Moscow: Progress Publishers.

Lindberg, Staffan, 1996, "While the Wells Went Dry: The Tragedy of Collective Action among Farmers of South India," mimeo.

Lipton, Michael, 1977, *Why Poor People Stay Poor: Urban Bias in World Development*, Cambridge: Harvard University Press.

Little, Peter and Michael Watts, 1994, *Living Under Contract: Contract Farming and Agrarian Transformation in Sub-Saharan Africa*, Madison: University of Wisconsin Press.

Lowe, Lisa and David Lloyd, eds, 1997, *The Politics of Culture in the Shadow of Capital*, Durham, North Carolina: Duke University Press.

Mackintosh, Maureen, 1989, *Gender, and Rural Transition: Agribusiness and the Food Crisis in Senegal*, New Jersey, Zed Books.

Madras Institute of Development Studies (MIDS), 1988, *Tamilnad Economy: Performance and Issues*, New Delhi: Oxford and India Book House Pub. Co.

Mahadevan, Raman, 1992, "The Process of Manchesterisation in Colonial South India: A Study of the Pattern of Textile Investment and the Growth of Indigenous Capitalists in Coimbatore in 1914–45," 12th European Conference on Modern South Asian Studies, Economic and Demographic History of South Asia, Berlin, Sept.

Mahmood, Saba, 1998, "Women's Piety and Embodied Discipline: The Islamic Resurgence in Contemporary Egypt,"' PhD dissertation, Ann Arbor, Michigan: UMI Dissertation Services.

Mallon, Florencia, 1994, "The Promise and Dilemma of Subaltern Studies: Perspectives from Latin American History," *The American Historical Review*, vol. 99, no. 5., pp. 1491–1515.

Marshall, Alfred [1890] 1986, *Principles of Economics*, London: Macmillan.

Marx, Karl [1867] 1967, *Capital: A Critique of Political Economy*, vol. I, New York: International Publishers.

Marx, Karl and Frederick Engels [1848] 1998, *The Communist Manifesto: A Modern Edition*, New York: Verso.

Manthagini, B., 1983, "The History of Hosiery Industries at Tiruppur," M.Phil. thesis, Coimbatore, Bharathiyar University, Coimbatore, India.

Massey, Doreen, 1994, *Space, Place and Gender*, Minneapolis: University of Minnesota.

May Day Manifesto Committee, 1968, edited by Raymond Williams, *May Day Manifesto 1968*, Harmondsworth: Penguin.

Mellor, John, 1976, *The New Economics of Growth: A Strategy for India and the Developing World*, Ithaca: Cornell University Press.

Miles, Robert, 1987, *Capitalism and Unfree Labour: Anomaly or Necessity*, London: Tavistock.

Mills, Mary Beth, 1999, *Thai Women in the Global Labor Force: Consuming Desires, Contested Selves,* New Brunswick, N.J.: Rutgers University Press.

Mines, Mattison, 1984, *The Warrior Merchants: Textiles. Trade and Territory in South India*, Cambridge: Cambridge University Press.

Mitra, Ashok, 1977, *Terms of Trade and Class Relations*, London: Frank Cass.

Mohanty, Chandra, 1984, "Under Western Eyes: Feminist Scholarship and Colonial Discourse," *Boundary* 2, 3 (12/13), pp. 333–58.

Moore, Barrington, 1966, *The Social Origins of Dictatorship and Democracy: Lord and Peasant in the Making of the Modern World*, Boston: Beacon Press.

Moore, Donald, 1993, "Contesting Terrain in Zimbabwe's Eastern Highlands," *Economic Geography*, 69, 4, pp. 380–401.

Moore, Henrietta, 1994, *A Passion for Difference*, Indiana: Indiana University Press.

Murphy, Eamon, 1981, *Unions in Conflict: A Comparative Study of Four South Indian Textile Centres 1918–1939*, Delhi: Manohar Publications.

Nadkarni, M.V., 1987, *Farmers' Movements in India*, Ahmedabad: Allied Publishers.

Nadvi, Khalid, 1992, "Flexible Specialization, Industrial Districts and Employment in Pakistan," World Employment Program Working Paper 232, Geneva: International Labor Office.

———, 1996, "Small Firm Industrial Districts in Pakistan," PhD. dissertation, University of Sussex.

——— and Hubert Schmitz, 1998, "Industrial Clusters in Less Developed Countries: Review of Experiences and Research Agenda," P. Cadène and M. Holmström, eds, *Decentralized Production in India*, New Delhi: Sage.

Neelakantan, 1996, "Change and Continuity—A Contrasting Account of Urban and Rural Transformation," Working Paper no. 139, Chennai: Madras Institute of Development Studies.

Nicholson, F. A., 1887, *Manual of the Coimbatore District in the Presidency of Madras*, Madras: Government Press.

O'Hanlon, Rosalind and David Washbrook, 1992, "After Orientalism: Culture, Criticism and Politics in the Third World," *Comparative Studies in Society and History,* vol. 34, no. 1., pp. 141–67.

Oi, Jean, 1992, "Fiscal Reform and the Economic Foundations of Local State Corporatism in China," *World Politics*, 45 pp. '99–126.

Omvedt, Gail, 1994, "We Want the Return of Our Sweat—The New Peasant Movement in India and the Formation of a National Agricultural Policy," *Journal of Peasant Studies*, vol. 21, nos 3–4, April–July, pp. 126–64.

Orru, M., 1991, "The Institutional Logic of Small-Firm Economies in Italy and Taiwan," *Studies in Comparative International Development*, 26/3, pp. 3–28.

Page, Brian and Richard Walker, 1991, "From Settlement to Fordism: The Agro-Industrial Revolution in the American Midwest," *Economic Geography*, 26, 4, pp. 281–315.

Paloscia, R., 1991, "Agriculture and Diffused Manufacturing in the Terza Italia: A Tuscan Case-study," S. Whatmore, P. Lowe, and T. Marsden, eds, *Rural Enterprises: Shifting Perspectives on Small-scale Production*, London: David Fulton Publishers.

Pandey, Gyanendra, 1984, "Encounters and Calamities: The History of a North Indian *Qasba* in the Nineteenth Century," R. Guha, ed., *Subaltern Studies III: Writings on South Asian History and Society*, New Delhi: Oxford University Press.

Pandian, M.S.S., 1992, *The Image Trap: M.G. Ramachandran, in Films and Politics*, New Delhi: Sage Publications.

Panitch, Leo and Colin Leys, eds, 2000, *Working Classes: Global Realities*, London: Merlin Press.

Parry, John and Bloch, Maurice, 1989, *Money and the Morality of Exchange*, Cambridge: Cambridge University Press.

Pavaskar, C.V., 1985, *The Problem of Dearness Allowance*, Bombay: Bombay Chamber of Commerce and Industry.

Pearson, Ruth, 1998, "Nimble Fingers Revisted: Reflections on Women and Third World Industrialization in the Late Twentieth Century," Pearson and Jackson, eds, *Feminist Visions of Development: Gender, Research and Policy*, London: Routledge.

———, and Cecile Jackson, eds, 1998, *Feminist Visions of Development: Gender, Research and Policy*, London: Routledge.

Peet, Richard, 1998, *Modern Geographical Thought*, Oxford: Blackwell.

Piore, Michael and Charles Sabel, 1984, *The Second Industrial Divide: Possibilities for Prosperity*, New York: Basic Books.

Portelli, Alessandro, 1998, "Oral History as Genre," M. Chamberlain and P. Thompson, eds, *Narrative and Genre*, London: Routledge.

Postone, Moishe, 1993, *Time, Labor and Social Domination*, Cambridge: Cambridge University Press.

Prakash, Gyan, 1990a, "Bonded Labour in South Bihar: A Contestatory History," Sugata Bose, ed., *South Asia and World Capitalism*, Delhi: Oxford University Press.

———, 1990b, "Writing Post Orientalist Histories of the Third World: Perspectives from Indian Historiography," *Comparative Studies in Society and History*, vol. 32, no. 2., pp. 383–408.

———, 1992, "Can the 'Subaltern' Ride? A Reply to O'Hanlon and Washbrook," *Comparative Studies in Society and History*, vol. 34, no. 1., pp. 168–84.

Prashad, Vijay, 2003, "Gujarat Cannot and Must Not Become the Future of India," Znet, http://www.doccentre.org/TOD/prashad.htm, posted May 03, accessed June 17, 2003.

Prieto, Norma Iglesias, 1997, *Beautiful Flowers of the Maquiladora* (Life Histories of Women Workers in Tijuana, by Norma Iglesias Prieto), translated by Michael Stone with Gabrielle Winkler, Austin: University of Texas Press, Institute of Latin American Studies.

Pyke, F., G. Beccatini and W. Segenberger, eds, 1990, *Industrial Districts and Inter-firm Cooperation in Italy*, Geneva: International Institute for Labor Studies.

Quibria, M.G., 1995, *Critical Issues in Asian Development: Theories, Experience, and Policies*, New York: Oxford University Press for the Asian Development Bank.

Rabinow, Paul and Richard Dreyfus, eds, 1982, *Beyond Structuralism and Hermeneutics*, Chicago: University of Chicago Press.

Reiniche, M.L., 1996, "The Urban Dynamics of Caste: a Caste Study from Tamilnadu," C.J. Fuller, ed., *Caste Today*, Delhi: Oxford University Press.

Raj, K.N., 1973, "The Politics and Economics of Intermediate Regimes," *Economic and Political Weekly*, 7 July.

Rajamani, T.M., 1993, *Anja Nenjan Asher Mill Palanisamy* (Dearly Beloved Asher Mill Palanisamy), in Tamil, Chennai: South Asian Books.

Ramachandran, V.K., 1990, *Wage Labour and Unfreedom in Agriculture*, New York, Oxford University Press.

Ramasamy, P., 1996, *Enadu Ninaivugal* (My Memories), in Tamil, Tiruppur: Jyothipriya Autoprint.

Rasmussen, Jesper, Hubert Schniitz and Meine Pieter van Dijk, eds, 1992, "Flexible Specialization: A New View on Small Industry?" special edition of *IDS Bulletin*, vol. 23, no. 3, July.

Rose, Gillian, 1993, *Feminism and Geography: The Limits of Geographical Thought*, Minneapolis: University of Minnesota Press.

Roseberry, William, 1989, "Agrarian Questions and Functionalist Economism in Latin America," *Anthropologies and Histories: Essays in Culture, History and Political Economy*, Rutgers: Rutgers University Press.

Roy, Tirthankar, 1993, *Artisans and Industrialization: Indian Weaving in the Twentieth Century*, Delhi: Oxford University Press.

Rubin, Gayle, [1975], 2000, "The Traffic in Women: Notes on the Political Economy of Sex," reprinted in Joan Scott, ed., *Feminism and History*, Oxford: Oxford University Press.

Rudra, Ashok, 1992, *Political Economy of Indian Agriculture*, New York: Oxford University Press.

Rukmini, R., 1993, "The Process of Urbanisation and Socioeconomic Change in Tamilnadu, 1901–81," Ph.D. dissertation, Madras: University of Madras.

Rutten, Mario, 1994, *Asian Capitalists in the European Mirror*, Amsterdam: VU University Press.

———, 1995, *Farms and Factories: Social Profile of Large Farmers and Rural Industrialists in West India*, Delhi: Oxford University Press.

Sabel, Charles and Maurice Zeitlin, eds, 1997, *World of Possibilities: Flexibility and Mass Production in Western Industrialization*, Cambridge: Cambridge University Press.

Sachs, W., ed., 1992, *The Development Dictionary: A Guide to Knowledge as Power*, London: Zed.

Salzinger, Leslie, 2003, *Genders in Production: Making Workers in Mexico's Global Factories*, Berkeley: University of California Press.

Sarkar, Sumit, 1997, "The Decline of the Subaltern in *Subaltern Studies*," in *Writing Social History*, Delhi: Oxford University Press, 1997.

Sathyamurthy, T.V., ed., 1995, *Industry and Agriculture in India Since Independence*, Delhi: Oxford University Press.

Saxenian, Annalee, 1994, *Regional Advantage: Culture and Competition in Silicon Valley and Route 128*, Harvard: Harvard University Press.

Sayer, Andrew, 1992, *Method in Social Science: A Realist Approach*, London: Routledge.

———, 1997, "The Dialectic of Culture and Economy," R. Lee and J. Wills, eds, *Geographies of Economies*, London: Arnold.

———— and Richard Walker, 1992, *The New Social Economy: Reworking the Division of Labor*, Cambridge, Mass: Blackwell.

Scott, Joan, 1998, *Gender and the Politics of History*, New York: Columbia University Press.

Schmitz, Hubert, 1989, "Flexible Specialization: A New Paradigm of Small-scale Industrialization," IDS Discussion Paper no. 261, Brighton: Institute of Development Studies.

Seidman, Gay, 1994, *Manufacturing Millitance: Workers' Movements in Brazil and South Africa: 1970–1985*, Berkeley: University of California Press.

Sen, Gita, 1992, "Social Needs and Public Accountability: The Case of Kerala," M. Wuyts, M. Mackintosh, and T. Hewitt, eds, *Development Policy and Public Action*, Oxford: Oxford University Press in association with the Open University, pp. 253–77.

Shaiken, Harley, 1994, "Advanced Manufacturing and Mexico: A New International Division of Labor?," *Latin America Research Review*, Spring, pp. 39–69.

Sharma, H.P., 1973, "The Green Revolution in India: Prelude to a Red One," K. Gough and H.P. Sharma, eds, *Imperialism and Revolution in South Asia*, New York: Monthly Review Press, pp.77–102.

South India Hosiery Manufacturers Association, 1958–1997, *Andarikkaigal* (Annual Reports), Tiruppur: South India Hosiery Manufacturers Association.

————, 1996–8, Accessed, File on "Labour Disputes for Increased Wages": Letters 1–28, Tiruppur: South India Hosiery Manufacturers Association.

Spivak, Gayatri Chakravorty, 1998, "Can the Subaltern Speak?," C. Nelson and L. Grossberg, eds, *Marxism and the Interpretation of Culture*, Urbana: University of Illinois Press, pp. 271–313.

Srivastava, Ravi, 1995, "India's Uneven Development and its Implications for Political Processes: An Analysis of Some Recent Trends," T.V. Sathyamurthy, ed., *Industry and Agriculture in India Since Independence*, Delhi: Oxford University Press, pp. 219–47.

Steedman, Carolyn Kay, 1987, *Landscape for a Good Woman: A Story of Two Lives*, New Brunswick, N.J.: Rutgers University Press.

Stein, Burton and Sanjay Subrahmanyam, eds, 1996, *Institutions and Economic Change in South Asia*, Delhi: Oxford University Press.

Storper, Michael and Robert Salais, 1997, *Worlds of Production: The Action Frameworks of the Economy*, Cambridge, Mass: Harvard University Press.

Strange, Susan, 1986, *Casino Capitalism*, Oxford: Blackwell.

Subrahmanyam, Sanjay, 1996, "Institutions, Agency and Economic Change in South Asia: A Survey and Some Suggestions," B. Stein and S. Subrahmanyam, eds, *Institutions and Economic Change in South Asia*, Delhi: Oxford University Press.

Swaminathan, Padmini and Jeyaranjan, J., 1994, "The Knitwear Cluster in Tiruppur: An Indian Industrial District in the Making?," Working Paper no. 126, Madras: Madras Institute of Development Studies.

———, 1999, "The Knitwear Cluster in Tiruppur: An Indian Industrial District in the Making," A.K. Bagchi, ed., *Economy and Organization: Indian Institutions Under the Neoliberal Regime*, New Delhi, Sage, pp. 94–121.

Tewari, Meenu, 1996, "When the Marginal Becomes Mainstream: Lessons from Half-Century of Dynamic Small-Firm Growth in Ludhiana, India, PhD dissertation, Ann Arbor, Michigan: UMI Dissertation Services.

———, 1998a, "The State and the Shaping of the Conditions of Accumulation in Ludhiana's Industrial Régime: An Historical Interpretation," P. Cadène and M. Holmström, *Decentralized Production in India*, New Delhi: Sage.

———, 1998b, "Intersectoral Linkages and the Role of the State in Shaping the Conditions of Industrial Accumulation: A Study of Ludhiana's Metalworking Industry," *World Development*, vol. 26(8) 1.

Thompson, Edward P., 1963, *The Making of the English Working Class*, New York: Vintage Books.

———, 1993, *Customs in Common*, London: Penguin.

———, 1993a, "The Moral Economy Reviewed," *Customs in Common*, London: Penguin.

———, 1993b, "The Sale of Wives," *Customs in Common*, London: Penguin.

———, [1967] 1993c, "Time, Work-discipline and Industrial Capitalism," *Customs in Common*, London: Penguin.

Tripathi, D., 1984, *Business Communities of India*, New Delhi: Manohar Publishers.

Tyabji, Nasir, 1989, *The Small Industries Policy in India*, Calcutta: Oxford University Press.

Upadhya, Carol, 1997, "Culture, Class and Entrepreneurship: A Case Study of Coastal Andhra Pradesh," C. Upadhya and M. Rutten, *Small Business Entrepreneurs in Asia and Europe: Towards a Comparative Perspective*, New Delhi: Sage Publications.

———— and Mario Rutten, eds, 1997, *Small Business Entrepreneurs in Asia and Europe: Towards a Comparative Perspective*, New Delhi: Sage Publications.

————, 1997, "In Search of a Comparative Framework: Small-scale Entrepreneurs in Asia and Europe," *Small Business Entrepreneurs in Asia and Europe: Towards a Comparative Perspective*, New Delhi: Sage Publications.

Vadivelu, A., 1915–28, "Diwan Bahadur Muthuramaswami Kalingarayar Avergal, Poligar of Uttukuli," a re-reprint from *The Ruling Chiefs Nobles and Zamindars of India*, Madras.

Verdery, Katherine, 1996, *What Was Socialism and What Comes Next?* Princeton: Princeton University Press.

Wade, Robert, 1990, *Governing the Market: Economic Theory and the Role of Government in East Asian Industrializiation*, Princeton: Princeton University Press.

Walker, Richard, 1989a, "In Defense of Realism and Dialectical Materialism: A Friendly Critique of Wright and Burawoy's Marxist Philosophy," *Berkeley Journal of Sociology*, vol. 34.

————, 1989b, "Field of Dreams," M. Goodman and M. Watts, eds, *Globalising Food: Agrarian Questions and Global Restructuring*, Routledge.

————, 2001, "California's Golden Road to Riches: Natural Resources and Regional Capitalism 1848–1940," *Annals of the Association of American Geographers* 91(1), pp. 167–99.

Washbrook, David, 1975, "The Development of Caste Organization in South India, 1880–1925," C.J. Baker and David Washbrook, eds, *South India: Political Institutions and Political Change 1880–1940*, Delhi: Macmillan Company of India Limited.

Watts, Michael, 1983, *Silent Violence: Food, Famine and Peasantry in Northern Nigeria*, Berkeley: University of California Press.

————, 1992, "Living under Contract: Work, Production Politics and the Manufacture of Discontent in a Peasant Society," A. Pred and M. Watts, eds, *Reworking Modernity*, Rutgers: Rutgers University Press.

——, 1994, "Life under Contract: Contract Farming, Agrarian Restructuring and Flexible Accumulation," Little and Watts, *Living Under Contract: Contract Farming and Agrarian Transformation in Sub-Saharan Africa*, Madison: University of Wisconsin Press.

——, 1996, "Development III: The Global Agrofood System and Late Twentieth-century Development (or Kautsky redux)," *Progress in Human Geography*, vol. 20, no. 2, pp. 230–45.

Wells, Miriam, 1996, *Strawberry Fields: Politics, Class and Work in California Agriculture*, Cornell: Cornell University Press.

Williams, Raymond, 1977, *Marxism and Literature*, Oxford: Oxford University Press.

Willis, Paul, 1977, *Learning to Labor: How Working Class Kids Get Working Class Jobs*, New York: Columbia University Press.

Wolf, Diane L., 1992, *Factory Daughters: Gender, Household Dynamics, and Rural Industrialization in Java*, Berkeley, University of California Press.

Wolf, Eric, 1966, *Peasants*, New Jersey: Prentice-Hall.

——, 1982, *Europe and the People Without a History*, Berkeley: University of California Press.

——, 2001, *Pathways of Power: Building an Anthropology of the Modern World*, Berkeley: University of California Press.

World Bank, 1993, *East Asian Miracle: Economic Growth and Public Policy*, New York: Oxford University Press.

Wright, Melissa, 1997, "Crossing the Factory Frontier: Gender, Place and Power in a Mexican *Maquiladora*," *Antipode* 29/ 3, pp. 278–96.

Yamuna, T.V. and N. Jaya, 1993, "Socio-economic Profile of Child Workers of Hosiery Industries in Tiruppur Town, Tamil-nadu," *Man in India*, vol. 73, no. 2, pp. 151–61.

Yule, Sir Henry, 1903, *Hobson Jobson: A Glosssary of Colloquial Anglo-Indian Words and Phrases, and Kindred Terms, Etymological, Historical, Geographical and Discursive* (new edn, ed. William Crooke), London, J. Murray (accessed on line at http://www.urdustudies.com/resources.html, last on February 28, 2004.)

Zacharias, C. W. B., 1950, *Madras Agriculture*, Madras: University of Madras, G.S. Press.

Index

318, 326, 335; labor 245, 330, 338; *see also* caste, Madaris
dedicated production 82, 114, 132–4
density of firms 30
development politics 33
differentiated labor arrangements 256; *see also* labor, wages, women
Dirks, Nicholas B. 297, 316
District Industries Centre (DIC), Coimbatore 286–8
DMK (Dravida Munnetra Kazhagam) party 235; *see also* Dravidian Movement
Dravidian Movement 3, 180, 181, 262, 335, 338
Duraisamy, S.V. 319
dyeing 60; *see also* bleaching and dyeing

economic liberalization in India 34–5, 44; uneven implementation 36
elite failures in knitwear industry 134–40; old guard business 135, 137; outsiders 135, 137–8; rural aristocracy 135–6
employment in factories, 1986–1996 27
Epstein, T.S. 41, 301
Erode, Tamil Nadu, periodic market (*cantai*) in 7, 58, 60, 61
exports 24, 52, 56, 79–80
exporters 56, 77; labor arrangements 124; problems 125; sister concerns 121, 232; *see also* TEA
ex-worker owners 114–16; *see* Gounder ex-workers, other ex-worker owners

fabric processing 66
fabrication machines 64, 310–11; ownership of 116; units 63–4; male workers in 64
family labor 104–5, 124, 152

family wage 100–1; *see also* wage rates
Fantasia, Rick 334
fashion garments, export of 79–80; global markets 80–1; uncertainty in price and quality 81–2
feminism in Tiruppur 262–3
feminization of labor 241–2, 245
fieldwork and consolidation of capital 264–8
firm size and growth 105
flexible specialization 297–9; 36–8, 52, 298–9
FOHMA (Federation of Hosiery Manufacturers Association of India) 95
"freelance" workers 107

Gandhi, M.K. 321–2
Ganesamurthy, N. 319
gender and accumulation of capital and labor 279–82; and work 104–6; and wages 105; *see also* women workers
gendered hegemony 240–2, 256, 265, 270–3, 282
gendered militancy 247–55
General Agreements between labor and capital 256–7
global fashion markets 80
globalization of capital 29, 32, 33–4
Goodman, David and Michael Watts 310
Gopalaratnam, P. 156, 319
Gounder caste 28, 49, 51, 52; accumulation strategies 112, 184; class mobility (in the 1950s) 210; consolidation of capital under TEA 242, 264; contracting 126, 127, 231–2, 265; control of labor and contracting 125; control of production networks 128–9; dedicated production 133; education levels 293; family

.